SPIDER WEB

NICK FISCHER

SPIDER WEB

THE BIRTH OF AMERICAN ANTICOMMUNISM

UNIVERSITY OF ILLINOIS PRESS
Urbana, Chicago, and Springfield

Publication of this book is supported by grants from
the Australian Academy of the Humanities and
from Monash University.

⊗ This book is printed on acid-free paper.

Printed and bound in Great Britain by
Marston Book Services Ltd, Oxfordshire

Library of Congress Cataloging-in-Publication Data
Names: Fischer, Nick.
Title: Spider web : the birth of American anticommunism /
    Nick Fischer.
Description: Urbana : University of Illinois Press, 2016. | Includes
    bibliographical references and index.
Identifiers: LCCN 2016003063| ISBN 9780252040023 (hardcover :
    acid-free paper) | ISBN 9780252081514 (paperback : acid-free
    paper) | ISBN 9780252098222 (e-book)
Subjects: LCSH: Anti-communist movements—United States—
    History—20th century. | Conservatism—United States—History—
    20th century. | Myth—Political aspects—United States—History—
    20th century. | Propaganda—United States—History—20th
    century. | United States—Politics and government—1919–1933.
    | United States—Politics and government—1933–1945. | BISAC:
    POLITICAL SCIENCE / Political Ideologies / Communism &
    Socialism. | HISTORY / United States / 20th Century. | POLITICAL
    SCIENCE / Labor & Industrial Relations.
Classification: LCC E743.5 .F476 2016 | DDC 324.1/309730904—dc23
    LC record available at http://lccn.loc.gov/2016003063

Contents

Illustrations

Acknowledgments

Spider Web represents the culmination of many years of work. The staff of University of Illinois Press and many mentors, friends, and relations have helped me greatly during this time and deserve my formal thanks in these pages.

I first thank the staff, faculty board, readers, and copyeditors who work at UIP or were engaged by the Press to work on the book. In particular, I thank Laurie Matheson for seeing potential in the book and in me, and for persevering with both. Jennifer Comeau has been a helpful production editor. Jennifer Holzner designed two tremendous covers, presenting me with a wonderful dilemma, which I think we got right. The design staff created a very attractive and easy-to-read manuscript. Rosemary Feurer of the Northern Illinois University contributed invaluable observations and generous advice at critical stages during the book's development, and I thank her and the Press's anonymous reader, an expert on the Industrial Workers of the World. Ellen Goldlust's eagle eye improved the syntax of the book and helped us both discover terms that have not crossed the Pacific Ocean. And Sheila Bodell created the useful and insightful index.

I conducted considerable research for this book in various archives, where I received valuable guidance and assistance, including at the Hoover Institution (especially from Remy Squires), the Newberry Library in Chicago, Loyola University of Chicago (especially from the late Brother Michael Grace), the Library of Congress, and the US National Archives and Records Administration. I also found valuable material in the National Library of Australia and the State Library of Victoria, and I thank manuscript staff at those institutions.

Much of my research was also conducted through interlibrary loans and the assistance of the document delivery librarians at Monash University, who promptly furnished me with every item I requested.

The School of Philosophical, Historical, and International Studies at Monash University, where I am an Adjunct Research Associate, has supported my scholarship for several years, and I particularly want to thank Clare Corbould and Andrew Markus for providing valuable advice and for arranging generous financial support for the book's publication. I also thank the Australian Academy of the Humanities for its generous financial support of the book.

Mark Peel has been a wonderful supporter, offering me advice and assistance whenever I have asked, notwithstanding the many claims on his time and his more recent physical distance.

A number of experienced scholars read chapters of the book and helped improve it. They include David Goodman of the University of Melbourne, Lois Foster, and Phillip Deery of Victoria University. Deery has also assisted me with various references, recommendations, and publishing opportunities, for which I am very grateful. I thank both him and Robert Goldstein, whose *Political Repression in Modern America* was an important reference for me, for their generous endorsements of the book.

Jacqueline Kent read a draft of the book, and Antony Williams read chapters and helped me plan to complete the book in the most insightful and practical way. I greatly appreciate their assistance and astute suggestions. Peter Elliot did his best to keep me healthy and productive.

Mary Cunnane provided indispensable advice about writing book proposals and communicating with publishers, and she also suggested the book's title.

A number of close friends read chapters of the book and gave me consistent encouragement. I particularly thank Sean Coley for his reading and great support and friendship, and I also thank Isabel Ashton, Jon Cina, John Rutherford, Paul Sendziuk, Joseph Fonte, Paul Brownrigg, Nadine Davidoff, Daniel Tofler, and Jerome Carslake.

Many members of my family have keenly followed my progress and welfare. I thank Shirley Hall, John Gomo, and especially Joshua, John, and Suzanne Wolf for reading substantial sections of the book and for their enthusiastic and caring support. My thanks go also to Daniel Fischer and Adrienne Garneau for their support and excitement about the book.

I am tempted to purloin a line from the noted historian of anticommunism Ellen Schrecker and describe my children Leo and Saskia as late-onset victims of McCarthyism, on account of the amount of time I have spent working on *Spider Web*, but in some respects this is not fair. When I wrote the first draft of the book at home I was able to spend a great deal of time with them, so we all have *Spider Web* to thank as well as to curse. They have been so excited for me, in the sweetest ways, and I am very grateful for their enthusiasm and love.

My mother, Sandra Fischer, has been a great support to me throughout the development of the book, and I thank her for her unconditional love and confidence in me and this project, as well as for studiously reading great chunks of the book and for putting things in the right perspective, so many times.

Inevitably I have not been able to produce this book as quickly as I had hoped, and as a result some people very dear to me will never have the chance to read it. I particularly wish that my late grandmother Marta Fischer had been able to. She led a remarkable life (1910–2009) through many of the events described in this book. Whereas her brother and his German-born wife settled in the United States, the Fischer clan has John B. Trevor (see chapter 6) to thank, in part, for having been born and raised in Australia. Marta had more horse sense than anyone I have ever met, and both she and my grandfather Bela were great influences on me, morally and intellectually.

My penultimate thanks go to Gabrielle Wolf. Her support has been crucial. She has taken joy in all my successes, shepherded me through disappointments, and made so many sacrifices, particularly to care for our children for extended periods, to enable me to write. A marriage is about so much more than achievements, trials, and single events, and I am very grateful to have Gabrielle's love and support, at all times.

Finally I thank my father, John Fischer, who has read the book more times than anyone but me. I know he is as excited as I am to finally see it in print. I am more grateful than he can know for the myriad ways in which he has helped me complete the book, including, above all, in introducing me to many wonderful historians and books, and in teaching me how to think as a scholar should.

Introduction

A great paradox lies at the heart of America's understanding of its anticommunist past. On the one hand, the man who stood at the head of the anticommunist movement in the late 1940s and early 1950s, Wisconsin senator Joseph P. McCarthy, is a household name the world over. For many, his career is synonymous with ruthless political opportunism and repression.

Yet McCarthy's own notoriety and that of the period of the Cold War to which he gave his name have distorted understanding of the origins and nature of American anticommunism. Anticommunism was not the product of this postwar environment. Rather, anticommunism originated much earlier and was created to a significant extent by an informal network of activists who strove to entrench their views in the core of American politics and society. Since Reconstruction, anticommunism has linked an antilabor and laissez-faire agenda with fears of subversion, influencing not only the evolution of conservative politics but even the bounds within which twentieth-century politics came to be practiced.

McCarthyism's prominence in the public mind has obscured an understanding of the lengthy genesis of American anticommunism in three crucial ways. First, it has focused too much attention on the activities of a handful of prominent men who abused their positions in the US government to restrict the constitutional liberties of thousands of American citizens. In fact, many organizations and individuals across government, the military, the intelligence services, the police, diverse industries, and civil society were complicit in anticommunist repression. Second, the focus on McCarthyism has overstated the significance of the US-USSR rivalry and the battle to protect US "national security" as determinative influences on the development of anticommunist theory and activity.[1] Third, the preoccupation with McCarthyism has narrowed the time frame through which the political events of the mid-twentieth century are generally understood and consequently has encouraged episodic interpretations of the significance of anticommunism. As a result, the significance of the doctrine and its hold on American politics has sometimes been understated, quarantined to particular and short periods of time, and explained as an aberration from a more durable political norm.

However, scholars recently have developed a more sophisticated understanding of the long and complex history of American anticommunism. Ellen Schrecker, Kim Phillips-Fein, and Ira Katznelson have shown that a broad range of organizations and individuals were involved in anticommunist repression. They have also explored the importance of depression-era developments to the emergence not only of Cold War anticommunism but also of the modern conservative movement more broadly.[2] This book builds on this scholarship by exploring the significance of the period immediately following the First World War to the emergence of anticommunism as a significant influence in US politics and culture. In particular, the volume focuses on the linkages, beliefs, and actions of a network of anticommunists that emerged at this time, particularly in response to the Russian Bolshevik Revolution of November 1917. With supporters in every field of government and industry, this network stretched from the highest echelons of power down to the smallest towns and farming communities. Seizing on the call for transnational socialist revolution issued by Russia's new communist government, the anticommunist movement devised the perfect metaphor both for describing the international communist threat and for spreading its counterrevolutionary message: the spider web. No image could better represent how the disparate strands of international radicalism—anarchists, socialists, Bolsheviks, labor unions, peace and civil liberties groups, feminists, liberals, aliens, and Jews—intertwined and terminated at one source: the Communist International in Russia.

Yet ironically, the image of the spider web perhaps most accurately describes the interwar anticommunist movement itself. Indeed, the anticommunist spider web was arguably a more powerful and influential "conspiracy" against American democracy. During the Red Scare of 1919 and then in the 1920s and 1930s, anticommunists fought organized labor, radical political parties, and numerous progressive causes, insisting for both sincere and opportunistic reasons that those movements formed part of a hideous Bolshevik and anti-Christian web. This inflammatory rationalization helped to justify anticommunists' extreme actions, which included murder, assault, political terror, the suppression of free speech and industrial action, interference with educational institutions, forced patriotism, immigration restriction, deportation, and the annulment of landmark social legislation.

To prosecute this war, anticommunists marshaled supporters in government, the judiciary, the intelligence community, police forces, the armed services, industry, the media, and what would now be described as society's conservative base. The "hard" power of the state, wielded to expel, imprison, and execute political "radicals," to destroy "militant" industrial unions, and to suppress unorthodox political and economic doctrines, was augmented and justified by the Anticommunist Spider Web's "soft" legacies: the ideology and mythology of anticommunism and, just as important, the personal contacts and data files from which McCarthy and other Cold War anticommunists so heavily drew.

This book's focus on the interwar years (roughly 1919–41) further expands the temporal understanding of American anticommunism as well as knowledge about its organizational origins. In particular, the volume broadens the time frame for examining the public-private and state-society networks that did so much to develop and spread anticommunism. Further, it demonstrates that the collaboration of the Federal Bureau of Investigation and the American Legion should be regarded as a prominent example of cooperative countersubversion pursued by a broad network of state and civic organizations as well as individuals. This book thus follows the lead of Alfred McCoy, Schrecker, and Roy Talbert, expanding knowledge of the scope of these networks by tracing the ways in which myriad interwar groups and individuals were interconnected and collaborated in the production and dissemination of anticommunism. It also extends the recent work of Phillips-Fein, Katznelson, and Nelson Lichtenstein and Elizabeth Tandy Shermer, tracing the origins of these networks beyond the hostile reaction to the New Deal into the first Red Scare and the Roaring Twenties.[3]

This volume also identifies the individuals and organizations that contributed to the conception and/or promulgation of anticommunism. Anticommunism was more elite-driven, or top-down, than has often been supposed, including in Richard Hofstadter's influential estimation and in other leading accounts of the Red Scare that attribute too much agency to a never-defined and amorphous "American people."[4] Specifically, international communism must be treated with great caution as an explanation for the rise of American anticommunism. While fear and loathing of communism was an important factor, many organizations and individuals deliberately coordinated this opposition to achieve diverse political, economic, and social objectives. Members of the Anticommunist Spider Web played a role in orchestrating the fear of communism even as many of them succumbed to it.

While the interwar Anticommunist Spider Web is significant enough to warrant dedicated study, the Web also illuminates several broader historical issues. Far from being an episodic phenomenon, anticommunism became a significant influence in American politics shortly after the Civil War. The doctrine of anticommunism was deployed, more or less unceasingly from 1871, in the service of laissez-faire economics and the suppression of labor organization as well as other forms of social, political, and economic activity that undermined dominant business and political interests. This deployment has important implications for historical debate about the origins of American anticommunism as a response both to hostile foreign influence and to domestic political, economic, and social conditions. Opposition to radical left-wing doctrines and organizations originating in Europe certainly provided one motive for antiradicalism. However, anticommunism became an important factor in American politics long before the socialist revolutions that empowered the international communist movement. The two were fully compatible and eventually melded, but anticommunism had emerged much earlier, primarily in response to domestic tensions that grew in significance as the US economy rapidly industrialized in the late nineteenth century.

These tensions played an important role in the emergence and sustenance of anticommunism because the same rhetoric and actions were used to suppress indigenous radical organizations and the anarchist and later communist parties that were more cosmopolitan in orientation and membership. These radical organizations and movements were maligned and attacked indiscriminately until the emergence of the USSR subsumed other strands of the Radical Left and simplified the crusade against the Left into a fight against (international) communism. The story of why and how the Anticommunist Spider Web of the interwar period advanced this crusade forms the core of this book.

The rise of American anticommunism also imparts important lessons about how politics in America has worked since the Civil War. Organized groups in the American polity have harnessed political and economic doctrines in the service of specific sectional goals. Anticommunism was the product of a marriage of private and state instruments, techniques, and philosophy used to promote laissez-faire and the antilabor "open shop." Anticommunism was applied with particular intensity during the McCarthy era and the Red Scare, but these periods have been emphasized only because anticommunist repression then spread beyond the labor movement and the Radical Left into broader society. Nevertheless, those two eras were thoroughly grounded in the politics of the preceding decades.

The evolution of anticommunism was an important element in the construction of the modern American state and corresponds with profound changes in state, social, and corporate methods of dealing with conflict, especially economic conflict. Over time, a reliance on brutal, physical repression of targeted individuals and organizations gave way to more sophisticated forms of repression and control.[5] What began with antistrike injunctions and the fatal beating of striking workers evolved into a political ideology that eventually claimed a greater hold on the concept of Americanism than any other competing force or notion.[6]

Army and intelligence personnel also were instrumental in developing and repatriating techniques and weapons of countersubversion that were first deployed in the Philippines. These personnel, together with other members of the Spider Web, played a crucial role in creating the public-private networks of political surveillance that spread across the country during the interwar decades. In describing these developments, this book enlarges observations made by researchers such as McCoy, Goldstein, and Schrecker, confirming the Philippine conquest and the First World War as crucial moments when government assumed principal responsibility for policing industrial relations and political subversives.[7]

This history extends recent scholarly arguments that since the Second World War, the Right has maintained a primary focus on economic power, particularly on regaining the power lost during the Great Depression and the New Deal. Nevertheless, many of these anticommunists were also caught up in or deliberately appealed to what Michael Rogin has termed the "countersubversive tradition." The lifeblood of their propaganda was conspiracy theory consistent with the "paranoid style of politics," which tended almost invariably to envision authoritarian and other radical means of restricting the franchise in America. Accordingly, this book emphasizes the economic motives for anticommunism but also examines its mythology and the antidemocratic dreams of many of its purveyors.[8]

Spider Web members such as Military Intelligence captain John Bond Trevor and Representative Albert Johnson, a Republican from Washington State, connected eugenics, immigration restriction, and anticommunist movements, seamlessly weaving ethnoracial and political objectives into doctrine and policy.[9] The Spider Web also melded anticommunism and evangelical Christianity, seeding the modern Religious Right. And elements of the Spider Web helped found the American Nazi movement and perpetuate racist eugenics research into the twenty-first century.

But perhaps the greatest achievement of the interwar anticommunist movement was to keep the fires of right-wing countersubversion burning during the discouraging years of the Great Depression and the first half of Franklin Roosevelt's presidency.[10] The commitment and in many instances fanatical passion of Web members helped to ensure that the forces of the Right were ready and able to reassert their political agenda from the late 1930s, especially in the favorable climate of the Cold War. Their knowledge, personal contacts, and countersubversive files made possible the rise of federal and state legislative committees investigating "un-American activities" and boosted the careers of such Cold Warriors as Richard Nixon and Ronald Reagan.[11] While Phillips-Fein and other scholars have focused on the role networks of businessmen played in undermining the New Deal and seeding the modern conservative movement, this book shows that these and other networks built on the activity and ideology of earlier campaigners, especially those in the Anticommunist Spider Web.

This book revives several important historical voices, including those of Trevor, a leading nativist; Jacob Spolansky, an immigrant from the Russian empire who enjoyed a thirty-year career in anticommunist espionage; and the founder of the US Army Chemical Warfare Service, Major General Amos A. Fries, who commissioned the original Spider Web Chart depicting the "interlocking directorates" of the communist movement. Although anticommunism became an expression of the "common culture" of the United States, activists continually shaped the doctrine to pursue diverse objectives.[12] The Spider Web demonstrates that even in the largest democratic societies, effective political crusades can be waged by very small numbers of people.

This book also disputes the distinction some scholars have drawn between right-wing, reactionary, authoritarian, and dilettante (or armchair) anticommunism on the one hand and its supposedly responsible, liberal, and commonsense respectable relation.[13] By distinguishing responsibility for the conception as opposed to the promulgation of anticommunism, this volume argues that while numerous liberals and conservative, craft-based trade unions were significant purveyors of anticommunism and anticommunist repression, it is far from clear that they contributed anything distinctive to anticommunist doctrine.[14] Similarly, while principled liberal opposition was an important element of American anticommunism, the values of social democracy were subsumed in the din of the immoderate antilabor and conformist precepts of Red Scare and Cold War anticommunism.

Finally, this book does not tell the story of the American Left. This broad heading encompasses many different ideological strands, but the members of the Anticommunist Spider Web did not distinguish among these strands. Instead, those in the Web sought to destroy all of these strands, primarily through the ideology and the label of anticommunism. Therefore, the book does not discuss at length the disputes that divided left-wing and labor organizations. Similarly, a comprehensive analysis and comparison of the relative defects of American and Soviet societies is beyond the scope of this volume. In addition, the book does not treat anachronistically criticism of the USSR and of American citizens who sympathized with it. Arnold Beichman, John Earl Haynes and Harvey Klehr, and other scholars have criticized Americans who kept faith with the Communist Party after the horrors of collectivization, Stalin's Great Terror, the 1939 Nazi-Soviet nonaggression pact, and the subjugation of Eastern Europe after World War II. Yet for much of the 1920s and even into the 1930s, knowledge about events in the USSR was patchy and, for many on the left, mediated by untrustworthy sources. Further, the members of the Anticommunist Spider Web typically had little information about or understanding of these events, and such knowledge was generally incidental to their anticommunism. This book tells a different story, examining how anticommunism mediated governments' and society's capacity to abide by the principles that inspired the foundation of the United States.

SPIDER WEB

CHAPTER 1

The Origins of American Anticommunism, ca. 1860–1917

> Though the people support the Government,
> the Government should not support the people.
>
> —Grover Cleveland

Anticommunism was a response to the failure of US political institutions and traditions to resolve the fundamental challenges of the latter nineteenth century. Anticommunism emerged from an edifice of economic and social inequality and stratification and from the ways in which different social, economic, and political interests sought either to explain and preserve or, alternatively, to reform the structure of American society.

At the most basic level, anticommunism helped justify long-standing practices of labor exploitation and the suppression of labor organization. But the doctrine was innovative in that it justified this exploitation and suppression by blaming foreign ideas and people for American economic and social tensions. These tensions began to emerge immediately after the Civil War, which had been fought not just to abolish Afro-American slavery but also to extinguish the threat the spread of slavery posed to the prospects of free white people throughout the Union. Apart from its moral wrongs, a slave society would destroy a growing nation's capacity to guarantee its citizens an independent living. Yet Union victory neither resolved the increasing incompatibility of republican ideology and America's political economy nor dislodged or revised the Jacksonian reform tradition that sought to deliver "equal freedom" rather than equality to citizens, and offered little remedy to the period's defining trends.[1]

In the decades following the Civil War, increasing numbers of Americans struggled to meet their basic needs. They did not make a living wage or work in a safe environment, and they had no safety net to sustain them when they became sick or disabled. The principle of forcing people to labor in intolerable conditions or for intolerable terms survived slavery to become a basic feature of working life. For millions of industrial and agricultural laborers, sharecroppers, and tenant farmers, life was defined by cruel patterns. They worked in dangerous jobs for subsistence wages, in constant fear of poverty and loss of livelihood. Booms and busts shook the economy periodically, and "average" workers bore the brunt of prolonged recession. Their every attempt to organize into cooperative or industrial associations was met with heavy opposition, penalties, and condescension.

Simultaneously, the economic dominance of corporations and the institutionalization of political corruption as the price of economic development increased with each passing decade. Many employers and magnates refused to negotiate with labor unions, and the state generally rose to the defense of property. As corruption closed off one reform after another, the historical practices of "criminaliz[ing] political differences" and stigmatizing "dissenters as social pariahs" became ever more important devices for marginalizing "those going under in the new America."[2] A rising tide of protest and civil, industrial, and political violence was blamed on the unprecedented numbers of aliens arriving on America's shores, allegedly bringing with them polluting notions of class warfare. This cycle of widespread and prolonged distress gave rise to competing responses. While some citizens acknowledged that the nation's political system and economy required reform, a corresponding conviction that distress did not warrant and should on no account receive any systemic redress emerged. And this conviction resulted in a distinctive and in some respects exceptional American form of anticommunism.

With astonishing speed, anticommunism became an effective and influential political doctrine and strategy. It was woven, sometimes uncritically but often with great craft and persistence, into America's "countersubversive" tradition of politics, in which fear of disorder, conspiracy, and tribal bonds give rise to violent and exclusionary rhetoric and action. As a form of countersubversive politics, anticommunism was prosecuted by a blend of corporate, government, and social entities comprising public-private or state-society partnerships of great power that were in many respects particular to the United States.

Capital and Corruption

The economic and social tensions that defined Gilded Age America were rooted in the fundamental direction in which the American economy had developed since the early nineteenth century. This direction was defined above all by the transition from an agrarian to an industrial economy dominated by corporations.

Although the United States initially relied on a partnership between capital and the state to finance and coordinate economic development, private corporations emerged as the principal engine of the American economy by the close of Andrew Jackson's presidency. After the Civil War, they also became the great political power. The rising power and concentration of capital resulted from numerous factors. Technology was an important spur, as was US integration into the global economy. Industrialization in agriculture revolutionized not only farming but also the demographic patterns of national life. As farming mechanized, it became a mass-production business where yields grew exponentially and unit prices fell dramatically. Farming businesses rationalized and sold huge volumes of stock, becoming major exporters. American agribusiness realized economies of scale that only Russia could rival. Independent farmers in both the United States and Europe were driven off the land, triggering mass migrations from the American heartland and from Europe to US industrial centers, placing unprecedented stress on the labor market, civil infrastructure, and social cohesion. From 1860 to 1890, the metropolitan population ballooned while rural centers declined.[3]

The postwar economy was dominated by industrialists and finance magnates. In the thirty-five years that separated the Civil War and the twentieth century, the wealth amassed by the great capitalists or "robber barons" gave them "such incommensurate power" that in the judgment of H. W. Brands, "the imperatives of capitalism mattered more to the daily existence of most Americans than the principles of democracy." Whereas more than half the nation's wealth had been held by the richest 29 percent of the population before the Civil War, just 1 percent owned the same amount a generation later.[4]

The barons amassed such enormous wealth as a consequence of the structural opportunities provided by the absence of a strong and centralized government (whose priorities might have differed from those of business) and a comparable absence of powerful social classes (particularly a hereditary landed aristocracy) whose interests might also have clashed with capital. American capital benefited, too, from the availability of vast tracts of fertile and accessible land that had been seized from its traditional owners. And the great capitalists also gained from government assistance in the form of land grants, tax concessions, and forcible resolution of its labor-management problems. American capitalists thus profited from many freedoms denied to industrialists and merchants in Europe and elsewhere in the New World: in global terms, these barons were uniquely fortunate and powerful.

Although American capital benefited from unparalleled freedom, the political economy of nineteenth-century America was characterized more by state capitalism than by free enterprise. In this system, governments doled out huge concessions to corporations and underwrote the costs of their expansion. Between 1850 and 1870, railroads received roughly two hundred million acres of land, "a gratuity equivalent to the size of France" and several times the acreage handed out for small-scale farming under the Homestead Act of 1862. Government attitudes toward the disbursement of public monies were epitomized by President Grover Cleveland, who in 1892 agreed to lower interest rate charges on a twenty-six-million-dollar government loan to the Union and Pacific Railroad but vetoed a ten-thousand-dollar appropriation for Texas farmers in need of drought relief. Citizens, the president said, had to understand that "though the people support the Government the Government should not support the people."[5]

Governments regarded subsidization of business as a necessary price for developing their jurisdictions. In the rush to develop competing regions, corporations could play towns, cities, and states as well as both the major political parties against each other, giving themselves over entirely to the service of capital. Legislators accepted bribes paid by railroad and finance tycoons, which fell "like snowflakes and dissolved like dew." And two-thirds of the holders of cabinet posts during the Gilded Age had rail clients, sat on railroad management boards, lobbied for railroads, or had relatives in the railroad business.[6]

Having embedded the major political parties within their corporate structure, plutocrats refused to brook any interference in their business, whether from government, consumers, or an increasingly desperate and growing labor movement. Whatever political measures governments instituted to arrest the death of free labor, the barons straightforwardly subverted. Thus, around 1900, the United States had been wholly transformed "from a nation of freely competing, individually owned enterprises into a nation dominated by a small number of giant corporations."[7]

Labor in the Gilded Age

The power the robber barons wielded over their workforces was multifaceted, structural, and opportunistic. The same geopolitical, technological, and market forces that drove the growth and concentration of capital entrapped many Americans in wage slavery and poverty. The industrialization of agriculture, the formation of a US national labor market (one of the Civil War's most important consequences), and the mass migration of European peasants created a glut in the labor market to the detriment of independent farmers and artisans as well as unskilled laborers. And while immigration and emancipation made labor cheap, technological advances devalued manual skills and knowledge. New migrants, both native (typically from the Deep South) and foreign-born, struggled to find decent and consistently remunerated work. They discovered that contrary to American mythology, they were locked into the working classes. Society was now stratified; upward mobility was exceedingly rare.[8]

Although the economic changes sweeping America need not necessarily have so harmed the prospects and condition of so many manual workers, customary and prejudicial practices and attitudes toward labor relations were determinedly and successfully pursued by capital and by its allies and servants after the Civil War. Important legacies of southern slavery and antebellum industrial relations practices in the North remained influential. During the war, while union ranks were depleted, industrialists formed employers' organizations, maintained blacklists of unionists, and pressured government for antilabor laws. Several states passed legislation outlawing not only strikes but also unions as "conspiracies to restrain trade." State and federal troops crushed strikes under martial law. The federal government also provided northern industrialists with scab labor, including freed slaves, while permitting employers to import and indenture European laborers, keeping native-born workers out of employment.[9]

Throughout the postwar period, fetters on free labor and labor organization became more prevalent and confining. Freed slaves were quickly entrapped by Black Codes that threatened the homeless with imprisonment if they refused to toil for planters. When the codes were outlawed, African Americans (and most white farmers) in the South had little option but to become tenant farmers and sharecroppers, a state "not far removed from slavery."[10]

In the North, the prevalence and severity of wage slavery also deepened. At the end of the war, workers had no minimum wage laws, but their living expenses had grown by about 70 percent. They owed their homes to the companies for whom they drudged. They were forced to pay inflated prices for life's necessities at company stores. They could appeal to no law to compensate them or their families for injuries or death suffered in the workplace. And the principal available jobs were perilous; working conditions for miners and steel mill, railroad, and textile workers were unhealthy, injurious, and too often deadly.

While working conditions produced great suffering, that suffering was magnified by the disproportionate burdens laborers bore during the prolonged, severe economic downturns that plagued Gilded Age America. The profound disruption to traditional economy and society meant that workers had little choice but to seek employment wherever it might be available. The itinerant nature of the workforce helped preclude the formation of labor unions and the establishment by unions of broad, local connections. Thus, as writer Jack London observed, capital could always call on "a large surplus army of laborers" that could easily be mobilized against anyone who refused to work under the terms offered.[11]

The Birth of Anticommunism

Such huge and growing disparities in wealth, health, and opportunity did not go unchallenged. Desperation and anger repeatedly led to major industrial conflicts that spread across vast regions and industries. Trade unions as well as farmer and farmer-labor alliances sought to redress economic inequities, with varying degrees of success. But the plight of the working classes also fueled fears of their latent, malevolent power as well as a powerful sense of resentment among some prosperous citizens, who concluded that their economic inferiors posed a revolutionary threat with which the state was ill-equipped to cope. With this resentment came with a trenchant denial that inequality was rooted in the fundamental conditions and relations of society; acknowledging the structural bases of poverty and inequality risked reinforcing an unwelcome "sense of the contingency and fragility of the American dream."[12]

This combination of fear, resentment, and denial culminated in the birth and support of a doctrine that styled labor organization, industrial action, and unemployment relief as illegitimate and even subversive threats to American civilization. This doctrine provided vital and effective political cover for a campaign of repression that was unleashed not only to suppress the working classes' industrial organizations and aspirations but also to altogether discredit the politics of class.

Although the characterization of labor organization as an expression of "communism" began before the Civil War, the rapid rise and fall between March and May 1871 of the Paris Commune (or city council), a socialist government that was ejected by the French regular army, first raised the serious prospect, in at least some Americans' minds, of a local workers' revolution. The reign of the Paris Commune had barely ended before a professor at the Union Theological Seminary in New York shuddered, "Today there is not in our language . . . a more hateful word than communism."[13] This "hateful word" came quickly to encompass an apparent breakdown of social order signified by the formation of labor unions; the widespread presence of indigent, unemployed men; and the congregation of recently arrived and ethnically exotic migrants in urban districts and industries. All these groups were rapidly and indelibly associated with foul terminology and rhetorically and physically attacked for their supposed inability and unwillingness to assimilate into decent society.

Communal Loyalty and Conspiracies

The hostile response of various elements of American society to economic disadvantage and social disorder had complex origins. It did not simply express anxiety about contemporary conditions and prospects. It also reflected the influence of venerable political narratives and practices that encouraged the demonization of marginalized groups.

The fear of disorder as a "distinctive American political tradition" first developed in the white majority's relations with people of color. This tradition defined itself against alien threats and sanctioned violent and exclusionary responses to them. Native Americans were the original emblems of this threat, and their conquest legitimized the violent subjugation of other alien groups. Aside from being represented as (noble or ignoble) savages, Native Americans also symbolized tribalism, which was thought to pose a menace to "private property and the family." Their subjugation was thus predicated on the need to undermine "communal loyalties as sources of political resistance." After the Civil War, "the group ties of workers and immigrants were [similarly] assaulted in the name of individual freedom."[14]

American political tradition was also intolerant of faction within the polity. The Founders' political theory did not accommodate "institutionalized opposition to popularly based government." This attitude later fed into middle-class distaste for labor unions, but it first fueled a tendency to equate institutionalized opposition to government policy with sedition. Here, intolerance of section melded with a rich tradition of fear of anti-American conspiracy. Since the Federalists alleged that agents of the French Revolution were conspiring with Freemasons and the Bavarian Illuminati to destroy their independence, Americans had detected national threats from Catholics, Masons, the Mormon church, the "monster-hydra" of the Second Bank of the United States, abolitionists, the "Slave Power" conspiracy, and "demon rum." These fears had biblical utopian and apocalyptic roots, but they also reflected a "dark side of American individualism" as well as the fluidity of antebellum society, where individuals had ample opportunity to represent themselves as something or someone they perhaps were not. Thus "pervasive role-playing generated suspicions of hidden motives" and of secret, nefarious centers of power.[15]

A principal response to the threat of subversion was to "domesticate American freedom." Revolutionary reformers such as Benjamin Rush hoped to transform citizens into "republican machines" who would "perform their parts properly, in the great machine of the government," exercising their freedom with self-control. For the middle classes, the most important institution reinforcing self-control was the nuclear family, supplemented by schools. Together, they helped to enforce an "ideology of domesticity [that] limited political dissent in scarcely measurable ways." When successful, this self-censorship "did not simply intimidate political opposition already formed but inhibited the formation of new opposition," resulting in the "suppression of politics at the pre-political level, through the transformation of potentially political discontent into problems of personal life." In this fashion, "reform practice turned conflicts of interest into problems of personal and social adjustment" and encouraged "the criminalization of political differences, the collapse of politics into disease, the spread of surveillance, and the stigmatization of dissenters as social pariahs."[16]

Yet the structural inequality of the Gilded Age produced political, social, and economic problems of a magnitude that patently could not be addressed by personal adjustment or "a therapeutic approach to social problems." In postbellum America, the full power of the state had to be coupled to the pressures of public opinion to subdue the "communist" threat of labor organization. Compared with other industrializing, Anglophone societies (where the franchise was steadily growing), the US state played an unusually great role in suppressing labor organization (and other subsequent forms of protest). Moreover, the state's adjudication of the distinction between legitimate and illegitimate dissent had since the eighteenth century often been hostile to a broad concept of political let alone economic liberty.[17]

Anticommunism as a form of countersubversion thus had great "symbolic power" that stemmed from a "demonological worldview" that had long formed part of "the core of American politics." Many of its proponents practiced the "paranoid style" and were mired in the "paranoid position" of politics. However, like earlier countersubversives, many of the most influential creators and proponents of anticommunism were "real conservatives, defending privilege," and were principally concerned with staving off economic redistribution. Anticommunism therefore traversed quite distinct fears and purposes, and anticommunists' paranoid fears and fantasies along with their material interests could "neither be reduced to nor separated from one another."[18]

The Political Purposes of Anticommunism

Notwithstanding the cold-blooded efficiency with which it was usually applied, anticommunism often expressed a primal fear that the forces of "communism" might succeed where all previous doctrines and people's movements had failed; "communists" might just meld the disparate elements of America's vast underclass into a united force that would rise up in revolution, as had occurred in Paris and later in Russia in 1905. Where Progressivism, Populism, Free Silver, homesteads, Free Soil, Redemption, Reconstruction, and emancipation fell short, "communism" might triumph. Under its banner, the huge urban and rural proletariats might sink their differences; so, too, might white and black laborers and sharecroppers, native-born and immigrant factory hands, Catholics and Protestants, Christians and Jews. Here was the nightmare.

However, a significant number of astute and ruthless business leaders and politicians also recognized that the specter of communism could be their greatest weapon in the fight to retain and enlarge their share of the national wealth and political power. "Communism" alone could help them to mount a crusade that would transcend socioeconomic, regional, party-political, ethnic, and religious barriers and crush all attempts to socialize net wealth or dilute the doctrinal sway of laissez-faire, individualism, and white Protestant solidarity. In short, "anticommunism" could be used to split the (now multiethnic and multiracial) working classes even more effectively than they had been before. The concept was sufficiently broad to subsume and then engulf the issues over which Americans had been fighting for generations. And like earlier conspiracies that had exercised the American mind, the threat of communism had an international dimension that could make opposing it a patriotic duty.

A variety of ideological, political, economic, and social strategies came to form the doctrine and practice of anticommunism. Throughout the Gilded Age, these strategies were used to resolve major industrial and political disturbances according to a basic pattern. First, dissent expressed by industrial and political elements was swiftly and brutally quashed by public and private forces, often at the behest of big business, using both legal and extralegal means. These means included police raids and crowd dispersal, infiltration of labor unions and other organizations by agents provocateurs, mass arrests on spurious charges such as vagrancy and disturbing the peace, and punitive legislation and judicial rulings. Official, corporate, and media agencies also conflated dissent with foreign—specifically Marxist and anarchist—ideas and immigrants from Europe. While Marxist and anarchist ideology did have some currency in working-class and migrant communities, proponents of such ideologies had only marginal influence among both groups. Nevertheless, enemies of labor seized on the existence of such ideas and of minority groups who subscribed to them to justify wholesale attacks on the notion of labor organization as well as the labor movement's principal goals. The conflation of "communism" and anarchism with labor organization and migrants was strengthened by fantastic stories told by the opponents of labor to supply irrefutable "proof" of "un-American" treachery and conspiracy among trade unions and migrant communities. Finally, successive incidents of dissent and protest were used to spread political terror among the working classes and immigrants, warning them of the danger of supporting unsanctioned economic redistribution.

The doctrine and practice of anticommunism thus did not evolve in the United States in response to the seizure of power by the Communist Party of the USSR or anywhere else. Rather, it evolved primarily to combat economic and political threats represented by a diverse array of movements and organizations that were greeted with uniform hostility by business magnates, the mainstream media, governments, the army, and the police for reasons of economic, political, and psychological expediency. This diverse range of movements and organizations was combated by an equally diverse range of strategies and instruments beginning with hostile rhetoric.

The Rhetoric of Anticommunism

Anticommunism first appeared in the United States as rhetoric used to attack and dismiss collective action by the poor, the unemployed, and labor unions during the 1850s. Yet prior to the Civil War, these appearances were sporadic. And immediately after the war, the labor movement even enjoyed the qualified support of Radical Republicans seeking to protect dignified and free labor with the power of the state. This support subsided, and anticommunist rhetoric both hardened and became a regular feature of politics during the depression of the 1870s. As the depression deepened, councils of unemployed workers formed across the nation, including in New York City, where the Committee of Safety petitioned authorities to provide public works programs, temporary pensions, and food for the unemployed and their families. These requests were refused. Mayor William Havemeyer, foreshadowing President Cleveland, declared, "It is not the purpose or object of the City Government to furnish work for the industrious poor. That system belongs to other countries, not to ours." In response, the committee called for a public demonstration on the morning of 13 January 1874. Although the committee attempted to obtain permission to hold the demonstration, the government and its business backers were determined to prevent the gathering, mobilizing the police and the mainstream media to immediately crush both the demonstration and the committee's political program. New York thus joined almost every major city in the United States in meeting the problem of unemployment with a "tramp" scare.[19]

Even before the demonstration, one labor representative described the committee as the cat's paw of "Communists, Internationalists, demagogues, and evil-disposed persons." The committee indeed had socialist members and was supported by a small group of radical French immigrants, the Societé de la Commune. Yet it also included antimonopolist reformers and trade unionists and was supported by thousands of desperate citizens. But conservative media, city officials, and prominent businessmen acknowledged no other purpose or agency in the committee than foreign-born radicals and their revolutionary desires. The *New York Graphic* attacked the committee's legitimacy, describing the demonstration as a "riot" while it was in progress. The "riot" was immediately quelled, and the press unleashed a torrent of abuse on participants in the march. The leaders of the committee were denounced as "enemies of society" and "loud-mouthed demagogues" who admired "the extreme red republic" of the Paris Commune and taught American workers "the favorite tactics of the worst class of European socialists." The *New York Times* led its 14 January issue with the headline, "Defeat of the Communists."[20]

In what became a standard anticommunist rhetorical trope, the press sought to divide the working classes between law-abiding, respectable Americans and slothful, treacherous, insincere foreigners. Committee members of Irish heritage were described as "miserable loafer[s]." And the police, the *Times* claimed, had "wisely refused" to permit a display with which "the great majority of the working men . . . had disclaimed all connection." The unfortunate events of 13 January, the *Times* continued, were wholly attributable to the "bad spirit . . . rife among the more worthless sections of the community" and "persons of the lowest class."[21]

Another political tactic that became a perennial ingredient of anticommunism was the campaign to portray the demonstration as part of a national conspiracy. In the case of Tompkins Square, this portrayal was abetted by the release of bogus documents and reports that furnished "proof" of revolutionary scheming. By publishing such material, the opponents of the labor movement helped to foster moral panic about labor organization. The police leaked material to the *New York Tribune* purportedly demonstrating that Parisian communists, "heavily-armed German revolutionaries," and atheists had planned to defenestrate Mayor Havemeyer from City Hall and to incinerate buildings "where gold was stored." "Communists" were also alleged to have smuggled into New York diamonds and precious gems purloined by Communards from Parisian churches to help finance the purchase by revolutionaries of ammunition and bombs. The *Times* also informed readers of "Communism in Cleveland, Ohio" and "Labor Troubles in Philadelphia." The put-upon denizens of the City of Brotherly Love, the *Times* asserted, had been subjected to a "Communist reign of terror" by "striking carpet weavers," who had threatened to kill "peacefully-disposed and hard-working weavers" if they failed to "leave their looms and join the strikers." Closer to home, even the most routine form of damage was blamed on the actions of exiled Parisian Communards.[22]

Charges of conspiracy obscured the denial by supporters of the government and the police of the role of structural disadvantage in provoking citizen unrest. The poor of New York and elsewhere had revealed "nothing more conspicuous," the *New York Independent* stated, "than their unfitness to share the privileges and immunities of a free government." In a nation where "republican equality, free public schools, and cheap western lands allowed 'intelligent working people' to 'have anything they all want,'" the poor had shown themselves to be "tramps." In the opinion of Yale University's dean of law, the indigent unemployed had brought before society the unfortunate "spectacle of a lazy, incorrigible, cowardly, utterly depraved savage." Such "disgusting" and "crazy . . . loud-mouth gasometers" required the harshest treatment. The *Philadelphia Inquirer* spoke for many when it advised public officials to "club" any spirit of the "American Commune . . . to death at the hands of the police or shoot it to death at the hands of the militia." After the demonstration had been violently crushed and nearly fifty demonstrators on charges of disorderly conduct, assault, and "waving a red flag," the *New York Herald* commented that "America, while the land of liberty, [was] not a safe place for the mischievous advocates of communism." American-born Chartist John Francis Bray reached a different conclusion. "If the word had been in use among us a few years since," he suggested, "every anti-slavery man would have been denounced as a 'Communist.'"[23]

The next incident of national importance to associate political and industrial radicalism with labor organization, immigration, and communism was the "long strike" of anthracite coal miners in Pennsylvania and the subsequent hanging of nineteen ethnic Irish men alleged to be members of a shadowy, militant miners' organization, the Molly Maguires. The strike lasted from January to June 1875 and resulted from long-standing ethnic and industrial tensions, the prevailing depression, and the determination of major corporations to transfer both the costs of their expansion and the financial downturn to their employees. The strike was marked by a series of industry-related murders that provided a public justification for the destruction of local miners' unions as "communist" and "terrorist" organizations.

The specific conspiracy with which members of the Molly Maguires were associated was the assassination, during the 1860s and 1870s, of sixteen men, most of them mine officials, as well as a number of beatings and acts of sabotage. At the time (and in a more measured way recently) the Mollies were charged with deploying a specifically Irish "strategy of violence" to settle their grievances. Modern scholars have acknowledged that the Mollies introduced a "rare, transatlantic [form] of violent protest" but have also declared that this protest was "transformed [in] the context of American industrial society." Contemporary critics such as the *New York Times* and the *Pittsburgh Gazette*, however, associated the Molly Maguires' actions with a peculiarly Irish "state of brutish ignorance and superstition" and with "the spirit of French Communism."[24]

The popular description of the Mollies as communists was, in significant part, the work of an ambitious young railroad president, Franklin Benjamin Gowen. After assuming control of the Philadelphia and Reading Railroad, Gowen determined to rival other railways as a producer as well as shipper of coal. To help finance his plans, he ordered workers to accept a massive pay cut and publicly associated their unions with the fanatical Mollies, whom he accused of directing a campaign of terror against anyone who opposed their nefarious plans. Constructing a "powerful and enduring myth" that denied Irish coal miners "all rationality and [any] motivation [other than] inherent depravity," Gowen implemented two cardinal political strategies. First, he portrayed the Mollies as "part of a national and international network" of murderous Irish militancy. Second, he portrayed the men implicated in murders of mine managers and owners as a well-organized and subterranean arm of the trade unions. In concert, these strategies enabled Gowen to entangle the Mollies and the miners' unions, justify the destruction of both organizations, and advance his attack on the legitimacy of labor organization.[25]

Gowen was careful to associate local union leaders with the Paris Commune and the International Workingmen's Association (the First International), the political arm of various socialist, anarchist, and trade unions founded in London in 1864. This assertion, he realized, would be invaluable in the fight he planned to provoke by cutting his workforce's wages. Aware that a major strike and violence would likely result from his strategy, Gowen blamed all ensuing violence on the Mollies. When the State of Pennsylvania arraigned twenty Irish American miners for murder, a media barrage of apocalyptic, antilabor, and anti-Irish invective confirmed the wisdom of his plan. The issue of the economic and physical violence meted out by the railroad to its workers and their community was overshadowed by the alleged psychotic "communist" leanings of the accused. In court, the Molly Maguires were presented as a primitive, bestial, anarchic threat to social order. On this basis, many commentators concluded that Pennsylvania authorities owed it to "civilization to exterminate [such a] noxious growth." This demonological imagery and vengeful language became a staple element of the anticommunist worldview and propaganda.[26]

Around the time that Molly Maguires were being hanged, another event of lasting significance to future anticommunism played out in the Great Rail Strike of 1877. The product of railroad managers' attempts to displace the costs of unsuccessful expansion strategies onto their workers, the strike spread across state and then national lines and resulted in striking workers' occupation and destruction of railroad property. To seize back company property and defeat the strike, rail bosses established numerous precedents for future corporate and government handling of labor disputes that would greatly influence the ethos and practice of anticommunism in the interwar period. Rail managers, the federal government, federal judges, and the US Army pursued a successful strategy of associating the strike with imported communism. A Hayes administration official pronounced that the strike was "nothing more nor less than French communism," and the mainstream media agreed. The *New Orleans Times* asserted that the strike was "America's first experience in communism." The *New York World* pondered whether the strike was "Riot or Revolution?" It mattered little that the strikers were not communists and that the strike was not coordinated by trade unions or any other organization. Instead, it was a spontaneous eruption of desperate citizens' rage, caused by foolhardy railroad competition, as the *New York Times* conceded—but not until doing so was no longer risky or important.[27]

Other major incidents in the 1880s and 1890s further strengthened the rhetorical association of labor organization and protest with communism. Ten years after the suppression of the Molly Maguires, opponents of organized labor seized on another terrorist act to associate unions and their goals with "communist" fanaticism and violence. An unknown and never-discovered assailant detonated a bomb amid a large crowd of citizens and police near Chicago's Haymarket Square on 4 May 1886, leading employers and their supporters to use the incident as a pretext for destroying the eight-hour-day movement and an emerging reformist form of labor organization expressed in the Noble and Holy Order of the Knights of Labor, America's largest and most progressive union. Like Gowen, the Knights' enemies used violence to associate both the union and its broadly supported goals and methods with the Revolutionary Socialist Party, a small anarcho-syndicalist group.[28] Opponents launched a two-pronged response to the bombing. A dubious trial of several prominent anarchists was held to dissuade radicals from emulating the anonymous bomber's feats. More important, the trial was broadened into a devastating assault on the philosophy and goals of the mainstream labor movement. The accused bombers were labeled Dynamarchists and Red Flagsters, and they and all anarchists and entire migrant groups were referred to as "the very scum and offal of Europe," coming to the United States "to terrorize the community and to exalt the red flag of the commune above the stars and stripes." The entire labor movement was damned as "anarchist" and "communist"; the association of organized labor with radicalism, violence, and aliens was cemented; and various forms of industrial action, including trade boycotts, were outlawed as "socialistic crimes."[29]

The Pullman rail strike of June–September 1894, the first national strike in the United States, constituted another defining moment in the evolution of anticommunism as a means of suppressing organized labor. What began as a popular and spontaneous response to wage cuts instituted by the Pullman Palace Car Company in the middle of a severe recession was dismissed as a radical, European-inspired stunt, and such antiradical rhetoric played a significant part in the successful efforts of railroad bosses, the federal government, the judiciary, and the army to defeat the strike. Although the press had initially excoriated the "Marquis de Pullman" for the cruelty of his wage policy, the supply by the railroads' General Managers' Association of copy to media organizations ensured that the strike was quickly portrayed not as a "fight of labor against capital" but as a "criminally injudicious attack of certain forces of organized labor on every other kind of labor and upon all popular interests in common." The General Managers' Association described the strikers' cause as one of anarchy, a charge echoed in major opinion organs, which proclaimed, "Anarchists on Way to America from Europe"; "From a Strike to a Revolution"; "Anarchists and Socialists Said to Be Planning the Destruction and the Looting of the Treasury."[30]

When General Nelson Miles led two thousand troops at the General Managers' Association's discretion to help crush the strike, he described industrial conflict in identical terms. Confronting the strikers, Miles gave them a clear choice: stand down "on the side of established government" or remain on strike and side with "anarchy, secret conclaves, unwritten law, mob violence, and universal chaos under the red or white flag of socialism."[31] The strikers did not stand down but were promptly pushed aside and their leaders imprisoned in one of the most consequential defeats of organized labor in American history. The strike became a key exhibit in a long list of "communist" outrages bedeviling America, and the rhetorical and ideological association of labor organization and industrial protest with perfidious and foreign doctrines was assured into the twentieth century.

Anticommunism and the Repression of Organized Labor

While hostile rhetoric was an important element of the "anticommunism" that began to emerge during the 1870s, it would have had less effect had it not been backed by other effective strategies, the most basic of which was physical force. Bray wondered if the fate of the Committee of Safety in New York in 1874 heralded "a new era of force meant to give the workingmen a taste of the 'wholesale discipline' in store for them, if they persist in their trade unions and other contrivances to resist the authority of their 'masters.'"[32]

The answer to Bray's question came quickly and was restated regularly. Wholesale discipline was indeed meted out to trade unionists, the unemployed, striking workers, and the small radical political groups that operated at the margins of the labor movement. All of these groups were regarded or characterized as constituting a revolutionary threat. Many Americans concerned about revolution (or simply a redistribution of wealth and opportunity) had grave doubts about the state's capacity to preserve the status quo. These doubts, along with fear of the working class and underclasses and the heavy emphasis on corporations to provide employment and economic growth, combined to produce a multifaceted approach to physically suppressing workers' expressions of militancy.

Congress gave corporations great power to manage their labor problems. In Pennsylvania, coal mining concerns were permitted to form special police forces. The partnership between the state and corporations was also remarkably intimate. The Molly Maguires were prosecuted by Gowen, who had previously been a Democratic district attorney.[33]

Corporations and business leaders also expended considerable energy anticipating and responding to labor and working-class organization. One enduring outcome of unemployment-related disturbances during the 1870s depression was the formation of state militia (soon redubbed the National Guard) to protect capital. Many Guard divisions across the nation were directly funded by industrialists and business groups that described themselves as "Citizens' Associations." Hoping that these organizations would convince skeptics of their concern for the common weal, employers used these associations to disseminate antilabor sentiment to sympathetic media and the middle classes. The associations were also used to channel funds into the construction of urban armories to supply militia with weaponry.[34]

Employers' other major private instrument for suppressing workers and left-wing political groups was private detective agencies. Gowen was a pioneer of industrial espionage, and he engaged the famed Pinkerton National Detective Agency to infiltrate mining unions and Irish American cooperatives. Although Pinkertons had been providing such services since the 1850s, their agents had never played so prominent a role in prosecution of workers as they did in the capital trial of the nineteen alleged Mollies.[35]

The ejection in 1894 of striking steel workers from Andrew Carnegie's Homestead plant and the subsequent neutralization of the steel unions was another major spur for the use of private strikebreaking and industrial espionage services. These services were sold under various labels, including "anticommunism," and were extremely lucrative. In Pittsburgh and other large cities, more than twenty agencies competed to supply industrial espionage, "audit," and "public relations" services. Nationwide, at the height of the Red Scare, the three largest security firms—Pinkertons, Burns, and Thiel—employed about 135,000 men in 10,000 local offices. The work performed by these firms became so important that numerous corporations, notably the Ford Motor Company, chose to bring their corporate antiunion operations in-house. Other companies, including Ford's major rivals, Chrysler and General Motors, preferred to engage private detective firms to perform such work in hopes of putting some distance between their brands and such activity; General Motors spent one million dollars on the services of Pinkertons between 1934 and 1936.[36]

The Homestead strike also had important consequences for the development of state and quasi-official anticommunist forces. Congress's subsequent ban on federal government agencies' engagement of private security firms created a vacuum filled by the Bureau of Investigation, Military Intelligence, and quasi-official organizations such as the American Protective League.[37] Prior to the emergence of these instruments, however, the state steadily built up its own labor-fighting capability by transforming state militias into the National Guard and the US Army into an industrial arbitrator. The rise of informal associations of unemployed workers along with terrorist incidents such as the Haymarket bombing encouraged civic authorities to invest more heavily in urban police forces and establish special antiradical "Red," "Anarchist," and "Bomb" Squads. And legislatures and the judiciary outlawed many strike actions and other forms of industrial and consumer protest.

This process began as soon as New York's Tompkins Square "riot" was put down. While one prominent journalist hoped that "cholera, yellow fever, or any other blessing" would rid society of its "imposter paupers," big business and government did not trust the future to nature. Instead, they took firm, lasting action to eradicate the "tramp" threat, passing laws that forbade travel "without visible means of support." In New York City, police made more than one million vagrancy arrests under this authority in just one calendar year. By the close of the century, forty states had antitramp acts. The Black Codes thus found a northern equivalent in the tramp laws that prevented the unemployed from "moving to better their condition."[38]

The suppression of the 1877 rail strike marked another turning point in capital's politicization of the emerging military and policing organs of state power: business began to fight industrial disputes not just with private detectives and police but also through civic organizations and fronts, urban police departments, the National Guard, and the US Army. In addition, the strike gave rise to the use of such important legislative and judicial strikebreaking instruments as the antistrike injunction and the legal precedent of federal guarantee of freedom of commerce, backed by military force. Although railroads received great and perhaps unprecedented assistance in suppressing the strike, the removal of strikers and sympathetic members of the community from rail premises remained difficult to effect, exposing the weakness of civic instruments of law and order when faced with mass disturbance. Authorities responded immediately by reviving and expanding the tradition of calling up the state militia to deal with temporary emergencies. Even so, community hatred for the railroads was so great that federal troops, thousands of special deputies, and urban police departments were also needed to crush the strike. The use of deputies was another outcome of the strike that directly influenced the prosecution of anticommunism in the interwar period, ultimately leading to the emergence of gargantuan private armies like the American Protective League, which was deputized by the federal government in the First World War to round up draft dodgers and suppress "communist" elements on behalf of business. And in the League's path followed more durable organizations like the American Legion .[39]

In addition to funneling money into the militia, the "Citizens' Associations" formed by business leaders supported police departments, which were fast becoming "aggressive partisans" of wealth. Industry also cultivated local army commanders and raised funds to construct forts in urban areas. Thus, when the railroad workers struck, the army was available and disposed to lend its muscle to their suppression, an inclination further strengthened when Chicago businessmen purchased General Miles a fifty-thousand-dollar home. Prior to the strike, the use of soldiers to quell industrial disputes had been unusual. But the strike began a trend, and with the Indian Wars winding down, military involvement in strike suppression became routine. Henceforth, at least until the Spanish-American War, federal troops' most important role was intervening in labor disputes for capital's gain. The same was true of the National Guard; some historians estimate that fully half of the National Guard's activity in the latter nineteenth century comprised strikebreaking and industrial policing. By contrast, Australian troops, for example, were called out to aid civil authorities a mere twelve times between 1860 and 1900.[40]

Yet the willingness of the army and the militia to help crush strikes did not in itself provide a firm foundation on which to base future assaults on organized labor. This foundation was instead provided by Judge Thomas S. Drummond of the US Circuit Court, who accepted the railroads' argument that they had a constitutional right to pursue their commercial activity without hindrance. Drummond not only upheld the legality of federal guarantees of railroad activity but also devised a new, powerful sanction against industrial action. Agreeing that railroads' essential role in "all the relations of society" meant that those who struck them committed "as great an offense against the rights of individuals and . . . of the public, as can well be imagined," Drummond established broader grounds for antistrike injunctions and their enforcement by military authority. His ruling empowered employers to contrive conditions under which federal guarantees of commerce could be invoked to stop industrial action.[41]

Having first been articulated in response to the Great Rail Strike, the concept and application of the antistrike injunction was considerably expanded to help end the Pullman strike. The US Supreme Court also issued two rulings immediately after the strike that ensured that antitrust legislation would very seldom be applied to corporations, and then only in the narrowest possible sense, but would be applied in the most extensive and restrictive manner to labor unions.

President Cleveland's attorney general, Richard Olney, was as instrumental to the defeat of the Pullman strike as Judge Drummond had been in 1877. Like

Drummond, Olney had spent his entire professional life in the service of railroads. In concert with the General Managers' Association, he devised a ruse to engineer antistrike injunctions and the dispatch of federal troops for strike suppression: the blockage of federal mails. Using dormant Civil War legislation authorizing presidential suppression of violent threats to federal law, and the (Sherman) Antitrust Act of 1890, Olney won from federal judges "the most severe . . . omnibus injunction . . . ever issued [against strikers] before or since." A blunt and powerful instrument, the injunction banned any action unions might take to maintain the strike. Transforming the English common law concept justifying an injunction—that is, the restraint of a party to prevent irreparable damage caused by its imminent actions—the judges ruled that the railroads' "expectancy" of future business and of the services of experienced employees were rights as concrete as their ownership of locomotives. Thus, the court ruled that unions were causing the railroads' "irreparable" damage through "malicious conspiracy." Men were imprisoned nationwide for refusing to turn switches or fire up engines. The day after the injunction was issued, Chicago officials wired Washington for federal military assistance, fabricating evidence of property destruction and the imminence of a general strike; General Miles and his soldiers arrived a week later. Troops and deputies killed more than fifty strikers and protesters. When protest was quelled, strike leaders were charged with criminal conspiracy to obstruct mails, interfere with interstate commerce, and intimidate citizens exercising their constitutional rights to work. Hundreds of strikers were indicted under federal statutes. The strike had a disastrous effect on organized labor. By granting antilabor injunctions, the courts destroyed the American Railway Union and seriously undermined labor organization in general for the next forty years. Between 1880 and the Great Depression, nearly two thousand federally backed antistrike injunctions were issued. Only Franklin Roosevelt's crushing victory in the 1936 presidential election—a "plebiscite" on the New Deal—finally created a political risk for courts and justices that continued to obstruct federal and state government efforts to regulate the power and behavior of corporations. For the bulk of the interwar period, however, courts played a crucial role in crippling unions and associating their programs with "un-American" and "communist" ideas, precisely as employers intended.[42]

Tarnishing the Labor Movement

Franklin Gowen's prosecution and the execution of Molly Maguires established a tradition of using politicized or show trials of radical groups to destroy not only those small sects but also, and more important, labor unions and other more mainstream instruments of political and economic opposition. Although at least some of the accused Mollies probably were guilty of murder, their trial and execution was procured in part via testimony of witnesses of low repute and dubious selections of both prosecutors and juries. From his extraordinary and official position in the court, Gowen associated the Mollies with the miners' unions and explained how the Ancient Order of Hibernians (a mutual aid society) had transplanted conspiracy directly from Ireland to the United States. Gowen also impressed on juries the importance of the accused's guilt by association, thereby establishing a crucial and long-standing precedent for the prosecution of radicals. Jurors in this and in all future such cases had to determine, Gowen stressed, not merely "the guilt of particular persons, but [also] the far more transcendent issue of the guilt of [their radical] society itself," which should by default be regarded as being "on trial for its life."[43]

The use of show trials to divide, unnerve, and tarnish the labor movement was one of Gowen's greatest triumphs. Desperate to differentiate trade unionism and the Mollies, leaders of mining unions dissociated the Mollies altogether from labor activism. But in robbing the Mollies of "any motive other than revenge or bloodlust," the unions only made it easier for labor's opponents to equate both unions and the Mollies with sociopathic violence. Gowen thus established a narrative in which labor unions and radical organizations could be portrayed as indistinguishable and responsible for all industrial and political disputation. He and his associates made the contradictions between republican ideology and an economy that enriched a minority an issue of "labor activism." They transformed a "limited matter of Irish collective violence" into widespread belief in general ethnic and working-class depravity.[44]

Show trials were used again in the wake of the Haymarket bombing to shatter the Revolutionary Socialist Party, to which the alleged bombers and conspirators belonged. More important, however, was the bombing's effect on the eight-hour-day movement and the Knights of Labor. The Haymarket affair, like the conflict in Pennsylvania coalfields, was the product of long-standing grievances and tensions. It was intimately connected with the movement in support of shortened working hours, for which demonstrations were staged across the nation on 1 May 1886. It was also the climactic event in a series of clashes involving strikers, employers, and the police in Chicago in the mid-1880s.[45]

State authorities immediately swung into action, ostensibly to find the culprits guilty of the bombing but more broadly to destroy both the Chicago anarchist movement and the Knights of Labor. The police arrested dozens of Revolutionary Socialist Party members, many of whom were beaten and tortured in jail. The Knights condemned the bombing and strove to dissociate themselves from revolutionary violence but nevertheless remained as much the target of authorities and industrialists as radical socialists and anarchists because they practiced forms of industrial and social protest that employers regarded as (worryingly appealing) socialism. By May 1886, the Knights counted seven hundred thousand members nationwide, more than all previous labor federations combined. The Knights had won recent victories against major railroads, reinstating wages and attracting legions of new delegates. Unlike its main competitors, the craft-based unions, the Knights looked beyond industrial action to improve workers' lives. They operated producer and consumer cooperatives. They agitated for helpful legislation, including land grants, the eight-hour day, the abolition of child labor, the institution of an income tax, and public ownership of railroads. The Knights also showed an ability to mobilize the working classes' power as consumers, instituting successful boycotts. The Knights' slogan, "An injury to one is the concern of all," proclaimed its anticapital philosophy and provided its members with a sense of "religious solidarity" that subsequent American labor organizations "have [never] been able to match."[46]

Authorities as far afield as Milwaukee, Pittsburgh, and New York incarcerated leaders of the Knights of Labor on conspiracy charges. The eight-hour movement "virtually disintegrated . . . and many who had secured the shorter work day in advance . . . saw the policy change rescinded." A business-led media backlash drove unions out of numerous industries for a generation. By early 1887, the prominent business organ *Bradstreet's* noted with pleasure that perhaps only fifteen thousand workers in the United States had retained the "communist" eight-hour day. Strike activity and trade union membership collapsed, and the Knights disappeared from American politics and industry.[47]

But the task of subduing the Chicagoan radical movement remained unfinished. City authorities and the business community prioritized not so much finding the people guilty of making and throwing the Haymarket bomb as devastating radical groups by making a capital example of their members. Eight Revolutionary Socialist Party members were swiftly brought to trial for conspiracy. Authorities knew that none of these men had actually thrown the bomb, but their trial made good publicity. Local and national media brayed for the blood of the accused, and made much of their foreign extraction.

Like the trials of the Molly Maguires, the prosecution of the Haymarket conspirators was intended to intimidate those who would oppose capital by showing them that even guilt by association could cost them their lives. The presiding judge ignored legal principles of fairness and impartiality by proclaiming to the press the defendants' guilt even before the trial began. Jurors "frankly conceded their prejudice against the accused but were permitted to serve anyway." They were bombarded with anarchist literature, indicating that the defendants' political and economic philosophy were as much the subject of the trial as their alleged crimes. Witnesses contradicted one another. According to one historian, "some obviously lied," and several had been bribed by the Chicago Citizens' Association, which also compensated the families of police slain in the incident, paid off informants, and hired Pinkerton detectives to help round up Revolutionary Socialist Party members. Five of the accused would not plead for clemency, and their death sentences were carried out in November 1887.[48]

The Haymarket affair had numerous and profound ramifications. When homegrown industrial unions and communist parties eventually emerged in the first decades of the twentieth century, they were still struggling to escape the legacy of Haymarket, hoping to realize the Knights' program and shrug off the association of European migrants with political violence and mayhem. The use of show trials as a means of making examples of radicals continued. The affair also had a pronounced effect on local and national policing and the future definition and enforcement of national security. One historian describes the institutionalization of radical hunting in America as the culmination of "historical stimuli beginning with the Haymarket bombing," a conclusion that the International Association of Police Chiefs also reached soon after the affair.[49]

For police, radicals became a catchall scapegoat on whom any major or miscellaneous disturbance could be blamed. Post-Haymarket suppression of radicals was entrusted to Red, Bomb, and Anarchist Squads established in many metropolitan police forces. These squads quickly created a class of officers who had great professional and financial incentives to stir up fear of "communists." These forerunners of interwar anticommunist agents kept themselves in the public eye and the public fearful of left-wing insurrection by publicizing (and sometimes fabricating) stories of dastardly, barely foiled plots against public safety. These stories appeared in newspapers and memoirs and circulated among business leaders and police chiefs to strengthen the case for the permanent deployment of Red squads. Squad commanders also began a documentary process by which the size of the domestic radical movement was obsessively recorded, usually with "wholly invented" and grossly inflated estimates. This information, when married with a "countersubversive specialty [for] self-promotion, power, fame, and profit," made this new class of anticommunist police an entrepreneurial phenomenon. Several infamous radical squad chiefs exploited the unique business opportunity their positions created by running extortion rackets in gambling houses and brothels; one Chicago captain also reputedly sold personal property and real estate stolen from the executed Haymarket convicts. Business elites tolerated these excesses in exchange for unstinting police protection of profits, and the police became an integral part of capital's "political machines [and] support network." Police forces in large cities "became the spearhead of the movement to control [any] unrest and protest." This movement, "fueled by a spirit of Babbitry," would permit nothing, especially "evil conspirators allied with foreign principles . . . to impede the steady expansion of a profit-yielding economy." Thus the police's post-Haymarket "embrace of the protection of national security as a prime mission" anticipated a "century of police repression" in which protest was defined "in such a way as to warrant the most freewheeling target selection and the most punitive modus operandi." Further, "in a society programmed for fear, this mission served as a protective barrier" against anyone who might challenge business's power to define subversion. In the Red Scare of 1919 and beyond, this power grew exponentially and was shared not just by urban police departments but also by newly empowered national security agencies.[50]

Organized Labor at the Close of the Gilded Age

By the turn of the century, decades of constant "anticommunist" repression had severely restricted the prospects and condition of organized labor. The degree to which the position of labor deteriorated in the latter nineteenth century is evident in comparisons of labor's fortunes in the United States with those of workers' movements abroad. Few societies provide a better benchmark for gauging the relative position of American workers than that of Australia, which in the late nineteenth century had won global repute as the (white) "workingman's para-dise." This was not a little ironic. The first two British colonies in Australia had been established to imprison the human "refuse" of Great Britain; by contrast, the United States represented the world's first experiment in mass democracy. Yet Australia's labor movement during the 1890s created a political party that within ten years grew strong enough to form the world's first national labor gov-ernment. The United States, for its part, continued to restrict workers' rights in a manner more comparable with the autocracy of Russia than its Anglophone cousin. This irony is further compounded by the fact that the protection Aus-tralian workers received from state and federal parliamentary labor parties was in significant part made possible by the American Revolution, from which the British Crown belatedly learned the importance of speedily granting autonomy to distant colonies. But as Robin Archer has shown, the late-nineteenth-century history of industrial relations in the two nations reveals the importance of corpo-rate control of various structural elements of the American polity in establishing employers' superior position and ultimately in paving the way for the emergence of Red Scare and Cold War anticommunism.[51]

American labor's ability to organize in its own defense was inhibited by the power of employers, who influenced the political executive, legislatures, the courts, the armed forces, the police, and the media far more than did the working classes. And while the tactical and strategic decisions made by various US labor organizations can be criticized, the obstacles they encountered were sterner and more diverse than those encountered by their brethren in Australia and arguably in numerous Western European nations.

This fact is made plain not so much because unions were judged to be illegal organizations but by the consequences of this judgment. The United States was not the only nation where unions were for some time regarded as criminal conspiracy. These judgments also occurred in Australia. However, the charge was seldom leveled in Australia, and as the power of organized labor grew through industrial action and parliamentary representation, such allegations fell into disuse. Similarly, striking workers were killed in Australia as elsewhere throughout the industrializing world, but Australia experienced just one such death between 1890 and 1894. Further, military personnel never opened fire on striking workers in the antipodes. By contrast, the Pullman strike opened a period of escalating violence against striking workers in the United States: between 1902 and 1904 alone, about two hundred union members were killed and nearly two thousand were injured in labor disputes. Industrial repression in the United States may not have been as savage as it was in tsarist Russia, but it was very harsh.[52]

The significance of corporate influence over the structure of the American polity is further illustrated by the judiciary's treatment of organized labor between 1870 and 1935. American judges treated organized labor so harshly in part because they were subject to greater political pressure than were judges in British democracies. Many American jurists had to run for election to their offices, bringing judges into the ambit of political parties and big business. The "vast majority" of judges elected to the bench in this era were former politicians or party officials selected for and confirmed in their positions by the president and the US Senate. Under different circumstances, judges' susceptibility to political pressure and influence might not have so harmed organized labor. But at this point in US history, the courts "were rarely subject to political pressure to act in the interests of labor." The courts "were acting in concert" with rather than in opposition to or in advance of the executive. Indeed, the executive branch usually initiated antilabor initiatives. Yet if the courts did not actually lead the executive to oppose labor, they had an ability to frustrate the sometimes prolabor will of the other branches of government that judges in British parliamentary systems did not share. In Britain and its dominions, parliamentary sovereignty ensured that courts deferred ultimately to the will of the people; legislators could enact bills to override unacceptable judgments. This situation gave labor unions great incentive to win control of legislatures. Though labor parties took some time to win majorities in the lower houses of Australian Parliaments, this prize also delivered the labor movement control of the executive. In the United States, however, the separation of powers and the constitutional primacy of judicial review enabled the courts to obstruct or override prolabor laws made by state and federal legislatures. This power, combined with physical repression, discouraged a majority in the labor movement from seeking to establish a presence in the US House of Representatives and state assemblies.[53]

The courts, big business, and the executive were careful also to mete out the harshest treatment to industrial or general unions that welcomed unskilled and semiskilled members. Their representatives understood that industrial rather than craft-based unions were the essential element in a viable, labor-based political party. In Australia, membership in industrial unions was high: more than 60 percent of unionists in the New South Wales Trades and Labor Council were affiliated with general unions. In the United States, just 15–20 percent of federated craft union members were affiliated with new unions. Thus in 1894, when the Australian labor movement voted to establish federal and state parliamentary labor parties, the American Federation of Labor did the opposite. This fateful decision did not constitute a capitulation, as it has sometimes been portrayed; federation members agreed "on the need to pursue . . . an unprecedentedly wide range of . . . goals through political action." Nevertheless, the decision left the union movement permanently on the defensive, always battling for the right simply to exist rather than winning power in the political system to achieve such objectives as the eight-hour day.[54]

The level of violence—rhetorical, judicial, and physical—to which organized labor was subjected, however, taught many workers in the United States a simple lesson: big business would never permit them to form their own political party. In the first decades of the next century, a militant general union, the Industrial Workers of the World, would learn the lengths to which the enemies of labor would go to prevent the spread of such unionism. And when the United States entered the First World War, organized labor and any other social group that opposed America's war commitment or its consequences learned the lengths to which the federal government would go to silence dissent. Moreover, the difficulty of prosecuting an unpopular war spurred the federal government to create an array of agencies, rhetorical arguments, and initiatives that in short order ushered in the next era of American anticommunism.

CHAPTER 2

The First World War and the Origins of the Red Scare

Don't you know that some man with eloquent tongue could put this whole country into a flame? . . . What an opportunity for some man without conscience to spring up and say: "This is the way. Follow me"—and lead in the paths of destruction!

—Woodrow Wilson

While anticommunism had been an important element of American politics since the 1870s, the US entry into the First World War in April 1917, contributed greatly to the next phase of its development, the Red Scare of 1919–20. The effort required to bring a reluctant nation into the war and quash dissenting voices brought the federal government into the business of systematic rather than ad hoc industrial and political repression. The civil liberties of citizens who protested either the commitment to war or its effects were suppressed. Cultural conformity was asserted with unprecedented force and consistency. The place of nativism and antiradicalism in American politics and society became elevated. The compact between the federal government and American citizens was mediated by ideologies of political conformism and industrial quiescence and enforced by federal and public-private bureaucracies and agencies. And the experience of war strengthened capital and weakened workers' and farmers' movements. It also set political precedents that helped to spawn a new movement devoted to promoting the cause of anticommunism in American life.

US participation in the war made possible the emergence of "modern" anticommunism in several ways. First, it expanded the use of draconian and quasi-legal methods of suppressing strikes and other activity that threatened industrial output. For example, the deployment of the US Army to put down industrial disturbances, which had not occurred since the Pullman strike, became standard practice. Second, it exacerbated social and political conformism by intensifying the association of nonconformists with treachery and subversion. This atmosphere of conformity and the widespread persecution of perceived rebels and dissidents soon carried over into the Red Scare and did much to establish the cultural censorship and repression associated with Cold War anticommunism. The war effort also provided political cover for big business to broaden its assault on labor organizations, beginning with the Industrial Workers of the World (IWW) and then continuing with conservative craft unions. Business further used the war crisis to destroy numerous cooperative associations, just as it had previously destroyed the Knights of Labor. Republican and Democratic leaders used the war to pit the state against rival and smaller political parties. The outright destruction or neutering of organizations such as the Nonpartisan League and the Working Class Union was reminiscent of the treatment meted out to Civil War draft resisters and paved the way for subsequent assaults on the Union of Russian Workers, the Socialist Party of the United States, and the Communist and Communist Labor Parties.

Finally, the war prompted the federal government to develop new techniques and instruments of repression that soon became crucial weapons of anticommunists. National security agencies, like the Military Intelligence Division (MI) of the US Army, either came into existence or, like the Department of Justice's Bureau of Intelligence (BI), were transformed into essential government organizations. Government surveillance of malcontents and militants grew to rival the espionage operations of major corporations, though the two invariably worked hand in glove. And the practice of deporting unnaturalized "radicals," like the political trials pioneered in the nineteenth century, became a favored method for decapitating political and industrial organizations, starting with the IWW and continuing during the Red Scare with the Communist Party.

The Origins of America's War

Important elements in the polity favored entering the war. However, the numerical disparity between the general populace and these elements necessitated the use of force to change the electorate's view. The essential supporter of American involvement in the European conflict was President Woodrow Wilson. For the United States, national advantage rather than security was at stake, and Wilson was anxious to partake of this advantage. He understood as soon as the war broke out that if the United States stood aloof from the conflict, the nation and he personally risked exclusion from dominance or even an important role in the peace negotiations that would follow.[1]

Wilson was fortunate to share his desire for war with the most powerful elements of society: the East Coast leadership of the Republican Party; Wall Street; chambers of commerce and industry; the party political press and new media; the leadership of the armed services; the most important members of his cabinet; and the congressional leadership of his own party. Each had their own reasons for wanting war, but the most influential rationales included the promise of great profit for manufacturers of war materiel, greater employer control of laborers' wages and conditions in America, and opened markets in postwar Europe. In addition to being financially desirable, the drive to expand foreign trade was regarded as an essential "hedge against unemployment and discontent at home . . . a solvent for radicalism." Mass deployment of troops would protect the nation from reform and radical movements. Yet when war broke out in Europe in August 1914, a majority of Americans saw little point in fighting. They had troubles enough of their own.[2]

There were few more important proponents of war than the congressional leadership of the Republican Party. Seeking to concentrate the power of capital at home and find overseas markets for US products and finance, Republican leaders realized that their only means of achieving these goals was to transform the zeitgeist. Few understood this as clearly as former senator, secretary of state, and secretary of war Elihu Root, who commented, "It isn't merely a willingness to fight that is required; it is a change in the whole attitude of the people toward government." Moreover, as Robert Bacon, another former secretary of state, explained to a French acquaintance, fifty thousand Americans understood the necessity of entering the war on the Allied side, but another one hundred million did not. The task of big business and the political class was to reverse these figures. They succeeded, but only with the aid of political, social, and economic repression unleashed by the Wilson administration, state governments, and prowar elements—first to bring the nation into the war, and then to prosecute it to their satisfaction. And because the principal "communist" groups and ideologies of the previous fifty years—industrial unions, left-wing political parties, and farmers' cooperatives—were identified with the antiwar cause, the campaign to destroy opposition to the war became a trial run for the Red Scare onslaught on domestic "communism" that erupted immediately after the war.[3]

Silencing Wartime Dissent

The effort to bring the United States into the war and then conduct an effective military campaign required the use of repressive techniques and agencies that government and industrialists had developed in the previous fifty years. In addition, other methods and agencies that had been tested in US colonial administration were repatriated with great effect.

The necessity of government engagement in political repression, an enduring strand in American political thought, was another device that the Wilson administration could deploy. The federal Alien and Sedition Acts of the late eighteenth century had once imperiled freedom of speech and the press in the United States. The Sedition Act criminalized "false, scandalous and malicious" statements that sought to defame government officials or excite public "hatred" against them. This enshrinement of the English common law of seditious libel was never fully rejected even by advocates of free expression. So while the legitimacy of political opposition was eventually accepted, a significant number of Americans continued to distinguish between legitimate and illegitimate opposition.[4]

President Wilson's efforts to stamp out illegitimate opposition also had two singularly important and more recent precedents. Around the turn of the century, several laws made by both the US Congress and the colonial administration of the Philippines imported the logic of the antistrike injunction into the political realm. These laws formed at least part of the basis for the repressive legislation enacted in 1917. The assassination of President William McKinley in September 1901 by an assailant with anarchistic associations was the immediate catalyst for the enactment of the first US domestic laws in more than a century to outlaw "opinions, affiliations and advocacy" of prohibited ideas. The most important of these laws, the Immigration or Anarchist Exclusion Act of 1903, barred from the United States immigrants who believed in, advocated, or associated with organizations advocating the forcible overthrow of the US government or any other form of government. Any prospective immigrant found to hold such views would be prevented from landing for three years, and any alien resident in the United States for less than three years found to hold such views could be deported. Four states also passed laws prohibiting the advocacy of anarchy. The anarchist laws were little used until the war—an average of barely two aliens were deported each year for political offenses. More significantly, however, these measures made the federal government a force in its own right for political repression. This governmental role was strengthened in 1908 when new federal legislation sanctioned the political censorship of the mail.[5]

Around this time, American administrators in the Philippines introduced a range of harsh measures to help crush native resistance to US rule: the Sedition Law (1901); the Reconcentration Act of 1903, which authorized mass incarcerations; and the Philippine Libel Law (1904), which proscribed statements that exposed government to "public hatred, contempt, or ridicule." With defendants having to prove the fairness, truthfulness, and public good of their utterances, the laws allowed the governor (future president and US Supreme Court chief justice William Howard Taft) to control the flow of information reaching Filipinos not just via native publications but also via the expatriate American press.[6]

These domestic and colonial sedition, anarchist exclusion, and censorship acts were reprised in 1917 at local, state, and federal levels as America first prepared for and then entered the war. Indeed, domestic authorities went to greater lengths even than Philippine colonial authorities to control opinion, not only censoring news and attitudes but also developing infrastructure to manufacture, shape, and distribute information. The long advance to war prompted various authorities to suppress antiwar and troublesome industrial activity. In August 1916, Congress had authorized the creation of national and state councils of defense. In urban and industrial centers where large numbers of European migrants resided, police bomb and anarchist squads redoubled their watch on ethnic and political groups. In March 1917, Idaho pioneered what would become one of the most important measures for promoting domestic repression over the next two decades, a "criminal syndicalism" statute. This law, which twenty-two other states and territories copied in the next two years, outlawed any organization committed to violently changing the control and ownership of industry or America's system of government. Though these measures aimed squarely at eliminating regional chapters of the nation's most prominent industrial union, the IWW, the acts were used after the Bolshevik Revolution and the armistice to "extend wartime censorship and [outlaw] any form of speech or protest deemed to threaten the prevailing economic interests." The fundamental industrial purpose of criminal syndicalism legislation was affirmed by the acts' indebtedness to older anti-anarchist statutes and by the Unlawful Associations Act introduced by Australia's conservative nationalist government in 1916 to destroy the IWW's Australian branch.[7]

As soon as Congress declared war on Germany on 6 April 1917, the federal government amassed great repressive power. With the declaration came authority to censor and monitor telegraphic and telephonic communication. The Espionage Act of June 1917 expanded these controls and gave the administration almost total discretion to define and proscribe conduct or expression that prejudiced the war effort or aided the enemy. The October 1917 Trading with the Enemy Act empowered the president to censor subversive literature and monitor mail.[8]

The Business of Loyalty

Though he did not ask Congress to support US participation in the war until April 1917, President Wilson had long been inviting Americans to police their own communities and "disloyal" criticism of his policies. In his annual message to Congress delivered on 7 December 1915, Wilson divorced criticism of his administration's foreign policy from any legitimate place in national life. He also displayed unmistakable candor in associating treachery with foreign-born Americans, stating, "The gravest threats against our national peace and safety have been uttered within our own borders [by] citizens of the U.S., I blush to admit, born under other flags . . . who have poured the poison of disloyalty into the very arteries of our national life."[9]

Wilson's rhetoric profoundly influenced subordinate levels of government and the prowar lobby. Dozens of mayors across America formed "defense commit-tees." Another state-society or public-private nexus in the tradition of citizens' alliances, "preparedness" societies, emerged to campaign for involvement in the war, catapulting from inconsequence into an influential interventionist "cru-sade." Several of them, including the National Security League, were formed by Republican luminaries. As war approached, they began to refer to themselves as "patriotic" societies, flooding the political marketplace with prowar propaganda. Calling for public bans on the German language, the American Defense Society sent vigilantes "to break up rallies of pacifists, protesters, and champions of the Irish independence movement." Former President Roosevelt coined the lobby's devastating epithet for those whose criticism revealed their "alien sympathies" and compromising origins: "hyphenated Americans."[10]

Thus, on 2 April 1917, when President Wilson implored Congress to send the United States to war, his simultaneous plea for "national unity of counsel" and a domestic war on "spies" perpetrating "criminal intrigues" was almost unanimously supported; to offer the president anything less was to be "pro-German" and "un-American." The intolerance for dissent so characteristic in war was manifest immediately. Before the United States had been at war for even a week, Root called for an end to politics, stating, "We must have no criticism now." Across the republic, police prevented or closed antirecruitment meetings to prevent "riots." State governors formed commissions of public safety to monitor and if necessary censor public discourse. And federal authorities began raiding the offices of antiwar organizations, seizing literature and subjecting suspects to interrogation without benefit of legal counsel.[11]

America's participation in the war had a particularly marked effect on the fortunes of the working classes as well as on political liberty. While the presi-dent's demand for "national unity of counsel" most obviously inspired suspicion and persecution of alleged pro-Germans, it had other effects in keeping with the countersubversive political tradition. For although the president brought the American Federation of Labor (AFL) into his political tent, the war gave rise to a fresh onslaught against organized labor and left-wing political groups led by the federal government and industrial and financial magnates on whom the admin-istration, by the president's own admission, had now made itself dependent.[12]

The transformation of the commitment to war into an exercise of mass censorship and industrial repression resulted from a disjunction between the Wilson administration's determination to win the war and its capacity to achieve this goal. While Wilson "centralized and expanded federal power as never before," the machinery and institutions of government remained inadequate to the task of coordinating a modern, national war effort. Consequently, the president sanctioned "a massive infusion of private power into public administration." As the government recruited academic, military, and business leaders to manage production, conscript an army and control public opinion, the "tenured bureaucrats of the merit civil service" were superseded by an "executive-professional government coalition" whose role was not to supervise and direct "the private sector from positions in a powerful state" but to mediate and coordinate "the actions of a powerful private sector in a weak state." As the bureaucracy became "infused [with] private sector concerns and techniques," the "scales of the intragovernment capital-labor struggle" in the powerful Departments of War, the Navy, and Justice were "tipped toward the [political] right."[13]

As government tipped rightward, industrial and political radicals were targeted as threats to society and state. War made their suppression particularly necessary. Because radicals "seemed the only ones to care" about immigrant working classes, "they acted as mediating agents in the process of Americanization and, not coincidentally, in the spread of socialism and anarchism" in migrant communities. Radicals also threatened production. These twin threats of radicalism and economic disruption were sometimes combined in the same organizations, especially the IWW. More than 40 percent of IWW members were immigrants, and the union made a concerted effort to organize immigrant workers. By the time war broke out, the IWW was becoming a significant force in such vital industries as shipping, agriculture, mining, oil, and lumber. It was also spreading into regions and industries that had not previously been organized. From April to October 1917, strikes cost industry 6.28 million workdays, one-sixth of them lost in strikes led by the IWW.[14]

The Rise of the National Security State

One of the federal government's primary tools to suppress "radicals" was the state security apparatus, which used strategies that had been pioneered in the industrial milieu at home and in colonial administration abroad. Two previously unobtrusive agencies were suddenly transformed into important investigative bodies. The Office of Naval Intelligence, long an obscure wing of the Naval War College, was revived and soon employed more than three hundred officers in Washington, D.C. The ranks of the BI, which formerly included just a few hundred "amateurish" sleuths with "no counterintelligence experience," swelled to fifteen hundred agents in a few months. And under the guidance of a veteran of the Philippine occupation, Major Ralph Van Deman, the US Army's defunct MI division was reformed shortly after the declaration of war. By war's end, Van Deman had elevated MI into one of four general staff divisions, with responsibility for espionage and counterespionage duties and a staff of around seventeen hundred officers, civilian employees, and volunteers.[15]

The war offered the booming but still lean national security state an opportunity to cement its place in the machinery of government. Since its establishment in 1908, the BI had depended on moral and political crises to raise its profile and justify its existence. For many years it concentrated on enforcing the White Slave Traffic (Mann) Act of 1910, working to frustrate criminal syndicates transporting female minors across state lines for prostitution and "other immoral purpose." Once the nation was committed to war, the bureau began to investigate the industrial workforce.[16]

Determining who comprised the urban working classes, what they believed and wanted, and what they were prepared to do to get it was an overriding concern of the Wilson administration. It called on state security services to "serve a panoptic function, to make the actions and intentions of foreign [and] radical workers intelligible . . . and thereby manageable." As Alfred McCoy has shown, "colonial innovations" were an important "influence on the formation" and methods of the US "internal security apparatus." This influence particularly concentrated in the person of Van Deman, who had served with the Philippine Constabulary, a paramilitary outfit staffed by American officers and soldiered by indigenes that infiltrated nationalist cells and subverted strikes, rallies, and meetings. Building comprehensive files on Filipino nationalists, the Constabulary pioneered the use of "psychological and information warfare," spreading misinformation and entrapping Filipinos on treason charges. Using surveillance, infiltration, and hostile propaganda, the constabulary pushed the Filipino independence movement "to implode amid suspicion and betrayal." Van Deman and his colleagues introduced the same methods into MI, the BI, and the Office of Naval Intelligence with the goal of weakening American industrial unions, community cooperatives, and minor political parties that threatened production levels, corporate profits, and the major parties' prowar consensus. And just as the army had learned to use Filipino operatives to help subdue the native independence movement, so too did US state security agencies reach into the community by co-opting hundreds of thousands of "citizen spies," principally the members of the newly formed American Protective League (APL). In this manner, the nascent national security state and the Wilson administration created a new and "distinctively American fusion of state agencies and civilian adjuncts" that evolved into "a sub rosa matrix that honeycombed American society with active informers, secretive civilian organizations and government security agencies." The Anticommunist Spider Web soon emerged from this fusion of state and civilian organizations. First, however, they had to subdue the German "Hun" and those Americans who, by design or default, would aid him.[17]

Waging War on Industrial Unions

For the Wilson administration and major employers, industrial or political organizations that threatened either production levels or sectional profits constituted assistance to the enemy. No organization felt the brunt of this view more than the IWW, whose treatment during the war demonstrated how effectively business interests used the bogeys of the Hun and subsequently, the communist to associate its enduring fight against organized labor with victory in Europe and "100% Americanism." The president's overwhelming desire to achieve military success led his administration to contribute unprecedented resources to big business's assault on labor organizations. And although hundreds of wartime strikes staged by the conservative craft union movement were mediated, industry never negotiated with a select group of organizations whose ideological and practical responses to domestic conditions were considered intolerable: by claiming that "the class struggle" was the real cause and purpose of the war, these organizations committed an unforgivable offense.[18]

Although never numerically large, the IWW was perhaps the most important union in the United States in the early twentieth century. Its philosophical stridency and practical effectiveness brought it the hatred and fear of employers. The Wobblies, as they were known, were avowedly anticapitalist, with no truck for compromise. Founded in 1905 by a small group of veteran unionists and socialists, the IWW strove to provide workers with an alternative model of industrial and political activism to that offered by federated craft unions. Unlike skills-based craft unions, the "syndicalist" IWW represented all workers across industry and ethnic lines. It emphasized worker control of job conditions and direct action as the best means to desired ends. Essentially uninterested in electoral politics, the Wobblies practiced rigorous internal democracy, dispensing with the autocratic, formal management structures of craft unions. The Wobblies thus offered a vision of class solidarity that had not been seen since the destruction of the Knights of Labor.[19]

The IWW came to national prominence by leading a textile workers' strike in Lawrence, Massachusetts, in 1912. Its success was built on its inclusive philosophy and innovative tactics. The Wobblies organized unisex and multiage picketing, ensured that strikers did not engage in violence, and coordinated a national relief effort. Adapting a socialist strike relief tactic from Europe, the union billeted children of strikers out of Lawrence. The IWW also led a nine-month-long "free speech" fight against the City of San Diego, which was abridging First Amendment rights on behalf of local businesses. By the time war broke out, the IWW was costing employers in seldom-organized industries and regions significant time and money. The IWW taught workers to abandon hopeless strikes in favor of crippling slowdowns in production. It secured wage increases and better conditions. And when it did organize a strike, it was seldom ineffective. Faced with such effective opposition, employers across the nation called on local and federal authorities, the press, and vigilantes to help obliterate the IWW.[20]

In addition to being courageous, the Wobblies were strategically capable. They generally ignored the antiwar movement, reasoning that organizing opposition to the war would only deprive the workers' movement of strength in all-important industrial struggles. But this wise posture provided no protection against employers' hostility. By mid-1917, a cross-regional assault on the IWW was in full swing. And the IWW failed to convince federal authorities of its disinterest in opposing the war. On the contrary, the BI, Office of Naval Intelligence, and MI remained convinced that the IWW was the linchpin of both labor agitation and antiwar activity nationwide, and their efforts to gather information on and root out "anti-American, pacifistic, and radical . . . agitators and societies" centered on the IWW.[21]

Notwithstanding federal suspicion and targeted persecution, the national assault on the IWW was instigated not by the Wilson administration but by business interests and their proxies in the APL and state and county defense councils. However, federal government involvement was a necessary and decisive precondition for the practical destruction of the union. The campaign to destroy the IWW hinged on the use of both federal military and civil forces. And it became a national crusade when the administration sanctioned the use of the military to suppress the IWW and coordinated national raids on its premises and arrested hundreds of its leaders. Anti-Wobbly activity had previously been organized at the local and state levels, though they had used fundamentally similar strategies that resembled nineteenth-century campaigns to destroy and discredit left-wing and industrial organizations. The IWW was constantly styled an anarchistic, violent, Teutonic, and later communist organization. Its members were portrayed as the Molly Maguires had been: alien, foreign-born, fanatically aggressive, and incorrigibly idle. The union's acronym was regularly derided as shorthand for "I Won't Work," "I Won't Wash," and "I Want Whiskey." Employers and the press beseeched governments to suppress the organization, and governments answered the call, charging Wobblies with breaching vagrancy, anarchist, and freshly-minted criminal syndicalism laws.[22]

Employers also used familiar methods to harm the IWW, feeding friendly media outlets stories that blamed routine equipment failure on Wobbly sabotage. Strikes that never eventuated were constantly prophesied. Employers refused to negotiate with the union and blacklisted its members. Timber companies arranged retail-dealer boycotts of eight-hour lumber and worked with the US Army to form a closed-shop company union of loggers. MI helped business to marshal local vigilante and "patriotic" associations to assault and forcibly enlist Wobblies and counter their influence among workers. Yet these measures did not bring employers the speedy solution they sought. So they began to deport, prosecute, and confine troublesome workers and unionists, using a combination of vigilantism, federal law, and military force. Employers were also not above arranging the odd murder when doing so seemed expedient. Mining corporations in Arizona showed particular initiative in stamping out industrial organization. More than sixty Wobblies in Jerome were herded at gunpoint by corporate heavies into rail trucks and shipped to the California border. This action was quickly outdone by vigilantes in Bisbee, who loaded almost two thousand suspected Wobblies and "radical" supporters into a train bound for New Mexico.[23]

Although vigilante terror did not solve all of industry's labor problems, the mass deportations created a precedent that employers and governments followed in subsequent political and industrial disputes. The Bisbee deportations demonstrated that the coordinated assistance and sanction of the state was needed if corporations hoped to rid their workforces of intransigents: although corporate forces removed the workers from the town, the US Army sheltered and fed them in a stockade for several weeks. Moreover, local repression of the Wobblies, helpful as it was, could not completely eradicate the union, and state authorities and major employers prevailed on the federal government to do so. When Idaho Wobblies threatened to stage a general strike on behalf of some imprisoned comrades, the governor called in federal forces. Mining interests similarly petitioned the Bureau of Immigration to cleanse its workforce of leading unionists. In Minnesota, former governor John Lind, a member of the public safety commission, urged local immigration inspectors to arrest all alien IWW agitators on the Iron Range. Deploying a strategy resembling the political trials of the nineteenth century, Lind orchestrated a surgical purge of a handful of union leaders while threatening to deport all alien workers. With labor scarce and production vulnerable, the removal of the region's leading Wobblies would, Lind reasoned, leave business with a malleable workforce, "brainwashed from their radical beliefs and divorced from their support of radical organizations." A series of raids on IWW premises and expulsions of Wobblies followed. Yet industry plans to use deportation as a broad industrial relations tool were ultimately frustrated. Furnishing proof of individual detainees' guilt was difficult, particularly when local police and vigilantes proved incapable of observing judicial rules for collecting evidence. And such proof was vexingly necessary: local bureau offices were shocked when Secretary of Labor William B. Wilson insisted that the government substantiate each individual deportee's guilt.[24]

Industry's final and most productive recourse against the IWW was the US Army, which became "an illegal posse comitatus" for federal, state, and local officials, who placed it at the disposal of any petitioning corporation. The federal government had made possible the use of the army as a corporate police force in March 1917, when the Department of War began directing regional offices to "sternly repress acts committed with seditious intent" and to protect public utilities essential to war. Commanding officers were instructed to consult with local officials and businessmen to determine which utilities required military protection. The previously ad hoc use of the military to enforce industrial agreements thus became a systemic practice. The military consistently and without presidential "proclamation or a declaration of martial law . . . assumed jurisdiction where the civil courts were functioning and where peaceable strikes were in progress." Although federal authorities generally reported that strikes were orderly and that the IWW had committed no acts of violence or intimidation, orchestrated campaigns in the press, in petitions to Congress, and in "manipulated mob violence on the local level" were used to justify the imposition of "veiled and illicit martial law" over entire regions. Under the pretext of preventing industrial violence, troops raided Wobbly camps and premises, arresting and detaining thousands, and denying them access to the common law right of habeas corpus. Federal and state civil authorities then took charge of cases where convictions seemed attainable or contrition was demonstrated, while stubborn men remained in military custody. The same practices prevailed on mining ranges. With commodities classified as utilities, industry routinely used the army to suppress labor organization on the pretext of restoring the peace and protecting workers. Federal troops then occupied copper camps in Arizona and Montana. Soldiers were quartered in company barracks and accepted all intelligence about dangerous subversives provided by company agents. For industry, the subcontracting of workplace security and intelligence operations to the army was immediately effective. By August 1917, the army reported that it was satisfied with the number of laborers returning to work.[25]

A series of coordinated raids across the nation on 5 September 1917 brought to a climax the federal attack on the IWW. Having prepared for the event by burglarizing and vandalizing the union's Chicago headquarters, federal and APL agents seized 166 Wobbly leaders in dozens of major industrial centers and cities. The raids had been planned by Lind; Charles Daniel Frey, one of the APL's governing triumvirate; and the head of the Chicago office of the Department of Justice. Although authorities in Washington, D.C., doubted the legality of such raids, Lind convinced them that "wartime hysteria" would drown out any protest. Eventually, 113 IWW leaders were tried for violating the Espionage Act, crippling the organization. Thereafter, local vigilantes and judges picked over its remnants. Meanwhile, the ringleaders of the Bisbee deportation escaped punishment for kidnapping and abridging deportees' constitutional rights because of the IWW's "revolutionary" character. Assistant attorney general William G. Fitts described the IWW as different "from every form of legitimate organization." Senator Thomas J. Walsh of Montana similarly pronounced that there was "no place in the American system for such an organization, in peace or in war." They meant every word: there was no place in America where the murder, torture, and assault of Wobblies were not sanctioned.[26]

Farmers' Collectives and Minor Political Parties

While the IWW was the most important labor organization destroyed by war laws and attitudes, Wobblies were not short of company in court docks and penitentiaries. They were joined by members of other organizations that dared to use their market power collectively as laborers, consumers, or producers. Following the creation of the draft, these organizations commonly opposed the conscription of their members, thereby providing local authorities and business groups with a pretext for their destruction. These extinguished organizations included the Farmers' and Laborers' Protection Association, the Working Class Union, the Socialist Party and Renters' Union in Oklahoma, the Growers' Protective Association, and the Farmers' Emancipation League.[27]

Another significant midwestern organization targeted by business and destroyed by war laws was the Nonpartisan League, an agrarian political party. After emerging from the Republican Party in 1915, the league quickly became a powerful force in North Dakota and a worrying example beyond. A decade of poor harvests and substantial profits for big business had convinced league members that their condition could be improved only by establishing state-owned banks, grain elevators, flour mills, and packing plants as well as not-for-profit credit and insurance agencies. League members were also angered by the unfair economic impact of the war; while their margins were squeezed by mandated, deflated wheat prices, produce dealers, banks, elevator operators, and railroads were not required to make similar sacrifices. Headed by Arthur Charles Townley, a bankrupt farmer, the league ran a full slate of candidates in North Dakota's 1916 state elections and won control of not only the legislature but also the governor's mansion. The league promptly established a national headquarters in St. Paul, Minnesota. Sensing a genuine threat to their political duopoly, the major parties set about obliterating the league, describing it as a "socialist conspiracy controlled entirely" by the godless, free-loving Townley, who wished to "establish a Socialist autocracy" with himself as "Czar, Kaiser and Sultan."[28]

Exhaustive monitoring of the league's public utterances ensured that numerous representatives were fined and sentenced to lengthy jail terms under the Espionage Act. For the league, the arrests were calamitous, preventing it from campaigning on its program of economic reform and permitting its enemies to portray its constituency as disloyal. These enemies, including the governor of the Minneapolis Federal Reserve, claimed to have received "substantial evidence" of league efforts "to defeat the success of the Liberty Loan campaign in the northwest." The German and Scandinavian heritage of many of its members cast further doubt on their loyalty. The Wilson administration's propaganda chief, George Creel, believed that the league "more than any other [organization], was impregnated with the lie about a 'rich man's war' . . . by reason of well-established lies and certain fundamental ignorances." Consequently, the administration turned a blind eye to violence against league members even though North Dakota had "heavily oversubscribed [its] liberty loan allotments . . . despite drought and crop failure." Creel later conceded that there was "no doubt as to the [party] political nature of the [league's] persecution," but it had already sustained fatal wounds. Within a few years, the North Dakota legislature was retaken by the Republican Party (masquerading as the Independent Voters' Association), the governor was recalled, and the league went the way of the Knights of Labor.[29]

National Security Agencies and Labor Organization

As industrial unions, economic cooperatives, and small political parties were being destroyed, the national security apparatus turned its attention to frustrating labor organization even by conservative craft unions and to interfering with government mediation of labor disputes. The BI, for example, dispatched agents to trouble spots such as Erie, Pennsylvania, to attempt "to prevent labor disruption and strikes, and to save General Electric from unionization rather than the country from revolution." Although the National War Labor Board had found that General Electric's wages were low and that its inefficient practices caused unnecessary staff turnover, the bureau prevented the board's findings from being publicized, prevailing on local newspaper editors not to print "any news relating to labor trouble, the IWW, or Socialist activities." Instead, the BI urged "the local manufacturers' association to step up its infiltration and surveillance of labor groups" and local police to confiscate and destroy radical material.[30]

As such actions became standard procedure nationwide, radicalism was increasingly conflated with labor organization and patriotism became intertwined with the prerogatives of big business. Further, as in Erie, the BI and other national security agencies called on a variety of local government and civic forces to help suppress "radicals" of every political and industrial stripe. Though readily available, such help took no more potent form than the APL.

Partner in Repression

The wartime destruction and frustration of unions, farmers' collectives, and minor political parties hinged on support provided to government and corporations by "patriotic" organizations. By far the most important such organization was the APL. No other civil adjunct of government rivaled it in size or in the amount of leeway authorities granted it. The suppression of undesirable unions and organizations, the drafting of tens of thousands of unenlisted "slackers," and the extensive surveillance of suspected "radicals," "anti-Americans," and later "communists" could not have been coordinated by the national security apparatus without APL assistance. Further, the APL's organizational and funding structure and the politics and demography of its personnel made it a template for the later "patriotic" societies that created the Anticommunist Spider Web.

For the Wilson administration, the creation of the APL was necessitated by two principal concerns: fear of pro-German espionage and the difficulty of enforcing an unpopular draft. Combined, these concerns were deemed great enough to require the formation of new volunteer auxiliaries, continuing a tradition antedating the Civil War. By 1917, the United States had become home to huge numbers of ethnic Germans, Austro-Hungarians, and (anti-British) Catholic Irish. Notwithstanding the rapid and substantial expansion of the national security apparatus, the administration and many citizens worried that government was ill equipped to monitor let alone combat these potentially disloyal elements. Mindful of the draft riots of the Civil War, the Democratic Party's mantra about limited government, and the efficacy of colonial paramilitary auxiliaries, the administration decided to devolve responsibility for enlistment and enforcement of the draft to local volunteers. A scheme of "supervised decentralization," depending on civilian appointees, would make enlistment more palatable to the public at large. Moreover, by building a distinct temporary bureaucracy, the administration reasoned, it could both avoid enlarging its payroll and swiftly dismantle a volunteer force when doing so became expedient. So when Albert M. Briggs, a Spanish-American War veteran, approached the Chicago BI office to propose forming a national volunteer force, the administration jumped at his offer.[31]

A vice president of Outdoor Advertising, Briggs brought business contacts and a suitable political outlook to the task. As soon as war was declared, Briggs received the go-ahead from US attorney general Thomas W. Gregory to form his auxiliary, which he dubbed the American Protective League after an older patriotic society and an Illinois insurance company. Within weeks, the league had attracted legions of volunteers. They included a former secretary of war, retired police commissioners, and numerous citizens' groups that were already aiding local law enforcement agencies. By June 1917, the league reported that it had put eighty thousand volunteers into the field to help advise and enroll draftees. In addition, the league was briefed to alert government of any suspicious activity or persons.[32]

Although the league was instructed not to detain suspects or claim official status, it habitually exceeded its mandate. This development was arguably inevitable, given the organization's ambiguous governmental treatment, diffuse structure, internal culture of secrecy, size, and corporate mentality. On the one hand, the Wilson administration tried to keep the volunteers at arms' length: the point of the league was to save the government money and effort, so it was subscription-based. On the other hand, the administration blurred the lines between its agencies and the league. It permitted league officers to carry badges emblazoned "U.S. Secret Service." The league's nine-member "War Board" included representatives from both the BI and MI. Several of its senior directors were formally commissioned into the national security apparatus. And Van Deman and BI director A. Bruce Bielaski collaborated to transform it into a powerful counterespionage auxiliary. The league was even authorized to refer to itself as an "Auxiliary to the U.S. Department of Justice" and granted the privilege of free mail.[33]

While the league was formed by and for government, it was a devoted servant of capital. From the outset, its labor-bashing purposes melded with its counterespionage function. The sudden materialization of this enormous posse comitatus carrying the authority of the federal government was a blessing for both big and local business. Briggs recruited "the cream of America's business and professional elite" to help run his private army: bank and railway presidents, managers of prestigious hotels, wealthy real estate agents, and so forth. With such men at the helm, the league had no trouble securing financial support from the individuals and corporations that "usually most benefited in a property sense" from the services the league provided.[34]

The Chicago office was the template for all other units. Comprising seven bureaus, its members were organized geographically by profession, trade, and social standing. From the head down, the branch "reflected the descending order of the social and economic hierarchy in Chicago, with patriotism, efficiency, and loyalty forming the only . . . criteria for selection." Businessmen headed each of the branch's intelligence divisions, ensuring that every sector of Chicago's industry was monitored for treasonous and eventually Bolshevik sabotage. Packing plants, the electrical industry, grain merchants, paint and chemical manufacturers, grocers, and producers of war materiel all received APL "protection."[35]

Senior officers typically shared English or Scots ancestry and were Republicans, "educated in prep schools and major eastern colleges, and members of fraternities and local social clubs." A few were Catholics, Democrats, or Irishmen, and at least one member was Czech. Further down the chain, the organizational profile became a bit more varied, including a few Jews and professionals hailing from "the old middle class of the progressive movement." Descending the hierarchy, farmers, credit agency representatives, town clerks, sales managers, postal clerks, and company managers comprised the rank and file. In this respect, the league constituted a down-market version of the Office of Naval Intelligence, and its plebeian elements differed somewhat from the BI, which favored former soldiers and private detectives, although such men also participated in the league.[36]

The league was not a cheap venture; the New York office alone consumed four thousand dollars a month. Yet compared with the cost of industrial disturbance and redistribution of wealth and profits, it was a bargain. Its rank-and-file members paid just seventy-five cents or one dollar to become government-accredited agents of big business, clearing industries of troublesome employees free of charge. The league even infiltrated labor unions, signing up their business agents as members. Across the nation, APL units helped local authorities raid IWW and Socialist Party premises and furnish employee blacklists to employers and the Bureau of Immigration. The APL's services enabled government and corporations to expand their assault on the IWW from its leaders to the entire organization. BI and APL agents conducted raids nationwide, arresting hundreds of middle-ranking union officials and thousands of rank-and-file members. Such persecution, together with censorship provisions that prevented the IWW from publicizing its plight and raising money, helped transform the aggressive and powerful workers' advocate into the "ex-champion of the radical world."[37]

After the league helped to suppress the IWW, the Wilson administration determined to make greater use of the APL to stamp out opponents of the war. Impatient with the jurisdictional and punitive constraints of the Espionage Act, administration officials sponsored an amending statute, the Sedition Act, which Congress passed in May 1918. The new measure proscribed the utterance or publication of "any disloyal, profane, scurrilous or abusive opinion about the U.S. flag, form of government, Constitution or armed services." The penalties for such infractions were twenty years in jail and fines of up to twenty thousand dollars. To help enforce the act, Bielaski formalized the APL's incorporation into government, ordering all BI agents to give "full cooperation" to the league's quarter-million-plus members, who swept across the country, free from scruple

Supplement to The SPY GLASS

ARNOLD HENKEL

German army officer; age, 35; height, five feet seven inches; dark complexion; gray eyes; dark-brown hair tinged with gray above, red below; weighs 150 pounds; right leg bowed; buckshot wounds in shoulder, six or seven buckshot still in left wrist.

JACOB BREUER

Sailor; age, 36; height, five feet nine inches; dark complexion; blue eyes; brown hair. Has following tattoo marks: bust of sailor boy on right forearm, anchor and initials K. B. between thumb and index finger of right hand. Weight 170; muscular build.

Get These *Dangerous* Enemy Aliens

FIGURE 1. Wanted notices for Arnold Henkel and Jacob Breuer, supplement to the *Spy Glass*, the American Protective League's official news bulletin, ca. 1918. Henkel and Breuer had escaped from Fort Oglethorpe, Georgia. It is doubtful that they represented or wished any harm to the United States. (Records of the American Protective League, Records of the Federal Bureau of Investigation, US National Archives and Records Administration)

and discipline. Throughout the final year of the war, as official and quasi-official intelligence arms of the War and Justice Departments continued to harass the nation's enemies, "slackers," "pro-Germans," and Wobblies were replaced by or morphed into "Bolsheviks," civil libertarians, and pacifists.[38]

Chaos and lawlessness resulted. League members perpetrated countless assaults on citizens' liberties. Operatives broke into and entered premises and stole what they took to be incriminating documents, exposing many illicit love affairs but little else. Agents routinely posed as BI agents to visit post offices and confiscate mail. Telephone companies facilitated unauthorized wiretapping on the league's behalf. Federal officers enlisted league members to help raid radical premises and round up enemy aliens, whose portraits were splashed across the pages of *Spy Glass*, the league's periodical (figure 1). Reluctant draftees and the "disloyal" were hauled before mobs and made to publicly support the war effort to avoid being lynched; at least one unfortunate citizen failed to convince and paid with his life. After April 1918, league operatives received bounties for each arrest they made.[39]

For the federal government, the league's huge size and reach gave it inestimable value. The league made possible various operations that could not otherwise have been contemplated, particularly national recruitment drives. The first of these drives, which took place on 5 June 1917, resulted in violent confrontations across the nation. Shootings and murders occurred as private scores were settled. Business groups that funded local APL chapters and vigilante groups directed them to attack organizations that discouraged enlistment.[40] A subsequent enlistment campaign held on 12 September 1918 was dubbed the Slacker Drive. Authorities and the league rounded up tens of thousands of alleged draft evaders, including 12,115 slackers in just five New Jersey cities. But league members were not very discerning, and only a tiny fraction of those detained were genuine draft dodgers: the New York City branch, for example, detained more than 60,000 men over three days but identified just 199 genuine draft evaders. Nevertheless, both Bielaski and Gregory declared that summary raids would continue, and the Department of War even envisioned an extensive role for league personnel in overseas missions, partnering with the Red Cross and YMCA.[41]

All told, the league made massive contributions to the war effort. Almost 1,500 units nationwide conducted perhaps 3,000,000 investigations for government, including almost 450,000 cases of suspected subversion. So prominent was the APL's role that it came to the attention even of the Australian government, which sent an official delegation to the United States in late 1917 to investigate the possibility of establishing a similar association. Far more lasting was the codependent relationship that had developed between national security agencies and patriotic societies. Although the league formally disbanded on 1 January 1919, its work continued for more than two years, as many operatives ignored their demobilization orders, renamed their units, and retained their invaluable files, contacts and personnel. The league thus made important contributions to new attorney general A. Mitchell Palmer's Red Scare and to ongoing state investigations of radicals. Only Congress's belated mid-1921 declaration of peace finally trimmed the APL's sails, and even then, its legacy remained potent for at least another fifty years, particularly during the interwar years, when national security agencies endured sweeping funding cuts and nominal restrictions on domestic surveillance.[42]

Cultural Repression on the Home Front

US participation in the First World War also set a crucial precedent for both the Red Scare and later Cold War anticommunism by creating a need for punitive federal legislation that not only compelled citizens to fight a foreign war but also forbade citizens from expressing any misgivings about the war or its conduct. The war effort also made modern anticommunism possible by encouraging and enabling the federal government to develop an official propaganda agency that not only censored but also manufactured and distributed political opinion. This political pressure, the sum of diverse political and industrial repression, influenced civil society to censor itself. Hence the United States experienced a mass cultural conflict that continued to influence postwar disputes about the parameters of a "free market" versus a "communist" society.

For more than a year after the United States entered the European conflict, the federal government's domestic war policy rested on three pillars: the Selective Service Act (May 1917), the Espionage Act (June 1917), and the Trading with the Enemy Act (October 1917). The military draft conferred far greater power on the government than the ability to impress all age-eligible male citizens and nonhostile aliens. It also authorized the judiciary to punish draft evaders and opponents. Goaded by major media outlets, which called on authorities to discipline "a certain insolent foreign element," the courts immediately began to sentence opponents of the draft. The passage of the draft act dramatically increased their case load. Judgments were typically swift and harsh.[43]

Yet the Wilson administration remained unhappy with continuing dissent. While it could muzzle conscientious objectors of draft age with twenty-five-year jail terms, people ineligible for the draft could still denounce participation in the war. Similarly, the revived Alien Enemies Act of 1798 merely empowered the government to arrest and deport unnaturalized subjects of an enemy power; it was useless against citizens and even long-resident socialist migrants from Russia. The Espionage Act, therefore, outlawed all opposition to the war, first by imposing fines of up to ten thousand dollars and twenty years' imprisonment for anyone who "willfully" made or conveyed false reports or statements that impeded the armed services' recruitment or operations or that "promoted the success of its enemies," and second by forbidding the distribution of any printed item "advocating or urging treason, insurrection, or forcible resistance to any law of the United States," on pain of a five-thousand-dollar fine and five years in prison.[44]

With this arsenal of legislative and judicial power, the president enjoined his Council of National Defense to enforce total national unity. The council pooled the resources of the president; the Department of Justice, the Department of Commerce, and the Department of Labor; the postmaster general; and the AFL. The council also coordinated the activities of similar state and local agencies. All of these entities played crucial roles in the war effort and in enforcing community support for the war. The AFL helped government and big business crush the IWW by denouncing it as an agent of the German government whose members ipso facto had no civil rights. It also spied on behalf of national security agencies on Labor's National Peace Council and the Wobblies. The Department of Justice, through the BI, infiltrated and subverted organizations such as the Philadelphia People's Council of Americans for Peace and Freedom, sowing discord and gathering evidence to incriminate its leaders for violating the Espionage Act. Bureau agents also strove to make life difficult for slackers in custody, feeding their jailers poor character references. Generally speaking, however, the contributions of the Department of Justice and the Department of Labor to political repression increased later in the war. In 1917, the postmaster proved most vital to the suppression of dissent immediately after passage of the Espionage Act. Albert Sidney Burleson, a seven-term congressman from Texas, held the post for the duration of Wilson's presidency. Burleson became notorious for his petty-minded zealotry, his disdain for the First Amendment, and his willingness to ignore or contravene opposing views and even judicial rulings.[45]

Burleson's chief weapon, section XII of the Espionage Act, was grounded in previous law made in the Philippines. The clause empowered him to withhold from circulation any publication that "inappropriately" criticized the nation's participation in the war, questioned US or Allied motives, discouraged enlistment, or discredited the armed services. Explaining his conception of inappropriate criticism, Burleson advised editors that they would exceed "the limit" of free speech if they stated that the administration "got in the war wrong" or was fighting "for wrong purposes." They could not state that the federal government was "the tool of Wall Street or the munitions-makers." And they had especially to avoid printing anything that was "calculated to dishearten the boys in the army" or that might "make them think" the war was not "just and righteous." Whenever the legality of Burleson's statutory power was tested, the courts almost invariably ratified his heavy-handed approach. And on the exceedingly rare occasions when they did not, the postmaster used abstruse rules and procedures to subvert rulings of the bench.[46]

A sensible bureaucrat who understood his role, Burleson shirked fighting the powerful and focused on suppressing weak and obvious targets. Though the Hearst newspaper chain strongly criticized various aims and the conduct of the war, its editors and publishers were unmolested by the postmaster. Burleson instead busied himself with running reform-minded and radical publications, particularly those issued in foreign languages, out of business. The largest foreign-language print community was German, and most of the community's publishers, with the exception of small socialist papers, trod carefully during this hazardous time. Nevertheless, intense pressure from superpatriots and state defense councils forced many German papers into protracted or permanent silence. Those who refused to submit to vigilante or legal pressure paid a severe penalty, prosecuted for treason and jailed under the Espionage Act for allegedly altering the meaning of reprinted material. English-language publications were also suppressed. *Public* and other periodicals were censored for urging the government to raise more of its wartime budget through taxation rather than loans; the *Freeman's*

Journal and Catholic Register ran afoul of the act by printing a statement by Thomas Jefferson that Ireland should be freed from British rule; and *Pearson's Magazine* succumbed as a consequence of its "discourteous treatment of the Allies."[47]

President Wilson, like his postmaster, believed that wartime made much or-dinarily innocent discourse "very dangerous to the public welfare." Accordingly, the administration further tightened its grip on freedom of speech, incorporating draconian restrictions on foreign language into the October 1917 Trading with the Enemy Act: editors were required to file with official translators any mate-rial dealing with government policy and the war. While the postmaster took the lead in stamping out unwelcome criticism of government policy, other arguably more important censorship and propaganda duties were performed by the major organs of news, opinion, and popular entertainment and by the administration's purpose-built Committee on Public Information (CPI). The federal government's propaganda machine was formed on 14 April 1917, just days after Congress de-clared war. Its purpose was articulated with unusual candor by Theodore Roo-sevelt, who remarked that a covert public relations campaign was required "to get our fellow countrymen into the proper mental attitude."[48]

As the head of his news factory, President Wilson chose George Creel, a jour-nalist, newspaper publisher, and Democratic Party publicist. The committee devoted much of its energy to "persuading" community leaders, as Creel later put it, to popularize the war effort and financially support Liberty Loan and Red Cross drives. The committee was particularly eager to offer minority and for-eign-language communities "co-operation . . . supervision [and] counsel," as they formed and promoted their own loyalty leagues. The committee "organized and directed 23 societies and leagues designed to appeal to certain classes and particular foreign-language groups, each body carrying a specific message of unity and enthusiasm to its section of America's adopted peoples." A domestic propaganda fleet of "Four Minute Men" gave pithy speeches to public assemblies across the nation. Seventy-five thousand speakers delivered more than 750,000 speeches to 315 million people at lodges, fraternal organizations, unions, granges, churches, synagogues, Sunday schools, women's clubs, and colleges. These or-ganizations and communities were typically addressed by their own members, who read identical scripts prepared by CPI staff. No American was too young to carry the committee's message. A youth branch of Junior Four Minute Men distributed more than 1.5 million copies of a War Savings stamp bulletin, and the committee organized prizes for the Junior Fourth Liberty Loan contest and Junior Red Cross Christmas roll call. It also published a School Service bulletin that was sent to subscribing schools.[49]

While the committee received extensive censorial power, it also relied on citi-zens' patriotism as well as fear to control public discourse. The CPI's ability to engender mass self-censorship and conformism and its mobilization of civilian auxiliaries perhaps constituted the committee's most important contributions to the war effort and to future anticommunism. Its hard power included the authority to edit newspaper copy, furnish its own advertisements and notices, and limit the distribution of information (figure 2). In this, the committee buttressed other agencies that controlled cables and radio, the censorship board, and the postmaster. It was also well equipped. Indeed, it might properly have been termed the Public Information Administration. Comprising dozens of departments, its "public relations experts" hired "artists, cartoonists, graphic designers, filmmakers, journalists . . . novelists, short-story writers, and essayists" to saturate "the country with war propaganda" in collaboration with "18,000 newspapers, 11,000 national advertisers and advertising agencies, 10,000 chambers of commerce . . . 30,000 manufacturers' associations, 22,000 labor unions, 10,000 public libraries, 32,000 banks, 58,000 general stores . . . 3,500 Young Men's Christian Association branches, 10,000 members of the Council of National Defense, 56,000 post offices . . . 5,000 draft boards [and] 100,000 Red Cross chapters." The Speaking Division "conducted 45 war conferences." The pamphlet division "prepared and published the war literature," enlisting "over 3,000 of the leading historians of the country" to carry "our defense and our attack" to millions. Under its direction, the "artists of America" produced "posters, window cards, and similar material of pictorial publicity for the use of various Government departments and patriotic societies." A weekly "Bulletin for Cartoonists" contained "from all the chief departments of the Government the announcements which they particularly wanted to transmit to the public." And the Division of Films carried images of "America's war progress, as well as the meanings and purposes of democracy . . . to every community in the United States and to every corner of the world."[50]

Although the committee's arsenal was formidable, it seldom had to engage its full artillery: a combination of commercial imperative, sincere political sympathy, and fear ensured that most mainstream newspapers and journals toed the administration line. Like the APL, the CPI was an ingenious means of economizing on the business of war. After the war, Creel calculated that each regional CPI branch distributed an average of 873 articles in the larger national papers each month—a total of fifteen thousand articles in media space that would have cost the administration $250,000. So faithfully did the mainstream press peddle sanctioned information that Creel was "surprised and gratified" by the ease with which he had been able to control public impressions of the war.[51]

Government pressure and self-censorship also transformed new media into an effective and important ally of the administration. Few purveyors of culture better aided the CPI than the movie moguls of Hollywood. While filmmakers were careful not to inflame prejudice against America's allies, including even

Have You Met This Kaiserite?

**NAIL LIES
LIKE THESE:**

THAT Red Cross supplies are being sold to shopkeepers by dishonest Red Cross officials.

THAT the Masonic orders have protested against allowing the Knights of Columbus to build recreation huts for soldiers.

THAT interned German prisoners are being fed five meals a day.

THAT this is "a rich man's war" or "a business man's war."

THAT farmers are profiteering.

THAT nine American warships were sunk in a disastrous engagement in the North Sea.

YOU FIND HIM in hotel lobbies, smoking compartments, clubs, offices and even in homes. He thinks it's clever to repeat "inside facts" about the war. He is a scandal-monger of the most dangerous type.

He repeats all the rumors, criticisms and lies he hears about our country's part in the war. He gives you names, places, dates. He is very plausible.

But if you pin him down, if you ask him what he really KNOWS at first-hand, he becomes vague, non-committal, slippery. He tries to make you think that the Government can fool you, if you are willing to let it—but it can't fool him. No, siree! He's too smart.

People like that are hurting your country every day. They are playing the Kaiser's game. They are fighting against this country. They are making it harder to win the war.

Through their vanity or curiosity or TREASON they are helping German propagandists to sow the seeds of discontent.

For every lie that has been traced originated with a German spy. Don't forget that.

There was the one about the President's Secretary. It was said, and said again, and spread broadcast, that Mr. Tumulty was convicted of treason and shot at Fort Leavenworth. That lie was easily scotched by a public statement from Mr. Tumulty himself.

But other lies are more insidious—harder to down. In another paragraph some of them are told. But they are only a few of many.

They are taken from a publication, issued by the Committee on Public Information, called:

**" THE KAISERITE
IN AMERICA"**

101 GERMAN LIES

This little book describes the methods of Germans here and quotes 101 lies that have been nailed by a newspaper which took the trouble to run them down. It will be sent to you upon request.

Get the Facts from Washington!

Get in the fight to stamp out this malicious slander. As you travel about the country or even in your social life at home, run down these lies. Call the bluff of anyone who says he has "inside information." Tell him that it's his patriotic duty to help you find the source of what he's saying.

If you find a disloyal person in your search, give his name to the Department of Justice in Washington and tell them where to find him. It is your plain and solemn duty to fight the enemy at home by stamping out these lies. Where shall we send your copy of this book? It's free!

COMMITTEE ON
PUBLIC INFORMATION
8 JACKSON PLACE
WASHINGTON, D. C.

CONTRIBUTED THROUGH DIVISION OF ADVERTISING   U. S. GOV'T COMM. ON PUBLIC INFORMATION

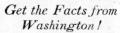

FIGURE 2. Committee on Public Information propaganda, *Literary Digest*, 10 August 1918.
(Papers of Herbert and Ivy Brookes, National Library of Australia)

the Japanese, they assiduously promoted hatred of Germany. Cecil B. DeMille, then a partner in the Lasky (Paramount) film company, approached the BI and offered "to organize the film industry all over" the United States to help stamp out "pro-German" sympathy. And while perspicacious trade journals advised filmmakers to avoid creating images "prejudicial to the government's prosecution of the present war," some had their pictures impounded, their liberty removed, and their wallets lightened.[52]

Thus, by the time the Bolsheviks seized control of Petrograd on 8 November 1917, a great program of domestic repression was under way in America.[53] The bogey of the Hun initially helped to justify this program, which continued to until the end of the war. However, conservative and reactionary forces in the United States soon found that the Bolshevik bogey offered a far more frightening and useful image for their political and economic purposes, and a new era of American anticommunism began.

CHAPTER 3

Here Come the Bolsheviks!

The Russian Revolution and the Red Scare

> The treatment accorded Russia by her sister nations in the months to come will be the acid test of their good will, of their comprehension of her needs as distinguished from their own interests, and of their intelligent and unselfish sympathy.
>
> —Woodrow Wilson

On 7 November 1917, revolutionaries from the Bolshevik (majority) faction of the Russian Social Democratic Labor Party seized power in Petrograd and proclaimed the world's first socialist government.[1] Government and business elites across the Western world received the news with dread and bewilderment. In the place of a military and commercial ally suddenly stood a socialist regime. It abruptly withdrew from the war, annulled the deposed tsar's treaties, and dishonored the debts of Russia's previous governments. More troublingly, the Bolsheviks' endorsement of violent, class-based insurrection and policies of land and resource nationalization promised a terrible future within and without the new socialist republic. Labor movements across the world drew strength from their Russian comrades' victory and announced their intention to follow along the same path. The Bolshevik threat was immediately perceived as the most serious menace to security and order, and American political elites and capitalists resolved to ensure that Bolshevism would make no domestic or international headway.

News of the Bolshevik uprising intensified the wartime atmosphere in the United States, in which fear of treachery was rampant. Political and business leaders understood that the revolution had broadened the opposition front from partisans of the Central Powers to large sections of the labor movement and anti-imperialist adherents of left-wing parties. These leaders also understood that events in Russia had given this opposition great encouragement. As the government enlarged its domestic policing powers, it attempted to isolate and militarily defeat the Bolshevik regime. Meanwhile, the business community widened its campaigns of political and industrial repression in the United States. Business had already smeared industrial unions as communists, and now it would do the same to the conservative craft unions.

In the months that elapsed between the US entry into the war and the Bolshevik Revolution, the fabric of American civil society frayed. Colleges expelled antiwar students and faculty. Elected officials were summarily dismissed for displeasing prowar elements of government and the community. Supporters of the war defended liberty by calling for the execution of naysayers. Vigilante control of local politics became so normal that it was bureaucratized. Reactionary judges saw themselves on the front lines of a battle against radicalism, and the punishment they meted out to unionists, opponents of war, and the foreign-born made vigilantism almost redundant. Whispering campaigns implicated citizens in high treason on the basis of their ethnicity. Citizens who spoke out against persecution were punished for their fealty to the First Amendment and habeas corpus. Conscientious objectors were imprisoned and grossly maltreated, pushed in many cases beyond the limits of psychological endurance. It became risky for émigrés from Eastern or Central Europe to meet in public and discuss even the politics of their lands of birth. Recalcitrance and every trace of foreignness were discouraged, and many citizens forfeited their legal rights.[2]

At the center of this maelstrom of political repression stood the president. As one of America's foremost political scientists, Woodrow Wilson had developed a decidedly European and medieval conception of the presidency. He regarded the president both as legislator in chief, like a British prime minister, and as the nation's paterfamilias, a kingly spiritual leader who literally and figuratively represented the body politic. Even in times of peace, such views might have proved awkward. But in a time of war they were profoundly damaging. Identifying with Abraham Lincoln, Wilson recognized that he carried within himself a "destructive danger . . . inseparable from his transforming public vision"; privately he admitted to "carrying a volcano about" inside him. This sense of creative destruction, married with his dictatorial vision of the presidency, provided Wilson with a justification for using extreme measures to engineer the US entry into the war and its successful prosecution. Later, as the war wound down and Germany quite abruptly collapsed in military defeat, Wilson helped to exacerbate the Russian civil war, by sending US forces into Russia to fight the Bolsheviks. This action belied the grandiose terms with which Wilson described his foreign policy and suggested that it was designed primarily to expand US global diplomatic, economic, and military influence.[3]

American Intervention in Russia, 1917–1920

When the First World War concluded, the United States "took over the leadership of the Atlantic heartland from London." The stated policy objective of the Wilson administration was to channel "democratic aspirations into arrangements compatible with Western interests." These interests were incompatible not only with those of the Bolshevik government but also with democratic reform in the former dominions of Russia, Ottoman Turkey, Austria-Hungary, and imperial Germany. Thus President Wilson's foreign policy, from his doctrine of self-determination and Fourteen Points to US participation in the Allied invasion of Bolshevik Russia, was arguably a "project of imperial global governance, in which nation-states carved from the defunct empires would operate as clients of the West against Bolshevism . . . while opening up other societies to free [Western] access, not just economically but also politically."[4]

In the summer of 1917, Wilson formed a policy group known as the Inquiry "to help formulate US strategy for structuring the post-war world." Equipped with detailed information about Europe's "national movements and demographic and economic data," the group drew up "frontiers that would grant self-determination" without creating new nations capable of obstructing Western interests. The Inquiry handed down its final report on 22 December 1917. Just over two weeks later, Wilson delivered his Fourteen Points speech, "with Points 6 to 13, on national self-determination and territorial questions, adapted from the Inquiry report." But the Bolshevik uprising threatened these plans. The same day the Inquiry wrapped up, peace negotiations between the Bolsheviks and Germany commenced. The Bolsheviks immediately annulled "the Tsarist 1907 partition of Persia with Britain, the partition of Turkey and the seizure of Armenia." They also appealed to the "labouring Muslims of Russia and the East" and the "oppressed and bled peoples of Europe" to join Russia in socialist revolution.[5]

The response of the Allied powers to Bolshevik diplomacy revealed that each intended not so much to make the world "safe for democracy" as to compartmentalize it into nation-states whose democratic aspirations would be sacrificed when they threatened Western interests. Hence, the United States and its European allies meddled in the affairs not just of Russia but also of Central Europe. So determined were they to ensure that "the unstable parliamentary systems created in the revolutionary aftermath of the Great War" did not fall into the hands of "socialists garnering majorities in elections" that they countenanced the replacement of parliamentary government in Hungary and Italy by right-wing and fascist dictatorships. They also selectively applied the program of national self-determination to create "a *cordon sanitaire* in Eastern Europe against revolutionary Russia." As the Bolshevik government pointed out, the Wilson administration supported independence for Poland, Serbia, Belgium, and peoples of the former Habsburg Empire but ignored identical aspirations among the peoples of Egypt, Ireland, India, and the Philippines. Further, against the advice of many of its own diplomats, army personnel, and aid workers, the administration interfered militarily in the internal affairs of Russia. This course of action "intensified, enlarged, and extended the [Russian] civil war, thereby [increasing] the material and human costs of the revolution." It also profoundly disturbed Russian leaders' attitude toward the West and influenced their fateful decision to build socialism in one country within a protective enclave in Eastern Europe.[6]

The Wilson administration spared little effort in trying to exterminate both Bolshevik doctrine and the Bolsheviks themselves. Yet the administration's policy was generally formulated in profound ignorance of Russia's political environment. Antipathetic to the perspectives and aims of Russian socialists, the administration's opinions of Bolshevism were founded on preconceived ideas that members of the US diplomatic service and their masters in Washington were disinclined to critique. Demonizing those they failed to comprehend, the administration's Russian policy comprised a series of ill-advised and provocative initiatives to destroy the Bolshevik regime.

Ignorance and solipsism had caused problems with the administration's policy toward Russia before Red October. The United States had invested heavily, financially, and diplomatically in pre-Bolshevik revolutionary Russia—for example, by becoming the first country to recognize Russia's provisional government after the abdication of Tsar Nicholas II in March 1917. But administration officials assumed that Russia would serve as a bulwark of US-style democracy in Europe. The Wilson administration backed its recognition of the provisional government with hundreds of millions of dollars. The disappointment felt in the United States about the failure of the governments of Prince Lvov and Aleksandr Kerensky was therefore acute and was further soured by the unexpected rise of the Bolsheviks. Yet the administration was oblivious to its own contributions to the Bolshevik ascendancy, particularly via the insistence that exhausted Russia should continue to fight Germany. This policy was driven in part by the influence of moral and philosophical as opposed to diplomatic and practical considerations. It also resulted from the incompetence of US ambassador David Francis, a successful businessman but an amateur diplomat who could not speak Russian. Isolated from embassy circles and important contacts and information, he sent communiqués that distorted Washington's political analysis.[7]

The administration received alternative high-level advice from the commander of the American Military Mission in Russia, Brigadier General William Vorhees Judson, and from Raymond Robins, director of America's Red Cross Mission. Prior to Red October, Judson and Robins consistently maintained that entente with the Bolsheviks was the only practical and clear-sighted course of action.

Judson argued that cooperation with the Bolsheviks, the strongest military force in the country, was the most efficient way to achieve long-term regional goals. He dismissed rumors that the Bolsheviks were in the pay of Germany. Indeed, he was concerned that Allied recalcitrance might drive Russia into the German camp. Further, Judson cautioned US secretary of state Robert Lansing that American support of anti-Bolshevik forces would worsen a civil war that would likely only benefit Germany. The administration did not welcome Judson's views, maintaining that the destruction of socialism was more important than defeating Germany. Lansing described Bolshevism as the "most hideous and monstrous thing that the human mind has ever conceived" and told the press that the Bolsheviks had "put one over" on Judson. For his part, the president, who had a feeble grasp of Russian history and culture, refused to engage with a clique of tyrants who opposed his diplomacy and had subjugated the Russian people, whose democratic aspirations he idealized beyond recognition.[8] The president's public support for national self-determination intensified his need to equate Bolshevism with perfidy, and helped to justify his hypocritical support of the Allied invasion of Russia just three weeks after the Bolsheviks seized power. After refusing to negotiate with the Bolsheviks, contrary to the wishes of the French government and the Bolsheviks themselves, the United States was at war with Russia.[9]

The Committee on Public Information (CPI) and the mainstream press vigorously supported the decision to make war on Bolshevik Russia. The manufacture of anti-Bolshevik propaganda had been government policy since July 1917, and the administration spent five million dollars acquiring and distributing information in the United States and in Russia despite knowing that the information was false. The most notable canard spread by the government was the accusation that the Bolsheviks had been paid by the kaiser to foment instability in Russia and take it out of the war. The administration's principal evidence supporting this claim were the "Sisson Papers," purchased in early 1918 by the president's envoy (and the CPI's second-most-senior officer), Edgar Sisson, editor of the archconservative *Chicago Tribune* and *Cosmopolitan* magazine, and according to Creel, an "organizing genius." The publisher of a Petrograd scandal sheet had conned Sisson, selling him documents purportedly showing that the "Bolshevik revolution was arranged for by the German Great General Staff, and financed by the German Imperial Bank and other German financial institutions" and that the Russian commissar for foreign affairs, Leon Trotsky, and Bolshevik leader Vladimir Lenin were working for German intelligence. The British government determined that the documents had been written on a single typewriter and were fraudulent, but the administration nevertheless decided to leak their contents to the press.[10]

The accusation that Russian Bolsheviks were controlled by Germany was spectacularly influential. The mainstream media overwhelmingly accepted the claims, denouncing Bolshevism and German meddling in Russia. Some papers, among them the *New York Globe*, admitted their inability to verify the Bolsheviks' treachery but nevertheless suggested that the Bolsheviks would transform both Russia and Germany into "a cauldron of hellbroth." Newspapers then began to urge the government to take immediate military action in Russia. A policy of containment was thought to be inadvisable, as the Bolsheviks would be easier to defeat sooner rather than later. And the United States would play an essential role in combating Bolshevism: the future of the world, according to the *New York Post*, depended on American (moral) leadership.[11]

The most influential articles concerning Bolshevik misrule concerned the destruction of the nuclear family. Newspapers in the United States and across the Western world printed chilling stories of the "nationalization" of women and children by "Commissariats of Free Love." Married and unmarried women were allegedly required to have sexual intercourse with random partners and surrender their offspring to the state. Although these stories had been taken from anti-Bolshevik Russian papers, the press and the administration claimed that they had been published in the Bolshevik paper *Izvestia*. The American public, for its part, remained generally ignorant that untruths or at best unverified assertions were being foisted on them. No retractions or corrections of manipulative or incorrect stories were made, even after more reasoned analyses of Russian affairs and radical philosophy became available. Congress took little interest in testimony that failed to corroborate the uniform, hostile impressions of Bolshevism it was determined to cultivate. The media similarly ignored the lonely voices dismissing charges of German control and cautioning against anti-Bolshevik military action on both martial and humanitarian grounds.[12]

In Russia itself, the CPI spread anti-Bolshevik messages in what was its most important external theater of operation. While Creel assured the Bolshevik government that the committee would do "nothing contrary to the wishes" of domestic authorities "or violative of neutrality," it abused these promises. Sisson closely supervised the committee's "continuous educational campaign," screening motion pictures under false titles, peppering the walls of Petrograd and Moscow with tens of thousands of posters and distributing inflammatory materials, including a reprint of the Sisson Papers, across swaths of Russian territory. While the committee distributed millions of copies of *The German Plot to Control Russia*, *Letters of an American Friend*, and President Wilson's 8 January 1918 message, it circulated just twenty-four thousand handbills combating a typhus pandemic in Siberia.[13]

At the same time, the administration continued to rely on jaundiced advice about the Bolsheviks' responsibility for myriad problems that in reality resulted as much from decades of tsarist misrule, Russia's disastrous war campaign, and a civil war that foreign powers were prolonging. Prominent engineer Herbert Hoover was an important provider of such advice. Appointed director of a visiting economic commission to Russia, Hoover shared the administration's strident anti-Bolshevism. Unlike Lansing and the president, Hoover at least recognized that real social grievances underpinned radicalism: Bolshevism, he noted, found favor only among the miserable and desperate, long oppressed by despots. For this reason, like many commentators in America, Hoover was initially sanguine about the risks of Bolshevism spreading to the United States. However, the horrors he witnessed in Russia sharpened his instinctive distaste for Bolshevism, influencing his assessment of the Russian people's liability for prevalent chaos. Faced with the ruin of Europe and the Russian Civil War, Hoover began to separate the unfortunate peoples he observed from himself and the United States, belittling their cognitive and ethical capacities. He argued that Russia's problems derived from particular racial and cultural qualities rather than from historical experience. When speculating on the rise of Bolshevism and its potential spread, Hoover suggested that Bolshevik conquest of Europe was unlikely because Bolshevism was a purely Russian product: no other race manifested "such a denseness of ignorance and such impressionism as the Russian people." The only universal quality of Bolshevism Hoover acknowledged was congenital degeneracy, manifested by "the criminal classes" in every society.[14]

Back in the United States, public support for charitable relief of Russia was similarly dominated by the anti-Bolshevik views of men such as Edward Egbert of the American Red Cross Mission. With personal contacts including Creel, Secretary of War Newton D. Baker, and numerous senators and congressmen, Egbert committed himself to securing American aid for anti-Bolshevik forces in Russia. Convinced that the Bolsheviks could not hold power if the Russian people received sufficient aid, Egbert remained a steadfast supporter of intervention in Russia, canvassing politicians and prominent "patriots" even after the collapse of counterrevolution. His principal vehicle was the Catherine Breshkovskaya Russian Relief Fund, which he founded and served as executive secretary. Formed on the advice of the president, who also instructed Egbert to liaise with the CPI, the Breshkovskaya fund won the support of the US Chamber of Commerce and the American Defense Society. The fund's executive committee comprised judges, senior political figures, educators, religious leaders, army officers, and industrialists. Yet the fund had little to do with the exiled Breshkovskaya or with conditions in Russia. Ekaterina Konstantinovna Breshko-Breshkovskaya, the "grandmother of the revolution," was a septuagenarian cofounder of the Socialist Revolutionary Party. Pan-Slavic, anti-Prussian, and something of a mystic, Breshkovskaya propagated an image of the Russian soul as primitive but incomparably pure, encouraging Americans to view Russia as a tragic, vulnerable victim of German expansionism. Fund supporters were led to believe that the Russian masses and the American people were kindred spirits. Breshkovskaya's public appeals did not describe the complexities of Russia's political environment but rather suggested that "far away" there lived "a true and honest democracy" ready to receive instruction in republican virtue. The fund prescribed the export of American education, a "remedy" that appealed profoundly to progressives. The fund planned to establish schools in territory held by counterrevolutionary White forces that offered instruction in modern farming techniques, trade, and elementary subjects. Graduates would then venture into Russian society and transform it. The best and brightest would even journey to America to learn advanced "technical and business methods." Thus, the fund's chief aims were commercial. Its organizers dreamed of making "English rather than German the commercial language of the new middle class of Russia" and of creating a new class of pro-American merchants that would "control the buying and selling for 180,000,000 people." It was perhaps fortunate that the fund's backers were never forced to reconcile the question of how they would smother Breshkovskaya's policies if the Bolsheviks were actually defeated.[15]

In short then, for both the US government and American corporations, commercial imperatives made dealing with the Bolsheviks unthinkable. American industrialists had valuable investments in Russia and expected the federal government to protect them. Dominant ideological tenets of American external strategy also demanded the defeat of Bolshevism. The Open Door policy, a marriage of industrial expansion and national imagery, expressed America's demand for unrestricted investment opportunities in foreign markets. Yet distressingly, the problem of Bolshevism persisted. Allied intervention in the Russian civil war never received adequate resources and was an abject military and diplomatic failure. The fight against Bolshevism would now have to continue primarily on the home front.[16]

Red Scare, 1919–1920

After the conclusion of the Great War, significant discord continued to shape political events in the United States as elsewhere. The fall of Russia's Romanov dynasty presaged the total collapse of the ancien régime in Europe. Nationalist forces staged a revolution in Turkey, hurling the Allies out of Anatolia. Communist governments were formed in Munich and Budapest, and the Spartacist workers' movement in Germany won substantial electoral support. Massive strikes broke out across the British Commonwealth and in Europe. The United States also experienced domestic chaos. While the war had not physically devastated America, it diminished most citizens' living standards and heightened social division. Inflation and a paucity of essential resources eroded wage increases and exacerbated tension between rural and urban locales; cities desperate for primary produce could not pay the prices farmers demanded. While the cost of basic necessities doubled from 1913 to 1920, corporate profits rose threefold from 1914 to 1917 and thereafter maintained an annual rate of increase of 30 percent; the war created more than forty thousand new millionaires. Confronted by collapsing social equity, the Wilson administration did little to help the needy. Privately acknowledging that rampant profiteering might distort the economy for a generation, the president dismantled his special boards and commissions and returned ownership and management of state-held resources to major corporations. Employers sought to prolong workers' wartime wage rates. Bitterly disappointed with the postwar economic settlement, more than four million workers (about 20 percent of the nation's workforce) took industrial action, staging more than thirty-six hundred strikes during 1919, more than the total number of strikers between 1923 and 1932.[17]

Barely two months after the armistice, workers' discontent became so acute that the United States experienced its first general strike, which took place in Seattle in early February 1919. When the government-owned Emergency Fleet Corporation refused to renegotiate the pay and hours of thirty-five thousand shipyard workers, a hundred unions walked off the job, responding to the call of the Seattle Central Labor Council. Although the strike was swiftly quelled, it nevertheless marked a watershed in the rise of fully fledged domestic anticommunism. While industrial action had long been associated with economic vandalism and imported discontent, events in Europe lent unprecedented force to descriptions of the strike as a "Bolshevik" revolution. And the suppression of the strike not only consolidated established means of repressing economic and political protest but also demonstrated how anti-"Bolshevik" officials could win unprecedented celebrity, prestige, and economic reward.

The "hero" who crushed the general strike was Seattle mayor Ole Hanson. The son of Norwegian immigrants, Hanson was a successful real estate agent, a former member of the Washington State assembly, and a failed candidate for the US Senate. When the strike broke out, business interests and local army commanders ordered Hanson to wipe out the local Industrial Workers of the World (IWW). Industry feared the economic costs of continuing worker mobilization, while the army worried that the Wobblies were using "German money" to procure "itinerant women" for enlisted men. Soldiers were also returning from furlough with antiwar literature. For the previous eighteen months, the Washington state branch of the Bureau of Immigration had sought to destroy the regional IWW by deporting all "undesirable" or "pro-German" aliens. Although the secretary of labor had insisted that proof of individual guilt be presented before warrants could be issued and that possession of Wobbly literature or adherence to Wobbly beliefs did not amount to advocacy of illegal principles, the bureau's Seattle office assumed the authority to perform mass arrests. Local businessmen and officials hoped that the bureau would rid the region of up to five thousand Wobblies. In two weeks of raids, two hundred people were seized. Yet the secretary reiterated that only activists who had personally violated immigration laws would be deported, and the program stalled. Hanson then provided local businesses with the names and addresses of Wobblies and their literature distribution points. He closed Seattle's IWW halls, confiscated Wobbly literature, burned union members' possessions, and broke up street meetings. In his sensational account of the strike cum political manifesto, *Americanism v. Bolshevism*, Hanson described this incident as the beginning of his campaign to destroy the "American manifestation" of Bolshevism. But it is more properly regarded as just one episode in local employers' ongoing battle with organized labor.[18]

Like most government officials, Hanson either could not or did not care to distinguish Bolshevism from anarchism, socialism, and industrial syndicalism. He simply equated all such "radical" movements with the collapse of civilization. As Hanson explained at length in *Americanism v. Bolshevism*, "with syndicalism—and its youngest child, bolshevism—thrive murder, rape, pillage, arson, free love, poverty, want, starvation, filth, slavery, autocracy, suppression, sorrow and Hell on earth." All left-wing parties and movements, he said, sought to establish "class government of the unable, the unfit, the untrained; of the scum, of the dregs, of the cruel, and of the failures." And as events abroad had shown, under radicals' rule, "freedom disappears [and] liberty emigrates" as "a militant minority, great only in their self-conceit, reincarnate . . . a greater tyranny than ever existed under czar, emperor, or potentate."[19]

Brandishing this catholic definition of Bolshevism, Hanson declared that Bolshevik spies had infiltrated the local radical movement and engineered the general strike. Within days, the strike was put down with the assistance of the army, the National Guard, and about one thousand special police deputies (de facto citizen militia). Hanson ordered Seattle police to shoot any "lawbreaker attempting to create a riot." Thirty-six alien Wobblies were expelled to New York for deportation. Once the strike was defeated, Hanson described it as the initial phase of "attempted revolution," orchestrated by revolutionaries from every corner of the United States acting on advice from visiting Russian dignitaries; this conspiracy was part of an international strategy built on simultaneous strikes, as a shipyard walkout in London confirmed. Hanson was immediately elevated to national celebrity and as would a future governor of Alaska abandoned the tedium of provincial office for the lucrative lecture circuit. Hanson gleaned more than five times his annual mayoral salary in just over six months of public appearances. His notoriety also elevated him to the platform of the Republican National Convention in 1920, by which time he had become an apostle for immigration reform and "Americanization" programs, dissociating domestic discord from its economic bases and linking it instead with ethnocultural qualities. He contrasted immigrants of the Reconstruction era, such as his parents, who had comfortably assimilated and become "real Americans," with inferior contemporary settlers who did not work the land, were itinerant, failed to raise families, and formed separate colonies in foul, congested, industrial centers. Whether radicals were Bolshevik, anarchist, socialist, or Wobbly, all were "irreconcilable agitating" aliens, "trouble-breeders [and] teachers of falsehood and sedition." They constituted "an ever-increasing danger," of no use to themselves "or to anyone else." Such Reds, Hanson thundered, had to "do right or starve," Americanize or "be sent out of this land of the free."[20]

Just as the Seattle strike was being suppressed, Congress began seriously to examine domestic radicalism, refocusing a Senate inquiry into German interests in the brewing industry into a wide-ranging investigation of left-wing radicalism in America. Plied with testimony from key witnesses who a few months later mounted one of the most lastingly influential legislative inquiries into "Bolshevism" in America, Congress concluded that all left-wing political, industrial, and social organizations were interconnected; were controlled by a new, hostile foreign power; and constituted a subterranean bloc that threatened America's system of government and free-enterprise economy. The Bolsheviks had become the greatest foe of not only the United States but also civilization, capable, Richard Slotkin notes, of deploying "both the conventional resources of a Great Power and the unconventional weapon of revolutionary agitation." As fanatical socialists, Bolsheviks "seemed [far] likelier than the Kaiser's secret agents to succeed in 'subverting' American industrial workers, Negroes, and the hyphenates of the urban slums." Congress had no doubt of America's urgent need to combat the Bolshevik regime with whatever weapons could be mustered.[21]

The information legislators considered in framing the measures they devised to target domestic and foreign "Bolsheviks" came exclusively from special interests and such partisan sources as Ambassador Francis, Egbert, antiradical attorney Archibald Stevenson, and the *Saturday Evening Post*. Even official American accounts of events in Russia came from Finland, often from obscure sources. Such accounts failed to analyze Bolshevism in relation to Russian history or contemporary conditions. Moreover, they were compromised by being introduced into congressional records alongside sensational accounts of socialism in the United States, such as a diatribe denouncing the Nonpartisan League delivered by Rome G. Brown, a Minneapolis lawyer. When one of the Senate's own, LeBaron Colt, a Rhode Island Republican, expressed his view of contemporary political chaos, he described conflict between socialism and capitalism as "a gigantic struggle between two world systems," between "the civilization of Europe and America" and "an old and dead civilization, the so-called civilization of Germany," which had been founded on "the blind worship of a soulless mechanism called the State, controlled by a military caste." Colt clearly missed the irony involved in his positioning of this existential threat in the idea of Prussianism while governments at all levels in America urged citizens to submit absolutely to the authority of the state.[22]

As the year proceeded, further industrial crises hardened antiradical opinion and strengthened conservative economics and politics. Mass walkouts by coal and steel workers, merchant sailors, airmail pilots, and the Boston police force were violently suppressed. Perhaps more important, strikers' demands for such elementary entitlements as the right to organize and an eight-hour day were uniformly dismissed as the thin edge of coming revolution and economic collapse. Big business ensured that the Bolshevik bogey put an end to the labor-organizing drives of the war period. On May Day, a series of red-flag parades degenerated into clashes and riots in which Socialist Party offices were destroyed. Summer witnessed the eruption of "race riots" in twenty-five cities, influenced by competition for jobs that had become increasingly scarce in the postwar economic downturn. The labor movement was hopelessly divided and ill prepared to navigate the industrial and political climate. In Chicago and other urban centers, returning white soldiers and retrenched white workers took out their frustration on the rapidly expanding African American community, which whites regarded as cheap scab labor. Black workers, in turn, did not trust or join white labor unions, leaving important industries patchily organized. The US Army's Military Intelligence Division informed Washington that "race war" and the mass casualties that accompanied it were the result of Bolshevik incitement of African Americans.[23]

Anticommunism in the Labor Movement

During this period, the AFL collaborated in government and business purges of radical unions and antiwar groups in the misplaced hope that doing so would insure the federation and its members against corporate and official attack. In part the result of AFL president Samuel Gompers's quixotic notion of radicals' loyalty to Germany, the federation's collaboration in domestic espionage and repression was consistent with its long-held strategy of pursuing incremental advance and eschewing risky alliances or principles.[24]

The federation's wartime and Red Scare collaboration drew mixed responses from contemporaries and continues to divide historians. Some scholars have recently argued that conservative labor leaders "thought seriously about the proper posture of the state toward domestic subversion." AFL bosses, in this view, "crafted a distinctly laborist politics of civil liberties that rejected statutory limits on speech and assembly and opposed the expansion of federal political policing," even if they did acquiesce in "ad hoc state repression of radicals." Modern scholars further assert that the federation's distinctive attitude toward civil liberty pioneered "a highly nuanced approach" to distinguishing "seditious conspiracy and militant but loyal labor protest."[25]

This conclusion is at odds with the AFL's historical cooperation with authority. Far from "producing a distinctively laborist conservatism that abided for decades," the federation's "anticommunist attitudes drove AFL leaders to support robust political policing at home and interventionist" foreign policies. This viewpoint featured very little nuance or principle. The federation's concern with repairing reputational damage caused by the infiltration of Labor's National Peace Council by a German spy led it to help the Bureau of Investigation (BI), the Military Intelligence Division, and the National Civic Federation, a business-friendly industrial relations consultancy, to spy on the IWW and other radical groups and individuals. The national security apparatus so valued the federation's assistance that the BI assigned Gompers a bodyguard. Ralph Van Deman hoped to establish a permanent liaison with the federation. The AFL eventually went beyond countersubversive espionage, accusing the avowedly anti-imperial Wobblies of being German agents, a ploy that even the federation's champions have described as cynical and "craven."[26]

The AFL's conduct toward the IWW, the Socialist Party, and other radicals stemmed from the federation's instrumental attitude toward First Amendment rights. Gompers and other federation leaders had no interest in protecting the free speech of Socialist presidential candidate Eugene Debs or Wobbly leader "Big Bill" Haywood. The AFL pleaded with the US Senate not to prorogue federal sedition and espionage acts but did not protest domestic political surveillance. Moreover, the AFL waved through state criminal syndicalism laws. The federation's position, therefore, was fundamentally compromised. It sought no real protection from the attacks of capital in democratic and republican principles but instead staked all on an appeal to employers and governments to invest in the AFL as the last and most effective bulwark against the radicalization of the American labor movement. By refusing to negotiate with the AFL, the federation argued, employers drove workers into the arms of the IWW and socialist and/or communist parties.[27]

This strategy failed. Like previous such efforts, the federation's attempt to dissociate itself from radical revolt failed to protect either it or the wider labor movement from corporate and government attack in the aftermath of the war.

In the coming years, the federation's wartime membership gains were swiftly reversed as big business banished organized labor from critical industries until after the Great Depression. The AFL's collaboration did not enable it to craft "a distinctly laborist politics of civil liberties" or to build a relationship with the "broader conservative movement" in which it had real ideological and political clout. On the contrary, the AFL's brand of anticommunism was indistinguishable from that of the conservative returned soldiers' league, the American Legion. Indeed, the AFL let slip an opportunity to create a broad, anti-Bolshevik workers' movement in America by warring with industrial unions that joined the federation in rejecting the Bolsheviks' (forced) incorporation of labor unions into the apparatus of what they understood to be a new, repressive Russian state.[28]

Strikes, Bombs, and Deportations

As the AFL fought to maintain its position, 1919 saw a steady procession of paralyzing strikes that offset whatever prestige the federation accrued during the war. The strikes aggravated reactionary sentiment and increased pressure on governments to immediately end civil strife by force. The mainstream press predictably described industrial disturbance as revolution. The *New York Times*, for example, claimed that even "the greatest coal operators in America" were "quaking" with fear at the prospect of thousands of miners "red soaked in the doctrines of Bolshevism, [clamoring] for a strike as a means of syndicalizing the coal mines without the aid or consent of the government, and even . . . starting a general red revolution in America."[29]

This message had several important effects. In numerous industrial districts it helped authorities to justify the mobilization of police, special deputies, civilian auxiliaries, and company toughs to crush strikes, and this mobilization usually swung the outcome of disputes in employers' favor. The smearing of strikers as Bolsheviks also helped persuade native-born and skilled workers to refrain from supporting industrial protest; the memory of Homestead and fear of losing their jobs to nonunionized immigrants further deterred rebellion. The association of strikes and especially foreign-born workers with Red revolution seemed also to make men such as West Virginia governor John J. Cornwell identify with the interests of coal and steel managers. Fearful of the social and political impact of "cheap foreign labor" in his state, Cornwell overlooked the fact that it was the corporations who had brought these "exotic" workers to his demesne. Instead, he opposed unionization in local coalfields while claiming that this contribution to staying "the tide of Bolshevism and Anarchy" would cost him his life.[30]

Cornwell's expectation of martyrdom was doubtless affirmed when a nationwide series of bombing attacks targeted prominent political and industrial figures. Starting with regional officials including the governor of California and continuing with the arrest and deportation of violent Italian anarchists, a fresh round of bombings targeted Hanson and a Georgia senator in late April. Soon thereafter mail bombs were discovered addressed to Postmaster Burleson, Secretary of Labor William Wilson, John D. Rockefeller, and J. P. Morgan Jr. On 2 June, eight bombs detonated simultaneously across the nation, killing two people. While one device damaged the Massachusetts legislature, another destroyed a considerable portion of US attorney general A. Mitchell Palmer's Washington, D.C., home. This botched assassination attempt critically influenced subsequent events. Before the bombing, Palmer had refused to become an advocate for superpatriots. The May Day disturbances had not convinced him that a campaign of postwar repression was warranted; on the contrary, Palmer publicly endorsed the citizens' right to lawfully change their system of government. The attempt on his life, however, irrevocably changed his attitude. As congressmen and senators filed through the wreckage of his home and urged the attorney to "run to earth the criminals who were behind that kind of outrage," the Radical Left gained a powerful enemy, encouraged by political circumstance and primal drives to seek the movement's total destruction. When President Wilson suffered a stroke in September, Palmer's cabinet colleagues urged him to take strong action. Palmer responded by declaring that national coal and rail strikes scheduled for November would constitute unlawful interference with the production and transportation of essential material.[31]

As attorney general, Palmer was singularly able to instigate a wholesale assault on radicals and aliens. He established the BI's Radical Division to compile intelligence about and direct investigations into left-wing and labor organizations. As division head Palmer chose J. Edgar Hoover, an ambitious young lawyer with family and college connections to the attorney and the BI's director, A. Bruce Bielaski. Meticulous, doctrinaire, and obsessive, Hoover set about establishing a card index system (much like that pioneered by Van Deman in the Philippines) that ultimately grew to contain profiles of more than sixty thousand individuals and two hundred thousand organizations. Congress allocated five hundred thousand dollars to facilitate radical hunts. With a mounting sense of frustration, the House invited Palmer to take definitive steps to apprehend and expel undesirables. Palmer soon obliged, unleashing a national anti-alien and antiradical campaign. Exactly two years after the Bolshevik uprising, Palmer authorized a raid on the New York offices of the Union of Russian Workers, where three hundred suspects were arrested. The following day, the New York legislature had a task force of BI and state police raid seventy-three radical offices and arrest nearly six hundred people.[32]

Inspired by the news from New York, other state police forces also worked with federal agents to seize alleged radicals and illegal aliens. Prisoners in several states were charged under criminal syndicalism laws, which were now described as "measures against Bolshevism, Communism, IWW-ism, socialism and radicalism." These measures were still used, for the most part, against Wobblies, but they were also deployed against members of the United Mine Workers in West Virginia, socialists in Ohio and Kentucky, and Japanese and Filipinos in Hawaii. Vigilante groups pledged to enforce all measures against "Bolshevism" and "un-Americanism"; to deport even "naturalized citizens convicted of any form of sedition or disloyalty"; to condemn strike activity by any member of a state service considered essential to the protection of property; and to denounce "the efforts of certain vicious minorities . . . to secure alterations in the basic laws of [the] nation by the use of sabotage."[33]

Across the nation, authorities, "patriots," and business interests mustered antiradical forces to destroy suspects' property and perpetrate human rights atrocities. Most infamously, on 11 November, Wesley Everest, a Wobbly and former serviceman, was brutally bashed with a rifle butt, castrated, lynched, and finally shot in Centralia, Washington. Congress and the mainstream press supported this savagery, regarding the resistance of Wobblies and socialists to vigilante attacks as insupportable challenges to national sovereignty: local congressman Albert Johnson led the defense of the Centralia vigilantes. Courts uniformly acquitted perpetrators of antiradical violence, while superpatriot organizations called for immediate, extensive immigration restriction.[34]

Powerful factions in Congress also sought to enlarge state powers to expel alien radicals. The House Committee on Immigration examined the number of alien radicals deported from Ellis Island between February 1917 and November 1919. Dissatisfied with the ratio of deportations to internments, the committee ensured that sympathetic bureaucrats would implement its objectives. Chairmanship of the committee had recently passed to Johnson, who had won election by advocating an extreme, antiradical, and severely restricted immigration policy. Johnson removed Ellis Island's administrator, Frederic C. Howe, criticizing him for his liberal attitudes and treatment of inmates. Major newspapers applauded Howe's removal, accusing him of harboring "a great tenderness" toward Reds and of being a "malign fairy" who had given "radicals and their sympathizers important and pivotal government positions." Supportive business groups and Spider Web organizations such as California's Better America Federation informed members that Ellis Island had been "a kind of headquarters for the 'Reds' in place of a prison" and that "scores of 'Reds' sent to the island" had been "permitted to 'escape'" to coal and steel districts, where they could foment revolution. Frustration with regulations restricting the Bureau of Immigration's capacity to expel aliens also prompted leading antiradicals to propose that responsibility for deportation be shifted to the Department of Justice. Doing what they could, immigration authorities declared membership in organizations proscribed by the attorney general, such as the Union of Russian Workers, a deportable offense. Accordingly, on 25 November, state and federal agents raided the Russian People's House in New York and claimed to have seized enough material to construct a hundred explosives. Russian radicals were also arrested in Pittsburgh and other industrial centers and accused of conspiring with the IWW. Antiradicals' greatest coup occurred in December, when 249 aliens and anarchists were banished to Russia. Political censorship, expressed through criminal syndicalism, immigration, espionage, and sedition acts, was augmented by legislation outlawing the display of red flags in thirty-two states and the cities of Los Angeles, New Haven, and New York: more than fourteen hundred people were jailed for contravening these provisions.[35]

Of the methods federal authorities used to suppress undesirable beliefs and persons, deportation was regarded as the most effective. Regular penal codes were regarded as unreliable, and congressional passage of a peacetime sedition bill seemed far from assured. The "full fury of repression" therefore was directed into "the one remaining channel of deportation." Now "freed from the restraining influence of wartime labor scarcity," the federal government initiated mass expulsions of aliens. Although obstacles remained—most notably, effective attorneys who secured the release of many Wobblies deported from Seattle—the Bureau of Immigration usually managed to ensure that its "canons of constructive intent" were used to determine an alien's deportability. However, these procedures were prohibited by the Department of Labor's most senior officers, William Wilson and assistant secretary Louis F. Post. Thwarted, immigration officials' antiradicalism became vengeful. In concert with the BI, they covertly arranged to exclude defense lawyers from the initial stages of deportation hearings for alleged members of communist parties. On 30 December 1920, three days before the Department of Justice carried out a nationwide raid to entrap thousands of members of these parties, the acting secretary of labor, John Abercrombie, advised that aliens could call on legal representation only after "government interests" had been served. Senior bureaucrats also realized that aliens' growing familiarity with government tactics would likely prevent the extraction of confessions. Raids were therefore ordered in the hope that authorities would capture radical groups' membership records before suspects could destroy them. Finally, the establishment of crippling bail terms would ensure that aliens would not be released prior to their hearings. Thus, as William Preston Jr. has memorably written, "Like a pig in a Chicago packing plant," alien detainees were "caught in a moving assembly line, stripped of all [their] rights, and packaged for shipment overseas—all in one efficient and uninterrupted operation [as] American knowhow . . . put an administrative procedure on a mass-production basis."[36]

To a significant degree, state persecution of aliens was a political sideshow intended to furnish authorities with token scapegoats for industrial and political disturbance. Most of the aliens deported to Russia were apprehended for innocent or innocuous behavior and were deported not because they constituted a public risk but rather because they were at risk of becoming public charges. Many deportees were single men or had not yet managed to bring their families to America. In short, they were vulnerable, unemployed aliens without strong ties to the United States. And although the BI possessed evidence indicating that most of the "communists" it considered dangerous were native-born, its Radical Division was anxious to deflect attention from its inability to charge any suspects with involvement in the June 1919 bombings. The simplest way to do so was to launch a public campaign against both the Union of Russian Workers and the Communist Party. This campaign was also influenced by circular thinking in the national security apparatus, whose members were so preoccupied with radical and Marxist labor groups that they overlooked the Italian anarchist cells that had actually carried out the bombings.[37]

While the Departments of Labor and Justice were rounding up and prosecuting Reds, conservative elements in Congress and the New York legislature decided that the Bolshevik crisis justified the abandonment of constitutional government. In December 1919 and again a month later, the US House refused to seat Victor Berger, a Socialist who had won a seat in Wisconsin. At the same time, the New York assembly barred five elected Socialists from taking office. However in taking such action, legislators and Palmer overreached. The treatment of the New Yorkers was roundly condemned as an unnecessary harm to democracy. Moreover, the arrest of such a large number of political prisoners, initially applauded by the media and numerous government officials, prompted the National Popular Government League, a panel of eminent lawyers and legal academics, to investigate charges relating to the impropriety of the mass raids and the use of coercion and torture by authorities. Once more in control of their department, William Wilson and Louis Post ensured that deportation cases proceeding on the grounds of casual membership or affiliation with a proscribed organization were discontinued. Palmer's enraged congressional allies, led by Johnson, attempted to impeach Post.

These events marked a turning point in the fortunes of the most visible opponents of "Bolshevism." Although enthusiasm for peacetime sedition bills remained, conservative legislators could not agree on the appropriate form for such a law, and compromise measures failed. At the same time, important judicial rulings criticized not only the denial of habeas corpus rights to aliens but also the very notion of Americanization. In addition, some powerful businessmen who employed many foreign-born workers publicly denounced the persecution of aliens. The impeachment proceedings against Post collapsed, while Palmer damaged his credibility by forecasting mass radical uprisings across the country. Authorities in various communities took the warning seriously, placing public buildings and important people's homes under armed protection, calling up militia, and imprisoning hundreds of suspected radicals as a precaution. Yet the day passed without incident, and the press hypocritically flayed Palmer as hysterical. Less than a fortnight later, the House Rules Committee, finalizing its investigation of Post, demanded that Palmer defend himself and his department against various charges of impropriety. Before he testified, the National Popular Government League issued its findings in a pamphlet cataloging the department's procedural abuses. Palmer made a final attempt to inflame anti-radical sentiment after a Wall Street bombing in September killed dozens and wounded hundreds. However, the bomb appeared to lack a definite target, and investigators could not be certain it was not a terrible accident, resulting in the failure of Palmer's attempt to pin responsibility on the usual suspects. His political career was dead. So, too, were the chances of proroguing the Sedition Act, which Congress finally repealed in March 1921.[38]

The End of the Red Scare

Palmer's fall and the release of the National Popular Government League report have generally been held to signal the end of the Red Scare and the end of the wartime period of authoritarian government and political repression. The election of plain Ohioan Warren G. Harding to the presidency and his stated desire to return the country to "normalcy" have also been interpreted as reflecting a broad desire to abandon the various crusades of the Wilson era and relegate politics to the back rooms of national life. Many historians have therefore concluded that the Red Scare "did not basically change the pattern of modern American history" and that "traditional consensus politics and individual economic advance" shaped the 1920s. Taken in isolation, neither of these conclusions is unreasonable. They are problematic not so much for what they say as for the impressions they convey. For if traditional politics and the doctrine of "individual economic advance" were reasserted in the 1920s, it was precisely because the war and the Red Scare had devastated unorthodox political ideas and organizations. Similarly, the Red Scare can indeed be interpreted as not having changed the pattern of American history provided that the repression by which it is characterized is regarded as an intensified application of long-standing practices. In this light, the judgment that the Red Scare "greatly" affected "certain subsequent developments" in American history becomes appropriate.[39]

In fact, the Red Scare did not sputter out. Nor did "the public," "the people," "many Americans," or "majority opinion" take stock in 1920 and suddenly realize the error of their ways. The country's politics changed not in spite of the Red Scare but because of it. Politics in the 1920s and in succeeding decades did not differ in kind from the politics of the Red Scare. The extent to which politics differed in temper has also been exaggerated. Although the pressure of war heightened public anxiety and conformism, government officials, business magnates, and journalists encouraged and directed the "patriotic" excesses of school boards, the American Protective League, and many other groups. And repression was willingly visited on its victims by people eager to curry favor with the powerful or to benefit personally or financially from the toxic climate. In the wake of the Red Scare, the members of a nascent anticommunist network made up for the absence of war fever by continuing to encourage and marshal anticommunist sentiment. The perpetuation of the Red Scare is charted in the policies and practices of government agencies, major industry, business advocacy groups, and "patriotic" societies; in the ongoing summary arrest of aliens and periodic deportation drives; in the continuing detention of political prisoners; in the retention of authoritarian powers by government; in the deepening collaboration between government and military intelligence agencies, police Red squads, and business and patriotic groups; in business' renewed assault on organized labor and its association of "100% Americanism" with unregulated labor markets; in the suppression of strikes with injunctions, judicial rulings, and physical force; in government and corporate obstruction of free speech; in the defeat of social welfare legislation; in the cultural campaign of "Americanization"; in recurring legislative inquiries into domestic communism; and in revolutionary changes to US immigration policy.[40]

The Anticommunist Spider Web recorded its first achievements in consolidating the Red Scare by obstructing Palmer's impeachment and, more important, by protecting and nurturing Hoover. Far from being absolved by an "apathetic" public, Palmer was protected by members of the Senate Committee on the Judiciary, including Lee Overman, whose inquiry into the brewing industry had mutated into the first legislative investigation of domestic "Bolshevism." This group obstructed all efforts to publish the committee's report on federal misconduct until February 1923. And even then, the report was read into the *Congressional Record* only on condition that the committee be released from any obligation to consider government misconduct in the Red Scare. Palmer destroyed most of his official and private papers when he left office in 1921, preventing any future reckoning. As head of the now renamed General Intelligence Division, Hoover dominated the bureau's recruitment and evidentiary practices, political orientation, and relations with kindred organizations. On his watch, three successive directors flowered and faded, brought down by unlawful excess, while they pursued operations that he wholly approved. Hoover wisely kept a low profile, made pleasing overtures to government figures, and was duly promoted. His apparent professionalism and organizational skills were widely interpreted as ideal management practice. His permanent appointment as BI director in 1924 was crucial to the fortunes of the Anticommunist Spider Web and the conduct of American politics for fifty years.[41]

CHAPTER 4

The Spider Web Chart

One can gain more in my estimation from examination
of such a chart than he can from reading voluminous
reports dealing with the same subject.

—J. Edgar Hoover

One of the most important and lasting effects of the Red Scare was that it created new alliances in the polity. Just as significant, it greatly strengthened cross-sectoral alliances that had long influenced political, economic, and industrial events. Representatives of government, big business, high finance, and the military were drawn into ever-tighter embrace by the rallying cause of anticommunism. And the Red Scare also brought other forces into this emerging anticommunist movement: wartime preparedness cum "patriotic" societies, leagues of returned servicemen, and venerable nationalistic orders, all representing what would now be referred to as the conservative base of society.

While the country feared domestic revolution, the political moment for anticommunists was pregnant with possibility. The specter of communism provided an all-encompassing bogey to aid in the fight against myriad unwelcome societal changes that anticommunists could blame on a grand pernicious doctrine associated exclusively with revolutionary and undesirable ethnic, religious, and social groups. The political activity of patriotic and veterans' organizations pushed the parameters of anticommunist activity beyond the political and industrial sphere into a broad range of social areas and issues. The work performed by these organizations—supporting the war effort and enforcing the policies of the federal government—transformed anticommunism from a military and economic exercise into a cultural crusade.

In the early 1920s, as the temperature of the scare cooled, the forces of anticommunism sought to coherently define their cause and promote it in the wider community. Soon enough, the movement produced its ideal propaganda in an image that satisfied its members' political and psychological needs: the spider web. The web offered the perfect vehicle for demonstrating how the disparate strands of international Bolshevism, including domestic movements on the left, intertwined and terminated at the Communist Third International (Comintern) in Moscow. From the threat of international socialist revolution, the anticommunist movement wove a story of a vast and deadly conspiracy against America mounted from within by Bolshevik spies, agents, and dupes. This narrative had already been recounted during federal and state legislative inquiries into domestic radicalism as well as in innumerable press reports, but it found its ultimate expression in what became known as the Spider Web Chart.

This chart was the first and best-known of many diagrams of the American "communist" movement that anticommunists produced. While the chart did not represent the entire US communist movement and was rather clumsily designed, it proved to be a scheme of unique power, ideal for spreading the message of anticommunism. Produced by the Chemical Warfare Service of the US Army, the chart depicted dozens of left-wing and progressive communist "front" groups, interlinked by a dizzying array of common personnel and causes. Not surprisingly, the chart reflected the particular preoccupations of the military, overemphasizing the role of pacifist and especially feminist organizations in the domestic radical movement. Even so, for the remainder of the century, America's battle with communism was dominated by the imagery of the Spider Web Chart, which spawned hundreds of imitations and underpinned a corpus of propaganda built on slanderous assertions, gross simplifications, stereotypes, and paranoid fantasies. Further, the chart performed an invaluable role in helping the anticommunist movement to coalesce and attract new members; it gave anticommunists a raison d'être so succinct and readily understandable that it refuted almost any need for justification or explanation.

The Creation of the Chart

When the United States entered the European war, the army hurriedly developed a chemical warfare capacity through a range of military and civilian facilities operating in the field and in laboratories in America. Within weeks of his arrival in France, the American Expeditionary Force commander, General John J. Pershing, centralized all field operations, research, and training in a special chemical warfare department. Turning as he customarily did to fellow Philippine veterans to fill critical posts, Pershing appointed Colonel Amos Alfred Fries to the position of chief of the force's Gas Service in September 1917 and made him responsible for offensive, defensive, and training matters in connection with chemical warfare.

Then, in the final months of the war, Fries was elevated to brigadier general in charge of the Overseas Division of the newly formed Chemical Warfare Service. Thoroughly invested in his new rank and mission, Fries was determined to ensure that the service would continue its work when the war concluded. Prevailing on powerful friends, Fries secured for himself a powerful satrapy in June 1920 when Congress authorized the establishment of a permanent Chemical Warfare Service under the command of a brigadier general.[1]

A passionate advocate of chemical weapons, Fries not only prolonged the life of his department but also used his "allies in Congress, the American Chemical Society, and various veterans groups" to halt "the ratification by the U.S. Senate of the Geneva Protocol outlawing the use of gas warfare." He had less success, however, in preventing Congress, influenced by progressive women's and anti-military lobbies, from slashing military appropriations after the armistice. By the midterm elections of 1922, these lobbies and the War Department were in direct conflict. In the fall of that year, Secretary of War John W. Weeks began to campaign to persuade the public of the importance of retaining strong armed services. The secretary, a former naval officer whose senatorial career had been derailed by suffragists, denounced opponents of large military appropriations as "groups of silly pacifists" whose "insidious propaganda" undermined the nation's capacity "to protect itself." Following his lead, a number of army officers, including Fries, began to denounce women's pacifist organizations "with increasing rancor." Fries had particular cause to denounce these organizations, for several of them had called for the closure of the Chemical Warfare Service since its establishment.[2]

Fries, the military hierarchy, and its supporters in industry and government were not prepared to close the service. The US Army's Military Intelligence Division (MI), which had fought off demobilization by becoming an integral part of the government's intelligence capacity, had come to rely heavily on the service for intelligence and analysis. After receiving instructions to draw up emergency plans to counter domestic revolution, MI's Negative Branch had asked Fries to evaluate the politics of feminists and female pacifist leaders as well as the organizations they represented. Fries duly advised that all such women and associations were "either socialists or Bolsheviks or doing the work of the Bolsheviks." The MI director received a report listing the prominent women's groups and alleging that they had ties to the Communist Workers' Party. The report further stated that "all women's societies and many church societies" varied from "violent red to light pink" and should be "regarded with suspicion." The army feared that all its hard work of "industrial and physical preparation for defense" would go to waste "if the younger generation [turned] out to be pacifists and internationalists."[3]

Fries therefore had the most compelling personal and institutional motives for combating advocates of peace. And perhaps under his direction, a librarian in the service, Lucia Ramsey Maxwell, compiled in May 1923 what became known as the Spider Web Chart. At the head of the chart sat a quotation from the 1920 report of the New York Joint Legislative Committee Investigating Seditious Activities (known as the Lusk Committee after its chair, state senator Clayton Riley Lusk): "The Socialist-Pacifist Movement in America Is an Absolutely Fundamental and Integral Part of International Socialism." Upon publication, the committee's gargantuan report immediately became an urtext for the forces of anticommunism.[4]

Maxwell's chart is an odd creation, a shoddily executed but nonetheless inspired piece of political, emotional, and psychological propaganda (figure 3). It features three columns, sitting below and connecting to two boxes that are meant to represent the heart of the chart but that actually sit above it, at a partial remove. These boxes refer to the Women's Joint Congressional Committee and the National Council for the Prevention of War. Below them sit just over three dozen other boxes containing information on assorted organizations and people. Most of the boxes are packed with words in such small type as to be almost illegible.

The chart presents an informal taxonomy of roughly seven types of Bolshevik-front organizations. In what might be termed the pacifist and antiwar group sit the Women's Joint Congressional Committee and the National Council for the Prevention of War along with the Women's International League for Peace and Freedom, the Women's League for Peace and Freedom, and the Women's Committee for World Disarmament. The suffragists' group features the reconstituted National American Woman Suffrage Association and the League of Women Voters. The Women's Trade Union League is classified in the Bolshevist trade union group. In the "uppity women's" group sit the American Association of University Women and the National Federation of Business and Professional Women. In the Puritanical and antibusiness group are the Woman's Christian Temperance Union and the National Consumers League. The women's advocacy group includes the General Federation of Women's Clubs, the National Council of Jewish Women, the Young Women's Christian Association (YWCA), and the Girls' Friendly Society. Finally, the "get government into the home" group houses the National Congress of Mothers, the Parent-Teacher Association, and the American Home Economics Association. Individual activists identified on the chart are also connected with one or many of these organizations.

Although Maxwell's tangle bears little resemblance to the symmetry of a spider web, it nevertheless constituted a considerable achievement. Maxwell seems to have been the first person to distill the dominant tenets of anticommunism, which had been circulating in enormous legislative committee reports and innumerable publications, into a powerful and highly memorable scheme that resonated on many levels.

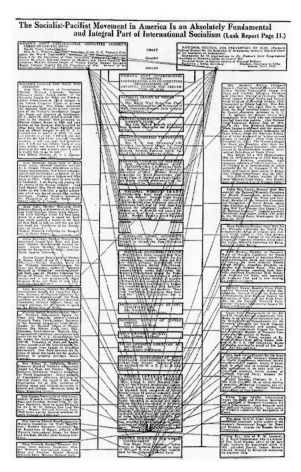

FIGURE 3. Lucia Maxwell's infamous Spider Web Chart, May 1923.
(http://womhist.alexanderstreet.com/wilpf/spider.jpg)

As a coda to her work, Maxwell reproduced two quotations from Soviet leader V. I. Lenin and his "commissar for free love," Alexandra Kollontai, about the importance of women to communism. Maxwell also appended a poem she wrote, "Miss Bolsheviki Comes to Town." Perhaps inspired by Irving Berlin's tune "Look out for the Bolsheviki Man," Maxwell's ode proclaimed:

> Miss Bolsheviki has come to town,
> With a Russian cap and a German gown,
> In women's clubs she's sure to be found,
> For she's come to disarm AMERICA.

She sits in judgment on Capitol Hill,
And watches the appropriation bill
And without her O.K., it passes—NIL
For she's there to disarm AMERICA.

She uses the movie and lyceum too,
And later text-books to suit her view,
She prates propaganda from pulpit and pew,
For she's bound to disarm AMERICA.

The male of the specie has a different plan,
He uses the bomb and the fire brand,
and incites class hatred wherever he can
While she's busy disarming AMERICA.

His special stunt is arousing the mob.
To expropriate and hate and kill and rob,
While she's working on her political job,
AWAKE! AROUSE!! AMERICA!!![5]

Maxwell used her official franking privileges to send copies of her diagram to a select (but not small) group of recipients. After mailing the original chart to President Harding, Maxwell sent facsimiles to the president's staunchly anti-labor attorney general, Harry M. Daugherty, and his special assistant, J. Edgar Hoover. The chart sent both men into raptures. The nation's most senior law officer later exclaimed that he did not know how he "should have got along without it," while Hoover described it as "a magnificent piece of work," more valuable to the anticommunist cause than all the "voluminous reports dealing with the same subject." The commander of Fort Bragg, Brigadier General Albert J. Bowley, was one of several military men to receive the chart, and he brandished it as he informed the Ohio Chamber of Commerce that the executive secretary of the National Council for the Prevention of War, Frederick J. Libby, was a Russian agent. Patriotic societies also received the chart. The manager of the Washington bureau of the American Defense Society, a Harvard-educated journalist, Richard Merrill Whitney, was so impressed that he urged the secretary of war to confer on Maxwell the Distinguished Service Medal; the chart underpinned all of Whitney's subsequent output, including his influential book, *Reds in America* (1924).[6]

For the next year or so, knowledge of the chart was restricted to its recipients and those with whom they shared it. Amos Fries, for example, made public appearances in which he customarily described the organizations featured in the chart as communist fronts; he also colluded with the American Defense Society in the surveillance of the National Student Forum, an organization he regarded not as "out and out Socialists or Bolshevists" but nevertheless as "doing the work of the latter." Then, in March 1924, Henry Ford's *Dearborn Independent* reprinted the Spider Web Chart in a two-part feature, "Are Women's Clubs 'Used' by Bolshevists?" The paper endorsed accusations of organizational treachery leveled by Whitney and Fries and leveled similar charges against the National Council of Women. The chart's publication in such a widely read paper pushed the debate to the center of ongoing battles between progressive and reactionary women's groups and among powerful corporate interests over female suffrage, feminism, and government provision of essential health and other welfare services. The reactionary women's groups, "patriots," manufacturers, and doctors' lobby alleged that the diverse goals of the progressive women's movement formed part of a political program devised by Kollontai in the International Secretariat of Communist Women.[7]

The progressive women's movement refused to permit such charges to go unchallenged and demanded a retraction from the *Dearborn Independent* and the military. A special committee of the Women's Joint Congressional Committee wrote to Weeks refuting the allegation that women's organizations were affiliated with or promoted the policies of Soviet Russia. Decrying the impropriety of permitting government employees to engage in such partisan conduct, the committee threatened the secretary with legal consequences and, more important in a presidential election year, the rancor of twelve million female voters. Weeks, a survivor of the discredited Harding administration, did not want to have to explain to the new president, Calvin Coolidge, why he might face such opposition in his reelection bid and consequently wrote a perfunctory letter of apology. Weeks claimed that he had instructed Fries to destroy the original chart and to inform anyone who had a copy that it was both erroneous and unauthorized. Weeks also attempted to distance his department from Maxwell, claiming that she had distributed the chart in her capacity as chair of the Patriotic Committee of the League of American Penwomen. For her part, Maxwell asserted that the chart was her private property and announced that she would produce an expanded and copyrighted version.[8]

Enduring Effects

Despite Weeks's order, the original chart remained in existence, though some copies were collected and destroyed. Others, however, continued to inspire imitation and to provide an important impetus to the Anticommunist Spider Web. The concept underpinning the chart also gained ever greater legitimacy. The editor of the *Kansas Woman's Journal* informed the Associated Industries of Massachusetts in late 1925 that progressive women's organizations formed an interlocking directorate of communist activism, emanating from the chief spider, the now elderly Jane Addams. Addams also featured prominently in a "corrected" spider web chart issued by a Massachusetts superpatriot, Charles Norman Fay. The following year, the president of the National Association of Manufacturers denounced the second Conference on Women in Industry, describing the economic theories of progressive women's organizations as Russian in origin, subversive, and spread by an interlocking directorate under the control of Commissar Kollontai. Patriotic women's associations nationwide received copies of the speech. Also in 1926, campaigning against the renewal of the federal Maternity and Infancy Protection Act of 1921, Senator Thomas F. Bayard Jr., a Delaware Democrat, entered into the *Congressional Record* an interlocking directorate chart produced by the Woman Patriots, which he mailed under his official frank to state officers of the Daughters of the American Revolution. It was fitting that the Woman Patriots were producing such charts: not only did the original chart carry a dedication to Mary Kilbreth, the publisher of *The Woman Patriot*, but Carrie Chapman Catt, cofounder of League of Women Voters, held the Patriots rather than the army chiefly responsible for the Spider Web Chart.[9]

The chart had already entered the realm of legend in patriotic and intelligence circles and had become a small burden for MI. The army regularly received unsolicited requests for copies of the chart, and although MI had no qualms about sharing intelligence within the Anticommunist Spider Web, it was eager to convince outsiders that it did not spy on citizens during peacetime. The division consequently was forced into uncomfortable exchanges such as one with Ida L. Jones, general secretary of the YWCA in Fort Wayne, Indiana, who wrote to MI in 1927 seeking verification of the existence of and a personal copy of the "Spider Web Chart of interlocking directorates of certain organizations deemed dangerous, sinister and subversive." An intelligence officer informed Jones that MI did not conduct "investigations of individuals or of organizations in time of peace" or lodge "adverse criticisms of any individuals or organizations." The officer also stated that there was "no truth" to the claim that the military had ever "issued" the chart and that all copies of it had been destroyed.[10]

But the Spider Web Chart would never die; it was far too useful. It had a permanent role inspiring the growing anticommunist movement with a vision of the political and organizational cohesion it should strive to realize. By helping to make real a communist conspiracy of progressive and radical agencies, the Spider Web Chart impelled the anticommunist movement to mirror the efforts of its imagined enemies. The chart's creator and sponsors certainly enmeshed themselves in the expanding Anticommunist Spider Web. Whitney used the chart to help him write *Reds in America*, which was published right around the time of his sudden death from heart failure in 1924. Maxwell continued to preach anti-communism with the Daughters of the American Revolution, as secretary of the Patriotic Women's Conference, and in *The Red Juggernaut*, which she published in 1932. While still in the army, Fries joined the advisory council of the Key Men of America, a patriotic society that was the brainchild of right-wing journalist Fred R. Marvin. Fries's fellow council members included not only Maxwell but Congressman Albert Johnson; Major General Eli A. Helmick, the inspector general of the US Army; and a subordinate officer in the Chemical Warfare Service. Fries also contributed to the corpus of anticommunism, publishing *Communism Unmasked* in 1937, after his retirement from the army.[11]

The Spider Web Chart had played an important role in helping these and many more anticommunists to find each other and forge a consistent political program. It not only amplified the reach and unity of the anticommunist movement but also, ironically, encouraged the emerging anticommunist movement to assume the form of what its members imagined to be the Bolshevik movement. In particular, the chart and other items of propaganda encouraged anticommunists to develop an extensive and highly connected network of kindred associations and a monolithic ideology.

CHAPTER 5

Mapping a Political Network

The Anticommunist Spider Web

> Every progressive spirit is opposed by a thousand
> men appointed to guard the past.
> —Maurice Maeterlinck

The American anticommunist movement that emerged out of the Red Scare believed that it had found the perfect metaphor for its mortal enemy in the spider web. Yet the anticommunist movement more closely resembled a spider web. Similarly, the members of the Anticommunist Spider Web formed a conspiracy against democracy that was far more influential than the "communist" conspiracy they fought.

A number of factors made the Anticommunist Spider Web a powerful and effective network. It achieved greater ideological cohesion than the notoriously sectarian parties of the Left. It enjoyed greater institutional stability than the communist conspiracy.[1] The organizations and individuals who constructed the web continued to hunt their prey from within its confines, avoiding the acrimonious defections that plagued left-wing parties. The Anticommunist Spider Web also enjoyed greater financial stability than the communist conspiracy. The child of the open shop movement, the federal government, the armed services, state policing bodies, mainstream media, veterans' organizations, the mature national patriotic societies (such as the Daughters of the American Revolution) and the conservative craft union movement, the Spider Web was never starved of resources, alliances, or oxygen. And although the constituent elements of the Web did not generally cooperate with the iron sense of discipline that they imagined the Left possessed, they nevertheless formed an "interlocking directorate" of significant size and breadth. The Spider Web thus constitutes precisely the sort of civilian network that liberal philosophers customarily describe as performing an essential function countering social and political tyranny. However, as Corey Robin (echoing Tocqueville) has observed, these networks have made a crucial contribution throughout American history to the emergence and consolidation of political repression.[2]

This is not to say that the interwar Anticommunist Spider Web was a numerically significant movement. Journalist and diplomat Norman Hapgood reckoned that the United States had about twenty-five thousand such "patriots" in the mid-1920s. He did, however, exclude from this number members of such giant reactionary organizations as the American Legion and the Ku Klux Klan, which supported anticommunism but had diverse members and purposes. Even so, some of the Web's leading organizations had large memberships, and many more of them forged close relationships with the enormous patriotic and business organizations that antedated the Red Scare, including the Daughters of the American Revolution (DAR), the Patriotic Order of Sons of America, and the American Bankers' Association. Many Spider Web members were sustained by close relations with big business, and several anticommunist organizations were fronts for business lobbies. Groups such as the Better America Federation (BAF) illustrate the anticommunist movement's origins in and strong ties to the antiunion, open shop lobby and its stalwarts, the National Association of Manufacturers, various Citizens' Alliances, and the National Founders' Association. As Hapgood put it, professional patriots represented "a large amount of money and a sensitive property nerve": their ultimate purpose was to promote "the status quo of property."[3]

However, protecting economic advantage was only part of the Anticommunist Spider Web's purpose. Business and political interests also used anticommunism as a tool to control foreign and domestic policy in the challenging environment created by the Great War, socialist revolutions in Europe, and the bitter industrial disputes of the postwar downturn. From the sanctums of America's most prestigious clubs and major political parties emanated legislative witch hunts of communists, conspiracies to deprive democratically elected socialists of their seats in the nation's legislatures, and "patriotic" societies that incited the populace against Reds.

A different sort of motive—fear—also encouraged the conservative craft union movement to ally itself with Red-baiting employers' organizations. Union leaders reasoned that the best hope for safeguarding their influence lay in abetting anticommunism, for which they might secure some reward from grudging employers and probusiness governments. Dread of mass migration was also a significant spur for members of the Spider Web, who mobilized to protect the political, economic, and cultural primacy of Protestantism and Anglo-Saxons. America's ethnic profile had been changing too drastically and rapidly for their liking in recent decades, and dominant conceptions of racial and religious identity associated communism with Central and Eastern European migrants, especially Jews, and minorities in the United States, particularly blacks.

Government intelligence operatives were among those most concerned by anticommunism, and the Red Scare put state and military intelligence services at the heart of the Spider Web. The Bureau of Investigation (BI), the US Army's Military Intelligence Division (MI), and the Office of Naval Intelligence maintained lengthy and strong associations with former agents, servicemen, and reservists; immigration and border security authorities; state, metropolitan, and county police; sympathetic politicians; business lobbies; and patriotic societies. These relationships, often informal by necessity, continued throughout the lean years between about 1924 and 1936, when both the Department of Justice and the armed services were officially barred from conducting domestic surveillance. Military and veterans' organizations were particularly enthusiastic propagators of patriotic propaganda. Their publications, such as the *Army and Navy Journal*, incessantly examined the concerns and promoted the objectives of the Anticommunist Spider Web, combating Red Peril conspiracy and constitutional reform and advancing the cause of the open shop. The BI was another vital strand in the Web, collating and distributing anticommunist propaganda as it both fed and fed from its wide network. The bureau's ties to the National Civic Federation (NCF) and Dick Whitney were especially strong during the tenure of director Frank Burns (1921–24), when the bureau, NCF director Ralph M. Easley, and the AFL forged an anticommunist alliance closer than any other in the United States or anywhere else in the world.[4]

The relationship between the BI, MI, and the private intelligence networks run by the Spider Web was reciprocal. Army officers campaigning against antimilitarism in educational institutions, for example, were influenced by Whitney. And in addition to distributing privately produced anticommunist material under the War Department's mail frank, MI wrote speeches for esteemed patriots and collected intelligence from employers' organizations such as the Minneapolis Citizens' Alliance. The BI's relations with private "patriots" were so close that some "professional patriots" like Whitney had as much access to its files as any senior agent. But scandal, particularly the surveillance of senators investigating the Teapot Dome affair, forced both the BI and MI to move their political surveillance operations underground. Yet new bureau director J. Edgar Hoover remained a national leader of the anticommunist, countersubversive movement, counting among his numerous interwar achievements Secretary of State Charles Evans Hughes's refusal to recognize the USSR and the creation of Congress's Special Committee to Investigate Communist Activities and Propaganda (1930). And in time, the domestic Communist Party's pro-Soviet activism and the rise of Nazism enabled Hoover to bring his surveillance program out of the closet when President Franklin Roosevelt authorized Hoover to again share with the executive the political intelligence that he had never ceased collecting.[5]

In addition to the military and civil intelligence arms of the government, the constituent organizations of the Spider Web fell into three categories. A taxonomy Hapgood suggested for these organizations ninety years ago remains useful. The most powerful handful of groups with national presence comprised the National Security League, the American Defense Society, the NCF, and mass member organizations such as the Sons and Daughters of the American Revolution, the American Legion, and national military societies such as the Reserve Officers Association. Beneath these organizations stood the "sectional" societies, devoted to single issues or the representation of employer interests and generally wielding influence only in their home cities and states. Several of these organizations still possessed considerable clout, however. Contemporary observers regarded the BAF as "the most active and highly organized" of these sectional organizations, but similar groups such as the Massachusetts Public Interests League stoutly defended the open shop and opposed progressive social reform. The final category of Spider Web groups comprised one-man bands "unlikely to continue beyond the individual's enthusiasm." Some of these anticommunists were also nationally significant activists whose enthusiasm sustained them well into the Cold War. They included journalist Fred Marvin and Harry Augustus Jung, "commissioner" of the National Clay Products Industry Association (an open shop lobby) and director of the American Vigilant Intelligence Federation. Another type of Web member not identified by Hapgood was the professional anticommunist spy or hunter, epitomized by Jacob Spolansky, an MI and BI operative who survived the budget and staff cuts forced on those organizations by working as a freelance journalist, recounting his anticommunist exploits, and organizing state and corporate industrial policing, espionage, and strikebreaking efforts. Numerous former intelligence operatives, among them Captain John B. Trevor, also established organizations to promote anticommunist objectives.[6]

The Spider Web's primary product was propaganda, which was created by larger, wealthier, and better organized groups as well as smaller and only sporadically effective associations. Consequently, as Hapgood observed, these groups depended strongly on staff "with some knowledge of newspaper publicity, compilation and printing"; moreover, many spider web activists were "former newspapermen or publicity agents." Web members who fell into this category included NCF director Ralph M. Easley, Marvin, Albert Johnson, Albert Briggs, and Spolansky. The American Protective League, National Security League, and American Defense Society enlisted famed author Emerson Hough, who interrupted his career mythologizing the Old West to mythologize the deeds of contemporary antiradical, nativist "patriots." Anticommunist organizations used their extensive contacts and expertise to disseminate their propaganda through major media outlets, in print, via the airwaves, and in public forums, working to materially influence elections, immigration policy, public conceptions of patriotism and citizenship, the treatment of political prisoners, and the enactment and enforcement of probusiness and open shop legislation. They also encouraged various forms of industrial and political repression. Spider Web propaganda thus was frequently used with great effect for much larger purposes.[7]

The Spider Web was an informal network whose members shared information in their frequently overlapping but distinct spheres of interest and influence. This approach ensured that messages spread far beyond the reach of any individual or group. While they could cooperate effectively to pursue such large goals as immigration policy reform, the members of the Spider Web generally pursued their objectives on their own or in concert with a few kindred spirits. Only on very rare occasions did they demonstrate the efficiency with which they credited the communist spider web, and they gained no insight from this fact, never questioning the human capacity for prolonged multilateral cooperation regardless of political belief. And if Hapgood underestimated the determination of even lone "professional patriots" to sustain for decades their political crusade, he correctly noted that many Spider Web front groups were vulnerable to the loss of critical personnel. Whitney's death, for example, also meant the demise of the American Defense Society's relationship with the BI. Similarly, the Massachusetts Public Interests League folded just one month after the death of its most charismatic leader, Margaret C. Robinson, in 1932. These changes in fortune, however, could result as much from the vicissitudes of government agencies and other powerful sponsors of anticommunism as from the health of any particular organization in the Web.[8]

The informality of the Spider Web was a logical outcome of the purposes and financial and institutional bases of its constituent organizations, which its members usually strove to obscure. The great majority of these organizations were publicly disingenuous about their aims and methods. Whether they were state and military intelligence arms that concealed and disavowed their illegal political surveillance and strikebreaking or commercial lobbies that cloaked themselves in Old Glory and the Constitution, Spider Web organizations operated on the basis of conspiracy. They functioned internally as rigidly hierarchical autocracies and externally as secretive, shadowy groups, refusing to divulge their financial affairs and principal sources of income even to their own members.[9]

This approach was not surprising: revealing such information would necessarily disclose the antidemocratic and elitist character of the anticommunist movement, which survived on subsidies from wealthy businessmen and corporations. A congressional investigation into the National Security League's affairs, for example, revealed that it had received contributions as large as thirty thousand dollars from Henry Clay Frick of US Steel, John Rockefeller, and T. Coleman du Pont, a former senator and chemical manufacturer who also served on the NCF's board. Such societies could therefore undertake considerable expenditures: the National Security League, for example, spent $235,000 in 1918, when it received $50,000 from Carnegie Corporation. The NCF, ostensibly an organization dedicated to the mediation of labor disputes, was "clearly a big business organization, and [had] been so," Hapgood wrote, "ever since Ralph Easley learned which class could write cashable checks." Most of its board, with the exception of Samuel Gompers, presided over corporations that actively discouraged collective bargaining by their workers and employed "spies and stool pigeons to rout any attempt at unionization." Easley had close relations with the labor espionage department of US Steel, providing it and the corresponding section of Standard Oil with sensitive information. And if, as Hapgood suggested, the NCF was the employers' organization most "intimately connected with Wall Street," it was distinguished only by the level at which it conducted its business, not by its character or associations. US Steel also had a hand in the affairs of the American Defense Society, and Judge Elbert H. Gary, one of the NCF's financial angels, supported the American Constitution Association, a front for West Virginia's most powerful coal operators. Corporate control of the American Defense Society was absolute. Aside from Robert Bacon (another representative of US Steel and a cofounder of the National Security League), its management board included the director of Great Western Chemical Corporation and Frederic R. Coudert Jr., a director of oil, real estate, and banking companies and the scion of a prominent New York legal family.[10] The BAF and the other most effective regional anticommunist associations were also dominated by commercial interests. The BAF's directors were "millionaire real estate, department store, and public utility captains of industry"; the leadership of the Los Angeles Merchants and Manufacturers Association and the federation were almost interchangeable. As Hapgood put it, a "mixture of patriotism, anti-radicalism, and privileged business [ran] through the larger and stronger organizations," while "only the small fry [were] patriots on principle," and even their motives were usually inseparable from profit.[11]

In spite of its formal lack of coordination, therefore, the Spider Web was a comprehensive network. And although its constituent groups did not always influence the political agenda quite as they wished, they still exercised considerable influence and contributed greatly to the creation of anticommunism as a coherent political ideology and movement. Even though many members of the

Web suffered from and peddled delusional conspiracy theories, their strong ties to the political establishment, their financial strength, and their access to government and military secret services enabled them to win numerous significant victories, including the defeat of a child labor amendment to the US Constitution; the institution of loyalty oaths for teachers and other restrictions on First Amendment rights; the draconian and racist reform of immigration policy; the continuing imprisonment, maltreatment, and even execution of political prisoners; and the enforcement of cultural homogeneity through "Americanization" programs. The Spider Web also had a profound effect on American politics, not just in the interwar era but also in the Cold War. Its redoubtable members, such as the BAF, John Trevor, Harry Jung, Major General Ralph Van Deman, Elizabeth Dilling, and Hamilton Fish Jr., nourished Cold War anticommunism and McCarthyism, briefing (and in Fish's case leading) various congressional committees and maintaining networks with MI; the BI and its successor, the Federal Bureau of Investigation (FBI); conservative labor unions; and employer lobbies. Fish and several others became the public face of the isolationist movement before World War II. And Trevor, Jung, and Dilling were among those who became important (if sometimes publicity-shy) supporters of fascism and Nazism.

"Interlocking Directorates"

Any attempt to map the connections among the members of the Anticommunist Spider Web risks looking like Lucia Maxwell's Spider Web Chart. This description of the Web thus focuses on some of the main groups and their associated members.

Captain John B. Trevor served as commander of the New York City branch of MI. A World War veteran, lawyer, long-serving trustee of the American Museum of Natural History, and member of the Atlantic Coast's best clubs, Trevor bridged the intelligence services, patriotic societies, and the scientific and congressional wings of the immigration restriction movement (figure 4). After helping to orchestrate the Lusk Committee's investigations and report, Trevor became the principal architect of the revolutionary Johnson-Reed Immigration Act (1924). Trevor then founded the American Coalition of Patriotic Societies (ACPS) to lobby for the maintenance of the act's draconian and racist provisions. His right hand at the ACPS, office manager Flora A. Walker, was one of the primary figures responsible for leading the DAR from broadly progressive to archreactionary politics in the 1920s. Trevor's antimigration activity led to his association with the American fascist and Nazi movement. He also became an anticommunist éminence grise for younger generations of Red-baiters, including Martin Dies and Joseph McCarthy.[12]

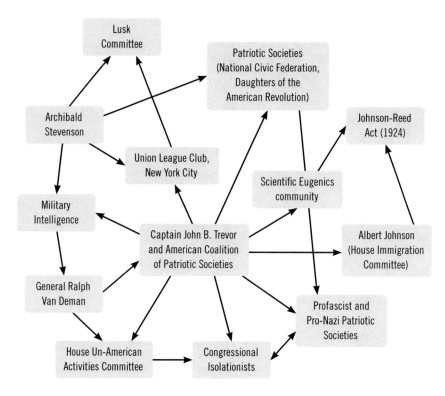

FIGURE 4. John B. Trevor and the Spider Web

The career of Jacob Spolansky, an immigrant from what is now Ukraine, illustrates the opportunities that the war and the Red Scare created for a new class of professional spies who were trained in anticommunism in the service of the state. Many of these spies worked intermittently for federal, military and state agencies while juggling assignments with the industrial espionage divisions of major corporations and employer lobbies. In Spolansky's case, state and corporate intelligence work also led to journalistic employment with industry and mass media. Spolansky's anticommunist activity began during the war with MI and continued with the BI until budget and staff cuts in the mid-1920s forced him into the private sector. Spolansky conducted corporate espionage for private detective agencies, Botany Mills of New Jersey, and Chrysler and General Motors. He performed similar service for such leading national advocates of the open shop as the National Metal Trades Association, for which he also published articles in *Open Shop Review*. County police and a grand jury in Michigan availed themselves of Spolansky's detective skills, as did numerous federal legislative

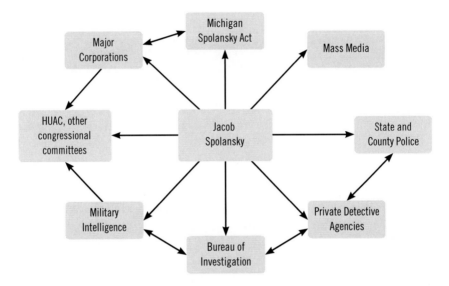

FIGURE 5. Jacob Spolansky and the Spider Web

inquiries into domestic radicalism, including the House Un-American Activities Committee in the interwar and World War II periods (figure 5).

The BAF was founded in 1917 by Harry M. Haldeman and Harry Chandler. The socially prominent Haldeman served as president of Pacific Pipe and Supply, with side ventures in real estate and oil. Chandler published the stridently antiradical *Los Angeles Times* and maintained significant investments in property and oil. Representing and funded by major industries, including steel, oil, real estate, utilities, department store, insurance and banking concerns, the federation became a major political influence in California immediately after its founding. Preferring, like so many Spider Web organizations, to conceal its primary function of agitating for the open shop and a laissez-faire economy, the federation sold its program as anticommunism, adopted an overtly patriotic name, and operated through patriotic- and democratic-sounding fronts such as the Americanization Fund.

An accomplished and industrious producer of open shop and anticommunist propaganda, the federation supplied workplace and other literature to regional industrial heavyweights, churches, Kiwanis and Lions Clubs, the Soldiers' and Sailors' Employment Bureau, the American Legion, the DAR and numerous smaller patriotic societies, the American Bar Association, and the US Department of Education (figure 6). Its work was esteemed and distributed by mass media outlets in print and on radio, and its roster of speakers and authors in-

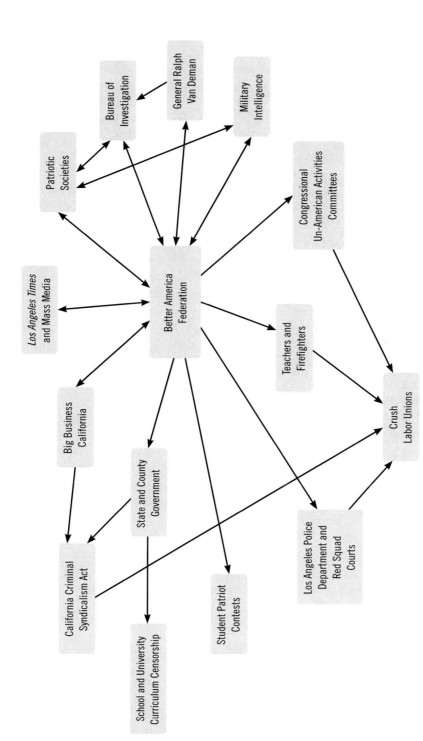

FIGURE 6. The Better America Federation and the Spider Web

cluded state politicians and exiled tsarist Russians. Together with the US District Court judge Martin Wade (who had conspired during the war with the American Protective League to imprison Socialist Party leader Kate Richards O'Hare), the federation sponsored student oratory competitions devoted to instilling the federation's interpretation of the US Constitution.[13] The federation sought repeatedly and often to influence electoral politics, law enforcement, school and university curricula, and the spread of unionism among California's workers. It placed particular importance on cultivating the Los Angeles Police Department's Red Squad to break strikes and dispense industrial terror and was one of the principal sponsors and beneficiaries of California's criminal syndicalism law. A long-standing and trusted source of information for anticommunist legislators in California and Washington, D.C., the committee ultimately followed the path of such other Spider Web members as Ralph Van Deman, turning over its gigantic collection of radical files to government and corporate subscribers in its final incarnation as the American Library of Information.

Though the Anticommunist Spider Web (figure 7) indeed resembles Maxwell's chart, the ideological and personal relationships among these protagonists was genuine and extensive. Exploring the broad connections of Trevor and others within the Spider Web reveals much about its workings. Into the 1940s, Trevor's ACPS maintained reciprocal ties with the DAR and the Sons of the American Revolution (members of both groups served on the ACPS board); Jung's American Vigilant Intelligence Federation; Walter Steele's newspaper, *National Republic*; and the Westchester Security League, an offshoot of the DAR. Trevor's chief confrere in MI and the prime mover of the Lusk Committee, Archibald Stevenson, headed up the NCF's Free Speech Committee in the 1920s before throwing in his lot with Merwin K. Hart, a fervent supporter of Spain's Generalissimo Francisco Franco who ran an open shop lobby, the State Economic Council (later the National Economic Council).[14]

Trevor's friend, Jung, had a background in corporate rather than military intelligence and put it to use running the National Clay Products Industry Association, American Vigilant Intelligence Federation, and other front groups. Aside from lobbying for the open shop, Jung distributed information from kindred groups and sold his expensive industrial espionage data to paid-up members of his associations. His strikebreaking and labor espionage service and his maintenance of a sizable radical card index ultimately saw him run afoul of Speaker of the US House Henry T. Rainey, who publicly attacked Jung in 1933 as a profiteer from labor disturbance. A traveling lecturer on the evils of communism and unionism, Jung had influence with local law officials, persuading Chicago prosecutors to file charges against twenty-six Communist Party members in 1929. A director of Fred Marvin's Key Men of America and the Industrial Defense Association,

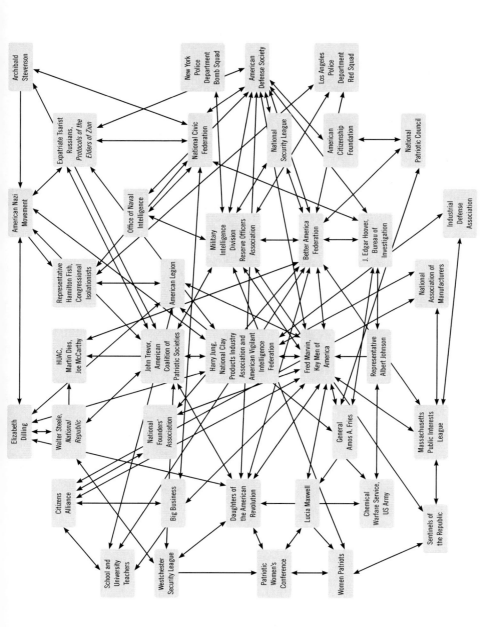

FIGURE 7. The interlocking directorates of the Spider Web

Jung was also an associate of the National Association of Manufacturers. His operations were subsidized by banks, industry, rich widows, and above all the publisher of the *Chicago Tribune*, Robert R, McCormick, whose family had long played a significant role in the suppression of "radicals." McCormick gave Jung financial support, free office space in the Tribune Building (which he shared with Illinois Klan leader Gale S. Carter), and a megaphone in the *Tribune*. Jung also became an important figure in the American isolationist and Nazi movements.[15]

Fred Marvin's ties to Johnson, Maxwell, Amos Fries, and other military figures represented only a small fraction of Marvin's involvement in the Spider Web. The advisory council of his Key Men of America also included judges, law school deans, American Legion post commanders, industrialists, Grange officeholders, and such important anticommunists and labor bashers as the BAF's "manager," Joseph Joplin, DAR president Mrs. Alfred (Grace) Brosseau (who also served as president of Trevor's APCS), Margaret C. Robinson, and Ernest H. Davidson, a wealthy real estate agent and president of the Ramsay and Dakota Counties chapter of the Minnesota Citizens' Alliance. Ben Affleck, president of the Universal Portland Cement Company, also divided his patriotic time between the Key Men of America and the American Citizenship Foundation. As a Red-baiting journalist, Marvin had cultivated relations with Spider Web members and big business since he covered the great disputes on the Coeur d'Alene mining range in Idaho in the late nineteenth century. As editor of Colorado's *Pueblo Chieftain* and *Mountain States Banker*, Marvin gave, in the words of his close friend Jung, "a large part of his life to the combating of radical activities and [the] defense of the principle of 'America for Americans.'" His work was distributed by open shoppers such as the Citizens' Alliance and the *National Republic*, which Marvin also coedited. Marvin's susceptibility to paranoid conspiracy fears cost him financially; libel suits issued by American Civil Liberties Union general counsel Arthur Garfield Hays and Rosika Schwimmer, the Hungarian-born vice president of the Women's International League for Peace and Freedom, bankrupted Marvin and his Searchlight Department, which exposed "subversive movements" in the *New York Commercial*. The Key Men of America brought Marvin back into solvency and prominence, allowing him to become a major source of anticommunist information for MI, which he supplied with a blacklist of more than two hundred socialist and communist organizations. The army, for its part, forwarded Marvin's diatribe against the Women's International League for Peace and Freedom, *Ye Shall Know the Truth*, to any correspondent who expressed interest in pacifism, feminism, or socialism.[16]

The military also was enmeshed in the Spider Web. In addition to their connections to the Key Men of America, Amos Fries and the US Army's Major General Eli Helmick spoke on behalf of the National Patriotic Council, along with Rear

Admiral W. A. Moffett, who split his anticommunist duties with the American Citizenship Foundation. Fries also commanded the Washington, D.C. post of the American Legion. Generals William H. Bisbee and Clarence R. Edwards sat on the board of the Industrial Defense Association with Jung and a host of college professors, clergymen, lawyers, doctors, society women, and business men. Retired general R. L. Bullard served as a director of the National Security League. Colonel Edwin Marshall Hadley joined with Elizabeth Dilling to establish the Paul Reveres. Most important, MI's founder, Van Deman, spent much of his long retirement amassing an enormous file on radicalism—more than a quarter million individual card entries—that made him a national antiradical clearing-house until his death in 1952. He maintained clandestine ties with his old unit, the Office of Naval Intelligence, and the FBI and exchanged information with the bureau on an official, funded basis after 1940. With close ties to the BAF, Trevor, the San Diego and Los Angeles police Red Squads, industrial associations in California, the Post Office, the Border Patrol, and the Coast Guard, Van Deman ran a "web of domestic surveillance" that penetrated the Communist Party and "a whole spectrum of liberal targets, including religious, civil rights, and labor organizations" and the motion picture industry.[17]

The membership rolls of Spider Web organizations also reveal the particularly active parts played by magnates in specific industries. The American Defense Society was run by Elon H. Hooker, founder of Hooker Electro-Chemical Company, which manufactured plastics and chemical weapons. A director of many corporations, Hooker sent General John J. Pershing on a national antipacifist speaking tour in conjunction with publicity given the issue by the *Dearborn Independent*. Hooker also sat on the board of the NCF, a gesture reciprocated by Judge Alton B. Parker, the NCF's president and the 1904 Democratic presidential nominee. Other chemical manufacturers were among the most enthusiastic supporters of the Spider Web. Erie Chemical, which manufactured tear gas, distributed more than fifteen hundred copies of Elizabeth Dilling's 1934 treatise, *The Red Network: A Who's Who and Handbook of Radicalism for Patriots*, supplying company salesmen, the National Guard, and hundreds of police departments "on the premise that its tear gas could be used to control crowds of communists and labor agitators."[18]

Dilling prolonged the lifespan of the propaganda of older anticommunists into the New Deal and beyond. A college dropout with a large store of carefully tended resentments, Dilling was sufficiently well-off to become a professional patriot. After traveling to Germany, the USSR, and Palestine in 1931, Dilling became an in-demand and well-remunerated lecturer for women's clubs, chambers of commerce, veterans' organizations, and Kiwanis and Lions Clubs. Her favorite shtick was to perform impressions of Eleanor Roosevelt, sometimes in a Yiddish accent, which reportedly sent audiences into hysterics. Dilling's first publication, *Red Revolution: Do We Want It Here?*, collected many of her newspaper opinion pieces. It sold well: the DAR distributed ten thousand copies. Her next volume, *The Red Network: A "Who's Who" and Handbook of Radicalism for Patriots*, drew heavily from the work of Spider Web members she admired, particularly the Lusk Committee, Marvin (who had by now become national secretary of Trevor's ACPS), the BAF, Steele, and Jung. A steal at $0.50 wholesale and $1.15 retail, the book sold two thousand copies in less than a fortnight and by 1941 had gone through eight printings with the support of the Ku Klux Klan, the Knights of the White Camellia, the German-American Bund, the Aryan Bookstore, the Silver Shirts, the Church League of America, the Moody Church and Bible Institute, the DAR, the American Legion, the FBI, MI, the US Army and Navy Officers' Club, the Women's Patriotic League, the Illinois Federation of Women's Clubs, the New York and Chicago police departments, and Pinkertons. Both the *Chicago Tribune* and the Hearst newspaper chain promoted Dilling's views and work. After cofounding the short-lived Paul Reveres, Dilling founded the Patriotic Research Bureau in 1938. Funded largely by Dilling and private individuals, the bureau also received substantial donations from manufacturing concerns in Cleveland and Boston, and Henry Ford bought Dilling office furniture and typewriters and "put her on his payroll at $200 a month for six months." Gradually amassing her own enormous card index of American radicalism, Dilling won the faith and inherited the files of other strident anticommunists, among them Francis Ralston Welsh, a Philadelphia lawyer and investment broker. Described by Upton Sinclair, one of the thousands of Reds she fingered, as a "pitiful, terror-stricken, hate-consumed candidate for an asylum," Dilling published additional books in 1936 and 1940, hoping to influence the outcome of presidential elections. She was by then well on her way to becoming the poster child for the Extreme Right, venerated by isolationists and pro-Nazis, in whose company she spent the rest of her long Red-baiting career.[19]

Despite the passion with which the members of the Spider Web pursued their calling, its significance or influence should not be overstated. Many of its adherents remained on the periphery of American politics, solidly imprisoned in the Web by their activity. At the same time, however, Trevor, Fries, Hoover, Van Deman, Johnson, Fish, and Haldeman occupied high civil, political, military, and business positions profoundly and materially influencing American politics, economics, and society. The structure of the Spider Web shows that significant crusades fashioned by very small numbers of people can strongly influence a democratic polity.

CHAPTER 6

John Bond Trevor, Radicals, Eugenics, and Immigration

In the annals of American anticommunism, if Joseph McCarthy is a leviathan, then John Bond Trevor is a minnow. Yet Trevor, who barely rates a mention in history, perhaps made the more substantial contribution to anticommunism and did so over a much longer period of time. Indeed, Trevor made history on several occasions.

Trevor is probably the only man who significantly influenced both the doctrinal evolution of anticommunism and the revolutionary immigration acts of the early 1920s. And he was a hinge that connected the theoretical and operational dimensions of anticommunism. As director of the New York City branch of the US Army's Military Intelligence Division (MI) during the Red Scare, Trevor directly observed and suppressed "radical" elements of the populace. His opinions about the sources of radicalism and the composition of the radical community were solicited by companion organizations, especially the Bureau of Investigation, and MI headquarters in Washington, D.C. Highly educated, intelligent, and articulate, Trevor knew how to talk politics and expected to be heeded. Politicians danced to his tune, not vice versa. Trevor was also a crucial proponent of immigration restrictions as a credible and practicable means of protecting the United States from Bolshevism. Together with his closest colleagues, he popularized the belief that radicalism was an inherent by-product of inferior races, who had to be prevented from migrating to the United States in the sorts of numbers experienced around the turn of the twentieth century. Between 1919 and 1924, state and federal legislative committees, which Trevor served as special counsel, drafter, and consigliere, provided him with a powerful medium for projecting his views on Bolshevik radicalism and race health. During this time, he helped engineer policing, surveillance, and immigration practices that dominated US politics and society for the next forty years.

Origins

John Bond Trevor II was a proud native American. Born in Yonkers, New York, on 19 November 1878, Trevor boasted an illustrious ancestry that included Thomas Willett, the inaugural mayor of New York; William Floyd, a member of the New York delegation that signed the Declaration of Independence; and Benjamin Tallmadge, who served on George Washington's staff and as a member of Congress from Connecticut. Trevor's father and namesake, a broker from Philadelphia, served as a Republican presidential elector in 1880 and as a director of Northern Pacific Railroad. At his death, his heirs received many millions. The younger Trevor received a master's degree from Harvard University in 1903 and a bachelor of laws degree from Columbia in 1906, two years after his admission to the New York bar. The guests at Trevor's 1908 wedding to Caroline Murray Wilmerding included Franklin and Eleanor Roosevelt. Caroline Trevor gave birth to two sons, John B. III and Bronson, before her husband embarked for Europe to fight in the First World War (figure 8).[1]

Evidently possessing martial qualities, Trevor returned after the armistice a chevalier of the French Légion d'Honneur. He also returned convinced, like Ralph Van Deman, that "a worldwide social and political revolution" was under way and could easily make its way to the United States. On his return to New York, Trevor became director of the city's branch of MI, helping to lead the army in what it considered "a state of war" with the foreign "Bolshevik" elements of the population. Trevor's appointment made him a principal official of the counterrevolutionary establishment, authorized to monitor and suppress radical activity. Trevor made the most of his position, undertaking exhaustive investigations into the links among domestic tumult, radicalism, and "Jewish" Bolshevism. Trevor believed that these investigations had discovered the location of radical strongholds across the city and prepared "elaborate contingency plans for putting down an insurrection."[2] He also claimed to have exposed the financial and ideological roots of radicalism, which he and many other MI officials located in a gigantic conspiracy, funded by wealthy German and American Jews and executed by radical activists. In the upper echelons of MI, the Bolshevik revolution had transformed Jews—particularly Jews from Eastern Europe—into a unique

Captain John B. Trevor, Military Intelligence

FIGURE 8. Captain John B. Trevor as he appeared in *Throttled!*,
the memoir of the chief inspector of the New York Police Department's
Bomb Squad, ca. 1919.

threat to America and its civilization. Eastern European Jews, as Richard Slotkin
has noted, were "the only immigrant group whose national origins linked them
to both the Central Powers and Soviet Russia. Of all the new immigrants they
were the most strongly marked as belonging to a distinct 'race,' maintaining a
distinct bloodline along with their cultural identity. They were also the only non-
Christian element in the new immigration."[3]

Within eighteen months of the US entry into the war, MI had swelled to include hundreds of staff in Washington and a great many field agents. Its Foreign
Influence Section monitored "the sentiments, publications, and other actions of
foreign language and revolutionary groups." New York's Jews were perhaps more

exhaustively monitored than any other group. Information gathered from such surveillance was intended to support "measures of prevention against activities and influences tending to impair [US] military efficiency by other [means] than armed forces." The division recruited Trevor during this expansionary period. One of a small group of officers on whom the intelligence establishment relied for raw data and interpretive expertise, Trevor produced reports and opinions and worked with a creative industry that underpinned state and federal investigations and legislation even after his return to civilian life. These inquiries and the laws they prompted entrenched Trevor's brand of anti-Semitism and racism in America's national security, intelligence, and immigration policies.[4]

When he surveyed the city under his protection, Trevor worried about the presence of immigrants, African Americans, and Jews in various boroughs that he fancied were becoming centers of radicalism. Radical forces in New York seemed so numerous that Trevor feared that local forces would be incapable of suppressing any uprising involving the most congested districts. To help prepare for Bolshevik insurrection, Trevor drew up ethnic "maps of New York City showing Racial Colonies," indicating where Germans, Italians, Austro-Hungarians, Irish, African Americans, and, most important, Russian Jews were concentrated. The charts also showed the locations of "radical meeting places" and estimates of the number of gatherings at each venue. Vouching for the accuracy of his maps "even in the small details," Trevor warned his superiors that the branch could account for "probably only ten to twenty percent" of the city's radical conclaves. The volume and severity of radical activity made urgent the dispatch of reinforcements and machine guns to New York.[5]

Trevor and his agents calculated that 90 percent of New York's active radicals were Jewish, a finding that accorded with the proof provided in the Sisson Papers that the Bolshevik Revolution had been orchestrated by German Jewish financiers. Moreover, elements in MI were convinced that the great majority of Bolshevik leaders (including the second-most-senior Bolshevik, Leon Trotsky) were Jews from New York who had flooded into Russia at the command of their German coreligionist paymasters to overthrow Aleksandr Kerensky's true Russian democratic government. A pernicious combination of "race" and "money," in the form of a rapidly growing American Jewish community, now constituted the gravest threat to the United States. Concluding that Jewish bankers had directed the policies of the Federal Reserve Board and the Wilson administration to "the advantage of Germany," Trevor and his colleagues believed that the same bankers had resolved to bankroll "the Bolshevik Secret Service" in the United States to replicate their recent seizure of power in Russia. The conspirators would achieve this goal and conceal their nefarious purpose by appearing to financially support the US war effort.[6]

In attributing control of the radical movement in the United States to an international Jewish conspiracy, Trevor betrayed the unmistakable influence of both the *Protocols of the Elders of Zion* and one of the men most responsible for popularizing the text in the United States, Boris Brasol. The *Protocols*, an urtext of anti-Semitic paranoia, describes a conspiracy for global conquest hatched by an international Jewish leadership cadre. It was introduced into the United States by tsarist Russian émigrés, including Brasol, who had been a leader of an ultranationalist and anti-Semitic organization, the Black Hundreds. Brasol, who began writing for Henry Ford's *Dearborn Independent* immediately after arriving in the United States, was probably introduced to American Defense Society director Charles Stewart Davison by Trevor, an old friend of Davison's. The society promptly published a translated edition of the *Protocols*. Although he was aware that the work might have been forged, Trevor was persuaded by its fundamental thesis. His colleagues likewise treated the *Protocols* and Trevor's conspiracy theories in general with the utmost seriousness. MI's new director, Brigadier General Marlborough Churchill (a distant relative of Winston), prized Trevor's "most valuable" reports and shared them with the Bureau of Investigation, the Immigration and Naturalization Service, Naval Intelligence, the State Department, and the US Shipping Board. MI headquarters also commended Trevor's ethnic maps, "ordered the master plate secured," and requested that he produce an identical map of Brooklyn. Trevor also gave copies of his map to the National Guard, the Adjutant General's Office, the New York City police commissioner, and the New York State Chamber of Commerce, of which he was a member.[7]

Archibald Stevenson and the Lusk Committee

One of Trevor's most important collaborators was another blue-blooded, well-connected New Yorker, Archibald Ewing Stevenson. A lawyer and engineer, Stevenson quickly built a reputation in the war years as a fanatical and dogged antiradical. As chair of the Aliens Subcommittee of the Mayor's Committee of National Defense of New York, Stevenson established America's first bureau for translating foreign-language media. Stevenson then became a special agent of the Bureau of Investigation in January 1918. After a short stint there, Stevenson joined MI, heading up its Propaganda Section. His tenure with MI was brief and dramatic. Like Trevor, Stevenson believed that radical foreigners and citizens should constantly be monitored as a precaution against the overthrow of the American government and the establishment in its place of "an industrial republic modeled after that . . . attempted in Russia."[8]

Stevenson also worried that the state was not deploying the requisite force against the revolutionary movement. Less than a fortnight after the armistice,

Stevenson unsuccessfully urged New York's attorney general to investigate local radical activity. Undeterred, Stevenson pursued this objective through other means. He started with his contacts in the prestigious and archconservative Union League Club. Initially formed to advance the Union cause in the Civil War, the club had long since functioned as an informal meeting place for the cream of society where important political work could be arranged. Stevenson and Trevor persuaded three fellow club members to join them in forming a committee to study the "Bolshevist movement." Stevenson chaired this Committee of Five (a name chosen to invoke the congressional subcommittee that had drafted the Declaration of Independence).[9]

As the committee collected evidence, Stevenson adjourned to Washington, D.C., to testify before a Senate Judiciary Subcommittee inquiry into wartime treachery in the brewing industry. Both Trevor and Stevenson had little interest in the committee's investigations: the war was over, the Hun defeated. Rather, they wanted to turn the committee's attention to the far more urgent problem of domestic Bolshevism. A finding by the senators that all left-wing political, industrial, and social organizations were interconnected, controlled by foreign powers, and dangerous to America's system of government and economy would be a great boon for the antiradical cause. It would focus legislators' and office-holders' attention, arouse public sentiment, and make much more likely the enactment of regulations and statutes to permit and fund censorship, surveillance, deportations, and other essential antiradical activity—including ideally restrictions on immigration.

Stevenson plied the subcommittee, chaired by Lee Overman, with facts and analysis, cajoling the senators to read into the public record the names of dozens of suspect organizations and individuals. And Stevenson apparently convinced the committee that the German kaiser had bequeathed to the Bolshevik high command in Petrograd control of a network of tens of thousands of unwitting agents whose every political thought, utterance, and act was directed toward the establishment of a Bolshevik regime in America. (If Stevenson accepted Trevor's contention that Jewish bankers and revolutionaries controlled the emperor of Prussia, he kept quiet about it.) When prompted by the committee to outline the "interlocking relations" that bound left-wing front groups, Stevenson explained how foreign powers had established and expanded an American radical network during the prewar, war, and postarmistice periods. Starting with the proposition that the entire US radical movement was "a branch of the revolutionary socialism of Germany," Stevenson explained that German propaganda had sought first to arouse opposition to shipping munitions to the Allies and then to incite domestic labor disturbances. Germans had also created "the great pacifist movement" to help discourage the United States from entering the war. When that effort failed, these propagandists stirred up "a revolutionary spirit in the radicals," as they had so successfully done in Europe.[10]

The German propagandists achieved their ultimate success by making "unwitting tools" of American citizens. Explained Stevenson, the "most conservative of Americans having pacifist leanings wound up in contact with the most violent radicals and merged directly into the present radical movement." German-Bolshevist propaganda, Stevenson emphasized, worked "like poison gas," lingering "after the attack is made." While this propaganda had affected "native-born" American citizens, Stevenson reassured the senators that those who had succumbed were, for the most part, hyphenated and Catholic Americans. The apparent popularity of this propaganda in large industrial centers was also attributable to the fact that "plain, common-sense American people" were actually a minority in America's great cities. One demographic, however, constituted a disturbing exception to this rule: the education profession. Throughout the tertiary sector, "a very large number" of professors, particularly of sociology, economics, and history, "subscribed to . . . dangerous and destructive and anarchist sentiments," preaching the "grossest kind of materialism" and deforming institutions of learning into "festering masses of pure atheism."[11]

Stevenson's emphasis on the German origins of Bolshevism differed somewhat from but did not obviously contradict other evidence provided to the committee by an American Methodist missionary whom the Bolsheviks had recently expelled from Russia. The Reverend George Simons, armed with a copy of the *Protocols*, shocked the committee and readers of the *New York Times* when he testified "not only that the Bolshevik leadership was predominantly Jewish, but that its cadres and coffers were filled by Jews from New York's Lower East Side." Standing at the head of a Red Army comprising Letts and "Chinese coolies," Trotsky, a "New York" and "Yiddish" Jew, guarded a regime that "decent" Russians regarded as "a German and Hebrew Government." The notion that Bolshevism emanated from New York changed some senators' attitude toward American Bolsheviks from one of bemused contempt to real fear. The committee was particularly exercised by the thought that East Side Jews and their propaganda "might rouse [American] hyphenates, Negroes, Mexicans, and Asians to rebellion." Further, Simons had suggested that the Jewish conspiracy against America was so strong that even federal officials were afraid to admit their knowledge of it. The committee seized on this fear of the international Jewish banker–revolutionary conspiracy, however genuine, to encourage public support for its policy prescriptions, which included curtailing the civil liberties of domestic radicals with sedition laws and reducing the subversiveness and size of "hyphenate communities through compulsory Americanization, forced deportation, and the radical restriction of immigration."[12]

Although Stevenson and Simons persuaded the senators that foreign enemy powers, New York Jews, and domestic radicalism were interlinked, Stevenson also got himself fired from the army. Inducing the (hardly reluctant) senators to officially record the identities of prominent alleged radicals, Stevenson outed Jane Addams and the president of Stanford University, David Starr Jordan, along with more than fifty other men and women. Sensitive to public outcry at Stevenson's slurs, Secretary of War Newton D. Baker informed the press that Stevenson had "never been an officer or an employee" of MI and summarily dismissed the Red-hunting lawyer. Baker technically told the truth: Stevenson was a volunteer who could not be considered an "employee" of the division. However, most MI administrative staff and secret agents were civilian volunteers, and the division could not have functioned without their help. Baker's implication that Stevenson had no connection with MI was sophistry, but few critics examined Baker's claims, particularly after he ordered the New York City branch of MI to close down its Propaganda Section and cease performing such work.[13]

Stevenson was now obliged to return to New York without either his position or a commitment from the committee to combat domestic Bolshevism. The best course, he and Trevor agreed, was to vest their hopes in a different and more dedicated group of public officials in their hometown. Back at work with the Committee of Five, Stevenson soon released its report on domestic radicalism. The Union League Club urged President Woodrow Wilson to call a special session of the US Senate to investigate the Bolshevik threat and implored the New York state legislature to do the same. The president, now at Versailles, was preoccupied with greater concerns. But in late March 1919, the state legislature approved the creation of a joint legislative committee investigation into domestic radicalism. The committee would examine the nature and extent of radicalism in the state, report its findings, and draft appropriate legislation. Along with all customary authority accorded to such bodies, the committee was given "extraordinary powers to compel the production of witnesses, books, and documents." The Union League Club's influence on the committee's terms of reference was clear, including the wording of the resolution, yet the legislature was farcically coy about the origins of its concern. In any event, the inquiry represented an invaluable opportunity for both Trevor and Stevenson to put into the public arena in unprecedented detail the information that Stevenson had laid before the Senate and that Trevor distributed regularly in his intelligence reports. When the committee's report, *Revolutionary Radicalism: Its History, Purpose and Tactics*, was issued the following year, it was identical conceptually and in its use of particular phrases and terms to the material that Trevor, Stevenson, and MI habitually produced.[14]

Even for such well-connected men, engineering a government investigation into their mutual obsession was surprisingly easy. The political situation was certainly propitious. A handful of officials across the country had been subjected to violent attack, seemingly by anarchist organizations. The Overman Committee had identified New York as the center of US radicalism. Nervous and ambitious city officials, eager to reassure the financial sector and conservative media, responded forcefully, raiding the offices of the Union of Russian Peasant Workers on 12 March and arresting 150 men. Hall owners refused to rent out their premises to foreign-language and workers' associations, which were forbidden to criticize government policy and to display the red flag. When the committee's formation was announced, the *New York Times* and the American Defense Society rejoiced.[15]

Amid genuine fear of disunity and even revolution, the ambitious opportunists who directed and headed up the committee confected and exploited these emotions. To a man, all of the members of the committee, known after its chair, freshman senator Clayton Riley Lusk, were self-promoters on the make. Lusk, with a background in business and foreign trade, had served just two months in the Senate and had no prior experience investigating radical organizations or activity. He had, however, the right opinions for the job, and he wanted to be governor, a dream that was eventually dashed by corruption allegations. Algernon Lee, a Socialist New York City alderman, regarded the committee with unconcealed contempt. Legislative committees, he remarked, came in two varieties, "whitewashing committees and committees for the discovery of mares' nests." The Lusk Committee, he said, would be "of the latter class," armed with ready-made conclusions and impervious to "any facts that do not tally with their purpose."[16]

While the legislature had been willing to establish the inquiry antiradicals sought, it did not give the Lusk Committee much of a budget. Yet this proved no obstacle to its effective operation. For one thing, whenever the committee ran out of money, the sympathetic state comptroller advanced it a bridging loan on his own security. The committee also received regular assistance from state and federal authorities, including district attorneys, police, the Department of Justice, the Bureau of Immigration, and the New Jersey branch of the American Protective League, which was commanded by Lusk's brother-in-law. But the most important ally of the committee was John Trevor. In addition to ensuring that MI would provide the committee with intelligence and logistical support, something the disgraced Stevenson could no longer do, Trevor had been appointed a special deputy attorney general with responsibility for managing relations between the committee and the state administration. He was the committee's point guard, sentinel, and indispensable advocate, protecting its interests and preparing the legal briefs to secure the search, arrest, and subpoena warrants the committee would require. He also provided each member of the state assembly with a survey of state laws on "anarchy, sedition, treason, syndicalism and kindred activities" and a copy of *Throttled!*, the sensational memoir by Thomas J. Tunney, commander of the New York City police's Bomb Squad (which featured a photograph of Trevor).[17]

The committee received a small staff of translators and an investigator, Clarence L. Converse. Stevenson officially served the committee as special counsel, but it was his rather than Lusk's baby. Stevenson routinely led the questioning of witnesses, and the committee's final report, submitted on 24 April 1920, stated that it had been "written and compiled" by Stevenson, "under the supervision of the committee." Trevor was also an important contributor to the report, which prominently acknowledged the special deputy attorney general and his "maps of New York City showing Racial Colonies."[18]

With the Lusk Committee under their control, Trevor and Stevenson orchestrated a campaign of political repression against New York's Radical Left. Stevenson communicated the committee's needs to the government, and Trevor ensured that those needs were met. While Clayton Lusk claimed that prosecutions resulting from committee activity were "incidental" to its investigative work, a more candid Stevenson boasted that the committee had spurred the state to prosecute violations of its criminal anarchy statute. And at the conclusion of its hearings, the committee initiated a comprehensive program of censorship and regulation of schools, colleges, and migrant education courses.[19]

Just as external events had encouraged the committee's creation, they continued to give it crucial impetus. The attempted May Day 1919 bombings of the homes and offices of three dozen nationally renowned antiradicals brought immediate and harsh suppression of suspect organizations. New York police raided Industrial Workers of the World offices. War veterans sacked the Russian People's House and the editorial office of a Socialist Party newspaper. Trevor declared that radical organizations were entirely to blame for the breakdown of law and order. The detonation of more bombs in eight cities across the nation on 2 June prompted the committee to bring forward its first public hearings to 12 June. To help publicize the hearings and to give the committee subjects to interrogate, Trevor secured search warrants for "centers and sources of radical revolutionary propaganda." In addition to Russian-language and socialist organizations, the committee set its sights on the Rand School of Social Science and the Soviet Bureau, the unofficial embassy of the unrecognized Bolshevik government.[20]

Trevor, Stevenson, and many other Red hunters refused to accept that the Soviet Bureau was a trade and investment arm of the Bolshevik government. Rather, they regarded it as a financial arm of revolutionary socialism that had to be stopped from funneling huge sums of Bolshevik money to (Jewish) supporters and sympathizers in New York. In fact, the bureau was broke, unable even to pay its staff. Further, its principal concerns really were commercial. The cash-strapped Russian Bolshevik regime was desperate to do business with American industry rather than subvert it. If these commercial links helped force political recognition of the socialist government, it would be a welcome development. But as the head of the de facto legation, Ludwig Martens, stated, the Bolsheviks were "not such fools to think that other governments can be overthrown as the result of outside interference" (a view that the Wilson administration did not share in relation to Russia). And there was no shortage of American businesses keen to cut a deal with the Bolsheviks. Investment in tsarist Russia by US firms had amounted to billions of rubles, and industrialists and merchants were concerned that German interests might steal a march on them. Notwithstanding a State Department directive discouraging trade with Bolshevik Russia, more than a thousand firms had contacted the bureau by mid-1919, and many had pledged to lobby for US recognition of the regime.[21]

The anti-Bolshevik lobby observed this situation with alarm. Trevor named and shamed businesses dealing with the bureau, deterring some firms from following through on putative contracts. But Trevor and Stevenson wanted to make a grand statement by putting the bureau completely out of business. The May Day raids had generated tremendous publicity and gave authorities an opportunity to attack the local radical movement. It was high time to administer similar treatment to the bureau. Stevenson led a posse comitatus of state troopers, company detectives, and friendly journalists to sack Martens's Soviet outpost. Martens fled to Washington, where he petitioned the federal government in vain to rescind the Lusk Committee's actions. Instead, the same subcommittee that had sought counsel from Stevenson months earlier now declared the bureau a propaganda operation. The bureau was finished. Stevenson and his confreres had bagged their first major scalp.[22]

Their next target, the Rand School, had much deeper roots and would prove far more difficult to dislodge. Founded in 1906 by the American Socialist Society, the school was a respected educational facility. Algernon Lee had been appointed educational director in 1909 and had instituted a program grounded in the liberal arts and sciences that featured regular talks from prominent guest lecturers. By 1918, the school had five thousand regular students, and its labor research department was a valued source of statistics for unions, libraries, government organizations, and corporations. Predictably, the school had earned the wrath of opponents not only of radicalism but also of labor organization, and it was attacked by "patriots" and veterans three times in the six months before May Day 1919.[23]

Barely a week after it closed the Soviet Bureau, the Lusk Committee hit the Rand School, simultaneously raiding the Left Wing Section of the Socialist Party on West 29th Street and the Industrial Workers of the World headquarters on East 4th Street. The committee arrived at Rand well prepared. Along with his search warrant, Converse brought three squads of uniformed police, three moving vans, and five hundred evidence tags. Three nearby hotel rooms were reserved for press briefings, where reporters were informed that the committee had terminated the school's revolutionary activity.[24]

Executives and friends of the Rand School were in no mood to lie down in front of the committee. Lee vowed that the "Luskers" would get "such a fucking" from the school that they "would be sorry they ever started" the fight. National Civil Liberties Bureau executive member Albert DeSilver attacked the entire proceeding, including the chief city magistrate, for approving the raid on the hearsay evidence of Converse. And when the New York attorney general (probably briefed by Trevor) persuaded a judge to order the school to show why it should not be placed in receivership and closed down, a friendly attorney forced the committee into court to substantiate its allegations. Coming up short, the committee stalled for time, attempting to reframe the charges against the school before the infuriated trial judge dismissed the case.[25]

Although the committee had failed to destroy Rand, its action still proved useful. The raids led directly to the arrest, incarceration, and deportation of several alleged radicals. The attacks had also put the issue of corrupt socialist educators on the political map, providing an essential justification for loyalty legislation that the committee soon drafted. More significant in the long term, particularly for Stevenson and Trevor, the committee publicized an important subject to underpin its mammoth treatise on domestic radicalism, which was intended to guide the policies and activity of governments, industry, and citizens for the foreseeable future.

The committee's report was designed to prompt executive government, legislators, the military, and policing bodies to more strenuously enforce current laws and to enact new ones to fill any breaches radicals had exposed. The report also sought to alert the general citizenry to their security duties by mobilizing public opinion and vigilance. It would help put a stop to industry flirtation with the Bolshevik regime. And it would empower government to monitor suspect groups and individuals, punish errant citizens, and deport aliens or better still prevent them from entering the United States. The product of more than six months of hearings and numerous raids and arrests, the committee's gargantuan report ran to almost eleven thousand pages and cost one hundred thousand dollars. It was the most comprehensive inventory of alleged radical activity in America that had ever been produced, and it created an ideological template for subsequent anticommunism. For the next thirty years, no serious anticommunist failed to consult its pages for inspiration and practical guidance. It provided the intellectual foundation for the Spider Web.

That the committee produced such a hefty tome so fast was a testament to its industry and, as Lee suggested, its precipitate nature. The committee simply could not have produced such a monumental volume so quickly if its authors and sponsors had not already had a fixed notion of their findings and a great deal of preparatory work ready for use. Indeed, the publication under Lusk's name of an article in the February 1920 *Review of Reviews* preempted the submission of the committee's report by three months.[26]

Revolutionary Radicalism took as its fundamental premise the idea that the United States was being threatened by "various" forces "seeking to undermine and destroy, not only the government . . . but also the very structure of American society." Indeed, Manifest Destiny had made the United States the primary target of these revolutionary forces, as the violent history of radicalism in America over the previous forty or so years had proven: the "number of unsuccessful attacks" made by "criminal anarchists . . . upon prominent and useful public men [was] unparalleled in any other country." The committee had no doubt that these forces were of foreign extraction. They had recently "shaken the foundation of European civilization" and were now dividing America, stimulating "class hatred and a contempt for government." Once ensconced, they had set about converting numerous softheaded, vulnerable, and seditious Americans to the revolutionary cause. These patsies and traitors—typically intellectuals and pacifists, liberal clergy, educators in the liberal arts, and "hyphenated" Americans—were to be found in militant trade unions, foreign-language clubs and societies, and educational institutions.[27]

Having established that the nation was threatened, the report explained who the nation's enemies were, why they were enemies, what the American people had to do in response to revolutionary threat, and why Americans should accept the committee's antiradical expertise and leadership. Not surprisingly, the committee declared that the revolutionary threat had been instigated "by paid agents of the Junker class in Germany as a part of their program of industrial and military world conquest." These agents had been active not only in the United States but also in Russia, Great Britain and its colonies, and Latin America. After entering the United States through New York City, these subversives had fanned out across the nation, creating and seizing control of left-wing radical groups of every stripe. Strident protests against social conditions were entirely attributable to the provocations of these Bolshevik agitators rather than to "critical [domestic] economic conditions."[28]

The committee did not merely blame aliens for America's unrest. It asserted that political radicalism could not survive outside communities of "foreign workers." To support this assertion, the committee emphasized the large numbers of foreign-born and unnaturalized members in radical associations. Strangely, however, the committee regarded the recruitment of such members as a ploy to escape "the attention of authorities." The committee also claimed that "less than five percent" of the radicals it arrested were "American citizens." Many were unable to speak English, "but all had been liberally supplied with radical propaganda." And as Trevor's depiction of the city's racial colonies had shown, the great majority of these aliens had been utterly unable or unwilling to disperse into the Melting Pot.[29]

According to *Revolutionary Radicalism*, radicals' political experiences, beliefs, and cultural customs made them not just unsuitable for citizenship but inassimilable. Through their conduct, radicals had shown an inability to distinguish between the unjust governments from whose jurisdiction they had fled and the US government. They had instead attributed to all governments the same "imperfections and vicious practices" and now anticipated, "with a fatuous and almost pitiful confidence, . . . the triumph in [America] of the radical theories." Radicals' infiltration of both traditional and more radical labor organizations had utterly corrupted the union movement. Most if not all labor unions were now attempting to revolutionize the United States, and strike action was now called "not with the idea of obtaining what is demanded but for the express purpose of failure—a failure that will leave the workman poorer and more embittered, will increase class hatred and make the workmen feel that only by violent revolution can they gain their demands." Events abroad further demonstrated that substituting general strikes for traditional bargaining practices was part of a "big destructive program" to destroy "present organized society."[30]

These assessments of the irremediable character of migrants were drawn verbatim from the Senate testimony of Stevenson and the lengthy intelligence assessments that Trevor continued to prepare for his former employers at MI after his demobilization in June 1919. In these assessments, Trevor postulated the inseparability of radicalism and specific ethnic groups. Like his counterparts in the New York Bomb Squad, he considered all Irish migrants allies of the Central Powers as a consequence of their "antipathy for England." Similarly, he believed that Indian and Egyptian nationalists were vulnerable to German and Bolshevik exploitation. Russian Jews were intrinsically dangerous as a result of their "almost universal" abhorrence of Russia's ancien régime and exposure to German Marxist socialism.[31]

If revolutionary desires had been limited to these groups, authorities might not have needed to act. However, the committee found that pacifism was another front activity "absolutely integral" to socialists' "triangular" plan of global conquest. Rejecting the notion that pacifists "opposed wars between all nations," *Revolutionary Radicalism* argued that pacifists covertly promoted "class consciousness" to help bring on "relentless class warfare." And the pacifist movement was merely the thin edge of liberal Pink treachery: "various so-called schools of social reform" were training "agitators" to undermine "respect for the institutions of the United States." The most notorious of these schools was Rand. But the committee worried that revolutionary ideas were increasingly prevalent among intellectuals, "university men," and their students. "Every single purely literary review" published in America over the previous two years, the report maintained, was socialist in character, and "four out of five college commencement day orations" in the same period had been "purely Socialistic." University discussion forums were spreading socialism, mutating from discussion groups into advocacy and propaganda organizations, while an advertising arrangement between a "self-confessed organ of Bolshevism" and the American Federation of Teachers further pointed to revolutionary subversion of the education sector. The committee discerned additional danger in the clergy. Across the nation, ecclesiastical support for revolution was growing. Pastors were affiliating with "pacifist and radical societies"; some reputedly even described the Industrial Workers of the World philosophy as the age's most perfect expression of Christianity. The church's malaise clearly reflected its subversion by internationalists.[32]

When it considered the radicalism of African Americans, the committee's anticommunism melded with more ancient fears. The Committee of Five had previously emphasized the fear that revolutionary ideas would take hold in black communities, and Clayton Lusk had previously drawn attention to the activity of "white radicals conducting a systematic campaign among the colored people of this country, especially among those of the South, for the purpose of 'changing,' as they call it, 'their race consciousness into class consciousness.'" While the committee conceded that African Americans had "just cause of complaint with the treatment they received," this fact had made them vulnerable to communist contamination. Now "various revolutionary agencies" were exploiting black complaints with "thorough skill" and were not alone in tapping the well of black "resentment." A raft of "well-to-do liberals, Socialists and other radicals among whites" were fanning the flames of revolution, supporting African American "uplift organizations." Disturbingly, African American activists were increasingly influenced by radical theory and were evincing pan-Africanism. This was a clear sign that the "Pan-Negro movement" was "looking to the consolidation of the Negro race throughout the world" and advancing a "broader movement," the "International League of the Darker Races," that sought to unify "the darker races, such as the Japanese, Hindus, etc., with the whites."[33]

The committee accounted for this shocking news in several ways. While fiendish Bolshevik agents "skillfully" manipulated the sentimental and misguided, the treacherous needed little encouragement to lapse into sedition. But organic allegories previously employed by Stevenson and Trevor provided other important explanations. Stevenson likened the effects of Bolshevism to those of mustard gas. Trevor similarly described Bolshevism as a contagion that "like disease neglected in the human body produce[s] complications more serious for the continued existence of our body politic than perhaps local manifestations indicate to the casual observer."[34]

Both of these motifs permeated *Revolutionary Radicalism*. Aside from their graphic power, they helped to sustain the committee's argument that socialism had no place in legitimate politics and that illegitimate beliefs and activity had to be crushed by the harshest means. A policy of tolerance had prevailed in New York. The 1902 law barring "criminal anarchy" had lain dormant, and such anarchy now ran "rampant throughout the state." Trevor had clear ideas about what action was required. Radical groups or activities could not be dealt with on an individual basis, since any reasons given to defend a particular action were invariably immaterial. A systematic revolutionary program demanded a systematic response that eschewed "soft" methods of conflict resolution. The repressive powers of the state needed to be strengthened, the too-liberal laws governing industrial protest revised, the duties of disparate intelligence agencies codified, the demobilization of the armed services halted, and restrictions on surveillance of civilians in peacetime removed.[35]

Trevor's program encompassed all the desires of the antiradical movement, and the committee could hope to realize only some of them. It was, after all, a legislative rather than an executive body operating at the state rather than federal level. Even so, the committee effectively wielded its power. First, its raids on alleged radical premises led to the deportation of three Finns, the incarceration of eight citizens, and the indictment of roughly sixty more men on charges of criminal anarchy. More significantly, the committee's raids helped to inspire the November 1919 and January 1920 Palmer Raids. The Soviet Bureau was closed down, and numerous businesses were discouraged from trading with and lobbying for diplomatic recognition of the Bolshevik government. The committee impaired freedom of expression and closed down numerous socialist and foreign-language periodicals. It aggravated religious and ethnic tensions in and beyond New York City, and it weakened democratic government. Its argument that socialism stood outside the realm of constitutional politics influenced Thaddeus Sweet, the Speaker of the New York State Assembly and a member of the Lusk Committee, to bar five lawfully elected Socialists from taking their seats. Four months later, on April Fools' Day, after taking counsel from both Lusk and Stevenson, Sweet took the extraordinary step of expelling the Socialists from the assembly, a move backed by 140 assemblymen and the Union League Club's Committee on Political Reform.[36]

However, the committee was most immediately influential in the sphere of education. The committee sponsored legislation that significantly curtailed freedom of expression in schools, colleges, and other educational institutions. The bills required all publicly employed teachers to certify their loyalty and mandated that all private secular schools obtain operating licenses from the Regents of the University of the State of New York. Mandatory Americanization classes were instituted at factories and community centers, with instruction courses prescribed for all state teachers. In addition, the state commissioner of education routinely invited principals to advise a special council about the loyalty of specific teachers. This council, whose executive included Stevenson, functioned like a star chamber, summoning teachers to closed hearings to determine whether they could continue to earn their livelihood: the council stripped twenty teachers of their licenses without stipulating reasons. After the Supreme Court of New York upheld the laws, Governor Al Smith repealed them in May 1923. But the acts had already inspired similar bills across the nation. President Warren G. Harding asked the US Senate to appropriate funds for "Americanization Work" in public schools in Washington, D.C. The state of Oregon instructed all children within a specific age group to attend public schools where the curriculum was stringently controlled "by a Klan-dominated coalition of interest groups." Ku Klux Klan chapters promoted similar bills in California and a clutch of states across the Midwest and the Deep South. Ohio Klansmen were also elected to that state's board of education. Although Lusk-style bills were generally repealed within a few years, the American Civil Liberties Union described schools as remaining "the most sensitive of all institutions to the fear of criticism of being open to radical thought." The direct interference in the administration of schools and universities pioneered by the committee became standard practice in the 1920s, as educational programs were consistently compromised by private pressure groups, often with the connivance or direct approval of government.[37]

The Lusk Committee's Soviet-style education acts constituted a far more serious attack on republican institutions and values than did even the Palmer Raids. Whereas the raids focused largely on social elements regarded as alien to the national community, the Lusk acts reflected a crisis of confidence in the wisdom and efficacy of liberal education and assaulted social sectors and ideals that had previously been considered integral to the nation. The Lusk acts left a legacy of repressive policies that violated freedoms of speech and conscience throughout America and constituted a direct precursor of the loyalty acts and regulations that policed employees' thoughts and associations in the Cold War era.

The other great legacy of the committee was its report. Although *Revolutionary Radicalism* did not bring to light fresh evidence of communist perfidy or uncover hitherto unknown laboratories of Bolshevism, the fundamental and supporting

tenets of anticommunism had never before been collected in such a comprehensive document that provided not only voluminous detail but also a coherent
taxonomy of the myriad, interconnected socialist organizations in America.
This taxonomy was key to the committee's long-standing influence on the next
generation of anticommunists. Its nomenclature, featuring such headings as
"Academic and Scholastic Socialist Activities," "Socialism and the Churches,"
and "Propaganda among Negroes," was both informed by and re-created in the
surveillance reports of the Bureau of Investigation and MI. A number of prominent superpatriots adopted the committee's classification scheme. Spider Web
member Fred Marvin distributed to members of the Key Men of America a *Daily
Data Sheet* that grouped articles under such headings as "Radicalism in Education," "Pacifism and Its Allies," "Liberalism and Its Work," "Propaganda Methods,"
"Radicalism in Women's Organizations," "The Youth Movement," "Radicalism
in Churches," and "Anti-Patriotic Movements." Elizabeth Dilling was similarly
influenced by the committee, regularly referencing its work in her publications.[38]

A new generation of legislators in the 1930s also found inspiration in *Revolutionary Radicalism*. The Special Committee to Investigate Communist Activities and Propaganda in the United States, named after its chair, Representative
Hamilton Fish Jr., a New York Republican, spent six months in 1930 gathering
testimony from nearly three hundred witnesses before issuing a report filled
with passages interchangeable with many of the sections of *Revolutionary Radicalism*. Throughout the 1930s, Martin Dies Jr., chair of the Special Committee to
Investigate Un-American Activities and its successor, the House Un-American
Activities Committee, also revisited the political tactics and treatise of the Lusk
Committee, seeking counsel from both Trevor and Stevenson.[39]

The political and psychological characteristics of the antiradical framework
established by the Lusk Committee were just as important and influential as
the virtual spider web it traced. *Revolutionary Radicalism* helped to entrench and
legitimize the characterization of alternative political views as foreign and treacherous and as the product of organized conspiracy. In so doing, it helped weave
conspiracy thinking and paranoid fear into the Anticommunist Spider Web. The
paranoid underpinnings of *Revolutionary Radicalism* are revealed by its internal
inconsistency and the antidemocratic convictions of its authors and sponsors.
Notwithstanding the gigantic size of its report, the committee was not much
concerned with proving its case. *Revolutionary Radicalism* never reconciled the
supposed Jewish and German (state-sponsored) origins of Bolshevism with the
demise of the Prussian empire. Nor did the report account for how Bolshevism
survived in America outside the foreign enclaves of New York City. The committee was not really interested in the causes of radicalism in the United States.
Establishing a pattern that would be repeated by official and private anticommu-

nists for decades to come, the Lusk Committee shirked the task of investigating how economic reform might improve social and political cohesion. Criticism and analysis of systemic problems in American society were confined to a mere two paragraphs of the report. The committee preferred to channel its energy exclusively into divisive activity and to lay the foundations for a more authoritarian society. In the place of genuine analysis came repressive laws; slurs on ethnic, political, and social groups; and in what would become a standard trope among anticommunists, an appeal to the general public to accept the superior political judgment of a leadership group in possession of "the complete knowledge."[40]

Trevor unquestionably conceived of himself as a member of this leadership group. And while he recognized that the Lusk Committee had identified radicalism with the foreign-born and the feeble-minded and had enacted important legislative reforms, he also understood that the ultimate phase of the antiradical project could be pursued only in Washington, D.C. It was not enough to establish the connection between aliens and radicalism and to use this information to deport unnaturalized radicals. The American public, Trevor had realized, had to be taught that radicalism was not merely the product of particular political, economic, or social conditions; rather, it derived from a racial, biological foundation that was impossible to correct. The exclusion of this biological contaminant from the nation would require nothing less than revolutionary changes to the US immigration system. Accordingly, Trevor traveled to the capital in January 1921 to join forces with the chair of the House Immigration Committee, Albert Johnson, and change America's immigration laws.[41]

Eugenics and Immigration

John Trevor drew two fundamental lessons from his experience with MI and the Lusk Committee. The first was that subversive political movements in the United States were essentially Jewish in origin, character, and personnel. The second was that an antiradical policy that focused on deporting aliens and educating citizens was fatally flawed. The deportation of aliens could never counteract the pernicious influence of radicals who escaped government dragnets or of the misguided civil rights lobby, which would always challenge antiradical action. These conclusions encouraged Trevor to seek out more effective solutions to America's Bolshevik problem, and he found those solutions in the pseudoscience of eugenics. English biometrist Francis Galton coined the term *eugenics* to mean "the study of agencies under social control that may improve or impair the racial qualities of future generations either physically or mentally." Eugenics aimed to systematically improve the condition of humanity by segregating its subspecies, or "races," which were distinguished by skin tone and cranial and facial characteristics. Different races displayed marked disparities in native ability and were arrayed in a complex hierarchy with "Nordic" Northern Europeans at its summit.[42]

The leading proponents of eugenics—a handful of prominent evolutionary biologists and geneticists—included Dean Worcester, a colonial administrator and spymaster who described Filipinos as the "lowest of living men" and the first step in man's evolution from "the gorilla and the orang-utan."[43] Trevor had known several of these scientists socially for many years. Long visible in the movement to restrict immigration, they found in Trevor a vital member of the intelligence establishment who was of their class and could give them unprecedented access to corridors of power. Trevor thus became a figure of singular importance, linking leading eugenicists and their allies in Congress. From January 1921, when he testified before both congressional immigration committees, until May 1924, when President Calvin Coolidge signed into law the landmark Johnson-Reed Act restricting immigration, Trevor synthesized and translated the scientific theories of the eugenicists into coherent legislation. He also devised the formula for selling a discriminatory and draconian immigration scheme to a nation whose political mythology celebrated its capacity to accept and shelter the downtrodden.

The Immigration Act of 1924 represented the culmination of more than thirty years of public debate and concerted lobbying by ardent restrictionists. The notion of limiting immigration to the United States had been an important element of American politics since the 1840s, when the Know-Nothings and other parties formed to oppose Catholic migration. Public support for restricting the immigration of arbitrarily defined racial groups, such as the Chinese, had also been expressed since the 1880s, and proposals to comprehensively regulate and restrict immigration by nationality were popularized and strongly endorsed first by lobby groups and then between 1907 and 1910 by the US Immigration Commission (the Dillingham Commission). The European war and the Bolshevik Revolution had seemingly improved the chances of effecting permanent and radical changes to immigration policy. Nevertheless, the creation of a comprehensive restrictive regime was not a fait accompli. The idea still represented a huge break with tradition and was opposed by immigrant groups and powerful business interests. In transforming US immigration policy, therefore, Trevor and his associates did much more than merely surf the latest wave of nativism. They kept the issue of immigration restriction before the general public and legislators, wore down the resolve of opponents and naysayers, campaigned incessantly for "a human blockade," and argued on behalf of the introduction of an annual quota system designed to preserve what they imagined was the racial mix of mid-nineteenth-century America. Further, they had more success than the Dillingham Commission did in associating the issues of race and radicalism not just with crime and idleness but also with genetics and destiny.[44]

The ideological seeds of the Johnson-Reed Act were sown in the 1880s, when the arrival of migrants in unprecedented numbers and from hitherto underrepresented regions first prompted native-born Americans to consider how undesirable migrants might best be categorized and barred from the country. Several organizations, among them the American Protective Association, formed to combat the admission of what they regarded as "unassimilable backward peasants from the 'degraded races' of Europe." The idea of immigration restriction coincided with the rise of eugenics. As eugenics began to take hold in the academy, the difficulty of assimilating large numbers of migrants (with perceived weaknesses for drink and vice) produced mounting calls for restricting new arrivals to the United States. Proposals to exclude adult male aliens unable to read and write in their own language were framed with "Italians, Poles, and Hungarians" in mind but were sold chiefly as a means of protecting native-born workers' jobs. Such literacy tests were not the exclusive preserve of anti-alien, crypto-racists (the same arguments were used in the South to justify the disenfranchisement of African Americans) or Americans (they were also adopted across the British empire to restrict nonwhite migration to South Africa, Australia, and New Zealand).[45]

At the center of the immigration restriction movement stood the New England and New York political and academic establishment. Harvard graduates and political leaders such as Boston Brahmin Henry Cabot Lodge (later the most influential member of the Dillingham Commission) and his close friend Theodore Roosevelt were deeply influenced by eugenic theories of "race psychology" and the "iterative character" of race. From French social psychologist Gustav Le Bon and others, Lodge, Roosevelt, and their peers learned that the "mystical" qualities of "initiative, tenacity, perseverance [and] energy" peculiar to Anglo-Saxons would be "enfeebled" by miscegenation, particularly with Jews, who "condemned to perpetual anarchy" any nation unfortunate enough to host them. Through vehicles such as the Immigration Restriction League (founded in 1894) and the Eugenics Record Office, the eugenics movement attempted to restrict immigration through literacy measures. However, these attempts were repeatedly frustrated by presidential vetoes exercised to protect business access to cheap labor from Canada and especially Mexico.[46]

But the restriction movement also won some significant victories. After the assassination of President William McKinley, restrictionists helped persuade Congress to pass the Anarchist Exclusion Act. The Naturalization Act of 1906 then stripped state courts of their century-old power to confer citizenship. At the same time, the eugenics movement gained important supporters through the work of the Dillingham Commission and in the academic disciplines of anthropology and psychiatry. The 1911 publication of *The Mind of Primitive Man* by German-born anthropologist Franz Boas inadvertently helped legitimize the idea that Europeans could be classified into "hereditary types" that clearly distinguished older from newer Americans. When married with genetics, Boas's theories helped eugenicists demonstrate that "a mixture of races physically" weakened "the stronger tribe." Psychiatrists' interest in biological influences on mental health similarly bolstered the restriction movement in 1914, when the National Committee for Mental Hygiene added to yet another federal immigration bill a provision to exclude foreign-born migrants manifesting "constitutional psychopathic inferiority." The politics of immigration had thus radically changed after the US Court of Appeals issued an 1874 decision striking down a California law barring entry to the "lunatic, idiotic . . . crippled . . . lewd and debauched" on the grounds that the measure violated the Equal Protection Clause of the Fourteenth Amendment, which was held to protect the rights not just of citizens but of persons in general. This change was finally cemented in legislation after war and revolution in Russia drastically hardened public opinion against immigrants. And in Albert Johnson, a feisty Red-baiter with a fanatical hatred of Asians and Jews, the eugenics lobby finally found a politician around whose commitment to the cause a comprehensive immigration restriction bill could be built.[47]

Born in Springfield, Illinois, in 1869, Albert Johnson led an itinerant life as a newspaper man before moving to Washington State at the turn of the century. As managing editor and owner-publisher of several newspapers, Johnson became an outspoken opponent of labor unions and immigrants. In 1912, Johnson stirred the citizens of Grays Harbor to expel striking Wobblies and to recall the mayor of Hoquiam for having released them from prison, propelling himself into the first of ten terms in Congress, where he advocated the open shop and immigration restriction.[48]

As soon as he arrived in the capital, Johnson joined the House Immigration and Naturalization Committee. As a minority member, Johnson had time to study "the immigration problem." Sensibly, he cultivated friendships with several of the nine Democrats on the committee; they gave him valuable support as his prestige grew. A fervent supporter of the war effort, Johnson resigned his seat in 1918 and joined the Chemical Warfare Service, where he doubtless met his fellow future Key Men of America director, Amos Fries. Johnson was also recruited by the Committee on Public Information as a Four Minute Man, delivering "19 addresses in 9 States" between December 1918 and February 1919. After "Captain Johnson" won reelection as part of the Republican rout in the 1918 midterm election, he became the committee's chair. Under his leadership, it "began to gather a mass of detailed evidence on which a new immigration policy might be based." According to Johnson's biographer, "Only two or three . . . out of the sixty-odd House committees" heard as much testimony or did as much work as Johnson's committee. Johnson's work ethic had already paid off in February 1917 when the committee helped push through Congress a new immigration law that finally introduced the long-desired literacy test, barring illiterate prospective migrants aged sixteen and above. The law also expanded the anti-anarchist laws of 1903 and established an Asiatic Barred Zone, prohibiting migration from what is now Indonesia, Malaysia, the Southeast Asian mainland, large swaths of China and Mongolia, the Indian subcontinent, the entire Middle East, and parts of the Caucasus and Turkey. Pleased as they were with this triumph, restrictionists regarded the literacy test as a stopgap measure with unavoidable exemptions: Japanese, illiterate relatives of admissible aliens, and Russian Jews fleeing religious persecution. Adopting the principle of racial or ethnic quota restrictions as its central policy, the committee accepted Lodge's advice to attempt its reforms with a new administration.[49]

Johnson's strident advocacy of immigration restriction and antiradicalism brought him to the attention of eugenicists. Trevor in particular saw Johnson as a valuable if rough diamond, a sympathetic and energetic confrere who, if introduced to the right ideas and advice, might just pull off the policy revolution the nation required. In addition to being on a first-name basis with the director of the Eugenics Record Office, Charles B. Davenport, and his right-hand man, Harry Hamilton Laughlin, Trevor introduced Johnson to the most significant eugenics proponent in the country, Madison Grant. Grant, like Trevor and Davenport, was a "lordly patrician whose family had adorned the social life of Manhattan since colonial times." Founder and chair of the New York Zoological Society, Grant served with Trevor on the board of trustees of the American Museum of Natural History. Grant's greatest contribution to eugenics was his 1916 volume, *The Passing of the Great Race; or, The Racial Basis of European History*, the most comprehensive and best-selling statement of racial nativism to date. Nevertheless, for all his familiarity with the relevant literature, Grant was an amateur, "well supplied with scientific information but free from a scientist's scruple in interpreting it."[50]

Rather than contributing any fresh ideas about biology or eugenics, Grant synthesized eugenic and anthropological ideas about race into a coherent theoretical and political program. In particular, he popularized the schematic division of Europeans into distinct Teutonic, Celtic, and Mediterranean races. While the knowledge that the Teutonic or Nordic race constituted the "white man par excellence" gladdened restrictionists' hearts, Grant sounded a gloomy note, warning of the dire consequences of Nordic miscegenation with Celtic or Alpine "peasants" and the moderately more accomplished Mediterranean race, let alone vastly inferior colored breeds. For Grant, it was axiomatic that "all the moral, social and intellectual characteristics and traits which are the springs of politics and government" were determined by hereditary racial qualities. Hybrid stock represented an existential threat to the Nordic race because miscegenation between superior and inferior races irrevocably corrupted and diluted the superior; chillingly, a union of a Nordic and a Jew would produce only a Jew (and probably a Bolshevik at that). Because race was the "superior force in history," political, educational, and economic attempts to resolve social conflict and inequality were futile. Indeed, political and religious doctrines of fraternity and equality had for centuries impeded the forces of history. American civilization, Grant insisted, would have to depend for its survival on "apolitical and scientific solutions"—that is, the rigorous segregation of Nordic and non-Nordic peoples and a comprehensive social engineering program of selective breeding, prohibition of miscegenation, and sterilization of "perverts, bastards, cripples, and feeble-minded individuals." In the wake of the Russian Revolution, Grant warned that special vigilance would be needed to turn back the great flood of Jews who would flee the inevitable overthrow of the Jewish Bolshevik regime and the equally inevitable, bloody reprisals that the Russian people would launch against their former overlords.[51]

Through Trevor's good graces, Johnson became acquainted with Grant and other leading eugenicists, including Henry Fairfield Osborn, president of the American Museum of Natural History; Grant's protégé, Theodore Lothrop Stoddard; and Laughlin from the Eugenics Record Office. All of these men testified before Johnson's committee or gave aid in kind, publicizing eugenics and the restrictionist cause; Laughlin was even appointed the committee's "expert eugenics agent." Trevor also introduced Johnson to Archibald Stevenson, and the two spoke together in public forums emphasizing the importance of crushing Bolshevism and curtailing immigration. While Johnson waited for the Wilson administration to expire, he led impeachment proceedings against Louis F. Post, charging him with insufficient zeal in deporting alien radicals.[52]

Encouraged by the support of eugenicists, important media voices, and the impending retirement of President Wilson, Johnson introduced a November 1920 emergency immigration quota bill to impose a two-year freeze on the immigration of all but close relatives of resident aliens. The bill was favorably received. In the latter half of 1920, European refugees had begun arriving in such numbers that by February 1921, passenger vessels were being diverted from Ellis Island to Boston. The racial quality of prospective migrants was also of grave concern, as nearly 120,000 Jewish refugees from Central and Eastern Europe received landing papers for the 1920–21 financial year. And since rising literacy rates in Europe were making the literacy test obsolete, Congress overwhelmingly supported the committee's demand for "a genuine 100 percent American immigration law." As far as Johnson and his supporters were concerned, only an immigration program based on principles of race health could keep the legions of Hebraic and Mediterranean subversives, "small in stature and low in intelligence," from settling in America.[53]

Trevor arrived in Washington and appeared before the House and Senate immigration committees, reinforcing the connection between alien races and Bolshevism and becoming a permanent fixture in the House committee's deliberations for the next three years. He "sat in on informal meetings of the restrictionist majority, fed ideas to it, and contributed to the drafting of reports." All this service was performed gratis: Trevor had the time, inclination, and financial means to assist the committee in any way and for quite as long as it required.[54]

Although the committee was heartened by widespread support for its plans, its task was complicated by big business's demand for cheap labor. An in-principle solution quickly developed: the movement of Canadian and Latin American workers would not be impeded, but the annual number of European migrants would be limited to a very small percentage of the number of each nationality that already resided in the United States. While the size of this percentage was subject to horse-trading, all parties agreed it had to be biased to allocate more permits to Northwestern Europeans. The new president approved the bill in May 1921, and the immigration revolution was under way.[55]

Trevor and Johnson were pleased with the act, anticipating that it would restrict total immigration in the next couple of years to around 350,000 per annum, down from nearly 1,000,000 in 1920 and with more than half of those arrivals coming from Northwestern Europe. For the first time, absolute numerical limits had been placed on European migration, and a nationality-based quota system had been introduced: only 3 percent of any given nationality's resident population in 1910 would be admitted. This provision would ensure that subsequent immigration could amount to only a fraction of prewar levels and that the proportion of the foreign-born in the national population would fall. Nevertheless, the two men felt that their work had really only just begun, and the committee resumed gathering data to support further restrictions, particularly on the immigration of inferior races.[56]

As the 1921 act came into effect, members of the restrictionist lobby soon realized that the law was not the rousing success for which they had hoped. Total immigration exceeded half a million per year, in part because foreign-born citizens were securing entry permits for their relatives. Johnson's committee therefore recommended that American consuls be empowered to require prospective immigrants to furnish essential information on family background, health, literacy, occupation, and criminal record, enabling officials summarily to bar the blatantly unsuitable and distribute visas evenly throughout the year. It also recommended that loopholes permitting the entry of distant relatives of citizens be closed and that aliens ineligible for citizenship be denied entry, thereby preventing any children these immigrants might have from receiving citizenship.[57]

While big business retained reservations about stricter immigration restriction, two factors wore down opposition to the committee's plans. Technological advances were reducing the need for unskilled labor, and industry officials faced enormous pressure from the restrictionist lobby to put patriotism above profits. The committee, therefore, could focus on developing support for its discriminatory program, an effort in which Trevor's political acumen proved invaluable. He realized that the key to bringing about desired reform was to present the committee's policy as conservative rather than revolutionary, emphasizing that the policy was an iterative development of long-standing procedures that would preserve the country's historical ethnic balance. The unbridled or lightly restricted immigration of Southern and Eastern Europeans thus could credibly be characterized as warping the national racial equilibrium relative to the previous three hundred years.[58]

To buttress this argument, Trevor prepared elaborate statistical tables outlining the origins of the US population. He divided the total population of 1920—precisely 105,710,620 souls—into a handful of categories. The "white population, native born of native parentage," totaled 58,421,957. "Foreign stock," whom Trevor defined as the "foreign born, native born of foreign parentage and native born of mixed parentage," amounted to 36,398,958, leaving 10,889,705 "native born of negro descent, some American Indians and a relatively small proportion of Asiatics." Trevor based these figures on "a perfected formula" of the Census Bureau, which had estimated the numbers of descendants of white citizens counted in the first census of 1790 at 47,370,000. The same formula allowed Trevor to ascertain that 1,716,402 additional citizens were descended from the 275,000 white immigrants who arrived between 1790 and 1820. From this total of 49,086,402, Trevor derived "the basic stock of the population"; happily, his own ancestors were among them, as were Grant's and Davenport's. He then divided this "basic stock" by national groups in the same proportions that each comprised of the national population. Taking into account migration after 1820, Trevor determined that in 1920, 75.4 percent of the US population derived from Northwestern Europe. Migrants from the "West Indies, Mexico, Central and South America, together with the Colored Races," accounted for 11.4 percent. This meant that Southern and Eastern European "stock" comprised 13.2 percent. These figures demonstrated the iniquity of determining racial quotas according to the 1910 census; on that basis, Southern and Eastern Europeans would be allocated 44 percent of the total quota, as opposed to 15 percent if the 1890 census was applied. Far from being unjust or discriminatory, a quota based on the 1890 census actually gave Southern and Eastern Europeans a 15 percent surfeit of visas.[59]

Like the Dillingham Commission, Trevor used questionable statistics that overstated the proportionate size of "nationalities" whose immigration he sought to encourage. However, the committee accepted his figures and arguments as the foundation for legislation introduced in March 1924. The bill proposed limiting the immigration of each ethnic group to 2 percent of the number of people from that group who were present in the United States in 1890. It also provided for the exclusion of aliens ineligible for citizenship, pointedly adding Japanese to the Asian nationalities that had been barred since 1917. However, residual concerns about discrimination forced the committee to apportion quotas directly according to the proportion that each group comprised of the present population as represented in Trevor's tables. Legislation framed on this "national origins" principle would be just as restrictive as a census-based scheme because it would establish an absolute annual maximum quota, which would also be divided in accordance with the proportionate origins of the white population. In common with a census-based approach, this scheme yielded seven times more Northwestern than Southern or Eastern European migrants. And by accounting for all Americans' ancestors, Congress would not have to use an arbitrary prior census. The national origins principle, as John Higham has observed, thus "offered a direct implementation of racial nationalism and an answer to all charges of discrimination. It gave expression to the tribal mood, and comfort to the democratic conscience."[60]

Congress agreed that the new system should come into effect in the 1927–28 financial year. Until then, a proposal for 2 percent quotas based on the 1890 census would remain in effect. Fewer than 300,000 total migrants would be admitted each year, not counting Canadians and Mexicans, who were exempted in deference to capital's need for labor as well as diplomatic and commercial relations with those countries. Other exemptions to quotas would be granted only to the wives and minor children of citizens, not of aliens. After 1 July 1927, a total quota of 150,000 would be parceled out in ratios determined by national origins in the white population as they stood in 1920. Although President Coolidge was reluctant to provoke a diplomatic crisis with Japan, he decided not to veto such a comprehensive and popular bill, and it became law on 11 May 1924.[61]

The eugenics lobby was ecstatic. Its retort to the Bolshevik Revolution had finally been made. And now that the bill had become law, all reticence about the legislation's eugenic purpose was abandoned. In his *Analysis of the American Immigration Act of 1924*, Trevor wrote at length about the relationship between the act and race suicide (the notion that inferior races bred at greater rates than superior

Nordic stock), the susceptibility of the Nordic race to degeneration through mis-cegenation and cohabitation, and the (now obstructed) desire of foreign states to dump their human waste on the United States. Americans could rejoice that Congress had "put an end, once and for all, to the immigration of those elements of foreign populations who may be classified as socially inadequate, criminal, anarchists or agents of revolutionary organizations, be this immigration volun-tary or stimulated by public or private agencies."[62]

Johnson also praised the act's role in regulating "the great problem of the com-mingling of races." "Our hope," Johnson averred, "is in a homogeneous Nation." Although America originally "welcomed all," and "all helped to build the Nation," times had changed. Now the Melting Pot would "have a rest," enabling America to unite itself "as completely . . . as any nation in Europe or in Asia" as its right of "self-preservation" demanded. Notwithstanding Trevor's claim that the act gave "effect to a policy slowly evolved since the early days of the Republic," neither Trevor nor Johnson could resist the temptation to boast of their contribution to history. For Trevor, the act marked "the close of an epoch in the history of the United States," while Johnson declared the new legislation "America's second Declaration of Independence."[63]

If the Immigration Act of 1924 was not quite so momentous, it indeed radi-cally transformed American immigration policy and instituted a new "system of racial classification and regulation . . . capable of circumventing the imperative of equality established by the Fourteenth Amendment." In this respect, as Mae M. Ngai has noted, the act completed the decades-long quest to find a lawful means of extending "the legal traditions that had [long] justified racial discrimi-nation against African Americans . . . to other ethno-racial groups." The various immigration acts of the early twentieth century had gradually achieved this goal through euphemism, by describing these undesirables as "aliens ineligible to citizenship." Trevor's schema solidified and extended this concept while adding arbitrary identity categories in its "national origins" clauses to rationalize ad-ditional exclusion. For this reason, Ngai has compared the Johnson-Reed Act with the Civil War, since in both cases "a confluence of economic, social, cultural and political factors . . . impelled major shifts in society's understanding (and construction) of race and its constitutive role in national identity formation."[64]

While Trevor's reforms "realigned" immigration policy and "hardened racial categories in the law," they also represented the culmination of international trends that began to coalesce during the European war, making the nation-state (as opposed to political philosophy) the primary guarantor and definer of the individual's right to belong. The war created new categories not only of state-less peoples but also of peoples of "enemy origin." Inalienable individual rights, Ngai has observed, now inhered "not in human personage . . . but in the citizen." As such, these rights could now be recognized and underwritten only by national governments. The concept of illegal rather than merely undesirable aliens emerged, and millions of aliens were dumped into "the same juridical no-man's land as refugees and the stateless." So while the postwar rush to "legislate restriction in Congress" was argued predominantly "in the domestic political language of racial nativism," it was also one of several administrative measures enacted at this time to tighten the "territorial integrity of the nation-state." The introduction of passport controls in Europe and the United States similarly began as emergency war measures but "became, without exception, the norm in regulating international migration." Thus among its many other strictures, the Immigration Act of 1924 established the requirement for prospective immigrants to produce "not only passports (documentary evidence of national identity) but also visas (documentary proof of permission to enter)." Passport control also became an important means of circumscribing the movement of communists. From 1928 to 1955, Ruth Bielaski Shipley, the sister of Bureau of Investigation director A. Bruce Bielaski, managed the US Passport Office, denying passports to Paul Robeson, Arthur Miller, and W. E. B. Du Bois, among others. Critics charged her with flouting due process in denying passports for political reasons; supporters applauded her defense of the nation against communism and subversion.[65]

Death and Legacies

The strict quota system of the Johnson-Reed Act remained intact until 1965. Its deliberate omission of refugee visas remained policy until 1948. Yet the restrictionist lobby feared that the measure would not sufficiently seal the country's borders and remained vigilant. Trevor zealously defended the national origins system and barriers to the immigration of inferior races whenever necessary.[66]

The work of preserving the act began almost as soon as it became law. In 1925, Trevor and Grant compiled the "Third Report of the Sub-Committee on Selective Immigration of the Eugenics Committee of the United States," extolling the virtues of examining "Immigrants Overseas, as an Additional Safeguard in the Processes of Enforcing American Immigration Policy." Trevor continued to influence legislators by forming front companies to give himself an institutional platform from which to lobby government officials on the importance of restricting immigration and combating Reds. At some point shortly before or during his tenure with the House immigration committee, Trevor persuaded the Chamber of Commerce of the State of New York to establish a "special committee on immigration and the alien insane" and to appoint him as its chair. In 1927 Trevor founded the American Coalition of Patriotic Societies (ACPS) to "coordinate the efforts of patriotic, civic and fraternal societies to keep America American." The coalition functioned as a holding company for Trevor's benefit. Although any society could join the coalition and more than a hundred organizations did, they were not required to pay any dues or contributions. They were required however, to delegate administration of the coalition to a board of directors, whose president, elected annually without opposition from 1927 until his retirement in 1950, was John Trevor.[67]

The establishment of the coalition cemented Trevor's move from an intelligence and legislative environment into the Spider Web of reactionary "patriotic" societies, where he remained in the congenial company of such old colleagues and friends as Ralph Van Deman, the Daughters of the American Revolution, Archibald Stevenson, Harry Jung, and particularly Walter Steele, whose collaboration with Trevor was so intimate that a contemporary investigator regarded their operations "as one." The pressure exerted by these Web members was instrumental, particularly during the Coolidge and Hoover administrations, in helping to transform the Bureau of Immigration into what the American Civil Liberties Union described as the "Bureau of Deportation." While the restrictionist lobby had previously focused on barring undesirable immigrants from the United States, it did not neglect to agitate for the removal of alien Bolsheviks. The expulsion of unnaturalized "radicals," in concert with the Johnson-Reed Act, reversed the total trend of migration. Between 1930 and 1935, almost twice as many aliens left the United States as new immigrants arrived. With the election of Franklin Roosevelt to the White House, however, the nation's purification program was instantly threatened. The total number of forced and "voluntary" departures dropped by almost half to around seventeen thousand per year. Employers were forbidden to threaten aliens with deportation in labor disputes. The Department of Labor was instructed to desist raiding suspected alien premises and stripped of its power to fingerprint aliens, and the Secret Service of the Bureau of Immigration was abolished.[68]

These reforms predictably aroused opposition, and it was led by "America's alien-baiter No. 1," John Trevor. So prominent was Trevor in the restriction movement that *Harper's Magazine* labeled him the greatest "patriot in America"—but only if "a man's love for his country" was measured "by his detestation of all who had the bad taste to be born elsewhere." Whenever he detected a threat to the integrity of his act, Trevor sprang into action. In 1928, when presidential candidate Herbert Hoover campaigned against the Johnson-Reed quota system, Trevor took out advertisements in the *Washington Post* defending the national origins formula as the only (nondiscriminatory) means of combating the intrigues of "hyphenates," who would "play politics with the nation's blood stream." With Mexicans and Canadians excluded from national origins quotas, Trevor also campaigned to institute a quota for Latinos. When congressional Democrats attempted in

1936 to pass a bill giving the secretary of labor discretion to offer citizenship to "hardship cases" (illegal immigrants of good character and means with American dependents), Trevor, Fries, and other leading restrictionists testified against the law, but they had lost Johnson, their congressional champion, in the 1932 Democratic landslide. As storm clouds gathered over Europe, Trevor, Laughlin, and the ACPS campaigned against legislative proposals to provide sanctuary to German Jewish children and called for a ten-year suspension of all immigration. These friends of the Nazis also urged the United States not to enter into combat with Germany, a position that likely contributed to MI's 1940 classification of them, together with Stoddard, as suspicious. In 1943, Trevor also opposed a proposal to allocate a token annual quota of 105 visas to Chinese as a gesture acknowledging China's struggle against Japanese imperialism and US support of the Kuomintang. Oblivious to irony, Trevor complained that the proposal had the backing only of a powerful pressure group. Such a move, he warned, would precipitate the dismantling of racial quotas and undo "the work of twenty years of immigration restrictions."[69]

That Trevor was not officially identified as a security risk testified to the value of his political and social connections as well as to the general sympathy his equation of Jewish racial qualities and Bolshevik anarchy found in government and intelligence circles and indeed the general population.[70] Trevor's anti-Semitic sympathies had drawn him into not only isolationist but also pro-Nazi circles by the early 1930s. In 1933, along with American Defense Society founder Elon Hooker, Ralph Easley, Jung, Steele, Stevenson, and Hamilton Fish, Trevor endorsed the book *Communism in Germany*, which featured a quotation from German chancellor Adolf Hitler. Prescott Dennett, the Washington representative for Flanders Hall, a Nazi-funded publishing house, worked with Trevor and Steele, both of whom had complete sets of the publisher's books. Trevor and Steele were also among the closest collaborators of John B. Snow, whose League for Constitutional Government did perhaps more than any other organization to encourage the notion that the Roosevelt administration was directed by Jews and communists. And while Trevor personally escaped accusations of treason, the ACPS was cited as a factor in the 1942 indictment of twenty-eight other pro-Nazi citizens for sedition. In addition, the ACPS's "honorary president," C. M. Goethe, also served as president of the Eugenics Research Association and a passionate advocate of Germany's eugenics program.[71]

With Johnson ousted from Congress, Trevor began to cultivate a new generation of anticommunists and immigration restrictionists, chief among them Texas Democratic congressman Martin Dies Jr. With the aid of the Hearst press, the *Saturday Evening Post*, and the ACPS, Dies rapidly rose to national prominence on the back of public speaking engagements and newspaper pieces filled, according to *Harper's*, "with Trevoresque facts and conclusions." By 1938, Dies had propelled himself into the position of chair of the newly established Special Committee to Investigate Un-American Activities, whence he hounded aliens, radicals, and left-wing government employees until 1945. Both a neo–Mitchell Palmer and proto–Joseph McCarthy, Dies publicly identified and called for the dismissal of hundreds of alleged communists and sympathizers in government employ. Trevor also assisted McCarthy and in the mid-1950s became a leader of Ten Million Americans Mobilizing for Justice, an organization campaigning to prevent the censure of the fading senator.[72]

Trevor also strove to ensure that the race "research" of Grant and (the now very elderly) Davenport and Laughlin (on whom the Nazis had bestowed an honorary doctorate) continued. Together with Laughlin and Wickliffe Preston Draper, "distant kin to three American presidents" and heir to a textile manufacturing fortune, Trevor founded the Pioneer Fund in 1937. Content to play the silent partner, Trevor took no official role with the fund. That task was left to his eldest son and namesake, who became its director and secretary in 1959. John Bond Trevor Jr. and New York tax attorney Harry Frederick Weyher Jr. controlled the fund for more than forty years. Dominated by wealthy New Englanders, Harvard graduates, and Boston Brahmins, the fund provided financial aid "for the education of children . . . of unusual value." Such value, the fund supposed, was found "especially" among children "deemed to be descended predominantly from white persons who settled in the original thirteen states prior to the adoption of the Constitution . . . and/or from related stocks." The fund's other fundamental purpose was to support "study and research into the problems of heredity and eugenics" to surmount "the problems of race betterment." Cloaking its white supremacism in the language of racial "difference" (a process begun in the 1920s by Stoddard) the fund now promotes a "better understanding of [human] similarities [and] individual and group differences . . . no matter how upsetting those findings may be to any entrenched religious or political dogmas." Committed to "freedom of enquiry in all matters, and generally, to an open society, broadly conceived," the fund finances "specialized 'niche' projects, which have difficulty attracting funds from government sources or from larger foundations." The fund's primary "niche" project, from its inception until well after the dismantling of segregation, was the "repatriation" of black-skinned Americans "back" to Africa. Reluctantly abandoning this fantasy, the fund continued to strive to prove the genetic inferiority of African Americans and to aid 1970s campaigns against "forced busing" and other forms of integration as well as investments in minority education. The principal evidence furnished to support these aims concerned "genetic aspects of educability."[73]

The elder Trevor's strident and very public anti-Semitism, white supremacist ideology, and anti-immigrant, anticommunist, and antilabor views had little if any effect on his social standing. He was commodore of St. Regis Yacht Club in the Adirondack lakes and a fixture of New York's Social Register, a listing of the most prestigious citizens of the city. Full reckoning of the ultimate consequences of eugenics-based policies did not come prior to Trevor's death on 20 February 1956 but would await the rights revolution of the 1960s. Fronting the ACPS (which was likely kept afloat solely by Draper) and the Pioneer Fund, John Trevor Jr. continued to protest the liberalization of immigration laws and attempted to confine refugee admissions to victims of communism until his death on 27 August 2006 at the age of ninety-seven. But the tide was finally turning against restrictionists and racists. Although some figures in the Pioneer Fund were important supporters of Senator Jesse Helms and Ronald Reagan in the 1970s, the unwillingness of so many funded researchers and fund directors to publicly discuss the organization indicates the lobby's defensiveness. The fund continues to shrilly deny its historical Nazi ties and ideological recidivism, and it is the sole surviving institution of John Trevor's making. But Trevor's less tangible and more important legacies remain. Support for pseudoscientific racism and anticommunism remained at the heart of public sentiment and policy for one and four generations, respectively, and Anglo-Saxon, right-wing warriors remain a significant force in American politics today. Thus, Trevor's underreported story is important to understanding the heritage of ideas and movements that continues to influence American politics.[74]

CHAPTER 7

Jacob Spolansky

The Rise of the Career
Anticommunist Spook

Communists will destroy the present institutions, eliminate all
public officials, liquidate your conception of family life, forbid
you to worship the Divine Creator, conscript your competence,
and exterminate every semblance of individual initiative.

—Jacob Spolansky

The growth of anticommunism during the First World War and the Red Scare
fostered the creation of a class of professional spies active both in law enforcement and political and industrial counterespionage. Few men better demonstrate the enduring and lucrative opportunities enjoyed by these spooks than
Jacob Spolansky, a migrant from Ukraine who arrived in the United States as a
young man around 1910 and was recruited into the US Army's Military Intelligence Division (MI) and the Bureau of Investigation (BI). Spolansky enjoyed a
thirty-year career, rotating in and out of government and corporate service and
spying on and infiltrating radical and labor organizations. An able self-publicist
with theatrical and journalistic training, Spolansky used legislative committees,
business associations, and media outlets to engender support for harsh measures
to deal with political and industrial radicals. His career highlights included coordinating the Palmer Raids in Chicago, arresting several CP leaders in Michigan
in 1922, formulating Michigan's 1931 "Spolansky Act" (requiring the registration
of all aliens in the state), and investigating for the House Un-American Activities Committee. A Red hunter of national significance, Spolansky, like John B.
Trevor, has nevertheless remained a historical footnote, an inhabitant of what
Alfred McCoy terms "society's shadowy interstices," ignored "in the writing of

national history."[1] This omission is unfortunate, for Spolansky's career illustrates how the Red Scare enabled committed anticommunists to prolong the practice of engaging mercenaries to bust unions and radical groups. Spolansky's career also illustrates how the Red Scare made the cooperative relationship between government and private anticommunist networks more intimate and far-reaching. Few organizations nourished these networks more than the national security and intelligence agencies, the urban and county police Red Squads, and the corporate plant protection forces in whose service Spolansky and others like him earned their keep.

Covert surveillance, infiltration, and manipulation of industrial and political organizations had been a function of policing since the mid-nineteenth century. For several decades, such policing was generally performed by private detectives employed by corporations. With official policing infrastructure slight, corporations paid detective agencies handsomely for any data they could furnish about employee performance and attitudes. The value of such data only grew as industrialization steadily eroded informal labor practices. Allan Pinkerton and several other entrepreneurs made big money detecting discontent in labor unions and radical organizations. This business model remained profitable throughout the Gilded Age and the Progressive period; corporate suppression of strikes peaked from 1911 to 1916. However, the US entry into the First World War abruptly ended this era of unaided and continuous labor surveillance by private detectives. Henceforth, the relationship between civil and military intelligence services and corporate detectives was inverted, as the former led the latter in an assault on forces that dared to challenge economic and political order.[2]

When Ralph Van Deman and other veterans of the Philippine Constabulary began to reform and rebuild the wartime national security apparatus, they repatriated countersubversion techniques they had used to destroy the Filipino independence movement. Civilian security adjuncts such as the American Protective League played an important role in this process, as did the recruiting of agents who possessed the linguistic skills necessary for understanding the "enemy." Just as the Constabulary had recruited Filipinos to spy on other Filipinos, US agencies engaged foreign-language-speaking migrants to observe their own kind in urban and industrial America. And this policy brought Jacob Spolansky, a young migrant from what is now Ukraine, to the attention of MI in Chicago in 1918.

The Migrant Becomes a Spy

Jacob Spolansky was born on 3 December 1889 in what he termed a "forsaken hamlet" near Kiev. The son of a middle-class pharmacist, Jacob and his five younger siblings received instruction in French, German, and grammar-school subjects from their resident governess. The name *Shpolyanskij* was reasonably common among Jewish inhabitants of the Pale of Settlement, in the Russian empire and Jacob was one of many immigrants named Spolansky who abandoned the Kievan provinces around the turn of the century. Spolansky's childhood idyll was shattered in 1903 when his father died of typhus. Spolansky left high school after a couple of years to help run the family dispensary but soon departed for Odessa to study drama, evincing a liking for public attention that frequently resurfaced during his later espionage career. After learning the actor's trade for about eighteen months, he joined a traveling repertory company that performed across southern Russia. After his mother received his father's life insurance payout, she sent him abroad, first to Switzerland, where he studied at a university for a year, and then to the New World. After landing in Montreal, Spolansky headed west to British Columbia and then across the border into Seattle. About twenty years old, he had just four dollars in his pocket.[3]

Spolansky spent several years working in a lumber camp in Washington before decamping to make his home in Chicago. There he studied English and resumed his dramatic activity at Hull House. He also began to pen stories for Russian-language publications, eventually establishing the city's first Russian newspaper, and served as vice chair of a Liberty Loan Committee. Initially popular, the paper expanded from a weekly into a daily until Spolansky's support for the Kerensky regime cost him so many radical readers that he was forced to sell the publication at a loss. Yet his time had not been wasted, for his journalism and patriotism led the local branch of MI to approach him as a recruit. The agency was also attracted by Spolansky's linguistic facility and knowledge, as he termed it, of "the concentrations of aliens in Chicago." Foreign-born, non-Christian, and multilingual operatives were still relatively rare in the national security apparatus, and although the Office of Naval Intelligence recruited among upper-middle- and upper-class families, the BI generally found recruits among what historian Thomas Klug has described as the "status and identity-seeking" lower middle class. That description applied to Spolansky, but while he lacked the military and labor espionage experience of many BI recruits, authorities in Chicago were sensitive to the invaluable intelligence immigrants could provide. The Chicago Police Bomb Squad, for example, had previously recruited a Russian émigré to help them infiltrate radical workers' groups. MI similarly put Spolansky in command of a large unit of spies and informants, handling "numerous military and civilian investigations relating to the war effort" for the antiradical "Negative Branch."[4] When the war concluded, Spolansky's talents were judged indispensable. The Chicago branch of the BI hired him and within a few months made him a special agent monitoring "Anarchists, Communists and other subversive elements." He rose rapidly to the position of head of the

Chicago District's Radical Division, which A. Mitchell Palmer soon reorganized into the General Intelligence Division. In this capacity, according to one historian, he coordinated the Palmer Raids in Chicago. Spolansky himself boasted of apprehending 650 people during the raids and of testifying "in every case" against an eventual four hundred or so radicals whom the government listed for deportation. Thereafter, Spolansky "concentrated almost exclusively [on] Communists and their organized webs." He also helped ensure that many other operatives concentrated exclusively on political repression. In a time of organizational expansion, when one-third of the bureau's entire staff was assigned to antiradical activity, Spolansky and other senior officers "indoctrinated the green agents" who knew "comparatively little about the radical movements . . . into the craft of trailing and investigating the enemies" of the United States. Spolansky was aided in this task by a steady stream of high-level CP communiqués and resolutions that flowed over his desk, including some from European government agencies working in concert with the bureau.[5]

When Spolansky joined the BI in July 1919, the country was experiencing massive postwar strikes. In response to this tumult, the Wilson administration sanctioned a campaign of violent repression. The BI and the Bureau of Immigration were authorized to infiltrate the ranks of steel and railroad strikers and engineer their arrest. According to historian Robert Weiss, the federal government, corporations, and their private armies "literally brought the war home," substituting organized labor and the "Bolshie" for the Hun. Leading the charge was Palmer, whose BI had by early 1920 amassed two hundred thousand dossiers profiling domestic radical activity, foreign-language newspapers, Irish American and African American nationalists, and numerous other subjects. The Palmer Raids were to a large extent made possible by federal subterfuge. BI, Bureau of Immigration, MI, and Office of Naval Intelligence agents infiltrated these groups and helped to organize simultaneous branch meetings held across the continent on 2 January 1920. The BI sought evidence to justify a standing peacetime sedition law. The Bureau of Immigration sought to deport whatever remaining foreign-born radicals were left in the country.[6]

While the antiradical investigations continued, General Intelligence Division boss J. Edgar Hoover broadened his agency's focus to include international, economic, and industrial affairs. And even though Congress declined to prorogue the Sedition Act in 1921, the division pursued its antiradical and antiunion objectives by deepening ties with private detective and strikebreaking agencies. The early 1920s represented the climax of what Weiss has described as "the golden age of private detective work." According to Louis Post, the division was already saturated with "labor spy interests" during the Wilson administration. Federal judge George W. Anderson similarly believed that the BI "owned and operated" the radical movement. Nevertheless, when US attorney general Harry Daugherty appointed nationally renowned private detective William J. Burns, a fellow member of Daugherty's "Ohio Gang" and his childhood friend, to serve as the BI's director, "the flow of personnel and influence from the private sector" into the bureau "reached an apogee." Burns's three-year tenure as bureau chief took the agency into "new depths of unethical and illegal activity." During the Harding administration, most newly appointed agents had previously worked as private detectives, and the General Intelligence Division and the private sector led "a two-pronged assault" on radical and labor organizations. The bureau "became the nation's political police, whilst private detective agencies specialized in shop-floor spying and picket slugging." An old-boy network of private and federal police was established, with public and private agencies routinely sharing information and employees and organizing joint operations. Daugherty's use of injunctions prohibiting striking railway workers from "interfering" with railway operations was buttressed by the deployment of bureau agents who offered strategic advice to railway company security forces and infiltrated strikers' ranks to foment unrest and amass evidence for prosecutions. A consortium of copper mines in Arizona also hired the Burns Detective Agency to infiltrate workforces and expose union organizers. Burns melded his public and private interests and instructed bureau agents to give his firm's employees every assistance. Bureau men acted as agents provocateur and distributed employee blacklists to mine operators in a flurry of correspondence among the Burns agency, copper company officials, police, and Department of Justice officials, including Burns.[7]

Spolansky never went to Arizona, but he did make national headlines for infiltrating the CP and orchestrating the arrest of several party executives. In mid-August 1922, Burns dispatched Spolansky and three other bureau agents to raid a secret national party convention in Bridgman, Michigan. They seized party materials and arrested party secretary Charles E. Ruthenberg and William Z. Foster, the party's trade union organizer, among others. Although the bureau's presence was unlawful (the party had not violated any federal laws), Spolansky and a posse of sheriff's deputies delivered their collars to state authorities for prosecution under Michigan's criminal syndicalism statutes. When Ruthenberg was brought to trial the following year, a disgruntled former colleague of Spolansky's in MI and the BI alleged that government and private agents had subverted numerous radical organizations at the highest levels. These agents, the former spy averred, had manufactured these organizations' propaganda, encouraged strike action and violent lawlessness (including bomb making), and engaged in mail fraud to frame radicals. Further, the agent accused Spolansky and other General Intelligence Division section chiefs of selling government information to private detective agencies. Spolansky was specifically accused of receiving payments from the Thiel Detective Agency and of regularly circulating government information to one of his cousins who was employed at Thiel and to another mutual relative working in the Chicago Police Bomb Squad. Outraged, Spolansky threatened to sue, though he ultimately did not. Spolansky testified that Foster had been present at Bridgman and later received favorable coverage in a *New York Times* exposé on agent "K-97," the mole who had allegedly organized the Bridgman summit and helped convince party leaders to keep the party underground. The *Times* even claimed that Spolansky "had studied the methods of the Russian Reds during the regime of the Czar."[8]

The Bridgman raid seems, however, to have been the high point of Spolansky's career in the bureau. The raid itself aroused concern among liberals and even the conservative Michigan Federation of Labor, which was persuaded by the BI's incursion into state law enforcement to call for the repeal of the state criminal syndicalism statute. When the Teapot Dome scandal terminated Burns's directorship, his successor, Hoover, was obliged to pay more than lip service to Attorney General Harlan Fiske Stone's organizational reforms. The General Intelligence Division was abolished and the practice of wiretapping and sharing information with businessmen and state officials ceased, at least officially. Henceforth, the bureau was directed to investigate only violations of federal law. The bureau's budget was frozen for the rest of the decade, and while the extent and effects of the resulting staff cuts have been exaggerated, including by Spolansky, the hero of Bridgman was soon out on his ear, possibly in part because of Hoover's anti-Semitism.[9]

The Professional Anticommunist

With a family to support, Spolansky quickly earned some cash—and some notoriety—by reviving his journalistic career with the *Chicago Daily News*, which published a series of breathless revelations about the Bridgman raids, communist plots to assassinate President Woodrow Wilson, radical bombing intrigues, communist fomentation of race riots, and Moscow's control of American radical organizations. Spolansky thus trod the well-worn path of Red-hunting diarists, who had been selling their tales since Allan Pinkerton published a series of ghostwritten detective novels in the 1870s. More recently, both William Burns and his predecessor at the bureau, William J. Flynn, had published novels glamorizing detective work. In his *Daily News* articles, Spolansky made his contribution to the evolving lore of radicalism, embellishing prevailing clichés about communists' beliefs and behavior. Spolansky's account of a raid on communists gathering in Chicago parkland portrayed them as cabalistic fanatics, obsessed by outward forms of fealty and arcane doctrine. A typical story, published on

17 October 1924, was headed, "'Reds' in the Woods Work Day and Night to End Dissension—Dramatic Scenes in the Chicago Forest Preserve at River Forest as Communists in Secret Convention Iron out Differences—Quarrels, Fist Fights and Weird Ceremonies Witnessed by Government Agents Hidden in the Leaves—Song Signalizes Reconciliation." Spolansky's revelations confirmed important suppositions about communists, demonstrating that even among their own they were compulsively oppositional and querulous and harbored grudges. During the conference, Spolansky reported, radicals argued "over everything . . . the selection of committees [and] the name to be adopted" for the merging Communist and Communist Labor Parties. Discord reigned, "each point" being "sufficient cause for eight or ten speeches and at least one violent quarrel, followed by general wrangling." Warming to his subject, Spolansky then described the convention's climax. With night falling, the delegates sat themselves "in a crescent about a small hillock which served as a dais"; then, "one after another, the delegates addressed their colleagues." A "weird ceremony" followed in which they sang the Internationale "like a group of school children learning a hymn," their voices at first "soft and earnest" but then "growing in volume as they progressed—to inspire the others to decide for unity." Then, as a majority formed in favor of unification, they "took hands and danced about the small circle of 'obstinates' who still continued their arguments hotly, their voices rising to a shout in order to be heard."[10]

Delighting in his writing, Spolansky apparently failed to grasp the contradiction at the heart of his anticommunist propaganda, in which the need to present communism as a dastardly foreign-backed threat to America's way of life fought with the desire to convince American citizens that the whole communist enterprise was infantile and ridiculous. In any event, Spolansky's journalistic activity had an important political and professional point. Like many other "federal agents groomed for a career in domestic counter-subversion," Spolansky was slotting himself into a "nationwide fraternity" that unceasingly warned citizens about the "Red Menace." Such activity, as Klug has observed, sought to "pressure Congress to provide money and a legal mandate for a renewed federal role in fighting communism" and to legitimize antiunion activity by the corporations and employer associations for whom Spolansky and other retrenched agents went to work after their government careers were abruptly terminated. Spolansky began publishing anticommunist pieces regularly for the *Open Shop Review*, the organ of the National Metal Trades Association and the National Founders' Association, right around the time of his departure from the bureau.[11]

The first corporation for which Spolansky publicly attested to working in his new career as an industrial consultant was Botany Consolidated Mills in Passaic, New Jersey. Though Spolansky hesitated to disclose the nature of his commission, circumstances strongly suggest that he was called in to supervise efforts to infiltrate labor ranks and provide strategic advice on breaking a major strike by Botany's workers. In his memoir, Spolansky elliptically describes the strike as a stunt pulled by communists "anxious to show their Moscow bosses" that they could cripple American industry. According to Spolansky, Botany's much-put-upon management had offered "time and again" to settle with strikers, only to be frustrated by communist agitators leading the strike, who were interested only in turning a mere "labor problem into a virtual civil war."[12]

But Spolansky neglected to tell his readers that the large mills in Passaic constituted hugely profitable industries that were shielded by tariffs and paid their fifteen-thousand-plus workers significantly less than a living wage. During and immediately after the war, Botany's assets grew from $3.5 to $28 million, necessitating a change of name and the formation of a holding company to hide its profits. In 1925, just before the major mills forced workers industry-wide to accept a 10 percent wage cut, Botany banked between $5 million and $6.75 million in net profits. At the same time, more than three-quarters of the company's sixty-four hundred workers toiled for less than $25 per week, often for ten or more hours a day, in dreadful conditions. Most had been recruited off the boats at Ellis Island and kept deliberately ignorant of English to help prevent them from organizing. Many men were employed on condition that their wives worked overnight; some women literally worked until their babies dropped newborn onto the factory floor. Passaic boasted the nation's highest rates of juvenile employment and third-highest illiteracy rates. Infant and child mortality and overall tuberculosis-related fatality rates outstripped the rest of the state by a great margin. The fact that the strike had been led by communists was not news by the time Spolansky published his memoirs. But the fact that 90 percent of Botany's workers struck for the best part of twelve months, braving the brutal attention of the police and the American Legion as well as job and financial insecurity, told a story of the Passaic dispute that Spolansky omitted, even a generation after the events. Spolansky also hesitated to discuss allegations that he was associated at the time of the strike with both Fred Marvin and the American Defense Society.[13]

After Botany settled with its strikers in late 1926, Spolansky continued hunting communists and combating labor organizations in Detroit, which served on and off as his base for the rest of his career. With typical discretion, Spolansky's memoirs hide the identity of the employers who commissioned him to investigate communist infiltration of their factories. The origins of Spolansky's commission, as he relates it, lay in the CP's desire to capitalize on its success in Passaic and find "new fields to conquer." The communists, according to Spolansky, quickly deduced that the most opportune site for their "mass sabotage methods" was the Detroit automakers' assembly lines. In early 1927, Spolansky began "uncovering the seat of the infection." He found that a thousand "militant, well-organized Communists" employed in important manufacturing plants had plunged the entire industry into chaos. This "military force" of "professional troublemakers ... all trained in Moscow" was holding hostage "more than a quarter of a million self-respecting workers" and their employers. Aside from seeking technical information for Russia, the communists were exploiting "real or manufactured grievances" to mount "a campaign to discredit the leading personalities in the auto industry, particularly Henry Ford, the symbol of American industry and might." The plan, Spolansky explained, was to shut down Detroit's economy by sabotaging products, driving up production costs, precipitating job losses, and driving a desperate workforce into the communists' revolutionary arms.[14]

The real story of Spolansky's employment was more complicated. And if any conspiracy lurked behind the economic disturbances wracking the city, Spolansky's employers had as good a claim on responsibility as anyone. When Spolansky was called in to Motor City, Detroit had one of the nation's least effectively organized workforces. The district's largest automotive and affiliated corporations employed around 285,000 people, scarcely any of whom were organized. Although more than 20 percent of Detroit's industrial workers had been union members around the turn of the century, the city's employers had formed their own representative organizations and used them to drive unions out of the plants. The presence and size of these organizations grew in precise proportion to those of laborers'. While membership in the AFL ballooned from around 275,000 in 1898 to more than 1.5 million in 1904, organizations such as the National Founders' Association and the National Association of Manufacturers were formed to obstruct and dissolve labor unions. Among the most important and militant of these employer associations was the National Metal Trades Association, for which Spolansky was again working.[15]

Detroit's employers had pried the shop floor open with immigrant labor. The use of such labor, already heavy in the nineteenth century, had increased with the rise of the motor car industry. As the city's population quintupled between 1900 and 1930, the proportion of foreign-born workers in manufacturing topped 40 percent; in 1917, 60 percent of Ford's thirty-five thousand workers were born outside the United States. But by the mid-1920s, industry's capacity to draw on this labor supply had been significantly curtailed by John Trevor's immigration reforms. At the same time, the local trade union movement was sponsoring efforts to restrict employment opportunities for migrants and had resolved to mount a fresh campaign to organize the automobile industry. Worse still, the CP, with significant support among the foreign-born, had taken control of the long-enfeebled Automobile Workers' Union and was distributing communist literature to a wide readership. The party seemed to be making itself a focal point for broader industry- and community-based organization, establishing links with neighborhood cells, mutual-benefit associations, and ethnic and work-ers' clubs. Such strategies were being employed in industrial centers across the nation. So a sizable group of Detroit employers affiliated with the Employers' Association of Detroit hired Spolansky to infiltrate the party and report on the nature and extent of radical subversion in their shops. Spolansky arrived as an emissary of the National Metal Trades Association, which provided "machine-shop tips . . . legal advice . . . plant guards, undercover spies, and strikebreakers" to member firms across America. In March 1927 Spolansky reported the names, addresses, and places of employment of nearly two hundred communists as well as "information regarding some 3,000 others." He must have been assisted in this work by the nearly three hundred industrial spies planted in the CP and kindred groups by the Corporations Auxiliary Company and the Railroad Audit Corporation, the two largest employers of corporate detectives in the region. At any rate, Spolansky called on the Employers' Association to "sponsor a per-manent counter-subversion operation" to secure material that would facilitate the deportation of "prominent leaders in the movement." As a member of what Klug describes as a national "professional counterintelligence establishment," Spolansky had a vested interest in promoting the Detroit business community's dread of "communist infiltration in order to fund, legitimize, and perhaps some-day legalize [a] red-catching network." Yet in spite of his worrisome findings, the association opted not to proceed with Spolansky's plan, reasoning that a purge of communist employees would cause workers to smell fear in their bosses and thus embolden the rank and file.[16]

While Detroit employers pondered their next moves, Spolansky busied him-self with winning public support for an anticommunist offensive by rekindling his journalistic activity in the local press. On 30 July 1927, *Detroit Saturday Night* published yet another Spolansky "scoop" on the Bridgman raid. Declining merely to rehash the circumstances of that raid, Spolansky also described the mock trial of a cofounder of the CP by leading party members, among them a Detroit resident. By outlining the circumstances of this "trial," Spolansky not only pro-vided another illustration of the party's bizarre culture but also demonstrated the "military efficiency" of its "organizational machine" and its leaders "supreme confidence" in daring to establish "an alien court to try a man for the offense of aiding" the country in which they all lived. This confidence was the product of an extensive spy network whose members had infiltrated government and the courts, and worked to subvert the prosecution of communists.[17]

Unfortunately for Spolansky and his supporters in the Detroit business com-munity, his confidential report and newspaper articles failed to persuade big business or its supporters in government to mount a vigorous anticommunist campaign. That campaign had to wait until the tipping point of International Unemployment Day, 6 March 1930. Huge demonstrations across the United States and Europe helped prompt Congress to form the Fish Committee, which arrived in Detroit with great fanfare to hold hearings in July 1930. Among those who testified to the high concentration of communists in Detroit labor organizations and their predominantly foreign derivation were police chiefs and detectives, corporate executives, and National Metal Trades Association emissary Jacob Spolansky. The importance of Spolansky's testimony to the committee can scarcely be overstated. Described by one modern historian as the country's "leading red-hunter specializing in the labor movement," Spolansky, the chief witness at the Detroit hearings, carried the authority not only of the National Metal Trades Association and the Employers' Association but also of the city's police department, whose files he conspicuously brandished and whose staff testified that the January 1930 creation of a covert operation "to work on the Bolshevik and Communistic activities in the city of Detroit" owed much to Spolansky's "great help." Further, the director of the Industrial Relations Department at General Motors indicated to the committee that its information about radicals in company plants was provided exclusively by Spolansky and the New York City police department.[18]

The arrival of the Fish Committee strengthened proponents of a witch hunt among local employers and directly inspired an investigation by the Union League of Michigan, a relatively new and elite club whose members included Governor Wilbur Brucker, two vice presidents of General Motors, and other local business leaders. Ten years after the New York Union League Club investigation had encouraged the formation of the Lusk Committee, the Fish Committee and the Union League of Michigan worked in similar lockstep. To conduct its own investigation, the Michigan league founded a Committee on Subversive Activities and appointed Spolansky its vice chair. The committee conducted public hearings in late 1930 and early the following year, while Spolansky warned the league's members on two occasions to remember that communists were seeking to "destroy the present institutions, eliminate all public officials, liquidate your conception of family life, forbid you to worship the Divine Creator, conscript your competence, and exterminate every semblance of individual initiative."[19]

In February 1931, the committee unveiled its legislative proposals. Closely mirroring the Fish Committee's recently announced program, the league called for the outlawing of the CP, the exclusion and deportation of all alien communists, the denaturalization of foreign-born communist citizens, and the banning of communist publications from the postal system and all interstate transportation. The league also introduced two recommendations of its own: disenfranchisement of native-born CP members and compulsory registration of all aliens in the state. These recommendations, which enjoyed the full support of conservative trade union locals, had a clear purpose: "political surveillance over the entire population," a goal that constituted "the standing objective of such militant anti-communists as Jacob Spolansky." As Klug observes, the registration of aliens would make possible the "systematic identification of communists, communist sympathizers, union agitators, and strikers." In addition, it would neutralize "the ability of radicals to travel, adopt pseudonyms, and merge imperceptibly into immigrant neighborhoods and the labor force. And it warranted the formation of a central file system, or political blacklist, under the control of the state police."[20]

The league's "Spolansky Act," as it was described by a contemporary labor attorney, passed through both chambers of the legislature by massive majorities and was signed into law by Governor Brucker on 29 May 1931. Brucker proclaimed it "protective welfare legislation," as it would prevent unlawful and unpatriotic Americans from taking the jobs of loyal laborers. Yet fearsome as it appeared, the Spolansky Act was a Pyrrhic victory. Less than a week after its proclamation, bureaucrats abandoned plans to register aliens as virtually impossible (as well as unpopular), and by the year's end, the measure had been ruled unconstitutional on the grounds that it usurped federal control of immigration. The decision destroyed anticommunists' strategy of using state legislation to obliterate the CP, and the act's failure undoubtedly helps to explain why Spolansky chose not to mention it or his Union League of Michigan commission in his memoirs. Instead, Spolansky alleged that the unemployed of Detroit were induced to protest by "huge sums" of communist money and the charms of "thrill-hungry" communist girls who "were used to bait the destitute." The ultimate aim of local communists, Spolansky insisted, remained the harnessing of class "hatred into a frontal assault on the citadel that Moscow despised most, Henry Ford's plant at Dearborn."[21]

After the excitement of producing the Spolansky Act, the man himself decided to remain in Michigan. Although the act had foundered, employment prospects for experienced Red hunters remained strong. The Fish Committee's hearings had cemented police ties to the district's right-wing and patriotic community, especially the American Legion, and the Detroit police had formed a new Special Investigation Bureau to monitor radical activity. Numerous former BI agents set up shop in Detroit, specializing in "industrial investigation [of] sabotage, parts theft, and wild cat strikes" for the automotive giants. Spolansky maintained his ties with the National Metal Trades Association and Employers' Association and overcame his legislation's defeat by testifying at the proceedings that resulted in the deportation of a Bulgarian-born communist who had led a community demonstration against the Spolansky Act. The man was just one of the more than 150 "well known Communists" Spolansky boasted of having expelled from the country, a figure that did not include "those who fled of their own accord when they knew of [his] interest in them." Having amassed a wealth of federal and private espionage experience, Spolansky decided to try his hand at state law enforcement, taking up an offer from the sheriff of Wayne County to establish a detective bureau to expose communist infiltration in this major manufacturing area.[22]

Businesses continued to solicit Spolansky's advice on detecting and removing radicals from their premises. Chrysler engaged Spolansky as a "consultant on plant protection" in 1935, when the "Communist threat" became "too ominous to ignore." By 1936, Chrysler had replaced Ford as the nation's second-largest automotive manufacturer (behind General Motors). Automotive unions accused Chrysler of maintaining "one of the most vicious and unspeakable spy systems ever employed in industry." Between 1933 and 1936, Chrysler spent more than $275,000 on the services of Corporations Auxiliary Service; it was also stockpiling tear gas for use on its employees. Pinkerton's biggest industrial client, General Motors spent even more on its services: approximately $1 million from 1934 to 1936. The *New York Times* reported that Spolansky was one of several former Department of Justice agents whom General Motors had engaged to replace Pinkerton's in investigating the mood of the automaker's labor force.[23] Moving back and forth between state and private employment, Spolansky rejoined the Wayne County Police as acting chief of detectives in 1937, probably as a consequence of corporate abandonment of labor surveillance following censure of the practice that year by the US Senate subcommittee headed by Robert La Follette Jr. that was investigating violations of free speech and the rights of labor. Spolansky's ability to swiftly change employers according to circumstance also demonstrates the importance of urban and county police forces as employers of career Red hunters and as proponents of antiunion, anticommunist activity.[24]

Spolansky's policing role immediately saw him confronting large demonstrations of strikers, who he later claimed had been worked up into "mass hysteria" by small numbers of "well-drilled [communist] agents." These demonstrations were significant enough to attract the attention of Martin Dies's reconstituted House Un-American Activities Committee. The committee arrived in Detroit in the fall of 1938 to investigate allegations that public officials, including Spolansky's immediate superior, had been influenced to overlook communist direction of the strikes. Claiming that the sheriff and anonymous callers threatened him with serious harm if he spoke to the committee, Spolansky not only testified with his customary enthusiasm but then took a party of like-minded citizens to Washington, D.C., to provide still more testimony to the committee. On his return to Detroit, Spolansky was charged with "crudely manufactured" offenses he declined to specify. Although the presiding judge had allegedly been paid two thousand dollars to find him guilty, Spolansky was acquitted. He resigned from the Sheriff's Department in December 1938 and released his resignation letter to local papers. Spolansky alleged that Sheriff Thomas Wilcox and prosecuting attorney Duncan McCrea had entered into an alliance with the CP, and in "an unprecedented move by an individual citizen," he asked the state attorney general to order a grand jury investigation. The following year, a one-man grand jury comprising Judge Homer Ferguson was convened, and Ferguson appointed Spolansky his "first investigator." By Spolansky's account, their "long and tedious, often dangerous, probing" unearthed enough evidence to send both Wilcox and McRae to jail; Spolansky could, it seems, be a dangerous man to cross. However, despite what Spolansky wrote, the 1939 grand jury in reality led to the disclosure not of communist infiltration of the police and the prosecutor's office but rather of an extensive bribery and payoff system that resulted in the indictment of the mayor, the county prosecutor, the superintendent of police, and eight officers as well as the reorganization of the police department and the abolition of the infamously corrupt Red Squad.[25]

With his legal affairs settled, Spolansky and the Un-American Activities Committee renewed their association. According to Spolansky, the committee's clerk, Robert Stripling, requested in May 1941 that Spolansky "prepare a full and detailed report on the nature and tenor of Communist tactics." Spolansky was sent to Chicago, where he investigated communist cells allegedly plotting strikes to cripple America's war production capacity.[26] Then, in 1943, Stripling dispatched Spolansky to Detroit following the eruption there of "communist manufactured" race riots, instructing him to "locate the roots [of the] tense racial feeling rampant over the Midwest." Echoing the conclusions of the Lusk and Fish Committees, Spolansky duly reported the existence in Detroit of a communist-controlled subversive movement "dedicated to the extermination of the white race." Exploiting "every incident . . . involving racial antagonism . . . on a wide scale as a means of aggravating" racial antipathies, Detroit communists had (mystifyingly and in contravention of official party policy) influenced white workers to strike rather than continue "to work alongside of Negroes." At the same time, "clever Communist propaganda" had convinced "the Negro" that the government and citizens of America "were engaged in a conspiracy to terrorize him, oppress him, discriminate against him and deprive him of his rights." According to Spolansky, he also provided the committee with "actual facts" pointing to the Japanese Secret Service's substantial role in fomenting the riots.[27]

By the time the war ended, Spolansky had reached middle age. With the Cold War heating up, he capitalized on the mood by publishing his memoirs. In April 1951, at the height of Joseph McCarthy's influence over national politics and culture, Macmillan released *The Communist Trail in America*, charging a respectable

$3.50 per copy. Written with the assistance of an attorney and aspiring playwright, Morton R. Sarett (whose musical, *Red, Hot, and Roman*, telling the story of the mad emperor Nero, opened later that year), *The Communist Trail* received extensive but tepid reviews. In his feature article on the book, *New York Times* critic Orville Prescott wrote, "One of the most repeated criticisms of literary critics is that they criticize a particular book for not being another kind of book. But there are books which ask for just such treatment. Mr. Spolansky's is one of them." According to Prescott, "as a contribution to an important, sinister and much-discussed subject," *The Communist Trail* was "superficial, disorderly and tiresome," containing too few "interesting revelations" and too much "elementary rehash of familiar material." Too often it was "impossible" for the reader to establish "for whom Spolansky was working at a particular time," what his sources of information were, and how he came to possess such information. And too often Spolansky indulged in "alarmingly sweeping statements." The old thespian in Spolansky could not resist rhetorical flourish. In one notable example of hyperbole, he claimed that the CPUSA ran its own secret police force every bit "as deadly" as the Soviet Union's, an overblown allegation that overlooked such Soviet atrocities as shooting turncoats in the head after forcing them to watch while their daughters were raped. Despite Prescott's review and others, *The Communist Trail* remains widely available and in 2012 ranked 4,352,216 on Amazon's bestseller list.[28]

Irrespective of his book's success, Spolansky seems to have found New York congenial, and he threw himself into local efforts to secure the 1952 Republican presidential nomination for the most stridently anticommunist and antilabor candidate, Senator Robert A. Taft. But Taft's bid failed, and Spolansky, now in his sixties, faded from public view. An aging and self-employed communist hunter had only limited employment opportunities in a field now crowded by the House Un-American Activities Committee and the FBI. Moreover, the reception garnered by *The Communist Trail*, the direction of Cold War anticommunism, and the desire to manage his posthumous reputation seemed to give Spolansky pause. In late 1954 he granted two interviews to historian Theodore Draper, sketching a more nuanced version of his beliefs and conduct than he provided in his memoirs. The two men shared a Jewish and Ukrainian background that may have created a sense of camaraderie, and Spolansky presented himself as a strident anticommunist but no enemy of organized labor. Describing himself as having supported not only Aleksandr Kerensky but also the Mensheviks (the minority faction of the Russian Social Democratic Labor Party), Spolansky painted himself as a believer in social democratic reform who held fast to the view that such reform should never be promoted by violence. Departing from his depiction in his newspaper articles of CP members as hopelessly fractious children, he suggested that "the majority" of the factional splits that had rent the party in the 1920s had been engineered by "clever agents." Claiming that the BI had planted half a dozen operatives in the upper echelons of the party, Spolansky stated that he had never believed in directing party activity to this extent because agents strengthened the party by orchestrating agitation. He also claimed that he had advised employers in Detroit that their troubles were rooted in the private detectives they had planted in the party and their shops: agencies such as Corporations Auxiliary charged firms between twelve hundred and fifteen hundred dollars a month but sent those firms miserably paid spies with criminal records who were entirely unreliable "professional troublemakers." Whatever his motives, the interviews form an interesting coda to Spolansky's career narrative, attesting to the inherently questionable character of counterespionage activity and its practitioners.[29]

In the final years of his life, Spolansky returned to Detroit, where he died in August 1966. A standard-bearer of "America's first generation of professional radical hunters," he is a largely overlooked figure who nevertheless occupied an important place in the Anticommunist Spider Web. While never a household name, he was a figure of national significance. He both expanded and strengthened the Spider Web, linking military and government intelligence services, federal and state legislative committees, police forces, big business, private detective agencies, and the media. His legacy was considerable. He helped to deport many unnaturalized "radicals" and imprison American citizens. He worked to crush the Far Left, hardened the anticommunist and antilabor ideology of national security and police agencies, gave crucial evidence and investigative services to congressional and state legislative committees, and facilitated employer involvement in government-led antiunion and antiradical campaigns. His career exemplifies the growing power of professional anticommunist agents in the Red Scare and the ways in which they transformed a wartime activity into a lifelong occupation of growing national economic and political significance.[30]

CHAPTER 8

The Better America Federation and Big Business's War on Labor

It is a labor of love, and surely there is no higher degree of civic patriotism than that which we are displaying in organizing the middle classes against the vicious attacks of vicious minorities.

—Better America Federation

O f all the civil organizations that promoted anticommunism in the interwar period, business lobby groups were among the most important. No other section of the community more effectively associated the fight against communism with the "open shop" and the suppression of labor unions. Business opposition to organized labor and radical political groups had been a consistent feature of American politics since before the Civil War. Indeed, as Ellen Schrecker has argued, "If there is any one element that, along with the targeting of foreigners, remains constant throughout the history of American political repression, it is the way in which those business groups that were most hostile to organized labor tapped into the countersubversive tradition to gain support for suppressing unions . . . without having to refer to economic issues."[1]

Business lobbies harnessed the passion and the infrastructure of the Red Scare to promote their economic and industrial agenda. They used anticommunism (and generous financial inducements) to revitalize and reorient urban police "Radical and Anarchist Squads," retaining them as a principal guarantor of business's influence and power. Industry officials manufactured propaganda and distributed it through friendly politicians, traditional media, their own publicity departments, and the increasingly diverse and widespread network of contacts they established in the Anticommunist Spider Web.

One of the leading business lobbies to emerge at this time was the Better America Federation, headquartered in Los Angeles. While neither as powerful nor as well known as the American Legion, the federation was still a very significant organization in the Spider Web, dominating anticommunism on the Pacific Coast from around 1920 until well into the Cold War.

Although the federation has received some scholarly attention, it has not featured prominently in studies of American anticommunism. Yet it should. As Howell John Harris, William Millikan, and Rosemary Feurer have shown, understanding the political, industrial, and social activity of regional employer groups and business lobbies is crucial to understanding how both regional and national business campaigns have developed throughout American history. In addition, just as Robin Archer has demonstrated the importance of the suppression of regional labor organizations in preventing the emergence of statewide let alone national labor political parties, the obverse pertains to the growth of anticommunism as a national phenomenon: without the activity and contribution of regional organizations such as the Better America Federation (BAF), the doctrine and practice of anticommunism in interwar America might not have assumed national proportions.[2]

The Open Shop Movement

Business advocacy groups formed vital strands in the Anticommunist Spider Web. Thinly disguised as "citizens'" and "public safety" committees and "law and order" and "liberty" leagues, they had been an important and often decisive factor in industrial conflict since the 1870s. For a time, these groups responded only to immediate circumstances. They assembled to help put down a strike or break a local union and then ostensibly receded from the political fray, all the while ensuring that police Red and Bomb Squads were adequately financed. After the economic downturn of the 1890s, however, employers felt the need to match the unprecedented labor organization that had developed. Employer lobbies emerged from industry organizations such as the National Founders' Association and its offshoot, the National Metal Trades Association. The National Association of Manufacturers, established in 1895, was the most important such organization, "the most powerful body of businessmen which has ever been organized in any land, or any age." The association and regional organizations such as the Citizens' Alliance (CA) in Minneapolis supplanted chambers of commerce, trade boards, and similar bodies, which could not cope with industrial unionism or after the First World War with general strikes.[3]

Whether national or local, business lobbies sought to uphold the absolute prerogative of managers to direct their affairs as they wished. Lobby members were implacably opposed to the eight-hour day, worker input into management, and any industrial agreement that mediated workers' output and remuneration. Business groups fought any union involvement in the determination of wages and conditions and refused to negotiate with striking workers. Implacably opposed to government mediation of industrial disputes , business associations even called for the assassination of federal arbitrators in some instances. Proponents of this unyielding approach to industrial relations justified their stance through various nostrums, most notably the "gospel of work as a moral imperative and the road to self-realization" and the "virtue of output." These ideas put a gloss on the economic imperative to run expensive capital equipment "as intensively as possible" and a concomitant belief, as Henry Ford put it, that "fear is a greater incentive to work than loyalty."[4]

While business lobbies' objectives did not vary, different schemes were used to achieve those objectives. These schemes were determined by the financial strength and size of the lobby and local political conditions. Most businesses could not afford to crush strikes on their own. Medium-sized and small manufacturers needed to cooperate to minimize the bargaining power of skilled workers and union influence. Accordingly, they formed the equivalent of industrial unions: organizations crossing shop and industry boundaries. The members of the Metal Trades Association in St. Louis, for example, established a regional labor market built on low wages and decentralized operations in poor rural towns that were prepared to guarantee open shop conditions. The Metal Manufacturers' Association in Philadelphia combated union influence by establishing its own employment bureau, which maintained detailed files of (proscribed) organized and (employable) "loyal" workers. Members shared information on hourly pay rates for dozens of job categories across hundreds of firms, sacrificing wage competition for common management of the supply and remuneration of labor. From roughly 1905 to 1924, the association used primarily these methods to break strikes and union locals. The direct costs of strikebreaking comprised just 4 percent of the association's expenditures, less than it spent on social events. Other employers' organizations suppressed labor more roughly. The Minneapolis CA imported strikebreaking workers, whom it housed and provisioned within fortified stockades and whose protection was vouchsafed by police. The alliance also formed its own industrial espionage service. And like the corporations that underwrote them, business lobbies purchased guns, gas bombs, and the services of toughs with criminal records.[5]

The assistance of city and police authorities was typically procured through outright bribery or threats of economic and political reprisal. Antiradical police squads had close ties with local business communities. Business lobbies also ran their own legal departments and committees, monitoring statutory developments that might impinge on their profits. Errant legislators were bombarded with correspondence and warned about enacting prolabor measures. The largest businesses also derailed social legislation by threatening to move their operations to more friendly locales. Various coercive measures also kept middle-class professionals and small business operators in line. Doctors, lawyers, and traders understood, as Louis Silverberg has noted, that they were "as dependent upon the corporate overlord [in an] economic fief as the workers on its payroll." Small proprietors could "nearly always be forced into the anti-labor camp" by a boycott of union-friendly employers or by a bank's denial of credit, heightening the economic pressure that could be applied to striking union members.[6]

Authorities sanctioned all of these measures. By contrast, severe court judgments continued to restrain union activity. In 1908, the US Supreme Court struck down laws prohibiting employers from forcing workers to sign "yellow-dog" contracts in which they promised not to join labor unions. That same year, the court also forbade all forms of union-led boycotts as "conspiracy" in restraint of trade.[7]

Having taken over the courts, business lobbies colonized government agencies. Associations reduced members' taxes by providing civic engineering and health services and by sponsoring vocational education. Some lobbies also arranged for limited unemployment relief to short-circuit the establishment of state-funded and -administered schemes. The CA and other organizations became an unelected branch of government, assisting in the preparation of city budgets and reform of the police force. By the 1920s, such activity had culminated in the enactment of a federal budget law and extensive collaboration between the US Chamber of Commerce and the Federal Reserve Board, the Farm Loan Board, and the Budget Bureau.[8]

To both buttress and cloak their influence, open shop lobbies invested heavily in their public image: theirs was a permanent political campaign. Around their crusading phalanges they deployed formidable auxiliaries: public works and institutions, social and cultural events, and economic theories and propaganda. The Minneapolis CA, one of the wealthiest lobbies, financed the construction of new libraries, universities, and museums, creating legacies that reflected well on its members and concealed the industrial violence and exploitation that paid for them. More important, however, was creating and manipulating opinion about laissez-faire and the open shop. Realizing, as Silverberg has noted, that "the invocation of patriotic symbols" was "far more effective . . . than any blunt assertion of basic purpose," business lobbies reached into the language of the Declaration of Independence, the Constitution, and republican virtue to define their cause. Incorporating property rights "into the right of liberty," they argued that these rights were indistinguishable. In combination, they formed the philosophical rationale for the open shop. The state, open shop lobbies explained, existed primarily to protect these two rights. Business groups in turn offered the state and these basic rights their protection. Open shop proponents also insisted that their views were shared by all who truly understood and valued "American liberty and American civilization." At the same time, leading economists provided scientific-sounding explanations for the (mal)distribution of wealth, arguing that labor and capital each earned the sum of their "marginal" product (the equivalent of what they contributed to production) and that the state had no legitimate reason to interfere with market forces.[9]

As industrial conflicts affected the broader social and political environment, business lobbies placed great importance on persuading middle-class bystanders to adopt an industry perspective. To make them fear the lower orders of society more than the top, open shop associations emphasized that the workers' program equally threatened middle-class and industrial interests. Business appealed, in Silverberg's words, to the "collective egotism, ideals, values and sentiments of the middle class," using the language of "'fair play' and 'Americanism.'" Discrete contests over industrial conditions were thus described as battles to preserve "the 'American system,' the 'capitalist system' [and] 'civilization' itself." And business sought to protect not merely itself but also "the 'public,' the 'consumer,' and the 'citizen.'" Business lobbies attacked the pursuit of social reform through government by emphasizing the virtue of "thrift." Pleading for "economy" in government, business undermined progressive faith in the state and influenced government to cut expenditure on the "extravagance" of social services as well as the business taxes that funded such services.[10]

In addition to broadening their appeal to the middle classes, business lobbies revived traditional pejorative terms for their opponents, juxtaposing "loyal Americans," the "backbone and sinews of [the] nation," against "agitators" and itinerant "tramps" who left a trail of "desolation and ruin," shattering the community's "natural harmony." Whereas proponents of the open shop fought in defense of "fundamental principles of government" and conserved "the best interests of all true American-loving [sic] citizens," organized labor and its "radical element" were "hostile to the interests of the people as a whole." So while corporations were "custodian[s] of a sacred trust," representing "the interest of the people from the richest to the poorest," unions stood for "labor monopoly" and would limit the production needed to "save the world from hunger."[11]

By the time the business community began to agitate for American involvement in the First World War, it had developed a powerful infrastructure of cooperative organizations and propaganda for suppressing radicals and organized labor. Prepared by twenty years' "successful self-assertion," the open shop lobby incorporated "the rhetoric of patriotism and the assistance of the wartime loyalty police into its defensive armor and offensive weaponry." And if the Bolshevik Revolution initially raised the morale of radicals and unionists, it similarly emboldened employers.[12]

The Open Shop Conquest of Patriotism

America's commitment to war had a marked effect on industrial relations. Not since the Civil War had the avoidance and timely settlement of industrial protest been so integral to the interests of the federal government. President Woodrow Wilson had placed employers at the center of his government's war effort, giving them a growing "sense of the legitimacy of their authority [and] the congruence between their personal interests and the national interest." Business had long emphasized this congruence, but the war made business's antirevolutionary message especially potent, helping it to persuade the middle classes and state agencies of the danger posed by organized labor and radicals. And business leaders began preparing their postwar open shop campaign, the American Plan, even while the European war continued to rage.[13]

Although Wilson had given conservative craft unions a place in his administration, business had far greater influence over his government. Business was also aided by the administration's tepid enthusiasm for enforcing industrial agreements. Business representatives outnumbered their labor counterparts on the National War Labor Board, ensuring that it could neither recognize unions nor compel companies to negotiate with them. Consequently, many employers treated the board with contempt, failing to appear at hearings or ignoring its rulings. Some federal officials accepted positions with employer organizations and coordinated propaganda campaigns against strikers. And when Secretary of Labor William Wilson criticized as traitors those unions that struck to "force the establishment of standards they [were not] able to force during normal conditions," employers argued that the secretary meant that all attempts by organized labor to extend its influence were seditious.[14]

Business also co-opted the repressive apparatus of the state. The Minnesota CA controlled that state's Committee for Public Safety: the alliance first persuaded the state to appropriate one million dollars for the committee's establishment and then stacked it with CA members. The alliance also financed and controlled state branches of the American Protective League. The employers' lobby in St. Louis, for its part, persuaded local officials to keep favored employees out of the draft and to place union organizers at the top of the list.[15]

As soon as the European conflict ceased, the US economy stagnated. Mass retrenchments and soaring unemployment devastated union membership and resources. Employers either held wages steady or lowered them. Firms that had concluded agreements with unions during the war tore up those compacts. And the suppression of major strikes across the country left the labor movement in its most abject state since the turn of the century. The Wilson administration did little to forestall turbulence. The president's 1919 Industrial Conference even took refuge in myth and nostalgia. Formulating uniquely "American" schemes, it spoke of establishing the "right relationship" between employers and employees, which it proposed to effect through fostering "unity of interest," "organized cooperation," and the "human relationship" of industry. But it insisted that no permanent government body was needed to impose any penalties on industry "other than those [of] public opinion."[16]

By contrast, the reexpansion of the war on radicals into a general campaign against labor commenced as soon as the armistice was proclaimed. In the 1920s, a succession of Republican presidents accommodated every industry request, turning business into what Robert Justin Goldstein describes as "virtually a national religion." The chief tenet of this religion was anticommunism, and its high priests were the open shop lobbies, which numbered nearly five hundred by 1920. According to the American Civil Liberties Union (ACLU), these organizations transferred "the whole fight" for civil and industrial liberty to the "conflict of organized capital and organized labor," leaving a new generation of "more practical generals" in command of industrial capital. While it was not the most important such practical general, the postwar growth of the BAF illustrates how business groups both developed and used opposition to communism for their great profit in the interwar period.[17]

Normalcy and the Practical Generals

Warren Harding's rallying cry in the 1920 presidential election was, "Back to Normalcy." Though a malapropism, the phrase "struck a responsive chord among voters." While Robert Murray has interpreted "normalcy" as signaling the restoration of "traditional consensus politics and individual economic advance" to "the center of American life," it signaled above all the domination by big business of economic and industrial policy. As Goldstein has observed, "Under the Republicans in the twenties, entire branches of the government, especially the Commerce Department, functioned as 'arms of business within government.'" According to Goldstein, "the regulatory agencies were packed with pro-business representatives; business concentration proceeded apace while antitrust laws were enforced stringently against labor; and Secretary of the Treasury Andrew Mellon, one of the richest men in America, devoted much of his time to reducing taxes in the highest brackets."[18]

The Harding administration's hostility toward unions was uncommonly severe even in the context of government's historic antipathy toward labor. Harding's attorney general, Harry Daugherty, put down strikes with federal injunctions. Arguing that unions were in the pay of Moscow, he achieved a near-permanent

SOME EMPLOYERS' IDEA OF "NORMALCY."
—Fitzpatrick in the St. Louis Post-Dispatch.

FIGURE 9. "Some Employers' Idea of 'Normalcy,'" cartoon by Daniel R. Fitzpatrick, *St. Louis Post-Dispatch*, ca. 1920. (Herbert C. Hoover Papers, Hoover Institution)

deployment of federal and state troops, police, and militia as strikebreakers. During the Harding-Coolidge term of 1920–24, Goldstein writes, "about 90 percent of all national guard active duty was related to strikes."[19]

Daugherty also connived with judges to suppress industrial action, corresponding regularly to arrange the prosecution of strikers for violating injunctions. Most judges were eager to help, particularly the majority on the US Supreme Court, who all but destroyed workers' rights to picket, boycott open shop products, strike for the purposes of organizing, and even collect relief funds for strikers. Under the direction of the newly appointed chief justice, former president and National War Labor Board chief William Howard Taft, the nation's highest court rescinded the section of the federal antitrust act that protected labor organizations from being considered interstate trusts in restraint of trade as well as numerous state anti-injunction laws. These judgments helped erode the AFL's wartime membership gains and left the entire labor movement with no defense for association other than the First Amendment's protection of the rights of peaceful assembly (figure 9).[20]

The conduct of Daugherty and the US Supreme Court are but two illustrations of the pro-business ethos of the Jazz Age. Half of the 1,845 strike injunctions issued between 1880 and 1930 were issued during the 1920s. And with government and judicial assistance, big business continued to kill, beat, and kidnap striking workers; evict them from their homes; intern them without trial; forcibly break up union meetings; and secure the deportation of unnaturalized "radicals." Strikers were routinely fined crippling sums for disorderly conduct and other spurious charges that had lain dormant for more than a century. Many were tried in kangaroo courts. Workers' rights remained under assault as the decade faded. According to ACLU figures, the number of prosecutions for industrial protest exploded from 418 in 1928 to more than 2,500 in 1929. In light of state criminal syndicalism laws, city ordinances restricting free speech, the censorship power of the post office, and "antiradical" vigilante violence, the ACLU described America as having descended into a "dictatorship of property in the name of patriotism."[21]

The craft union movement had hoped that distancing itself from "radical" political prisoners and collaborating with industry's campaign against "Bolshevik" workers would enable unions to escape what AFL president Samuel Gompers described as "the mightiest onslaught of reaction through which our nation [has] ever passed." But they miscalculated badly. In spite of its wholesale adoption of corporate ideology, its collaboration with national security agencies, and its own purge of radicals, the AFL was unable to prevent the departure of more than a million members between 1920 and 1923. Regional union locals abandoned decadelong efforts to organize open shops. The entire Political Left paid a heavy price for AFL's industrial policy, as open shop lobbies had no effective opposition and thus set the parameters of industrial action and economic and political debate.[22]

The Rise of the BAF

Although big business's power was rising as the Wilson administration faded, the postwar eruption of general strikes still left employers feeling insecure. The BAF and other organizations emerged to lead the open shop and laissez-faire movement, eternally vigilant against threats to business's dominance. An exemplar of the "historical origins and inner mechanics of postwar superpatriotism," the federation typified how open shop lobbies responded to the challenges of progressive reform and labor and left-wing activism by reasserting long-standing business policies in novel and effective ways.[23]

Based in Los Angeles, the BAF, like many other open shop lobbies, was founded as a patriotic association in the spring of 1917. According to an unusually candid federation document, the organization was born, perhaps fittingly, "in the drawing-room of [a] Pullman car." Originally known as the Commercial

Federation of California, it was the brainchild of two leading businessmen, Harry Marston Haldeman and Harry Chandler. Haldeman was a "plumbing magnate" with substantial oil and real estate holdings. At the height of his career, the real estate board described him as "the most useful citizen of Los Angeles." A prominent supporter of Red Cross and Liberty Loan fund-raising efforts, Haldeman also served on the federal War Industries Board. A cofounder of the Hollywood Bowl, Western Airlines, the Western Raceway, and the Salvation Army Advisory Board, Haldeman mixed with the social elite of Los Angeles. Chandler, the publisher of the archconservative *Los Angeles Times*, emerged from obscurity through extortion and marriage. Having run a business that monopolized the distribution of the *Times* with the aid of thugs who dispossessed his rivals of their delivery routes, Chandler married the daughter of the paper's publisher, Harrison Gray Otis. The "unquestioned leader of Los Angeles' . . . Anglo power structure" in the interwar period, Chandler served on more than fifty company boards, backed conservative causes through "countless dummy corporations and secret trusts," and was reputedly the largest real estate baron in the United States.[24]

The BAF was strongly grounded in a "tradition of business solidarity in Los Angeles" that had been reenergized by the dynamiting of the *Times* building in 1910 and the passage of laws protecting workers and regulating business. The federation's vice president for Los Angeles County, Reese Llewellyn, owned a steel mill that had been blown up by the same plotters who targeted the *Times*. The federation campaigned for members and funds through patriotic appeals. It prioritized the recruitment of former Liberty Bond sellers and ran its first membership drive at a banquet honoring bond sellers. The federation also promoted its agenda through its many patriotic-sounding community fronts: the Americanization Fund, the Association for Betterment of Public Service, the Associated Patriotic Societies, the Taxpayers' Association, the People's Economy League, the Tax Investigation and Economy League, the Committee of One Thousand, and the Committee of Ten Thousand. Contemporary critics alleged that the federation was itself a subsidiary of the Los Angeles Merchants and Manufacturers Association, which, with Chandler's *Times*, ran Los Angeles as "a de facto dictatorship." The federation consummated its attempt to disguise its sectional nature in May 1920, when it jettisoned its original name in favor of the Better America Federation and dubbed its newsletter *The Commonwealth*.[25]

Although the federation declined to bluntly state its purpose, all of its activities—lobbying, advocacy, propaganda, political and industrial violence—were directed toward the advancement of laissez-faire economics and the open shop. BAF leaders firmly believed that business served as the nation's backbone and that business leadership in all industrial and government affairs was essential for stability and progress. Yet persistent opposition from labor unions and radical political organizations convinced the federation that although public opinion "strongly opposed" labor and "Bolshevik" policies, it was "not consolidated." The federation strove to effect such consolidation by providing the public with the political education it required. In this endeavor it anticipated New Deal–era organizations such as the Du Pont dynasty's American Liberty League and took up the Lusk Committee's call to provide anticommunist community leadership. But while the federation claimed to offer its leadership to the general community, it was, as Progressive journalist Norman Hapgood noted at the time, "dominated by a small group of ultraconservatives." Like other Spider Web organizations, the BAF was a hierarchical autocracy. Its internal structure and administrative arrangements reflected its authoritarian political views, depriving members of any real means of influencing its policies. To contemporaries such as Hapgood, the federation's activities were "shrouded in secrecy." It refused to divulge its financial affairs and principal sources of income. Its executive committee put forward slates of preapproved candidates for "election" to internal positions. And the committee obscured its conduct by operating erratically through the federation's many fronts. Around 1920, the executive committee comprised Haldeman and nine other prominent California capitalists who represented manufacturers, fruit distributors, lumber companies, the Great Western Electrical Chemical Company, and the San Francisco Pacific Foundry Company: a simple majority of the committee—just six men—thus could control the entire federation. Its other most significant members led steel, oil, real estate, utilities, department store, insurance, and banking concerns and brought with them the support of financiers, manufacturers, wholesalers, retailers, professionals, and semipublic clubs such as the Rotary and Kiwanis and the Los Angeles Chamber of Commerce.[26]

While it had little interest in engaging the community in policy development, the federation was determined to politicize and mobilize the business community, a task it regarded as urgent. In the BAF's view, the nation remained on the verge of a Bolshevik revolution triggered by unchecked labor disturbances. This danger, which could only be averted by "active work on the part of federation workers and others," was being stoked by "unduly timorous . . . professional politicians." Disillusioned by the postwar turn of events, the federation voiced what it claimed was "a growing desire throughout the country" to select "the next president . . . from the ranks of industry." Yet the nation seemed reluctant to select such a man for its highest office, and if the federation could not elevate a businessman to the presidency, it could at least ensure the election of pro-business candidates by stressing the "duty of businessmen" to get into politics: the country "must no longer elect a representative to the Legislature because he is a Progressive, a Democratic [sic] or a Republican, but because he is a man who is not committed to Class-Legislation and who is ready to give all our people a fair deal and protection for their property rights under our Laws and Constitution."[27]

The care with which the federation emphasized its opposition to "class legislation" and its members' "patriotism in support of good government and democracy" demonstrates that such rhetorical tropes were as standard for business groups after the war as before it. And the federation effectively promoted these sentiments, backing slates of receptive candidates. In the 1918 Los Angeles County elections, the federation endorsed eighteen candidates, twelve of whom won. In simultaneous ballots for the city's administration and board of education, six of nine and four of seven candidates, respectively, won office. Once elected, the federation's "legislative bureau" provided officeholders with ideological guidance—for example, analyzing more than two thousand bills during one legislative session. The bureau also alerted federation members to the introduction of legislation "hostile to business interests" and property rights.[28]

The central tenets of the federation's political platform were simple, consistent, and invariably explained through the Manichaean opposition of "100% Americanism" and "Bolshevism." Any interference by government in relations between employers and employees or in the economy more generally amounted to communism. Any public ownership or control of a utility or any other essential service amounted to communism. And no interference with any business could be justified on the grounds that it served a public interest. In practice, these ideas translated into opposition to antitrust laws, regulatory boards and commissions, the Single Tax, higher taxes on utilities and the largest banks, social insurance, workers' compensation, absentee voter laws, attempts to abolish the Electoral College, and the direct election of senators. The BAF also opposed the "Social Creed of Churches," a statement of industrial principles that was endorsed by the Federal Council of Churches and the Catholic War Council of Bishops and that called for the abolition of child labor, regulation of working hours for women, the eight-hour day, the forty-hour week, a minimum wage, and collective bargaining.[29]

Foreshadowing the Red-baiting of Martin Dies and Joseph McCarthy, the federation also insisted that communists had infiltrated and were perverting the federal government. Seizing on allegations leveled by Indiana senator James E. Watson, the BAF reported that the Federal Commission on Trade had been penetrated by "more than a dozen . . . 'Reds' and syndicalists" who used their positions "to preach radicalism and Bolshevism to the employees of the plants which they inspected." Worse, one high-ranking commission official was "an alien" who was passing purloined "trade secrets" to his country of birth, "one of the chief trade competitors" of the United States. These cases represented merely the tip of a treasonous iceberg. Hundreds of "radical propagandists" had "flocked to Washington" to take employment "under government commission," supported by organized labor and a craven administration. Claiming that the number of federal employees had ballooned to 1.5 million during the war, the federation insisted that between one-third and half of them "were draft dodgers" and that they were protected by corrupt officers such as Secretary of Labor Wilson, a former union business agent sympathetic to "radicals and the reds." Frederic C. Howe, the administrator of Ellis Island, was another favorite target of the federation, as he was for so many members of the Anticommunist Spider Web. The BAF accused Howe of creating a "Red Paradise" on Ellis Island and permitting "scores" of Reds to escape to "coal and steel districts," where they could "stir up industrial trouble." Closer to home, the federation fingered the California Bureau of Statistics, whose workers were organized, as "a propagating station for radicalism." The federation thus targeted as treasonous those government agencies that directly regulated business or that administered highly controversial areas of public policy such as industrial relations, immigration, and taxation.[30]

The federation further used the Bolshevik bogey to demonstrate that the American economy was free from structural problems and would perform at its best if government would stop cosseting lazy and disloyal workers and turn over management of the economy entirely to employers. It dismissed the significance of high import rates on falling living standards, attributing these woes to strikes, for which Bolsheviks, saboteurs, and slackers—"paid agitators with transcontinental records"—bore full responsibility. Similarly, the federation scoffed at accusations of profiteering by big business. Business's critics were not only looking in the wrong places for the causes of inflated prices but also spreading "misleading statements and insinuations . . . on which Bolshevism feeds." According to the BAF, the United States desperately needed not a minimum wage or some similar contrivance but rather a businessman in the White House who would halt the slide of interventionist policy into Bolshevik government. The federation cautioned government to cease interfering with "finely adjusted" market forces lest it destroy the balance of the economy. And the BAF denounced the instruments with which government might attempt such disastrous interference—legislation and arbitrative bodies—as unconstitutional and ill conceived, violating employers' liberty to seek growth, the natural "organic law" of supply and demand, and workers' rights of "free contract."[31]

The federation mobilized another business shibboleth, that of waste in government, to promote laissez-faire, often pushing this argument through its Taxpayers' Association front but also promoting it in *The Commonwealth*. Under the banner "Still Wasting Money," *The Commonwealth* complained that the federal Internal Revenue Department employed more than fifteen thousand agents at an annual cost of $25 million. When that sum was combined with an annual compliance cost to business of $100 million, the federal government was squandering $125 million each year "without benefitting any one but a group of Federal employees," a display of "crass inefficiency" with "few parallels" in history.[32]

FIGURE 10. Better America Federation letterhead, June 1920. The inclusion of Baja California within the continental United States illustrates the federation's support for aggressive external military and trade activity. (Margaret Ann Kerr Papers, Hoover Institution)

The federation's free market convictions were extreme even by the standards of employer lobbies. Whereas some comparable groups, among them the Philadelphia Metal Manufacturers' Association, recognized that an unimpeded "owning and managing class" had an obligation to "best serve the interests of all classes" by reducing unemployment and providing for the (blameless) unemployed, the BAF recognized no responsibility for employers in the social contract. However, the federation's commitment to the free market was highly selective. Decrying the inflationary effects of trade imbalances with Europe (notwithstanding the attribution of such inflation to workers' laziness), the federation called on government to address this particular fetter on American manufacturers. In fact, the BAF fervently backed two forms of government intervention in the economy: external military conquest to open up foreign markets, and the forcible suppression of organized and radical labor (figure 10).[33]

The Red Squad and the California Criminal Syndicalism Act

One of the most important state agents on which the federation relied to suppress labor was the Los Angeles Police Department's Red Squad. In time, the federation became arguably the squad's most important sponsor and the squad the federation's client. Nationally renowned for cruelty, the Red Squad closed alleged radical union meetings, enforced injunctions, and subjected radicals, union members, and even children to unconstitutional brutality. The federation financially supported the squad and fed it information from the BAF's substantial antiradical dossiers.[34] Like other antilabor police squads, the growth of the Los

Angeles unit was encouraged by "the hysterical radicalism of World War I and the postwar red scare," which provided enough momentum," according to Frank Donner, to sustain the squads "through the 1920s until the next major burst of radical activity in response to the Great Depression. As in the prewar period, urban Red Squads generally maintained close and often corrupt relationships with local business interests, and their lack of clear direction or definition provided them virtual carte blanche to engage in uncontrolled surveillance of radicals, labor unions, and anyone else who struck their fancy." The Los Angeles squad was "above all characterized by an undiluted nativism and a blatant patron-client relationship with local business interests, which was openly proclaimed and implemented . . . over the years, with only minimal concessions to changes in the political climate, accountability requirements, reform movements, recurring corruption scandals, and adverse court decisions."[35]

According to Donner, the "extraordinary bias, power, lawlessness, and resistance to reform movements" of the Los Angeles squad hinged on its "unique support structure in the private sector." The squad's value to the BAF and the broader business community was demonstrated repeatedly in the interwar period. During a 1923 waterfront strike, hundreds of "radicals" and Wobblies were arrested without warrant, held in congested and unsanitary conditions, beaten by squad members, and charged with fabricated offenses. Five years later, the BAF had the squad round up alleged alien radicals to be handed over to the Bureau of Immigration for deportation. The federation was also directly responsible for a squad raid on a children's camp in San Bernardino. In June 1933, the ACLU reported that fourteen cases involving squad brutality were awaiting trial, with suits pending against squad Captain W. F. Hynes, six of his deputies, and the BAF after a raid on the John Reed Club rooms in Hollywood; the assault and battery of an ACLU attorney; two further claims of battery; the forcible closing of a Workers' United Front Election Campaign Committee function; the imprisonment without charge of a man held on suspicion of criminal syndicalism; seven further allegations of false imprisonment; and unlawful search of premises.[36]

Important as the Red Squad was, it was only hired muscle that enforced the law. The federation's most important labor-suppression instrument was the law itself, particularly the state Criminal Syndicalism Act. California's 1919 antisyndicalism act was one of twenty-three such laws enacted by states between 1917 and 1920, while nine other states and the US Congress considered such laws. The Golden State saw far more prosecutions than any other state and far more injustice. Its particularly draconian provisions inspired four other state acts or bills and helped California authorities destroy Industrial Workers of the World (IWW) locals and other industrial and political organizations. Like a series of ordinances that the Merchants and Manufacturers Association sponsored in

response to the bombing of the *Times* building, the criminal syndicalism statute "institutionalized the use of pretexts to screen what was essentially a form
of [antilabor] guerrilla warfare." The BAF was an influential supporter of the
legislation and used any opportunity to argue for its retention. The federation's
enthusiasm for the law was well founded. Between 1919 and 1924, more than five
hundred members of the IWW were charged under the act's broad ambit. And in
the early 1930s, after several years' slumber, it was wielded against communists,
convincing one federation director that "the biggest thing that the BAF has done
is to get the criminal syndicalism act on the books and to keep it there against
the efforts of those who are trying to repeal it."[37]

The efficacy of the criminal syndicalism statute derived from a clause that
proscribed membership in any illegal organization. Prosecuting authorities thus
had a single task: to establish a defendant's membership in such an organization. Doing so was generally not difficult, as defendants seldom denied their
associations. And the revolutionary character of these associations was easily
established from generic literature and the testimony of former radicals and
(ex-convict) Wobblies whom the BAF put on its payroll. Other jurisdictions
that broadly defined criminal syndicalist activity incarcerated troublemakers:
employees who simply slowed down on the job breached Idaho's definition of
sabotage.[38]

California's antisyndicalism act was widely used from immediately after its
passage. The police arrested thousands of men and women on suspicion of having contravened the act, including more than 770 between November 1922 and
May 1923. More than 500 men and women (all but 14 of them Wobblies) were
charged with committing offenses against the act; the remainder were members
of the Communist Labor Party, the Socialist Party and the Canadian One Big
Union. Of this number, 264 were tried, 164 were convicted, 128 were sentenced
to between one and fourteen years in jail, and 23 others received suspended
sentences. But even though more than half of those charged under the act were
never tried and a similar fraction had their convictions overturned on appeal,
the act more than served its purpose. The BAF, the Los Angeles Chamber of
Commerce, and the American Legion had demanded the eradication of IWW-
ism, and by 1920, every IWW hall in the state had been closed and dozens of its
leaders imprisoned. While the number of prosecutions tailed off between 1920
and 1922, this drop reflected the union's inability to organize in the face of the
American Plan and an economic downturn. When the improving economic climate gave rise to an upsurge in industrial action in late 1922, the state responded
forcefully. The main battlegrounds between business and the Wobblies were
Los Angeles and Orange Counties, the vicinity of San Francisco, and the Pacific
Northwest coast. In Los Angeles, a series of raids were carried out, and four

hundred longshoremen were arrested on charges of vagrancy, traffic violations, and criminal syndicalism. The Red Squad was unable to accommodate these men in overflowing city jails, so the surplus were held in a hastily constructed stockade. Sixty-five men arrested between November 1922 and May 1923 were charged with criminal syndicalism, and forty were convicted and sentenced to jail terms. Although twenty-seven Wobblies won their freedom on appeal, all but one of their convictions were reaffirmed by the state supreme court. Another forty-two men were arrested on charges of criminal syndicalism in 1924.[39]

Effective as it was, the war against the IWW was not without cost. First, trying suspects was an expensive process, particularly when so many defendants were acquitted by jurors disinclined to convict on the basis of the "ridiculous falsehoods" alleged by the BAF-financed and "self-confessed criminals" whom prosecutors habitually used as their chief witnesses. Sections of the general public also expressed unease with the Criminal Syndicalism Act's effects on civil liberties. However, the most important factor in the declining use of the act was the development of a cheaper method of suppressing unions. A July 1923 injunction issued by Judge Charles O. Busick of the Superior Court in Sacramento County seemed finally to provide an economical means of destroying the IWW. Busick's temporary restraining order prohibited the IWW from violating the antisyndicalism act. A month later, the order was converted into an injunction empowering any judge "by the simple process of calling any crime a public nuisance" to imprison any person considered to have violated the injunction; trial by jury for industrial offenses was thus subverted.[40]

Although the injunction was an unreliable means of securing convictions, state authorities and their business backers felt little concern. Even if only half of the cases covered by injunctions resulted in convictions, hundreds of potential troublemakers would be immobilized for years, either in prison or tied up in lengthy judicial procedures, and hundreds of other citizens would be deterred from becoming involved in "criminal syndicates." This rationale prevailed elsewhere, too. In Oklahoma, two Wobblies imprisoned in 1923 for violating the Criminal Syndicalism Act eventually won their freedom but did so only by contesting the legality of their trials rather than the act itself and only after more than two years behind bars. Similarly, while a test case, State of Idaho v. Moore, established that work slowdowns and advocating or committing nonviolent and noncriminal acts did not constitute criminal syndicalism, Wobbly Richard Moore lost five years of his life proving this point.[41]

In California and elsewhere criminal syndicalism statutes remained in effect for many years. Of the twenty-three jurisdictions that passed such acts, only three repealed the statutes or allowed them to lapse. Further, challenges to the validity of the statutes usually resulted only in Pyrrhic victories. Moore's suit prompted the amendment of Idaho's statute, making it the only criminal syndicalism law to outlaw nonviolent acts of sabotage, including "work done in an improper manner, slack work, waste of property, or loitering at work." In California, every legislative session except one between 1921 and 1939 considered a motion to repeal the Criminal Syndicalism Act, but all foundered on the opposition of the BAF; railroad, shipping, logging, and agricultural corporations; governors; attorneys general; liberal groups; church leaders; and newspapers such as the *Los Angeles Times* and the *Sacramento Bee*. Concerns about the state's ongoing ability to imprison Wobblies also prompted the American Legion, the BAF, and the attorney general to defeat a 1927 initiative to repeal the clause penalizing membership of a "criminal syndicate." Such a measure would have rendered the act useless because almost all convictions had been secured via this clause. Shortly after the defeat of this repeal measure, employers revived the law to prosecute communists who were organizing agricultural workers.[42]

The BAF relied heavily on state assistance to wage its war on labor but also more directly prevented workers from affiliating with trade unions. Its approach to industrial negotiation was aggressive and threatening: cajolery took a back seat to bribery and threats of retribution. When Los Angeles firemen organized and then sought registration with the AFL, they were persuaded not to affiliate in exchange for salary increases secured by the federation from the city council. The federation then undertook one of its most important campaigns, preventing teachers from affiliating. The BAF combined praise with shame, exalting teachers for their role in educating the nation's youth, but simultaneously pronouncing the education of minors "too sacred to be dragged through the mire of labor disputes." As "guardians of public education and the morals of boys and girls," teachers had a special responsibility not to "ally themselves with industrial trade unions." Those who did so would "degrade the profession" and betray "the trust that the community reposes in them." This accusation bled naturally into the federation's claim that organizing was a Bolshevistic act completely at odds with the vocation of education, "the greatest civilizing force the world has ever known" and the "most effective weapon against Anarchy and Bolshevism." If teachers were to make "the public schools of America . . . true cradles of liberty" and "impart instruction without prejudice," they had to "hold aloof from any form of class or labor organization." Like "soldiers," they owed "their first and only allegiance to the State" and should cleave to the American way. "Trust the whole community to give you better pay," the federation implored; "do not be deluded into believing that an alliance with industrial unions will help you. Why seek the support of a small part of the population when you now have the support and the confidence of the entire community? Maintain your independence; do your duty; teach in your school room the justice and utility of American institutions and the blessings of Liberty under the Law. Do this, and every reputable interest in the State will support you." The federation's campaign bore much fruit. The school boards of San Francisco and Los Angeles prohibited the formation of school teacher unions, while San Bernardino's teachers' institute condemned affiliation with the AFL. Various delegations of teachers, such as those of Visalia, "voluntarily" renounced their association with the workers' movement. The federation's only policy failure in this field occurred when the bill it sponsored to tie a loyalty regime to the employment of teachers was defeated.[43]

The federation professed concern with education merely to conceal its desire to destroy unions and provide its members with cheap malleable labor. For while the federation declared that the "most dangerous peoples in the world are those without adequate public schools," it also fought appropriations for schools as a means of restricting the number of teachers in schools for migratory workers. Contending that the IWW was developing these schools, the federation argued that better-educated workers were more likely "to succumb to radical doctrines," contradicting its claim that the example of Russia demonstrated the twin dangers of a Bolshevized teaching workforce and uneducated pupils. However, such contradictions aroused little concern as long as the federation, the Criminal Syndicalism Act, and the Red Squad were on hand to suppress the "un-American activities" of "disloyal groups."[44]

Regardless of the sincerity of its pedagogical concerns, the BAF's antiunion activity inspired other open shop lobbies like the Minneapolis CA, which pressured police into disaffiliating from the city's Central Labor Union in 1927. The federation was sufficiently vociferous and active in the suppression of industrial and civil liberties to be prominently mentioned in annual national surveys conducted by the ACLU during the 1920s and into the New Deal. Indeed, the ACLU described the federation in 1930 as a member of the "Big Five" "patriotic" or open shop lobbies, alongside the National Civic Federation, the American Legion, the Daughters of the American Revolution, and Harry Jung's American Vigilant Intelligence Federation. Hapgood also described the federation as America's "most active and highly organized" regional professional patriot group.[45]

The suppression of labor was an expensive business, and the federation raised enormous sums to fund it. In 1920, the federation announced its intention to raise two hundred thousand dollars a year for five years from Los Angeles County alone. Seven years later, Hapgood confirmed that since 1922, the federation had raised roughly eight hundred thousand dollars in the county through its Americanization Fund. The bulk of this money was contributed by "the open shop, power and other public utility corps of California" in the form of "substantial annual subscriptions" disguised as "miscellaneous general" and "office supplies" expenses. Another contemporary historian noted that a "California law and order league," almost certainly the federation or one of its fronts, received pledges totaling $1.25 million in 1921 "to fight the unionized building trades." From 1922 to 1925, the BAF "spent some two millions to destroy labor unions" and was believed to have raised "thrice that amount." Such sums elevated the federation into the ranks of the most powerful open shop lobbies alongside the Minnesota CA, which also used front groups to raise between $1.5 million and $2 million each year.[46]

A Cultural War against Bolshevism

The BAF's financial strength enabled it to provide its donors with a comprehensive union-busting service. Clients were encouraged to delegate the conduct of their industrial relations entirely to the federation. A circular issued by the Committee of Ten Thousand to company directors emphasized, "You don't want to be burdened with a lot of political work, do you? That's why this Committee was organized, so that busy men like you and your business interests can be properly safeguarded."[47]

The services the federation provided included industrial suppression, legislative oversight, and just as important workplace propaganda. The BAF created a large infrastructure to spread its open shop message to laborers, school and university students, and the general public. Like many major corporations and business lobbies, the federation sought to embed its principles in public consciousness, to exempt its values from political debate, and to encourage workers to equate loyalty to state and nation "with loyalty to one's employer, teacher, or leader."[48] One of the most important elements of the BAF's propaganda infrastructure was its Workers' Message Department, which produced publications instructing laborers in the virtues of laissez-faire. According to the federation, these publications, which included a booklet, "Mutual Interests of Labor and Capital," were "purchased in the main by manufacturers to distribute to their employees." One of the department's most significant products was a series of *Straight Shooter* circulars (figure 11).

Commencing in 1922, the *Shooter* was marketed to subscribers as "THE REMEDY" to the "mass of radical literature" circulated by schools for "instruction in radical oratory." Warning that it was pointless for employers to try to communicate with workers through such conventional means as newspapers and public speakers, the *Shooter* explained that the employer's most "practical, inexpensive and tremendously effective" method of communication was direct mail. A worker, the *Shooter* intoned, "receives but few letters in his home. Most of them are from his grocer, his dentist, his doctor. They ask for money. You may receive many letters; he does not. The workingman will read any letter that is mailed

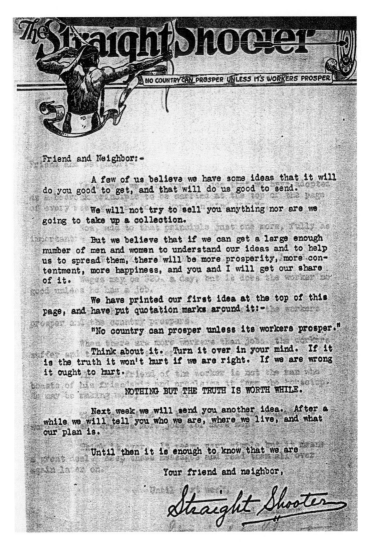

FIGURE 11. The Better America Federation's industrial propaganda sheet,
The Straight Shooter, ca. 1922. (Margaret Ann Kerr Papers, Hoover Institution)

to him. If it pleases him he will read a second letter from the same source. He
will continue to read succeeding letters if they appeal to his interest. [This] is
a proven fact." Every issue of the *Shooter* strove to explain to American workers
that the United States possessed the greatest industrial and political economy
the world had ever seen and that America could only be bettered by reinforcing
the economic principles on which the BAF believed it had been founded. Written

"by a man who [had] devoted the last twelve years of his life to writing and speaking on the subject of labor and capital," the *Shooter* "set forth in simple language the great fundamental truths with which" employers could "successfully combat radicalism." The *Shooter* circulars were "so worded that they at once attract attention [but] do not offend. They are fearless in exposing false doctrines and in presenting truth. Yet they do it in so kindly and fair a spirit that they arouse no opposition, excepting among the extreme radicals, and many of them have expressed a change of heart."[49]

The San Joaquin Light and Power Corporation (also an important supporter of the American Protective League), the Los Angeles Railway, the Union Oil Company of California, the Southern California Gas Company, and the Farmers and Merchants National Bank bought the *Shooter*, though it seems improbable that workers considered the circulars "kindly and fair" in spirit. The *Shooter* unquestionably perpetuated what Harris describes as the "individualistic-moralistic [and] hereditarian explanations of poverty and inequality" that many business leaders seem to have held.[50] The *Shooter* blended folksy homilies with simplistic language and imagery to persuade workers to accept certain "truths" about industrial relations and the distribution of wealth and resources. Its masthead depicted a Native American shooting an arrow into the center of a round mounted target. The arrow flies over a legend, "No country can prosper unless its workers prosper." Below this image, each circular began with the salutation "Friend and Neighbor" before moving on to make the same two points: first, capitalism was "natural," and second, economic success depended on native intelligence and work ethic. The *Shooter* defended capitalism through "historical" allusions intended to convince skeptical readers that they were just as much capitalists as were plutocrats. Capitalism, the *Shooter* explained, was an age-old economic practice that had facilitated the development of civilization: "CAPITAL is what men and women have SAVED and ACCUMULATED. One wise man said, "CAPITAL is what was LEFT OVER from YESTERDAY. . . . If there was no CAPITAL we would all be living in the jungle or the wilderness like savages, without houses, or clothes. . . . Every man who saves becomes a CAPITALIST, great or small. The system that permits men to save and give employment to others is called CAPITALISM."[51]

Anxious to correct the "misconception" that capitalism enriched an undeserving few at the expense of the masses, the *Shooter* noted that the capitalist instinct was a gift given only to a special few but enabling them to raise the living standards of all. "Thousands of years ago," according to one circular,

> Men and women lived under the shelter of rock and caves. They used stones and clubs and sticks . . . to catch fish and game. Each man kept all that he produced. But

they often went hungry, for they had no CAPITAL. . . . It took thousands of years to learn to tame sheep and goats and to keep them in herds. Nearly all of these early savages and barbarians lived from hand to mouth, consuming each day what they had in hand, just as most of us do now. Here and there was one who strived and saved, denying himself many things to-day, in order that he might have more to-morrow. . . . [S]uch men increased their herds until they were able to employ a neighbor's son to help to herd them. The owner of the sheep was benefited and the neighbor's son was better off. As the owner of the sheep grew richer, more neighbors' sons had jobs. . . . Did the owner of the sheep and the neighbors' sons look upon each other as enemies? No. Each needed the other and the world needed both. And so it is to-day.

Thus the idea that capitalists' inordinate share of surplus product harmed employees was simple nonsense. Rather, the capitalist was best understood not as the workers' employer but as their "friend," as a "tall man" who could reach far up into a tree, "gathering the most fruit." Those who worked for capitalists were "shorter men," jostling and competing with each other "for the fruit that hangs lower down." This did not mean that the tall man was immeasurably better off than his smaller companions. While the tall man gathered all the fruit he could reach, "human nature" dictated that he could "eat no more than the short man." God "in His wisdom" had "so limited the use of wealth, that no man can use more than his share, whether he be rich or poor. The tall man eats all that nature allows one man to consume, then he hands the surplus on down to the shorter men below, by giving them employment and opportunity, just as the old sheepowner used to do." Social betterment, the *Shooter* concluded, was available to all if the shorter men followed the example of their taller friends. In time, the shorter men, too, would "strive and save and give employment to others"; then everyone would be "prosperous and happy."[52]

Nearly 150 firms subscribed to the publications of the Workers' Message Department in the early 1920s, receiving weekly letters, special pamphlets, and other material. The federation complemented these publications with a fleet of lecturers who spread its message in schools, universities, churches, and Kiwanis and Lions Clubs as well as at the Soldiers' and Sailors' Employment Bureau and among chapters of the American Legion, the Daughters of the American Revolution, and the American Bar Association. The BAF's roster of speakers included state senator George W. Cartwright, who wrote most of the Workers' Message publications (perhaps including the *Shooter*), and an émigré White Russian, Baroness Otilly de Ropp, who lectured on "applied Bolshevism in Russia and America." In addition, Harry F. Atwood, president of the Chicago-based Constitutional Educational Association and author of several books, including *Back*

to the Republic and *Keep God in American History*, undertook a nine-month feder-
ation-sponsored lecture tour in 1923. They and other speakers claimed to have
addressed hundreds of organizations and hundreds of thousands of people. The
federation's material was circulated as far afield as Boston, New York, Philadelphia, Chicago, Denver, Cincinnati, and Indianapolis. One subscriber distributed
copies of federation pamphlets to every member of Congress, prompting several
legislators to commend the work. The *Saturday Evening Post* spoke in glowing
terms of the federation, as did California newspapers, particularly the *Los Angeles
Times*, and anticommunist publications like the *Boston Transcript*, Fred Marvin's
New York Commercial, and *Buddy*, the official bulletin of the Disabled Veterans of
the World War. The federation esteemed Marvin as highly as he did them, citing
his inventory of 617 openly published radical papers and magazines as unim-
peachable evidence of the hold of radicalism in the United States. Other Spider
Web members in receipt of federation material included the American Defense
Society and the National Security League. Alert to the potential of modern technology, the federation provided the Zenith Radio Corporation of Chicago with
"whatever anti-red material" it requested, reaching millions of listeners in the
United States, Canada, Mexico, Cuba, and Central America.[53]

Aside from California's workers, the federation expended most of its energy
to reach high school and college students and adults who could influence education policy. As in other areas, the federation's views on education countered
the "kindly and fair" spirit to which it lay claim. In addition to promoting cuts
to the public school budget, the federation sought to restrict the state's educational expenses by opposing the mandatory education of all children up to the
age of sixteen, justifying this position on the grounds that there was no point in
educating children who did not intend to take up vocations "requiring a superior
education" beyond the eighth grade. This stance also reflected the federation's
desire to preserve the juvenile labor force. In addition, the federation sought to
mold school and college curricula for those students it deemed worthy of further
education. It sought to ban the works of muckraking author Upton Sinclair (a
future Democratic candidate for governor of California) from schools, universities, and public libraries. The BAF prevented the distribution in educational
institutions of the liberal journals *Nation* and *New Republic*, attempting clumsily
and ultimately unsuccessfully to substitute a federation pamphlet, *America Is
Calling*, that attacked public ownership. Not content with banning alleged radical
publications, the federation, quietly supported by the University of California,
recruited a network of student spies. As Haldeman gushed, the federation put
"the children of the best business families throughout the land" to work watching "students of radical tendencies." Through them, BAF leaders learned about

the activities of students and teachers who upheld "radical doctrines and views," including Arthur M. Schlesinger Sr.[54]

Following its failure to introduce *America Is Calling* into curricula, the federation found a more suitable vehicle for its educational message in the US Constitution. Using yet another front group, the Southern California Citizens' Committee, the federation instructed school students in the history and purpose of the Constitution using material written by Atwood. Collaborating with Martin J. Wade, a former Iowa District Court judge and one-term congressman, the federation established a "Gigantic Oratorical Contest" in which secondary and tertiary students debated the Constitution. The competition quickly became national in scope, with contests held in seven regions. Finals were judged in Los Angeles, and large cash prizes were awarded to all finalists: some lucky winners even received a "*de luxe* summer tour of the Mediterranean." With the help of supportive members of Congress, the contest eventually became headquartered in Washington, D.C.. The federation promoted an entirely originalist or rigidly preservative interpretation of the Constitution, reflecting the goal of using the foundational document as a powerful means of combating objectionable reform. This approach, the federation told its members, offered "the highest form of business insurance": "The hard job is not to amend the constitution to keep up with the people, but to amend the people to keep up with the constitution."[55]

The federation's propaganda was both collegial and pioneering. Other open shop lobbies employed similar means to disseminate propaganda; the Citizens' Industrial Alliance of St. Louis (a Metal Trades Association front) sponsored lectures and civic events and recruited men of the cloth to combat worker organization. Before joining forces with the federation, Wade had officiated newspaper contests and essay competitions debating the Constitution in his home state with the help of the American Legion and the National Security League. Yet the federation's propaganda prefigured and outdid many of its brethren. Minnesota's powerful employers' movement also arranged essay contests in state high schools but did so only during the depression. And even the National Association of Manufacturers' "American Way" propaganda blitz in radio and cinema and schools and churches followed the federation's lead, intentionally or not.[56]

One respect in which the federation's propaganda was certainly collegial was in its authoritarian approach to industrial relations, social welfare, and First Amendment issues. Like the Lusk Committee and myriad open shop groups, the federation always sought to drive a wedge between union leaders and the rank and file by describing the former as "'foreign' agitators or outsiders who inspire social conflict for their own personal and dishonest ends" and the latter as native-born loyalists "wholly satisfied with [their] working conditions." In the steel industry, the federation claimed, foreign radicals "actually controlled" the major unions and forced "the Americans" in the ranks to participate in strike action they opposed for fear of being labeled scabs. To this boilerplate the federation added a distinctive hereditarian argument, differentiating conservative "American" union leaders, "the men of brains," from the dull, radical mass of union members. Hence it argued that unions with higher proportions of "American" leaders, such as the railroad engineers, were "more intelligent as a class than the coal miners and steel workers [because] the radical foreign element [was] missing." These and similar arguments had been popularized and endorsed years earlier by the Dillingham Commission, which "characterized foreigners as unskilled and accident-prone." This rationale also explained management's superior position and the inherent flaw of Bolshevism. Seizing on press reports, the federation claimed that an appeal for foreign investment issued by V. I. Lenin proved that even the Soviet leadership recognized that "shop committees cannot conduct . . . business successfully." According to the federation, the Bolshevik supremo "really wanted" not just foreign capital but capitalist management to run industries: he had finally realized that "modern industry cannot be conducted successfully without a different quality of brains than that which is necessary to swing a hammer or operate a machine."[57]

The federation ignored the concerns of those workers whose brains were capable only of swinging a hammer, giving "grudging approval" to the idea of guaranteeing all workers a day of rest, but only as long as it was restricted to "those possessed of 'lofty ideals' and 'worthy ambitions.'" Deaf to the prevalence and catastrophic effects of workplace injury, the federation stated, "The industrial heavens are not so black as the alarmists paint them." Death and injury resulted from "the carelessness or malice of the workmen." And the federation advocated extreme measures to suppress those incorrigibly disloyal and malicious workmen, praising the castration and murder of Wobbly Wesley Everest for giving "the reds a taste of direct action that they [could] understand." The federation's "kindly and fair" "tall man" seldom appeared outside the pages of *Straight Shooter*.[58]

BAF publications regularly excoriated nonindustrial organizations that dared to contradict this worldview. Like other Spider Web groups, the federation mistrusted and slandered liberal churches. When the Federal Council of Churches of Christ described "industrial ownership and management" as a "class conscious ruling group" and insisted that workers be given greater reason to believe in the judicial system, the federation concluded, "Many of the churches have fallen victims to propaganda circulated by certain union labor leaders . . . seeking to secure the co-operation of the churches in a political movement to secure the adoption of legislation forbidding the issuance of injunctions against labor unions." Before dismissing the council's program "in the main [as] a strong plea for law and order," the federation advised, "it may be just as well for members . . . to observe how far this propaganda is being pushed in their respective communities. The good intent of the churches and ministers to aid the working classes makes them fall easy victims to scheming radicals." Even President Wilson was subjected to this treatment. When he was quoted as saying that he opposed violent revolution but not "orderly radicalism," the federation commented that the president was advocating "parlor Socialism." Federation members were reassured, however: "It is very probable that the President was misquoted," a problem he had "suffered frequently."[59]

The federation felt no need to substantiate these claims and pronouncements. Rather, its members and the general public were expected to accept the veracity and good sense of the federation's position by virtue of their proper respect for authority, which ran direct from the federation's executive through to the federal government, presidential misstatements notwithstanding. The federation believed that it merely needed to assure members that its information was gleaned from "government channels of a most authentic nature," with the provision of further information or specific details neither necessary nor advisable. To a large extent, this position attempted to cover the federation's "lack of dialectical skill." Like other Spider Web societies, the arguments the federation mustered in support of its beliefs were, as Edwin Layton concludes, "scarcely better than copy-book maxims." Yet while the federation's reliance on appeals to prejudice and hierarchy reflected its leaders' capacity for logical and empirical disputation, the tactic remained politically effective. For although it was the only kind of argument that offered them "any prospect of success," it was also the type of argument that yoked unionism and progressivism with Bolshevism and created an environment in which the IWW could be destroyed and the open shop preserved in Southern California. As the 1920s wound down, the BAF appeared poised to continue to dominate California politics. But the federation and especially Harry Haldeman had not reckoned on the wrecking ball of the Julian Petroleum Company (JPC) and the disastrous effects of a decade of unbridled capitalism.[60]

Scandal, Death, and Resurrection

In September 1926, Haldeman invested heavily in the JPC, run by Courtney Chancey Julian, a clerk, oil driller, and speculator. Julian capitalized the JPC after acquiring a lease on a Santa Fe oil field and borrowed vast sums from private investors, which he secured with generous stock issues. Promising his investors huge returns, Julian used their loans as security for additional borrowings from financial institutions—in short, a Ponzi scheme. When the company's financial affairs became so complex as to threaten its survival, Julian consolidated its myriad small pools and loans into one general group of investors, later dubbed the Millionaires' Pool or Bankers Pool No. 1, which would buy up and hold the outstanding stock until the company's outlook improved. Members of the pool were guaranteed either massive returns on their initial investment or, if the stock value rose, even greater returns through a managed liquidation of pool stock. A host of wealthy and prestigious investors bought in, including Haldeman, who loaned JPC $20,000. By the time JPC finally admitted to issuing too many shares, pool investors had cashed in their shares and divided total payments of more than $750,000.

Any joy Haldeman and the other members of the Millionaires' Pool might have felt at their financial gain was short-lived. As the JPC began to collapse, the Los Angeles city prosecutor decided to make an example of the BAF leader and charged him with "collecting interest rates prorating at 228% annually." Although Haldeman tried to argue that stock transactions could not be considered usury, a grand jury indicted Haldeman and fifty-four other JPC directors and investors for conspiracy to violate the corporate securities and state usury acts and for obtaining money under false pretenses. Haldeman spent three years fighting charges of violating the usury act (escaping conviction only because of a lack of incriminating evidence) and a civil suit for pool profits. In March 1930, while testifying in an unrelated matter, Haldeman collapsed in a courtroom and died.[61]

The golden age of the open shop died with the BAF president, as the shock waves of the great stock market crash of October 1929 flowed through the US economy and polity. The postwar suppression of labor and concentration of market power (and wealth) into ever fewer hands arguably had disastrous consequences. Corporate profits and dividends had skyrocketed, while oligopolies and high tariffs inflated consumer prices to artificially high levels. Organized labor and proponents of an alternative economic vision had no influence on economic policy, as what Goldstein has called a "distorted economic structure . . . literally ran riot." Much as the BAF and other business lobbies complained about the tough times they endured at the hands of "Bolsheviks" and labor unions, they had the run of the country and made a hash of it. "Seeing all problems from the viewpoint of business," government, and industry "had mistaken the class interest for the national interest," ushering in "both class and national disaster."[62]

Like other open shop lobbies, the Great Depression forced the BAF to change its business model. The downturn ate into the federation's membership and revenue, diminishing its capacity; even the mighty National Association of Manufacturers lost 70 percent of its members, as did the Metal Manufacturers' Association in Philadelphia. Business support for welfare capitalism, private employment bureaus, and vocational education courses collapsed as corporations sought to insure themselves. A state commission on immigration and housing had also exposed the federation's dependence on private utility interests. With business's national reputation at perhaps its lowest level ever, the timing of this revelation could not have been worse. And economic pressure and scandal were not the only forces sapping the federation's strength. The federation's choleric authoritarianism had finally brought it political grief. Its opposition to the Social Creed of Churches was particularly unwise, alienating otherwise sympathetic individuals and associations. So the federation hunkered down, narrowed its rhetorical and organizational focus, and became a purveyor of information to other members of the Anticommunist Spider Web, the US Army's Military Intelligence Division and the Bureau of Investigation, corporations, and the Los Angeles Police Red Squad. Here it had an edge on less well-resourced agencies, including the National Civic Federation, which had been reduced to a shadow of its former self.[63]

This transformation had in fact been under way since the late 1920s, when the federation emerged as one of the most important employer groups that dabbled in industrial espionage and published "intelligence bulletins." The federation became a particularly important if irregular contact for a depleted Military Intelligence Division, whose 1927 "Study on Subversives" (compiled by Major Richard Charles) was drawn principally from information provided by the federation and the American Defense Society, the Key Men of America, the National Security League, and the Daughters of the American Revolution. By the time the federation testified before the Fish Committee, its chief public raisons d'être were sponsorship of its patriotic oratorical contests and the collation of data on subversive movements. The federation had now created its own spider web chart, "The Tie That Binds," which it submitted to the committee. Fully caught up in renewed panic about radicals' political influence, the BAF obtained copies of planned routes for hunger marchers in 1932 and warned the US Army's chief of staff, General Douglas MacArthur, about the revolutionary intentions of the Bonus Expeditionary Force of war veterans that descended on the capital that year. The federation also became a valued contact for retired Major General Ralph Van Deman, whose private counterespionage network was nourished by reports the federation gleaned from its covert operatives and data files.[64]

While much of the information shared among the federation, other professional patriots, and the intelligence bureaucracy focused on alleged threats to national security, profit remained a constant and essential motive for antiradicalism. The BAF and its partners were always on the lookout for lucrative antiradical opportunities. In 1933, for example, the Military Intelligence Division supported a consortium of business interests that included federation members, who were hoping to seize control of food cooperatives responsible for feeding Los Angeles County. Although fear of communist infiltration and capture of the cooperatives motivated the formation of this coalition, profit was the most compelling cause.[65]

The federation's second-generation leadership arrived during the depression in the form of Margaret Ann Kerr, who served as secretary and then manager for the next thirty-plus years. The energetic Kerr associated the federation with conservative women's and Christian clubs and became a great support to congressional and federal authorities rooting out communists. Retaining its opposition to the Social Creed of Churches, the federation continued to harangue the YMCA and YWCA and other progressive Christian organizations, admonishing them for their lack of vigilance in fighting communism from within and without. The federation also suborned the judicial process by supplying confidential reports to grand jury members, hoping to influence these and other legal proceedings. This activity constituted an important means by which several open shop lobbies combated the New Deal: the CA in Minnesota similarly strove to influence grand jurors, county attorneys, and state police, regularly addressing their professional associations. Other anti–New Deal strategies of open shop lobbies, including the formation of business alliances with sham farm lobbies, had roots in the BAF's rhetorical campaigns of the 1920s.[66]

The federation remained a greatly esteemed informant and public relations ambassador for the Los Angeles Police Department. Chief James E. Davis commended to large corporations the BAF's "data and confidential information on Communism and allied activities." In a letter to the California Oil and Gas Association, Davis described the BAF files as "invaluable to the Police," furnishing "the background for necessary action" against myriad individuals and organizations that the police could not monitor, restricted as they were by "inadequate financial appropriation," warrants, and other constitutional annoyances. The federation, however, kept "abreast of the developments in the Communist program of destruction" so that "public sentiment" could be "built up to support . . . action and legislation to enable the authorities to handle it."[67]

As the anticommunist crusade progressed through the 1930s, the BAF influenced a new generation of Red-baiting legislators. In 1935, Charles Kramer, senior counsel for Congress's Special Committee to Investigate Un-American Activities, effusively praised Kerr for having "diligently and constantly engaged in the preparing of material for the consideration of the House Judiciary Committee" and for having "personally called on a very large number of the members of the House and Senate, and . . . furnished valuable information for which we are all most grateful."[68]

Although Kramer was undoubtedly flattering one of the committee's most ardent supporters, the federation indeed provided valuable services. Communist Party membership lists and similar material compiled by the BAF and other Spider Web members saved Cold War Red-baiters the trouble of researching their case and provided them with important evidentiary and psychological support.

The federation continued to give material to the House Un-American Activities Committee and the Immigration and Naturalization Service, into the 1950s.

Nevertheless, despite Kerr's valiant efforts, the prestige of the federation gradually slid during the 1930s and 1940s, a fact reflected in the composition of its executive. Around 1939, the federation's vice presidents were Richard Colyear, a motor salesman, and Lloyd L. Austin, vice president of the Security-First National Bank. While respectable and well-to-do, these men neither represented nor walked with the Los Angeles business elite. And by the 1950s, the federation had morphed into the American Library of Information, which worked "to collect, correlate, evaluate, and maintain a library of factual information concerning organized movements subversive to American principles of government as expressed in the Constitution of the U.S.A." The library claimed to possess files on 2,500,000 radical individuals, movements, and organizations, including the names of more than 600,000 supporters of the legalization of the Communist Party. Its holdings were buttressed by Van Deman, who forwarded all the antiradical information he received to a select group of recipients and advised the Military Intelligence Division to acquire the federation's "excellent records." The library was kept financially afloat by powerful corporate and government subscribers, including Douglas Aircraft Corporation, Lockheed Aviation, Northrop Aviation, American Potash and Chemical, the General Petroleum Corporation, Shell Oil, Western Gulf Oil, Union Oil Company of California, the Immigration and Naturalization Service, public utilities such as Edison Securities and Southern California Edison, Pacific Mutual Life Insurance, the University of Southern California, Fox West Coast Theaters, Cecil B. de Mille Productions, the Los Angeles Turf Club, the State of California, and lumber, transportation, and cement firms. In 1951 these subscriptions totaled more than $100,000. The federation battled on through the 1950s (led by Major General W. A. Worton of the US Marine Corps) before death finally retired Kerr.[69]

The BAF made one further significant contribution to US politics by providing Harry Marston Haldeman's grandson, Harry Robbins Haldeman, an entrée into Vice President Richard Nixon's inner circle in the 1950s. Three-year-old Bob Haldeman had been among the mourners at the funeral for Harry Marston Haldeman, whose politics and activism had been continued by the boy's parents. Encouraged, Bob Haldeman later recalled, by his family's "interest in the BAF [and] concern about communism and creeping socialism" in the United States, he identified Nixon "as one among a number of political leaders in which [he] could become interested." Moved by Nixon's political difficulties—controversy surrounding his prosecution of US State Department official Alger Hiss and allegations that Nixon had received tainted campaign contributions—Haldeman volunteered for the Eisenhower ticket's 1956 reelection campaign. Haldeman wrote the vice president a letter, outlining his "background and . . . *bona fides* as an anti-communist" and drawing attention to his grandfather's formation of the BAF and his parents' continuing friendship with the Chandler family. A generation after Harry Marston's passing, the Haldeman name and the reputation of the BAF were still strong enough to set aspiring, anticommunist activists on their way to the pinnacle of American politics. Bob Haldeman went on to become President Nixon's chief of staff—and "a plumbing expert of a different sort" who was jailed for his role in the Watergate burglary. Harry Marston Haldeman thus was the first in a familial line of Republican activists with a distinctive conception of the ethics of citizenship in a democracy.[70]

By the end of its long career, the BAF had for forty years appended the cause of anticommunism to its open shop and laissez-faire crusade. In its heyday, the federation played a crucial role in making Southern California a stronghold of antilabor practices. It also played a leading role in business's national campaign to destroy Progressivism, "radicalism," and the labor movement, gifting Jazz Age America an industrial and political "normalcy" of fierce hostility to labor and other civil rights. And while the federation did not survive the post–New Deal era of Keynesian public policy settings, its role in entrenching laissez-faire economics at the heart of anticommunism remained significant for the duration of the Cold War.

CHAPTER 9

Political Repression and Culture War

For ourselves, under the legal principle that every man is presumed *to intend* the *consequences* of his own acts, we cannot believe that the Bureaucrats *have* good intentions in seeking unlimited centralized control over all American youth. But *we do not care what they intend*. The *results* of their actions will "hurt just as much" as if Moscow were paying all their salaries.

—*The Woman Patriot*

The notion that the 1920s was a time of liberated mores, dress, and behavior can be as misleading as the notion that it was a time of political apathy and private wealth accumulation. Like any cliché, these ideas have some basis in fact. Although the already wealthy benefited most from economic recovery, an unprecedented number of Americans enjoyed discretionary income and the leisure time in which to spend that money on new consumer goods and products—the "normalcy" that Warren Harding had hoped his presidency would bring. Yet the 1920s also witnessed the expansion of wartime and Red Scare repression into a general cultural war on "Bolshevik" causes, individuals, and organizations targeted by the Anticommunist Spider Web. Spider Web members and their supporters created a repressive infrastructure of blacklists, witch hunts, loyalty oaths, and compulsory patriotism. As the national political economy grew ever more corporatized and as homogeneous culture emerged and was packaged into consumable products, the Spider Web strengthened its influence not just on the doctrine of anticommunism but also on the nation's political culture. Goaded by big business and the Web, governments continued to suppress industrial and political freedom and tighten the regulation of cultural institutions as well as individual morality and behavior. If the 1920s was to witness any return to cultural "normalcy," members of the Spider Web hoped it would herald the normalization of militarism, isolationism, conformism, and superpatriotism. In addition, they hoped, the ascendancy of anticommunism would make the ostentatious demonstration of industrial quiescence, national loyalty, and conservative morality a permanent condition of citizenship. Even modest social reform, such as federal funding for maternal and child health care, could then be obstructed by patriot-led coalitions of commercial, professional, and citizens' societies.

"Patriotism" and Free Speech

Regulation of political thought and expression remained a paramount concern for public officials and reactionary "patriotic" societies throughout the 1920s. While federal and state authorities remained preoccupied with suppressing "communist" organizations and alien radicals, the eradication of unorthodox political ideas associated with communism also occurred at a local level, where officials, conservative pressure groups, and police forces played significant roles.

A combination of federal, state, and local ordinances effected political repression. The federal Sedition Act remained in force until 1921. More important, the Trading with the Enemy Act was never repealed, and the postmaster general retained censorship until 1930. Interception of mail, therefore, was routine. The postmaster general collaborated with the Bureau of Investigation to create lists of banned radical publications, most of which were printed in foreign languages or served African American communities. Police also routinely disrupted unwholesome meetings and rallies. Legal action was often necessary to protect radical gatherings, particularly in Pennsylvania, where hall owners were required to submit the names and programs of prospective speakers to police. The mayor of Johnstown attempted to use this regulation to prevent local antifascist meetings in 1924, and when the American Legion closed a memorial meeting for recently deceased Russian leader V. I. Lenin, the mayor declared that permission to stage all similar meetings would in future be subject to the Legion's approval.[1]

In 1928, police broke up more meetings, made more arrests in free speech cases, and enforced more injunctions than they had in any year since 1921. Moreover, American Civil Liberties Union (ACLU) statistics on these civil rights violations excluded incidents perpetrated against African Americans, who were most subject to attack. Records of these attacks, generally also the most ferocious, were compiled by the National Association for the Advancement of Colored People. Excluding the 2,000-plus indicted strikers, 1928 witnessed 418 prosecutions involving free speech and 53 reported meeting closures, a fourfold increase from the previous year. After the 1927 execution of alleged anarchist murderers Nicola

Sacco and Bartolomeo Vanzetti, a wave of prosecutions targeted many of the thousands of people who expressed disgust with their executions. Exactly one year later, St. Louis police broke up a memorial meeting with tear gas. A Boston man was imprisoned for criminal libel for holding a placard that called Massachusetts governor Alvan T. Fuller a "murderer." The situation remained similar in 1929. The ACLU reported that police broke up fifty-two meetings, forty-three of them involving the Communist Party (CP) or its affiliates, but remarked that the figures probably represented a quarter of actual incidents. And the number of political prosecutions returned to levels not seen since the mid-1920s: one defendant was a fifteen-year-old schoolboy sent to a reform institution for having participated in a demonstration by the Communist Young Pioneers against the Boy Scouts. The new president, Herbert Hoover, declined even to meet with a delegation seeking the restoration of citizenship for wartime political convicts. Like his predecessor Calvin Coolidge, he required each prisoner individually to petition for pardon.[2]

With the onset of the Great Depression, political conflict sharpened. While the number and range of citizens protesting the economic status quo grew, so too did reaction to such protest. Excluding strike cases, the number of prosecutions involving free speech mushroomed from 228 in 1929 to 1,630 in 1930. Interference with meetings more than doubled. Communist groups faced savage repression for their political and union activities, while the suppression of socialist meetings increased as well. The Fish Committee, which met for six months in 1930, helped to foster this reaction, interviewing 275 witnesses at hearings across the nation. It concluded that the communist menace was immense and dangerously unchecked and unanimously recommended the full reinstatement of the powers surveillance bodies had lost in 1924. The committee's legislative and administrative recommendations were not implemented, but its actions emboldened police, district attorneys, patriots, and militarists, and the ACLU reported that the Fish Committee had "tremendous" effects in stirring up prejudice, encouraging vigilantism, and causing arrests. Into the new decade, repression of civil liberties remained severe. In 1931, police killed four workers during demonstrations against the Ford Motor Company in Dearborn, Michigan. In Chicago, eight demonstrators were wounded when police turned a machine gun against them. At the Japanese Embassy in Washington, D.C., and the country's consulate in Chicago, police attacked protesters decrying the Japanese invasion of Manchuria. While the number of major prosecutions involving civil liberties fell, a huge increase occurred in the number of minor cases pertaining to strike activity, particularly in cities with a communist presence. This repression continued until Franklin D. Roosevelt took office as president in 1933.[3]

Although brutality against labor activists was appreciably curbed during the New Deal, anticommunism had by this time redefined the boundaries of civil liberty. Violence against union organizers and sympathizers remained prevalent, if concentrated in industrial trouble spots: Harlan County, Kentucky, for example, was notoriously deadly in the 1930s. In addition, communists and their ilk were routinely denied various constitutional freedoms, as even the ACLU balked at defending the rights of citizens so widely regarded as Soviet minions. During the First World War and throughout the Red Scare, the ACLU had played an important role protecting citizens' rights in the face of significant official and vigilante opposition. In an atmosphere that cowed even such committed social reformers and peace advocates as Jane Addams, the organization stood firm in its defense of the First and Fourth Amendment rights of even CP members. ACLU cofounder and executive director Roger N. Baldwin insisted that the CP was legal and that "mere advocacy" of revolution was constitutionally permissible. He argued that outlawing the party would "drive the movement into underground channels, with the inevitable tendency to secret conspiracies and to violence." His words, Jennifer Luff has observed, constituted "a classic statement of the civil liberties credo developed in the early 1920s." And the group backed up its words with its actions: after Baldwin suspected that the raid on the CP's Bridgman, Michigan, meeting was illegal, the ACLU's legal and public relations assistance to the Bridgman defendants exposed this illegality.[4]

The political climate of the interwar period, however, eroded the union's commodious concept of liberty. Like the American Federation of Labor (AFL), the ACLU began to police itself, adopting a position that Luff describes as "voluntarist anti-communism" and exposing, removing, and prohibiting communists from its ranks. And while the ACLU initially opposed statutory limits on communists' civil liberties, the August 1939 Nazi-Soviet nonaggression treaty finally led the ACLU to regard the American CP as a Soviet agency whose members did not qualify for the protections of the First Amendment. This position led to the expulsion of ACLU cofounder Elizabeth Gurley Flynn, a suffragist, Wobbly, and latter-day communist. Thus, well before the start of the Cold War, a restricted notion of political liberty was fast becoming political orthodoxy, helping to usher in federal and state citizen-loyalty programs in the late 1940s and to reconcile liberal conceptions of political freedom with anticommunist repression. As sometime Marxist and former organizer of the American Workers Party Sidney Hook argued (from his chair in the Department of Philosophy at New York University), communists could justly be repressed through antidemocratic means in a liberal democracy because they aided and abetted conspiracy against that democracy. Their suppression, Hook stated, was "a matter of ethical hygiene, not of politics or persecution."[5]

Conferring pariah status on any and all communists led to unanticipated outcomes, chief among them the encouragement of the CP's habitually furtive and disingenuous behavior, even in its dealings with allied or broadly sympathetic industrial, cultural, and political groups. As Ellen Schrecker has noted, party members cleaved to a "revolutionary identity" not just because they remembered "when the threat of deportation and criminal prosecution made legal operations impossible" but also because they knew that even during the friendlier climes of the New Deal (when the United States finally recognized the USSR), coming out as a communist could very likely result in the loss of one's job, particularly for teachers, college instructors, or lawyers, occupations pursued by many middle-class party members.[6] Party members also suspected—correctly—that the AFL and even the ACLU would acquiesce in the party's subversion by the national security apparatus. Thus, ceaseless persecution in the interwar period did much to engender in the CP a toxic organizational psychology that marked its approach to politics and activism throughout its existence. If the CP's failure to assist the Industrial Workers of the World stemmed from the party's obdurate sectarianism, its attempts to subvert mainstream unions were rooted in a mutual antagonism that was both philosophical and responsive to political maneuvering by both the party and the craft union movement. In any event, for the broader Left, the antagonism between the AFL and the CP restricted the parameters of political, industrial, and social reform that could be debated, let alone adopted, in interwar and then Cold War America. And anticommunist repression had considerable influence on the division between the CP and the craft union movement.

During the 1920s and 1930s, repression spread beyond political and industrial arenas. The interwar period was marked by religious reaction. The city of Boston became a stronghold of anti-birth-control advocacy, with mayoral decree prohibiting the right to promote contraception. In Massachusetts and elsewhere, police raided birth control clinics and confiscated patient and employee records. In 1925, eleven states issued compulsory Bible-reading laws. Tennessee legislated against the teaching of evolution, and after the law was upheld by the state's supreme court (following the infamous Monkey Trial of high school biology instructor John Scopes), the Mississippi legislature followed suit. Administrative regulations in other states produced similar outcomes. Two Kentucky high school teachers were temporarily dismissed on charges of teaching evolution, while a Christian fundamentalist high school principal in Tennessee was forced to resign for defining the word *evolution* for his pupils.[7]

Technological change heightened anxiety about social mores and hastened the expansion of repressive bureaucracy. The invention of movies with sound in 1928 prompted eight states to introduce censorship boards. Public opinion was exhaustively monitored. Works such as Theodore Dreiser's *American Tragedy*, a novel based on the lives of Sacco and Vanzetti, were banned for "obscenity." Conservative media interests restricted the amount and range of material in the public domain. Bureau of Investigation director William Burns gave speeches in person and on the radio in which he attacked the ACLU for its defense of Reds, yet the American Telephone and Telegraph Company refused to allow the ACLU to rebut Burns's charges. Others to feel the weight of corporate censorship included the Reverend Hermann J. Hahn, whose depression-era broadcasts were abruptly canceled after he advocated taxing the rich and the creation of federally funded unemployment insurance. All the while, few stones were left unturned in the search for sedition. A barber from Lynchburg, Virginia, found himself in contempt of court for expressing sympathy with railway strikers. In 1930, two women running a communist children's summer camp were convicted and jailed for three months on charges of "desecrating" the American flag after they refused a mob's demand that they run one up a flagpole.[8]

"Patriotism" and Americanization

The ostentatious display of "loyalty" became critical not only to enjoying peace as a citizen but in the case of immigrants to qualifying for citizenship. Would-be citizens were subjected to loyalty tests, judged largely by hearsay. The Bureau of Investigation muscled in on the naturalization process and ordered its agents to sound out local "business people" to evaluate a prospective citizen's "general character, reputation and attitude during the war." Other relevant factors included the migrant's marital status, occupation, purchase of (or failure to purchase) Liberty Bonds, membership in radical societies, length of residence in the United States, whereabouts of spouse, and reasons for immigration. As an afterthought, the prospective migrant's criminal record in his or her country of birth might also be considered. Finally, the bureau rendered its opinion on whether the alien would make "a desirable resident."[9] Another important way that migrants and their expatriate communities could demonstrate their loyalty to America was to abandon the use of their native tongues. The wartime insistence that Americans express themselves and educate their children only in English continued well into the interwar period.

The vetting of potential migrants and the eradication of foreign tongues from public discourse was important work, but these tasks were too passive to guarantee that migrants would make good citizens. Rather than hoping for good character and settling for compliant behavior in a prospective migrant, many patriots decided that a process of Americanization was required to assure each migrant's (political) assimilation. The concept of Americanization, like the notion of "100% Americanism," was vague in the particulars but absolute in emotional terms. Like other conceptions of patriotism promoted by 100-percenters, it was largely defined by what it was not rather than by what it theoretically was. For the Ku Klux Klan, Americanization was fundamentally anti-Catholic.[10] But for business and patriotic lobbies that emerged during the war, 100% Americanism was fundamentally about anticommunism. As far as these groups were concerned, immigrants were expected to accept the structure of the political economy as they found it, knuckle down and work hard, and assimilate into the mainstream culture as defined by governments, corporations, and professional patriots. Universities and schools were regarded as a principal battleground for the control of American politics and culture. Hence, anticommunists legislated loyalty oaths for teachers; created Bolshevik-style star chambers to assess teacher loyalty; influenced school and college curricula and interaction with the general community; suppressed teacher organization and affiliation with peak labor bodies; and used cultural events to foster the values of conservatism and laissez-faire. The techniques and values fostered by this Americanization were embraced across the nation in the 1920s.

Among the more important sponsors of Americanization in formal education settings were the Ku Klux Klan and the American Legion. Klansmen were elected to the Ohio Board of Education, while a Klan-dominated faction in Oregon legislated mandatory attendance by all children aged eight to sixteen in public (as opposed to a religious) schools. Similar laws were debated in several other states. Yet the American Legion's program of Americanization proved more durable, largely because it basically concerned anticommunism. Its message was more inclusive and easier to sell than the Klan's religious and racial discrimination. Compared with other patriotic organizations, the Legion also went to considerable trouble to articulate principles for and a program of Americanization. Its inclusivity was apparent in the group's commitment to the traditional mission of welcoming migrants into the nation. The American Legion also recognized the importance of constitutional freedoms of religion and thought and of providing civic assistance for new migrants; the program explicitly acknowledged newcomers' need for help with orientation and developing a sense of belonging. At the same time, the program betrayed great mistrust for the role of public institutions in this process. And tremendous hubris underpinned the notion that a veterans' association should play a fundamental role in immigration and citizenship processes.[11]

The Legion's Americanization program was run by its National Americanism Commission. Modeled on the Committee on Public Information, the commission had an authoritarian structure. Control was vested in the Legion's unelected National Executive Committee. The Americanization program promoted "the basic idea" of "100% Americanism through the planning, establishment, and conduct of a continuous, constructive educational system." This system would "combat all anti-American tendencies, activities and propaganda"; "inculcate the ideals of Americanism in the citizen population, particularly the basic American principle that the interests of all the people are above those of any so-called class or section"; and "spread throughout the nation information as to the real nature and principles of American government." The program did not define its notion of Americanism or the "real" principles of government, but they boiled down to two phases: "making Americans of the arriving and newly arrived residents, and of aliens who [were] in America but not of it . . . who for one reason or another . . . failed to appreciate that the form of government under which this nation has grown great is the form under which it must grow greater."[12]

The fundamentals pertaining to immigration included selection, assimilation, and rejection. In relation to selection, the Legion spoke with the same voice as its prominent supporter, Albert Johnson, calling on the federal government to "apply more rigorous standards governing the admission of aliens" and to "inquire more painstakingly into the history and antecedents" of prospective migrants. With regard to assimilation, the Legion proposed "to station its agents at the ports of debarkation," where they would "receive rosters of incoming immigrants" and their destination. Local legionnaires would then "extend the hand of welcome to these selected newcomers" and help them "appreciate the advantages of life in America and start them on the highroad which leads to American citizenship in fact as well as name." Legionnaires would be "the alien's friend, confidant, defender and critic," helping him find employment and learn English and "settle his grievances, explain his difficulties [and] show him how to make use of libraries, playgrounds, schools and other community benefits." As long as he respected "America's opinions as expressed in [its] form of government," he would be left free to vote, worship, and think as he saw fit. If these measures failed, the Legion reserved for itself the right to eject any alien who failed "to respond to the assimilation process." Migrants had to understand that they entered the nation "on probation" and that if it was "apparent that after sufficient time [they were] not on the way to real Americanism, out" they would go.[13]

The Legion did not propose to ignore "the millions already admitted to residence and . . . citizenship" or the native-born citizens it believed needed Americanizing. Assimilating these people, too, would be "gone about by the same way." In some cases, however, "the destruction of preconceived and false ideas [had to] precede the constructive work," a process that would require education and "the elimination of the cause; the deportation of . . . radical firebrands who prey on the ignorance of the aliens and implant in their minds false conceptions of American institutions before the alien has had the opportunity to learn the truth."[14]

Across the nation, the Legion's Americanization program resulted in a range of repressive actions. The Legion orchestrated the dismissal of ideologically unreliable teachers, even joining the federal Board of Education to jointly sponsor American Education Week 1924 and ensuring that federal education guidelines encouraged compulsory patriotism. The Legion dominated the agenda of educational conferences, while the board was relegated to the sidelines, an erosion of independence that led many organizations to boycott the event. By 1925, more teachers were being dismissed for "unpatriotic" utterances and opinions than during any previous period. Several states required their superintendents of education to provide daily patriotic exercises for schools. Educational decrees in Washington, New York, and Colorado mandated participation in patriotic activities. In the early 1930s, Washington, Michigan, Montana, and Delaware passed laws, formulated by the Legion and the Daughters of the American Revolution, requiring teachers to swear oaths of loyalty.[15]

The Legion also stifled students' freedom of expression. Student protest at New York's City College against compulsory military training prompted the college president to forbid student publications from discussing the subject. At the University of Minnesota, thirty-six students were expelled for objecting to military drills. The president of the University of Virginia barred from campus any speaker not approved by the Daughters or the Legion.[16]

The Legion's Americanization program spread well beyond the confines of educational institutions. The National Americanism Commission also sponsored youth activities and community services, citizenship schools for the foreign-born, vocational guidance services for boys, flag history and etiquette classes, and activities in observance of patriotic days. Other "advancement" schemes included an annual junior baseball program that brought more than four hundred thousand boys into "Legion sponsorship" and a School Award Medal.[17]

Thousands of smaller societies also spread the dual message of anticommunism and Americanization. One such association was the Westchester Security League of New York, founded by Mrs. Frank (Agnes Ely) Hawkins, national defense chair of the Daughters of the American Revolution and a subscriber to Fred Marvin's *Daily Data Sheet*. Hawkins began her anticommunist career addressing her chapter of the Daughters before forming the League to concentrate more fully on radicalism. The League distributed material to all corners and comers. It joined the Women's Patriotic Conference on National Defense and attended annual gatherings in Washington, D.C., beginning in the mid-1920s. Here the League forged relationships with the Committee on American Education, which was affiliated with John Trevor's American Coalition of Patriotic Societies and broadcast weekly programs from New York on the "Machinery, Principles and Aims of Our Government."

Like all anticommunists, the Westchester Security League was anxious about education. Leading by example, Hawkins formed a student discussion group at a high school after reading of its difficulties with Young Pioneers. "As a reward for the best work in citizenship," she took two of its members to the Women's

Patriotic Conference gathering. The Daughters of the American Revolution soon took over the League's patriotic program, running classes in public schools and new clubs for "Jr. American Citizens." The League also supplied schools and youth groups with subscriptions to approved literary matter, including Walter Steele's *National Republic*. A teachers' group challenging the Teachers' Union received information every month on how to combat "Progressive Poison in Public Education." And the League established a partnership with the Sons of the American Revolution to monitor "un-American" textbooks.[18]

The Westchester Security League monitored subversive adults, too, and was a trusted source of information for government and judicial authorities. The special congressional committee investigating subversive activities (1934) and Congressman George H. Tinkham, who was sponsoring a bill to revoke recognition of the USSR, used the League's resources, as did the Arizona legislature when it investigated "disloyal activities." The League also furnished material to an Arizona judge who was trying alleged communists. Within the Spider Web, the League corresponded with Steele, Harry Jung, Marvin, and the Better America Federation while cultivating support from the US Army's Military Intelligence Division, the War Department, and the US Catholic Conference.[19]

As the regulation of migrants' and students' activities and beliefs was steadily institutionalized, it became increasingly difficult to oppose Americanization programs and their growing crassness. Sections of industry, lamenting the spread of the American Plan into the national immigration program, expressed frustration regarding the identification of ethnic minorities with radicalism. Yet they felt powerless to contest the dominant concept of Americanization. The Inter-Racial Council, the National Founders' Association, and the American Constitution Association (Judge Elbert Gary's front group) all tried to put the antimigrant genie back in its bottle. But having so consistently denigrated "radical" migrants for their "communist" beliefs, industry officials lost control of the immigration debate to racist zealots like John Trevor. Similarly, their attempts to reach out to immigrants were drowned out by the Daughters of the American Revolution and the National Americanism Commission. With the encouragement of state education authorities, these patriotic associations worked through traditional settlement houses to educate migrants in the ways of anticommunism. In this respect, like the Better America Federation, the associations built on wartime infrastructure (created in this instance by the Committee on Public Information), which pressured ethnic communities to form their own Americanizing bureaus.[20]

No Americanization program was benign, and even the most moderate Americanization activities abused their educative and civic purposes. These programs were designed to engender conformity: the first words of English students at Henry Ford's company schools learned were, "I am a good American." Americanization also generally sought to entrench the political and economic status quo. Professional patriots and restrictive immigration policies helped to create an atmosphere in which some of the most prominent Americanization efforts were sponsored by migrants anxious to demonstrate their loyalty and gratitude. Many strident antiradicals were recent migrants or hailed from conspicuous ethnic minority groups. Jacob Cash, a Russian Jewish migrant, veteran of the Spanish-American War, and marshal of New York City, was one conspicuous ethnic loyalist. Prompted by "a deep sense of gratitude to the land which afforded him opportunity," Cash feared that untutored migrants were "heading for Bolshevism." In response, Cash formed the American Patriotic Society, which took as its chief activity the distribution of a monthly magazine, *The Patriot*, numerous booklets, and Cash's book, *What America Means to Me*; public lectures were available on request. Such activity sought "to enlighten others, and make them feel a sense of their responsibilities" to the United States. It also sought to prevent immigrants from being influenced by communists, radicals, and soft liberals. Cash advocated distributing the Constitution through the US consular service to help dissuade prospective immigrants who were unhappy with its contents. Identifying the gulf between the promise and the reality of America, Cash worried about the frustration migrants felt "because opportunities [did] not open up right away." He also worried about native-born Americans' failure to provide immigrants with a positive experience of Americanization.[21]

Although his was a small operation, Cash found ready support in government and business circles—from Theodore and Franklin Delano Roosevelt; from long-serving secretary of labor James J. Davis; from the governors of Oregon, Vermont, and Kentucky; and from numerous state and federal representatives. Cash received commendations from a host of judges, among them US Supreme Court Chief Justice William Howard Taft. Never shy about expressing its antiradical convictions, the AFL congratulated Cash on his determination to "offset Bolshevik propaganda." Business leaders, particularly in banking and insurance, were eager subscribers, as was the Americanization secretary of General Electric. Scout troop leaders, an administrator of an African American orphanage, the International Baptist Seminary, the American Legion, the Daughters of the American Revolution, and the Department of Justice rounded out Cash's support group.[22]

Educational institutions also played a considerable role in enshrining antilabor values in the doctrine of 100% Americanism. Few cultural institutions paid greater dividends to big business than the nation's most prestigious colleges and universities, whose boards of trustees were by the early twentieth century dominated by corporations. Corporate control of college finances translated directly into great institutional hostility to organized labor. Indeed, in Stephen Norwood's estimation, college presidents "rivaled the corporate 'robber barons' in their antagonism toward labor." Faculty tenure was not common in the United States until 1938, so professors with pro-labor tendencies were constantly vulnerable to dismissal at the request of wealthy donors and boards of trustees. Noted professors had been fired for criticizing authorities during the Pullman strike and for speaking against the prevalence of child labor. During the Red Scare, Harold Laski, a British historian and future chair of the British Labour Party who was then a young instructor at Harvard, was attacked by prominent donors, alumni, and students for publicly supporting striking Boston policemen. *Harvard Lampoon* called Laski a "Bolshevik" and "scum" and printed anti-Semitic poems and caricatures belittling him. The school's president, A. Lawrence Lowell, himself a strident anti-Semite, hesitated to sack Laski but privately told him that he had no future at Harvard. Laski promptly resigned.[23]

Lowell also recruited students to help break the policemen's strike. Organized labor regarded Lowell's predecessor, Charles W. Eliot, who ran the university from 1869 to 1909, as "the greatest labor union hater in the country." Eliot began the Harvard tradition of encouraging students to suppress labor rights, exalting the figure of the strikebreaker as a hero willing to risk life and limb in the defense of American values. For their part, college students of the period seldom thought about politics, and when they did, they sided with conservative and antilabor forces, viewing modern society as "rotten with altruism."[24]

College students voted for Calvin Coolidge in greater proportion than any other social cohort. However, they did not embrace strikebreaking merely to advance their preferred political agenda. Students also attacked labor organizations to demonstrate their manliness at a time when the proliferation of sedentary office jobs created what Norwood has described as a "crisis of masculinity" among America's upper and middle classes. While the rise of vicious initiation rites and football provided some outlet for the "craving" many of these young men experienced for "violent experiences," the Boston policemen's strike, according to Norwood, "provided students with probably the closest approximation to the atmosphere of combat for which they longed." Taking from the police the role of the "thin blue line" shielding decent society from Bolshevik hordes "intent on murder, rape, and robbery," Harvard strikebreakers were "energized by massive public support . . . in the atmosphere of hysteria that prevailed during the Red Scare."[25]

Given the great enthusiasm an appreciable number of college students showed for attacking labor unions and ideals, it is remarkable that the fear of communist subversion of institutions of higher learning emerged as such a salient feature of anticommunist dogma: the Lusk Committee's education laws were formulated while Lowell's legions helped force an entire police force into involuntary retirement. The place of rational thought in anticommunism was, however, often very limited.

The Collapse of Progressivism and Obstruction of Social Welfare

Outside the realm of formal and community education, anticommunism also impeded social welfare initiatives, particularly efforts to legislate protections for some of society's most vulnerable and exploited members. Conservative values and priorities were expressed in very selective regulation of personal health and criticism of sexual irregularity. Political, big business, professional, media, and patriotic organizations shrewdly conflated the prohibition of alcoholic and narcotic substances with other materially different incursions by the state into public health, to which they objected and labeled "Bolshevik." Federal maternal and child health and education programs were the main targets of such anticommunist agitation. Opposition to such programs was frequently disingenuous and still more commonly inconsistent, deriving less from republican and libertarian traditions than from status anxiety: fear of loss of income, professional prestige, and cheap labor. These concerns were masked by specious appeals for the protection of states' rights. Libertarian opposition to federal involvement in social welfare was typically contingent on the cause and intended targets of a particular measure. Opposition to government mediation of private substance use, for example, was patchy. Social conservatives were indifferent to the Harrison Narcotics Act of 1914, the first federal law, Alfred McCoy has noted, to restrict "individual rights over the body." But whereas conservatives regarded the use of opiates and coca-derived products as the concern only of degenerates, the Woman's Christian Temperance Union apparently deserved a place in the Spider Web Chart. Opponents of Progressive organizations also used private (and fabricated) information about the sexual practices of members of these organizations to disarm them. That such information was covertly gleaned from internal security agencies similarly did not trouble conservative libertarians. Rather, the threat of social reforms that threatened entrenched "respectable" interests necessitated the targeted use of sexual smears and the promotion of the ideology of domesticity, in which the family stood isolated and inviolate from the state "as both a refuge from and a solution to social disorder." Thus, legislative regulation of narcotic substances and the use of sexual smear as a political weapon became two more political practices repatriated from the Philippines.[26]

Opposition to "communist" social welfare initiatives, especially when they were achieved through constitutional reform, emerged only slowly. Although the introduction of federal income taxing power, direct election of senators, and even Prohibition and female suffrage engendered such opposition, these reforms were ineffectively opposed. However, the passage of the Nineteenth Amendment proved a high-water mark for (pre–New Deal) social reform. It quickly became clear that female suffrage had not been the first conquest of a strong and united

Progressive army but a relatively harmless change that had garnered backing from a broad coalition of interest groups. Social conservatives realized that support for additional reform was largely restricted to the ranks of Progressive women's organizations. These conservatives also understood that they could capitalize on discontent aroused by recent constitutional amendments and discredit further reforms by associating them with communism and feminism. The lobby that best understood this strategy was the antifeminist women's movement, which transcended its defeat on the suffrage question.[27]

The conferment of the franchise on women paradoxically gave a new lease on political life to women's organizations that campaigned against it. Leaders of the National Association Opposed to Woman Suffrage believed that the suffrage amendment resulted from the failure of men to protect the nation's patrimony: the republic of the Founding Fathers, where men and women, whites and blacks, and citizens and immigrants had been assigned a rightful station. The middle-class white women who ran the association now felt compelled to embrace the full rights of citizenship that had been thrust upon them and provide the conservative political leadership that had been missing when the amendment had been debated. The association was reborn as the Woman Patriots, and they assembled a broad-based coalition to oppose feminist social welfare and reconstitute the conservative movement.[28]

In the view of historians such as Kim Nielsen, gender identity "lay at the core of Red Scare understandings of healthy Americanism" and expressions of anticommunism. Opposition to social welfare was similarly oriented around traditional gendered imagery. People accused of radicalism were believed to hold beliefs and behave in ways that corroded social as well as political roles and structures. Conversely, men who upheld "patriarchal gender roles" while suppressing radicals were the "measuring stick of patriotism." Ole Hanson was one antiradical whose deeds were widely praised in masculine terms. Contemporary media described this modestly built and oval-faced scourge of the Seattle Reds as a "two-fisted, square-jawed man" whose backbone "would serve as a girder in a railroad bridge." Much was also made, including by Hanson himself, of his procreative prowess, which encouraged his supporters to compare his response to Bolshevism with that of a lion whose pride was threatened by an intruder.[29]

Antifeminist women's organizations amplified the association of gender perversion with radicalism, arguing that social welfare "feminized liberalism by promoting a political culture characterized by dependency." As Nielsen has observed, these groups maintained that the liberalism of Progressive women's groups created Bolshevized feminist women, "weak men, and a federal government that impinged upon male domains of power." Such was the view of Margaret C. Robinson, a veteran of the antisuffrage movement who became an important opponent of a proposed constitutional amendment to empower Congress "to limit, regulate, and prohibit the labor of persons under eighteen years of age." For Robinson, feminism spurred women to neglect their families, morals, and religion. She worried (strangely, given her own iron will and stern heart) that women were "very easily influenced" by political appeals pitched "in a humanitarian guise." Gullible women, unable to refuse the entreaties of communists and other covert revolutionaries, could be cheaply persuaded to support political and bureaucratic solutions to social ills that would encourage women's economic independence and deprive men of the "steadying and civilizing influence" of providing for a family. Robinson believed that a world shaped by Progressive feminists would leave no man "master of his home because of the constant supervision of Government agents." And men who lost their grip on the patriarchal family, the institution that most strongly tethered them to society and nation, were ripe for conversion to Bolshevism. This reason, according to Nielsen, primarily explained why Progressive women's organizations and women's colleges were regarded as "feeder societies" and "recruiting stations for extreme Radicalism among the educated classes." According to Robinson and her Massachusetts Public Interests League, women's colleges had been subverted by socialists and communists. Robinson's investigations into this subject caught the eye of Vice President Coolidge, whose three-part essay in a women's magazine, *Delineator*, focused on the role of female tertiary students in the radical movement. The influence of these women and high society hostesses sympathetic to socialism (so-called Parlor Pinks) should be particularly feared, Coolidge argued, because they could "drive home the pernicious propaganda of Bolshevism in circles where the I.W.W. type" could not enter.[30]

If proponents of social welfare could win neither the heart nor the head of a patriotic American woman, their next resort, antifeminists maintained, was to appeal to her crotch. The antifeminist women's lobby drew an absolute connection between social reform and debauchery. On the eve of the European war, the National Association Opposed to Woman Suffrage proclaimed that "polygamy, free love and the disruption of the home" would be the legacies of suffrage. In the grip of the Red Scare, citizens were again told that the new existential threat extended beyond political and economic matters into gender and sexual upheaval. Widespread reports of the establishment of a Russian Commissariat of Free Love and the nationalization of women were regarded as the inevitable consequence of the Bolsheviks' abolition of private property. The American Defense Society summed up this view: "Show me a Bolshevist and I will show you a potential robber and free-lover."[31]

Accusations of free love had been wielded with great effect against reformers and nonconformists throughout American history. Such claims had helped destroy Frances Wright's Nashoba Commune in the 1820s and twenty years later had forced theologian John Humphrey Noyes to relocate his "Perfectionist" commune. "Comstockery," a national campaign for the suppression of vice in the 1870s, similarly charged feminists with advocating free love. None of these people had promoted sexual license. They disavowed private property and monogamous marriage as instruments of sinful possessiveness and championed women's right to escape exploitative marriages. Nevertheless, in Red Scare America, the fact that Alexandra Kollontai held these same views spelled trouble for any group that Red-baiters could associate with communism.[32]

The Nonpartisan League was one organization that suffered greatly from free love smears. In addition to being described as socialist, Wobbly, Bolshevik, and atheistic, the League was constantly assailed for preaching free love. One Republican front group, the Independent Voters Association of North Dakota, issued a "free love bill," claiming that it was the work of the League: scores of anxious women asked the governor if they would be required to have sexual relations with returning soldiers. The slur of free love was as politically lethal for men as it was for women. Male members of the Nonpartisan League were mocked as weaklings unsexed by uppity, loose women. A man advocated free love only if he could not control his woman or was a feckless, polygamous Bolshevist. As Hanson explained, an intrinsic link existed between a man's loyalty to a woman and his country: whereas Americanism stood "for one wife and one country," Bolshevism stood "for free love and no country."[33]

The cultural attack on Progressive feminism and other radical doctrines was motivated in significant part by economic concerns. Yet more than one contemporary observer erred in dismissing groups like the Massachusetts Public Interests League as employers' organizations. In fact, antifeminist activism involved a significant element of status anxiety. Whereas the movement was outwardly concerned by the plight of emasculated men and debauched women, it was gravely concerned, as Nielsen has observed, that the growing ranks of professional and employed women would rob its constituency of access "to positions of influence and prestige." Accordingly, antifeminists rationalized as an attack on American democracy and values "the process of early twentieth-century state formation in which the federal government took over much of the moral authority and responsibility for social welfare from middle-class white women." Thus, social welfare proposals were styled "part of a larger socialist effort to use bureaucracy to nationalize women and children." This "purposeful contamination of . . . sexual politics with the radioactive quality of class warfare" enabled the movement to associate Progressive women's causes with "un-American connotations." Yet despite deploring the activism of Progressive women, antifeminist female activists found much (unacknowledged) fulfillment and purpose in their own activism. They certainly resisted offers of affiliation with or incorporation by male-led patriotic societies. And learning from each successive battle, antifeminist female organizations wielded their electoral influence and Red-baiting propaganda with considerable skill, routing their Progressive foes.[34]

The antifeminist women's movement rediscovered its mission opposing the Sheppard-Towner Maternity and Infancy Protection Act of 1921. A bipartisan initiative that sought to reduce America's high infant and maternal mortality rates, the act nonetheless had modest aims and scope. It provided $7.5 million in national funding over a six-year period, allocating the bulk of the money on population- and fund-matching bases. The scheme had miniscule administrative costs, and assistance was not forced on states, which were required to pass enabling legislation and were free, along with individuals, to reject aid. Yet Sheppard-Towner set off a firestorm of indignant reaction. While much of this reaction emanated from the American Medical Association, states' rights advocates decried the act's alleged Bolshevik origins and persuaded antifeminist and patriotic lobbies to do much of the arguing.

The American Medical Association opposed Sheppard-Towner as an insidious form of "state medicine." The association sought to maintain absolute control over the provision of medical services and total community adherence to a fee-for-service delivery model. Adapting the National Association Opposed to Woman Suffrage's strategy, the American Medical Association described Washington, D.C., as "a hotbed of Bolshevism." Sheppard-Towner and similar bills proposing the establishment of federal departments related to health and education, providing money for rural sanitation, and promoting physical education were condemned as elements of an "imported socialist scheme" that would ruin America. Like the antifeminist movement, the American Medical Association held Progressive women's groups chiefly responsible for its failure to prevent the passage of Sheppard-Towner. States' rights opposition to Sheppard-Towner was opportunistic. Those states that refused to pass enabling legislation accepted federal funds to build airplanes and roads, conduct soil surveys, eradicate arboreal disease, and finance (strikebreaking) state militia while insisting that Sheppard-Towner violated the Tenth Amendment.[35]

Important as the American Medical Association's opposition was, the most effective opposition to Sheppard-Towner was orchestrated by male and female patriotic societies backed by big business, which popularized the view that social welfare was Bolshevistic. Just as the National Association Opposed to Woman Suffrage had denounced the suffrage amendment first as a pro-German and then as a Bolshevik-feminist plot, the Woman Patriots insisted that Sheppard-Towner had been "masked as 'welfare' and 'women's' measures" by "certain women's organizations" that had been "entrusted to engineer" the adoption of "straight

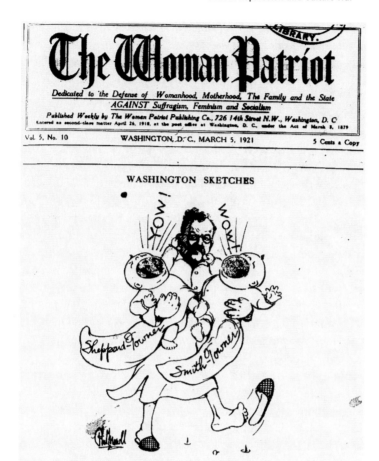

FIGURE 12. Representative Horace Mann Towner and his two "babies," bills to establish a federal department of education and federal funding for maternal and child health, reprinted on the cover of the *Woman Patriot*, March 1921. (Gerritsen Collection of Women's History, State Library of Victoria)

imported communism" (figure 12). For good measure, the Patriots called for the dissolution of the Children's Bureau, alleging that it, too, was "socialistic, dangerously bureaucratic, and largely staffed by subversive and childless women."[36]

Opposition to Sheppard-Towner reinvigorated the antifeminist women's lobby and cemented its relations with the Anticommunist Spider Web. The subsequent crusade to prevent ratification of the child labor amendment transformed the lobby into a powerful national political force. Like Sheppard-Towner, the 1924 amendment was born out of long-standing frustration with inadequate local and state labor regulation and an obstructive US Supreme Court. According to the 1920 census, 4.5 million school-age children received no formal education, and more than a million of them aged ten to fifteen were known to be employed in agricultural operations; textile, iron, and steel mills; clothing and shoe factories; and coal mines. In the South, about 20 percent of youths were employed; Rhode Island's textile industry elevated the state's percentage to near 15. Workplace injury was rife, especially in machine shops. In 1919–20, on-the-job accidents killed 38 children and disabled 920 for life in just three states. Nine states had no minimum age limit for factory and store work. Twenty-three states with a minimum employment age of fourteen weakened these laws with exemptions. Thirty-five states permitted children to work without obtaining a common-school education. Nineteen states did not make physical fitness for work a condition of employment; eleven permitted children younger than sixteen to work between nine and eleven hours per day. One state did not regulate daily hours for child laborers; four more allowed children to work at night. Thus, the many advocates of child labor regulation saw an obvious and palpable need for a constitutional amendment as a last resort. Congress agreed. A bipartisan proposal sailed through both houses by massive majorities, albeit with tepid presidential support. Supporters hoped that three-quarters of the states would quickly ratify what would become the Twentieth Amendment.[37]

Yet it was not to be. After four states ratified the proposal, it ran aground in a disastrous referendum result in Massachusetts. This defeat resulted from numerous causes. The scope of the amendment was overly ambitious, more stringent than all existing state regulation. It was clumsily framed, substituting the ambiguous word *labor* for the more obviously extrafamilial *employment*, allowing opponents to assert that the amendment eroded parental authority. The absence of a powerful coalition of labor and welfare organizations also deprived the amendment of the coordinated and broad support it required. The trade union movement was weak, and opponents easily characterized amendment supporters as "organized minorities," wielding undue influence through "lobbying and intimidation." The fact that the amendment's highest-profile supporters included the inaugural and current director of the Children's Bureau, both of whom were unmarried, and Florence Kelley was also problematic. Kelley was a particular liability. The most prominent individual in the Spider Web Chart, she was a settlement house worker, a factory inspector, an acquaintance of Friedrich Engels (and had even translated some of his work), and an instructor at the Rand

School. Perhaps worst of all, Kelley was a divorcée with a Slavic married name (Wischnewetsky) that allowed opponents to further associate her with radicalism. The ease with which amendment opponents associated this feminist trio and the proposal with Bolshevism proved decisive first in Massachusetts and subsequently across the nation.[38]

Massachusetts had seemed a fertile field for child labor regulation. Yet while the state legislature and the governor supported the amendment, the Catholic Church, the National Association of Manufacturers, and a host of Spider Web organizations led by the Massachusetts Public Interests League did not. The Massachusetts Public Interests League, the Woman Patriots, the Sentinels of the Republic, and the Constitutional Liberty League shared interlocking directorates, and Margaret Robinson's home was the mail center of the Citizens Committee to Protect Our Homes and Children, the "Paddy-Brahmin united front" that Harvard's President Lowell formed with Catholic leaders to coordinate opposition to the amendment.[39]

The committee was better financed and coordinated than its Progressive rivals. With support from industry, its campaign budget was more than five times the size of the funding enjoyed by the amendment's proponents. The Citizens Committee was also supported by government and national security officials. Delaware senator Thomas F. Bayard Jr. inserted whatever material the committee supplied into the *Congressional Record*, while the Department of War and the US Army's Military Intelligence Division continually referred interested citizens to the committee for information on the amendment and its Soviet origins. The committee's other important supporters included southern textile interests. Having helped to overturn previous federal child labor laws, they now created the Farmers' States Rights League, which influenced the American Farm Bureau Federation and the Grange to oppose the amendment. Southern farmers were anxious to avoid losing their competitive advantage in a national labor regulatory scheme: workers under sixteen years of age generally earned between a quarter and half of an adult woman's wage. As more than 60 percent of the nation's child laborers worked in agriculture, the farm lobby joined with the National Association of Manufacturers in arguing that the definition of *labor* and the expanded age of "childhood" would prohibit all children from contributing to their families' economic welfare. Coupled with a Children's Bureau pamphlet advocating "compulsory registration of pregnancy," the antiamendment lobby's arguments influenced many Massachusetts citizens, who voted down the amendment by a majority of three to one. National momentum for the amendment collapsed. By early 1925, only four of the sixteen state legislatures that considered the amendment ratified it, and opponents of child labor regulation had won a massive victory. The United States did not meaningfully regulate child labor until Congress passed the Fair Labor Standards Act of 1938, which the employers' lobby denounced as "a step in the direction of communism, bolshevism and Nazism."[40]

The irony that opposition to the amendment was led by upper-middle-class and industrial interests whose families did not depend on child labor apparently was lost on many voters. Of the hundreds of organizations described by the *Woman Patriot* as opponents of the amendment, not one represented a workers' or bona fide children's welfare organization. Yet the portrayal of the amendment as licensing children to shirk their chores around the home surprised and out-maneuvered proponents. Supporters of change also had no retort to opponents' association of the measure with creeping federal power. As F. Dumont Smith of the Citizenship Committee of the American Bar Association declared, opponents of the amendment succeeded in associating it with "the greatest danger" to the United States, which came "not from below but from above [and] not from the Reds and Anarchists but *from the Bureaucrats.*" Bureaucracy could be regarded as the "most odious of all tyrannies," the committee argued, "because it is anonymous." The Woman Patriots' conclusion that proponents' intentions were irrelevant consequently resonated with voters. The results of the amendment, the Patriots insisted, would hurt America "just as much as if Moscow" had designed and financed the reform because anonymous tyrants in Washington, D.C., would decide what work was fit for every child in the United States.[41]

The amendment's defeat had much larger significance. After this setback, Nielsen has written, "progressive-minded women were [put] on the defensive . . . the pace of legislation for working women slowed to a crawl or retreated, and the Sheppard-Towner Act was repealed and lapsed in 1929." Numerous leaders of the Progressive women's movement understood that the attack on the amendment had been a stalking horse for an assault on the entire cause of feminist reform. They had passed into an era when almost no women's group could be conservative and respectable enough to escape censure for treachery and poor morals. Anna Garlin Spencer of the National Council of Women had no doubt that "powers of evil [feared] a United Womanhood, organized for definite social progress, and [wished] to destroy the unity" of the Progressive women's movement. That unity broke down under assault from big business and the Anticommunist Spider Web. The Women's Joint Congressional Committee was forced to combat budget cuts for the Women's and Children's Bureaus. Adverse commentary from Amos Fries helped to force the Women's International League for Peace and Freedom out of the National Council of Women, while the General Federation of Women's Clubs, having lost conservative branches of its own, withdrew from the National Council for the Prevention of War. Several women's organizations began to enforce blacklists on their membership and guest speakers. The Daughters of the American Revolution had by far the most extensive and rigorously enforced blacklist, which featured six categories, including "labor organizations," "organizations interlocking with radical groups," and "workers schools and colleges," that covered more than three hundred organizations and two hundred individuals. These lists were compiled from information received from leading Spider Web members, among them Marvin, the Industrial Defense Association, the Better America Federation, and the Massachusetts Public Interests League. Moreover, according to Nielsen, feminism revealed an inability on the part of "antiradicals and Red Scare antifeminists to imagine women belonging, not to men or to the state, but to themselves." From the belief that "patriarchy and patriarchal thinking" were essential to "a sound state" came a defeat for Progressive feminism as crushing as the earlier defeat of organized and radical labor. The feminization of the American conservative movement, particularly in the leadership of the Christian Right, and the undermining of "the female citizen as an autonomous political actor" thus emerged as long-standing legacies of the Spider Web's cultural war.[42]

Veneration of the Constitution

Another important if less permanent legacy of the defeat of the child labor amendment was the impetus it gave to a nascent movement whose goal was to fix in stone the US Constitution. This movement found expression in an amendment designed to make constitutional change virtually impossible. The proposal had the support of several Spider Web organizations: the American Constitutional League, the American Defense Society, the American Legion, the Constitutional Liberty League, the Massachusetts Public Interests League, the National Association of Manufacturers, and the Woman Patriots, among others. Although the amendment did not garner enough support to pass Congress, its proponents were among those who worked hardest for the repeal of Prohibition.[43]

A longer-lasting expression of constitutional conservatism that began at this time was that of "originalism." During Woodrow Wilson's presidency, the Constitution had been revised four times—more than 20 percent of all the amendments passed since 1791. In 1913, Wilson stated that Progressives sought the freedom "to interpret the Constitution according to the Darwinian principle; all they ask is a recognition of the fact that a nation is a living thing." But within a few years, war and the threat of communism diminished the allure of constitutional reform and heightened the appeal of its patriotic perfection. Only in response to Red October was the Constitution quite literally dusted off to assume its new role as a rallying point for conservatives. In 1919, the recently formed National Association for Constitutional Government published fifty thousand copies of a pocket edition of the Constitution, frequently distributing it with a complementary pamphlet investigating the influence of socialists in American colleges. In 1921, when President Harding called the Constitution divinely inspired, he ordered the librarian of Congress to take the aged parchment out of storage and placed on display. Soon, the National Security League was distributing free copies of books written by James Montgomery Beck, Harding's solicitor general, warning that the Constitution now stood "in graver danger . . . than at any other time in the history of America." By 1923, twenty-three states had mandated constitutional instruction in schools; in 1931, this number had risen to forty-three. Much of this instruction reinforced Red Scare norms. A 1929 study, for example, found that around three-quarters of high school students believed that an American citizen should be prohibited from saying whatever they pleased even when they were neither committing nor urging actual acts of violence. During the New Deal, debate over the status of the Constitution intensified to the point where Thurman Arnold, later an assistant US attorney general, commented, "Hopeful people today wave the flag. Timid people wave the Constitution . . . the only bulwark against change." The interwar years saw the establishment of the restricted terms that even now define constitutional debate.[44]

The Restriction of Economic Liberty

If the defeat of the child labor amendment was a triumph for constitutional originalists and opponents of Bolshevik social reform, it also presaged the 1930s defeat of important labor rights and other social welfare initiatives by economic and political interests that used the charge of communism to obstruct the introduction of a national minimum wage and restrictions on the violent suppression of labor unions.

When the Roosevelt administration assumed office in 1933, it carried a mandate to take unprecedented action to help relieve the distress of millions of destitute Americans. The more liberal members of the administration and of Congress regarded the civil liberties of citizens as inseparable from prevailing "economic conflicts of interest," as Senator Robert La Follette Jr. put it. For committed New Dealers, the protection of civil liberty required new instruments such as the National Industrial Recovery Act's fair-practice codes that set wages and prices. Yet from the outset and with increasing success after Roosevelt won reelection in 1936, both Republicans and Democrats from both the North and especially the South formed what was later described as the "conservative coalition" and obstructed social and industrial reform. The members of this coalition sought to protect the prerogatives of their business constituents and to counter the New Deal's growing threat to southern racial order. In addition, to protect the economic privileges and social power of employers and of white Americans in general, they invoked the specter of communism to limit the scope of national labor standards and the organizing rights of workers.[45]

President Roosevelt's signature of the 1935 National Labor Relations Act marked the first time that federal law unambiguously recognized the right of workers to organize. Nevertheless, this right was often honored in the breach. Federal power to regulate the labor market was weakened by the exclusion of domestic and agricultural workers from the provisions of the National Industrial Recovery Act, primarily at the insistence of southern legislators determined to exclude southern blacks from federally mandated minimum-wage and maximum-hours standards. The definition of agricultural work was also broadened to include "industries related to it, such as canning . . . citrus packing and cotton ginning . . . which were low-paid and had many black employees." Even within industries that were covered by the act, wage codes recognized "differentials, with lower minimum wages authorized for southern workers." An industry could also be classified as southern if most of the workers in that industry in a given state were African American. For example, "fertilizer production in Delaware, where nine out of ten workers were black, was assigned a southern code, while workplaces in that state were coded as northern when their workers were overwhelmingly white."[46]

In addition, the administration's principal instrument of industrial arbitration, the National Labor Relations Board, was almost strangled at birth by roughly eighty injunction proceedings brought by employers challenging the board's jurisdiction. Employers had been encouraged in this endeavor by the recently formed business lobby, the American Liberty League. Unlike the issue of differential pay for African Americans, big business's interference with worker organization soon roused concern in Congress, and in March 1936, the Senate Committee on Education and Labor was authorized to investigate "violations of the rights of free speech and assembly and undue interference with the right of labor to organize and bargain collectively." A subcommittee was formed under the leadership of Robert La Follette Jr. to determine the "full extent to which the rights of labor to organize [were] being denied and the extent to which civil liberties [were] being interfered with." According to La Follette, these aspects of the investigation were inseparable. In his and fellow reformers' minds, "the most spectacular violations of civil liberty [had] their roots in economic conflicts of interest," and employer frustration of collective bargaining and association had "a fundamental bearing upon the economic, social, and political welfare of the people." According to the committee, the right to associate and organize as workers was "simply the result of the exercise of the fundamental rights of free speech and assembly."[47]

The La Follette Committee focused its investigations on four antiunion practices that had long impeded labor organization: industrial espionage, industrial armories, strikebreaking, and the employment of corporate police. The committee initially exposed the widespread use of industrial espionage and lethal violence in the steel, auto, and mining industries, functioning "simultaneously as protector of the Bill of Rights, instrument of government labor policy, and adjunct to a militant labor crusade." However, business responded swiftly to the bad publicity the committee created, abandoning the use of strikebreakers and detectives (tossing aside men such as Jacob Spolansky) in favor of sophisticated public relations campaigns to organize community sentiment against labor organization. A new generation of "citizens' committees of professional and business people flooded the channels of communication," denouncing "mob rule" by outsiders and communists. This sophisticated opposition soon rendered the La Follette Committee impotent, changing it "almost imperceptibly, from participant to observer," as it, "like the New Deal itself," "fell victim to the narrowing of possibilities which circumscribed the Roosevelt administration within a year after the 1936 electoral landslide."[48]

The La Follette Committee soon found not only that it had been neutered but that it had a new enemy alleging that the committee's "origins, composition, and direction evidence[d] affinity for communism." This enemy was the House Un-American Activities Committee (HUAC), formed on the initiative of Vice President John Nance Garner and placed in the charge of his fellow Texas Democrat Martin Dies Jr. Commencing hearings the day after the La Follette Committee concluded its investigation of "oppressive labor practices," the Dies Committee smothered every initiative the La Follette Committee sponsored. The conservative coalition rallied behind the Dies Committee to destroy the La Follette Committee and its final piece of work, the Oppressive Labor Practices Bill. Reaching the Senate floor in the spring of 1940, the bill was transformed by both southern Democrats and northern Republicans into a national security measure. Stoking fears of Nazi and communist "Trojan horses" and "fifth columns," La Follette's junior partner from Wisconsin, Alexander Wiley, insisted that employers retain the right to interrogate employees about their political beliefs, while Robert Taft "conjured up a picture of [invading] German troops" and a vulnerable America where employers would not be able to arm themselves to repulse them. Democrat Robert R. Reynolds of North Carolina amended the measure to stipulate that no more than 10 percent of a company's workforce could comprise aliens and that communists or Nazi Bund members could not be employed. The bill ultimately died in committee and with it, in Jerold S. Auerbach's view, "the La Follette Committee's final effort to aid the American worker."[49]

While the neutering of the La Follette Committee in some respects represented a typical action in defense of big business, the threat that the committee's activity posed to the preferred racial order of a majority of members of Congress was also significant. Each element of the Roosevelt administration's broad labor rights program—the La Follette Committee, the National Labor Relations Act, and after 1938 the Fair Labor Standards Act—caused southerners in particular to pay "ever more attention to the impact labor organizing might have in the region." The resulting schism in the Democratic Party became steadily "more visible as southerners began to mount a furious campaign" to undermine the administration's labor rights framework. The Fair Labor Standards Act had been watered down by the creation of differentiated minimum-wage rates set by industry boards that could consider "competitive conditions" to protect the South's advantageously low wage rates. This advantage, southern politicians made clear, depended on a race-based division of wages and labor rights. As Representative James Wilcox, a Florida Democrat, put it, "there has always been a difference in the wage scale of white and colored labor." Since the federal government was prohibited from making "any distinction between the races," Wilcox argued that investing "a federal bureau or board [with] the power to fix wages, of necessity [would] prescribe the same wage for the Negro that it prescribes for the white man." Such a prescription, he warned, "just [would] not work in the South." It was not possible to "put the Negro and the white man on the same basis and get away with it." Without differentiated wage codes, Wilcox insisted, the fair labor bill, like an antilynching bill, would be "another political goldbrick for the Negro."[50]

Soon after the weakened Fair Labor Standards Act passed, Virginia Democrat Howard Smith became chair of a House special committee to investigate the National Labor Relations Board. Operating until 1940 (when the Oppressive Labor Standards Bill was aborted), the committee built "opposition to the labor board and [framed] legislation to scale back recent union gains," deploying, what Ira Katznelson has described as "tropes that almost immediately came to dominate the southern orientation to labor in Congress and beyond. Their themes, which became common during and just after World War II, included accusations of a government bias favoring the Congress of Industrial Organizations and its anti–Jim Crow racial agenda, subversion by Communists, and a growing class bias against business and for labor." The committee's success in passing a range of amendments to the National Labor Relations Act that significantly curtailed the board's independence and capacity was aided by Smith's claims that the board was "honeycombed with employees who do not even believe in our system of private ownership of property, upon which our whole industry is based." Such rhetoric effectively began the Cold War practice of accusing federal employees with pro-labor or Progressive sympathies of being communists.[51]

The Federal Theatre Project

While the dilution of the New Deal's labor program was the main order of business for Congress and industry, anticommunists were sensitive to the importance of stamping out social and cultural manifestations of communism, especially if they also happened to subvert America's racial order. HUAC's swift destruction of the Roosevelt administration's Federal Theatre Project (FTP) demonstrates the conservative coalition's determination to use the issue of communism to roll back any Progressive advances in racial and economic equality through cultural forms. And the coalition's success in pursuing this aim paved the way for Cold War assaults on Hollywood and the arts.

The FTP was one branch of the Works Progress Administration's employment program for artists. The agency's Federal One Division employed writers, painters, musicians, and actors and directors in four separate departments. While conservatives were appalled to see public funds supporting all such activity, the FTP attracted singular opposition for several reasons. Some opposition was created by the influence of communists in the theater, but it was also aroused by the inherently subversive character of theater itself.

Communist Party members and supporters played a leading role in the New York Federal Theatre and influenced productions that addressed social issues. Historian Susan Quinn has estimated that these productions comprised about 10 percent of the FTP's total output. Communists also made trouble for the FTP by turning out publicity material, organizing picket lines to oppose staff and budget cuts, and introducing the character of CP leader Earl Browder into one particularly notorious play. Yet this influence was hardly revolutionary. Rather, it was consonant, Quinn has argued, with "the larger intellectual community." In the mid-1930s, when capitalism's reputation and survival were in dispute, communism appealed to an unprecedented number of Americans as an alternative to fascism in Europe and racism and crony capitalism at home. The CP had further broadened its appeal by joining the Popular Front. Hence longtime *New York Times* theater critic John Gassner noted that for many artists at the time, "Marxist theory was just one more attractive piece of driftwood in the current of fashionable intellectualism, along with amateur Freudianism, and hazy, antibourgeois romanticism."[52]

This artistic and cultural ferment partly explains conservative opposition to the FTP. But conservatives were also unsettled by the particular processes by which theater is made and the unique effects it can have on audiences. Performance study theory describes the ways in which theater transports audiences into a virtual, timeless reality in which they can reassess the validity of social norms and values. Richard Schechner and Emmanuel Le Roy Ladurie compare this "liminal" state to a public carnival, where people vicariously experience the breach, exaggeration, and inversion of social conventions and "satisfy desires" and "enact social relations" that are unacceptable in the real world. At the conclusion of a stage performance, the liminal state ends, and spectators are invited to find resolutions to problems posed in the production. This description of the impact of theater seems particularly relevant to the work of the FTP, which according to its director, Hallie Flanagan, "was educating the people of its vast new audience to know more about government and politics and such vital issues of the day as housing, power, agriculture and labor."[53]

Even before coming into HUAC's sights, the FTP had come under intense attack from the Hearst press. William Randolph Hearst, a pioneer of yellow journalism (and described by some historians as a bona fide fascist), saw the FTP as a useful means of attacking the Roosevelt administration for what he regarded as its lax defense against communist infiltration. Accordingly, Hearst paid FTP employees large sums of money to leak him theater scripts. He also bribed Flanagan's personal secretary and persuaded her to sign an affidavit stating that Flanagan's mail was "incendiary, revolutionary and seditious." This information fed such Hearst-paper headlines as "U.S. Contributes to Reds through Theatre Project."[54]

Approving Hearst's battle with the theater, HUAC member J. Parnell Thomas announced his intention to conduct a "sweeping investigation" into the FTP's political behavior. Citing "startling evidence," Thomas alleged that the FTP was "a branch of the communistic organization" as well as "one more link in the vast and unparalleled New Deal propaganda machine." Promising a "thorough cleaning" of the theater, the committee called numerous material and immaterial witnesses. Flanagan's secretary testified that Flanagan was either a CP member or a sympathizer, ensuring that FTP plays promoted communism, and that the theater employed only communists. The secretary's husband testified that communist propaganda was sold at theatrical performances and in rehearsal to raise funds for loyalist Spain. AFL president John L. Frey gave testimony of more peripheral relevance, averring that the labor movement had been communist-free before the formation of the Congress of Industrial Organizations. He also outed nearly three hundred alleged communist organizers in the union movement. The most inflammatory evidence the committee received, however, came from stage managers and actors employed in the FTP, who informed Congress that the theater was promoting interracial fraternization both on and off the stage. The "star witness on race mixing," according to Quinn, was Sally Saunders, "a dainty blonde of Viennese origin" who advised the committee that a black fellow cast member had invited her on a date and that theater staff had mocked her outraged response to this assault on her racial dignity. The media seized on the story, publishing many images depicting Saunders as an Aryan goddess alongside headlines reading, "Reds Urged 'Mixed' Date, Blonde Tells Probers." The committee regarded race mixing and communism "as two sides of the same coin." The committee also regarded the success of African American production units and the racial integration the project engendered among both performers and audiences as signs of communist infiltration. Quinn has argued that for the members of HUAC as well as for several people who testified before it, "the racial policies of the FTP struck a deeper note of alarm than the alleged Communist infiltration," particularly after some black ex-CP members employed by the Works Progress Administration testified that they had been sent to Moscow with dozens of other American communists to study urban guerrilla fighting. Congress thus confirmed the Lusk Committee's prophetic warning of communist-inspired "Negro" revolution.[55]

The committee called for the immediate abolition of the FTP, with Reynolds adding the stock charge of promoting free love to the list of the theater's sins. Congress cut the project's funding, and President Roosevelt declined to veto the cuts. On 30 June 1939, after four "febrile" years, the FTP closed its doors. It had been found guilty of underwriting Red revolution "at the expense," as Reynolds put it, "of the god-fearing, home-loving American taxpayer." FTP employees and much of the theater world bitterly resented the closure. Producer and writer Lee Simonson spoke for many when he declared, "The common peepul that the same Congressmen bray their devotion to, were seeing and enjoying theater for the first time at prices they could afford. So the benighted bastards had to deprive them of it." In the end, any and all arguments supporting the FTP were trumped by conservative horror at Saunders's story. Dies had promised that his committee would not "look under every bed for a Communist," and in a sense he was true to his word. The HUAC did not look under every bed—but it did find communists in every theater and performance associated with the FTP. And it was interested in prescribing only one remedy. Some contemporaries may have judged Dies the most "cynical" member of Congress, but with regard to white Americans' fundamental right to resist dastardly communist plans to promote racial equality and miscegenation, he had no capacity for cynicism or indolence. Such facets of Dies's character impressed John Trevor and other old Spider Web members, who did all they could to aid him in his anticommunist (and eugenic) crusades.[56]

CHAPTER 10

Anticommunism and Political Terror

Do not look for evidence as proof that the accused has acted or spoken against the [state]. First you must ask him to what class he belongs, what his social origin is, his education and profession. These are the questions that must determine the fate of the accused.

—Martyn Ivanovich Latsis

Although the comparison may be somewhat uncomfortable, several incidents of political terror that occurred in the United States after the Great War were grounded in the same attitudes as those prevailing in revolutionary Russia. These attitudes, characterized by a determination to eradicate unorthodox and heretical political ideas, were expressed in definitions of deviance that emphasized political beliefs rather than criminal actions. They were also expressed in the prosecution of leaders of revolutionary and nonconformist organizations. Above all, they were expressed in the interminable incarceration and even execution of symbolic scapegoats. The purpose of such activity was avowedly political: to intimidate and prevent people from supporting certain ideas and organizations by destroying the lives of a select few. And while the incarceration, deportation, and execution of these unfortunate souls called into question America's professed notions of justice, the need to set an example overrode all other considerations. Such is the nature of political terror.

The political nature of this terror was made apparent not just by the identity of its victims but also by the identity of those orchestrating their punishment. The former were invariably members of anarchist, anarcho-syndicalist, social-ist, and communist organizations or of industrial unions. Some had run afoul of draconian wartime restrictions on free speech. Others dared to speak up in defense of the rights of such people. The orchestrators of punishment were often powerful businessmen eager to stamp out labor organization and radicalism or public officials eager to expunge opposition to political and economic order. The use of political terror in the interwar period thus represented another weapon in the industrial campaign waged by proponents of the open shop and laissez-faire. But the use of political terror came at great cost. It created significant social tension and psychological turmoil for numerous individuals involved in or disturbed by the process, and it contributed to an environment of moral and ethical difficulty. Yet for a significant number of Americans, the gulf between the nation's ostensible ideals and its political reality aroused a primitive and defensive insularity that was released through repression rather than expiation.

Persecution of Political Prisoners

As soon as America's war effort concluded, calls for amnesty for political prisoners were issued, particularly for conscientious objectors. By early 1919, amnesty committees had been formed in many cities. They called for the release of political prisoners and the immediate repeal of restrictions on free speech and assembly. But the federal government was headed by hard-hearted men. Secretary of War Newton D. Baker turned down all such requests. Outgoing attorney general Thomas Watt Gregory maintained that America had no political prisoners: because its jails held no inmates incarcerated for "the expression of their views on social, economic or political questions," no general amnesty could be granted. There was no cause in whose name such an action could proceed. And Woodrow Wilson, whom Walter Karp has described as a "terrible ruin of a man," remained implacably opposed to the release of anyone who had dared to question his rule. Having "pity only for himself," the president refused even on his last day in office to pardon Eugene Debs, "rotting away his life in a federal penitentiary."[1]

The last conscientious objector was released from jail on 27 November 1920, but prisoners locked up for violating the Espionage and Sedition Acts remained trapped in Kafkaesque limbo. The administration wanted to deport all unnaturalized violators of these acts yet could not do so as a consequence of its reluctance to review the convictions or release from captivity such persons. The head of the Justice Department's War Emergency Division, John Lord O'Brian, reduced some sentences and commuted others to time already served but was prevented from reviewing any cases pertaining to Wobblies because they had been prosecuted by a special section of the department. Alien Wobblies soon came to believe that deportation represented the only path out of indefinite detention. Dozens of them agreed to be expelled in exchange for a group amnesty or commutation within a reasonable time frame, but the Pardon Office insisted that they serve full terms of imprisonment.[2]

Wilson's departure from the White House occasioned moderate changes in the treatment of the 475 or so prisoners convicted under federal espionage and sedition statutes. Just before Christmas 1921, President Warren G. Harding released Debs, hoping to defuse the political issue. The tactic worked, causing the AFL, hitherto a significant supporter of the amnesty drive, immediately to cease its campaign. True to its sectarian form, the AFL declined to speak up for imprisoned Wobblies.[3]

Around the time of Debs's release, the Harding administration offered to commute alien prisoners' sentences on condition that they submit to deportation. Some other prisoners who had served five years were freed in early 1922. However, the Bureau of Immigration immediately arrested aliens who had not agreed to be deported or to recant their beliefs. A District Court judge dismissed writs for habeas corpus pursued by the arrestees, ruling that Congress had the right to remove aliens "at any time for any reason or for no reason." District courts also rejected the argument that a conditional commutation comprised a pardon or formed grounds for blocking deportation. In addition, the US Supreme Court allowed the government discretion to find any alien unsuitable for citizenship on the basis of ex post facto legislation and wartime convictions. The Court subsequently tempered this discretion by ruling that the government could not denaturalize political convicts who had become citizens well before joining subversive organizations, thereby invalidating claims that citizenship had been obtained under false pretenses. Calvin Coolidge, like his predecessor, tended to grant presidential pardons only for prisoners who renounced all their radical beliefs and political activity. The Bureau of Immigration and the courts supported this stance by determining that membership in the Industrial Workers of the World (IWW) and citizenship were incompatible: the Republican administrations of the Jazz Age granted citizenship to no alien Wobblies. The hard-line pardon attorney in all these administrations, James A. Finch, was reluctant to recommend a pardon for any radical convict lest such measures "encourage" radicals. According to the American Civil Liberties Union (ACLU), every president from Wilson through Herbert Hoover had "little knowledge of the cases . . . and in a general way [reflected] all the current newspaper prejudices." All of these men were discouraged from exercising clemency by the hue and cry that erupted among the mainstream press and the patriot lobby, every time the release of a prisoner was merely contemplated.[4]

Deportees' suffering did not end with expulsion, for the government had difficulty removing them to such countries as Russia, Armenia, Turkey, the Ukraine, and Austria. Yet the Bureau of Immigration persisted in attempting to deport aliens to these countries. One Ukrainian man was deported and then returned to the United States three times. On each occasion he was provided with false papers issued by the "Ukrainian Diplomatic Mission," an entity dreamed up by the bureau. The bureau did not cease trying to deport political convicts to their homelands until 1932, after the policy had brought many refugees into mortal danger. Further, only in 1932 did alien political refugees finally receive the right to seek asylum in the USSR. Throughout the 1920s and into the 1930s, immigration authorities were accustomed to using material that was seized, often illegally, through raids and the mail to justify deportation procedures on political grounds. Moreover, officials commonly justified the removal of aliens via charges of dubious relevance.[5] The Bureau of Immigration periodically embarked on deportation drives against political targets, usually at the behest of employer lobbies such as the Better America Federation. In 1931, when a departmental scheme for the compulsory registration of aliens failed to pass Congress for a second time, mass raids were belatedly undertaken in its stead. Whenever deportation was infeasible, the bureau became obstructive, refusing to cancel deportation orders or bail bonds. The net effect of these policies was the callous, needless destruction of families and the creation of welfare dependency. A small group of alien Wobblies who for various reasons could not be deported remained in limbo, not deported but still facing active deportation warrants. Placed on a political behavior bond, they remained trapped in "the twilight zone of a suspended sentence," always subject to rearrest or expulsion if they again transgressed. The use of deportation threats by employers in labor disputes and raids on alien quarters were not outlawed until the summer of 1933–34. The Bureau of Immigration's Secret Service was then abolished and government's right to fingerprint aliens revoked.[6]

A spirit of vengeance extended not just to the treatment of violators of federal statutes but also to individuals and organizations who dared to offer prisoners the assistance to which they were legally entitled. Three men in Syracuse, New York, published a leaflet describing the horrific treatment some prisoners were receiving. They attempted to hold a public meeting on the issue but were arrested and charged with violating the Espionage Act and using disloyal and scurrilous language. Although the war had been over for nearly fourteen months, they were sentenced to eighteen months in jail. Prison sentences were cause for concern: between the enactment of the espionage statute and 1931, more than thirty men imprisoned for opposition to the war or radical activity died, many from criminal negligence and not a few in unexplained, suspicious circumstances.[7]

Activists working on behalf of other causes and victims also suffered. J. Edgar Hoover threatened the livelihoods of at least two of the authors of the National Popular Government League's May 1920 *Report upon the Illegal Practices of the U.S.*

Department of Justice. The head of the General Intelligence Division doubted the loyalty of Harvard law professors Felix Frankfurter and Zechariah Chafee Jr. and connived with Harvard officials to attempt to secure Chafee's dismissal. The Washington State Supreme Court disbarred a lawyer who represented the Centralia Wobblies in 1925 on the grounds that his public speeches had advocated IWW principles; five years elapsed before he was readmitted to practice.[8]

The pursuit of political outcomes through judicial activism was also evident in the selective prosecution of the leaders of civil liberties and political associations. A silk workers' strike in Paterson, New Jersey, was transformed from a routine labor battle by the criminal prosecution of ACLU head Roger Baldwin. During the winter of 1924–25, police closed workers' strike meetings as well as a subsequent protest meeting at which five hundred protesters were also physically attacked. Eleven people were charged with spurious offenses, and although most of these charges were dismissed, defendants were fined twenty-five thousand dollars for disorderly conduct and indicted for unlawful assembly, an English common law charge disused since 1796. The cases were tried in the Court of Common Pleas, in the absence of a jury and stenographer. After withholding a verdict for three and a half months, the trial judge found all defendants guilty without rendering an opinion on relevant law or the specific facts of the case. However, only Baldwin was sentenced to imprisonment, receiving six months; the other defendants received fifty-dollar fines. An advertisement for a book on birth control became the means for incarcerating another prominent radical, Carlo Tresca, a former Wobbly leader, anarchist, and publisher. At the behest of Italy's Fascist government, against whom Tresca had steadfastly campaigned, American authorities incarcerated him for four months.[9]

The treatment of violators of federal statutes and state ordinances pertaining to lawful assembly and morality constituted an important form of political terror in America. Yet the most important cases of political terror did not involve violators of the Espionage or Sedition Acts or victims of state antisedition and criminal syndicalism statutes. Rather, they involved a group of men who were either members of or were identified with anarchist, socialist, and industrial labor organizations and who were framed and incarcerated on charges of murder and conspiracy to murder. So controversial were these cases that they exposed the United States to international protest and infamy. They also divided opinion in local, state, and national communities.

Nicola Sacco and Bartolomeo Vanzetti

On 15 April 1920 in the small town of South Braintree, Massachusetts, two assassins shot dead the paymaster of a shoe company and his guard and relieved them of sixteen thousand dollars in cash. A few weeks later, Nicola Sacco and Bartolomeo Vanzetti, Italian immigrants known to be anarchists, were arrested in nearby Brockton and charged with the murders. Although serious law enforcement officials were convinced the robbery was the work of professionals and that the accused were extremely unlikely to have been involved, the US Department of Justice had long held an interest in the two men, classifying them as "radicals to be watched." Although officials wanted to deport the men, the District Court in Massachusetts had belatedly begun to apply the principles of habeas corpus in deportation proceedings, jeopardizing authorities' use of such means to rid the nation of foreign-born radicals. Accordingly, the Boston branch of the Justice Department and the district attorney decided to prosecute Sacco and Vanzetti for murder. They were ideal fall guys: radical immigrants who admitted to dodging the draft and to being atheists.[10]

From the first, the facts of the case did not support the two men's guilt. And for two men supposedly guilty of murder and theft, Sacco and Vanzetti behaved strangely in the aftermath of the shootings. They had not kept any of the stolen money, their material circumstances had not appreciably improved, they had not changed their daily movements or behavior in any way; and they had not gone into hiding, absconded, assumed false identities, or left town. Not even the prosecution alleged any of these things. However, on the day of their arrest, they had lied about their movements on the day of the murders. In addition, Sacco lied about possessing a firearm during his arrest and transportation to a police station. But those lies had nothing to do with evading capture for murder, since they had been told that they had been arrested as "suspicious characters" and questioned solely regarding their membership in radical organizations. They had no reason to believe that they had been apprehended for murder and robbery.[11]

The state manipulated evidence and judicial procedure to secure convictions of the two men. Prosecutors did not rely on witness testimony or material evidence to make their case because they had no such testimony or evidence. Numerous defense testified that the defendants had not been at the crime scene. Prosecution witnesses positively identified the men only after police lined each man up by himself. A ballistics expert later swore in an affidavit that he had intended only to confirm that a lethal bullet had come from the same make of gun as Sacco was found carrying, not that the bullet had definitely been fired from his gun, as the prosecution inferred. Jury members were selected by from Masonic meetings and the WASPy ranks of the upper middle class. The jury foreman commented prior to the trial, "Damn them, they ought to hang them anyway!" The trial judge, Webster Thayer, directed the jury to "be loyal to the government" and to "seek courage in [their] deliberations such as was typified by the American soldier as he fought and gave up his life on the battlefields of

France." Not surprisingly, Sacco and Vanzetti were found guilty and sentenced to death. Then trouble began for the State of Massachusetts.[12]

The defendants, their defense team, and large sections of the general public refused to accept the court's verdict. As soon as the sentences were handed down, Sacco and Vanzetti launched an appeal process that ultimately took the better part of seven years. As time wore on, disturbing evidence of official misconduct surfaced. Government officials swore to chicanery on the part of the Department of Justice, an allegation that was disputed neither by the department nor by the district attorney. Much incriminating correspondence between federal and state agencies had been destroyed and the state attorney general refused to release what survived. Yet all these revelations did not secure a retrial or the release of the men. Judge Thayer rejected repeated appeals and boasted in 1924 of having kept "those anarchistic bastards" incarcerated. In addition, the peculiarities of the Massachusetts justice system not only permitted but required the judge who presided over the trial to hear every subsequent application for a retrial. The state supreme court similarly had no power to inquire whether a trial record justified its verdict, a power possessed by courts elsewhere, including New York and Great Britain.[13]

The trial had enormous cultural impact. Writing in the *New Republic* in June 1927, Bruce Bliven noted that the case "occasioned a controversy of extraordinary bitterness." Not since "the slavery dispute before the Civil War" had any issue in American life "created such violent differences of opinion among persons who would ordinarily think alike." In at least two prominent Boston clubs, "members [had] been forbidden by formal rule to talk about the 'S-V affair.'" Broader public discussion was also strongly discouraged. Most Boston bookshops would not display Felix Frankfurter's *Atlantic* volume about the case, producing it only on demand. Teachers and school officials banned students from discussing the case. Attorneys and other professionals suffered professionally and financially for expressing disquiet about the verdict. Journalists convinced of the men's innocence were reassigned by editors who opposed judicial review of the trial. Newsworthy reports pertaining to the case were buried, written "with utmost brevity," or printed under innocuous headlines. Among Boston's upper crust, Bliven wrote, the desire to see the men die was "tremendously powerful"; fund-raising efforts for the Harvard and Yale Law Schools suffered as a consequence of faculty members' involvement in defense activity and criticism of the trial.[14]

As the appeal process wound down, only executive clemency could spare the men. Massachusetts governor Alvan T. Fuller was eager to have the men executed but worried about his reputation. Accordingly, he sought cover in the appointment of a review committee chaired by Harvard president Lawrence Lowell. Sensitive about recent criticism of his patriotism in connection with his membership of the National Council for the Prevention of War, Lowell and the other two committee members endorsed the proceedings, salting their report with gratuitous pronouncements on the evil of the defendants' "socialistic" and "communistic" beliefs.[15]

In addition to comparing the divisions caused by the case with the issue of antebellum slavery, Bliven suggested that only the Dreyfus scandal offered a true international parallel. Yet international condemnation of the "S-V affair" seemed only to arouse puerile and stubborn defensiveness among proponents of execution, who attempted to paint all opposition to it as the contrivance of domestic and foreign labor and communist organizations. Defenders of the guilty verdict also argued that the fundamental issue at stake involved state and national sovereignty rather than justice. Editorials and cartoons complained that American institutions were being held ransom by internationalists, and the public became outraged at the impudence of "world radicals." *Detroit Saturday Night* maintained that Sacco and Vanzetti were privileged to receive American as opposed to Russian justice, arguing that an almost-interminable period of time and deliberation separated the defendants' sentencing and their execution (figure 13).[16]

The comparison of Sacco and Vanzetti's treatment with Russian justice was revealing, though not in the intended sense. Despite the length of Sacco and Vanzetti's appeal process, their conviction and its review had been hardly less cynical than a Soviet show trial. And its outcome was precisely the same: the inhumanely conducted execution of victims targeted on the basis of their class and beliefs and killed in flagrant violation of procedural propriety. As Howard Zinn has concluded, the determination to kill Sacco and Vanzetti "was too persistently fanatical to be an oddity of Boston or Harvard, an unfortunate judicial slip [or] a prejudice of one person or another." Rather, "it is best explained by the powerful resolve of the American capitalist system after World War I to eliminate all radical threats on the eve of a new and uncertain era in world history." This "fear of opposition," according to Zinn, was ridiculously exaggerated, but "the American ruling class, with so much at stake—control of the greatest aggregate wealth in the world—[took] no chances."[17]

The Centralia Wobblies

At the height of the Red Scare, on Armistice Day 1919, violence erupted in the small town of Centralia, Washington, between local members of the IWW and the American Legion. In what became known rather hyperbolically as the Armistice Day Massacre, three legionnaires were killed while assaulting the local IWW hall during a commemorative parade, and another was killed while pursuing fleeing Wobblies. These events led to the beating, castration, and lynching

Justice in Cruel America and Lovely Russia

FIGURE 13. Sacco and Vanzetti cartoon, *Detroit Saturday Night*, 31 July 1927.
(Dorr E. Felt Papers, Loyola University, Chicago)

of Wesley Everest and the arraignment of twelve more Wobblies for murder and conspiracy to murder. Superficially, the case differed from Sacco and Vanzetti's, because the shooting of legionnaires by Wobblies was undisputed. Fundamentally, however, the Centralia Wobblies were treated just like Sacco and Vanzetti. Denied a fair trial, they were prosecuted and sentenced as class enemies, receiving unconscionably harsh jail sentences in what Alfred McCoy has described as a "war of extermination" waged by the American Legion on the IWW in the Pacific Northwest.[18]

The incident represented the climax of a campaign of vigilante repression orchestrated by powerful local businessmen against Wobblies. In the spring of 1918, Centralia's IWW hall was destroyed by a posse of hired thugs and patriots. In June 1919, a blind newsdealer who sold IWW literature was kidnapped, driven out of town, and advised to find another home. At a meeting of the Elks Club a month before the Armistice Day Massacre, employers discussed how to permanently rid the town of Wobblies. The nervous owner of the hall that the IWW had rented appealed in vain to the police for protection of her property. The local IWW secretary similarly appealed to the mayor, and an IWW attorney asked the governor for protection, also to no avail. The authorities clearly hoped that the hall would be sacked on 11 November and the Wobblies within subjected to violent assault and perhaps even killed. Immediately after the incident, the local American Legion post placed Centralia under martial law and, according to the *Centralia Daily Chronicle*, assumed "complete control of police affairs." The local Legion commander directed all investigations of the arrested Wobblies and organized manhunts for IWW members who remained at large, resulting in the death of one vigilante who was shot at close range by two colleagues who mistook him for a radical fugitive.[19]

After all of the Wobblies had been apprehended, the local county bar association resolved that none of its members would defend or aid in the defense of anyone charged in the incident. The special prosecutor who took the case, C. D. Cunningham, was the attorney for a local lumber baron whose nephew had been killed pursuing the Wobblies. Cunningham reportedly approved torturing the prisoners following their arrest, resulting in the mental breakdown of nineteen-year-old Loren Roberts. The Wobblies' attorney, George Vanderveer, was prepared to prove that Cunningham had also been present at Everest's lynching, and Everest's body had been placed in view of the prisoners for two days after his murder, mutely threatening his comrades. The Centralia Legion Post established a fund for the prosecution of the Wobblies. It received contributions from the local Citizens' Protective League and businesses. Some of the monies collected financed the transportation of large numbers of legionnaires to the courtroom in Grays Harbor County (home of Albert Johnson) where the Wobblies were eventually tried.[20]

The trial was moved to Grays Harbor because it was impossible to conduct a fair trial in the vicinity of Centralia, though the defense disputed whether Grays Harbor was far enough away. While not quite the travesty that Sacco and Vanzetti's trial had been, the Washington State proceedings were compromised by biased judicial rulings on the inadmissibility of certain evidence and the probable bias of some jurors: at least one juror reputedly stated his intention to "hang every God damned one" of the Wobblies. More important, the judge prohibited the defense from discussing the destruction of the IWW hall in 1918, the violent eviction of Wobblies from the town, and the threats issued to the new hall in the lead-up to Armistice Day. Roberts pleaded insanity but was denied a separate trial, and his confessions, though they had been extracted by force and had precipitated his breakdown, were used against him.[21]

The jury's verdict and the sentencing were as compromised as the trial proceedings. On the morning of 13 March 1920, the jury was directed to reach a verdict. By evening they had: two of the now ten men on trial were found guilty of third-degree murder (manslaughter). The court refused to accept this verdict and recalled the jury. Two hours later, the jurors found eight of the Wobblies, including Roberts, guilty of second-degree murder but acquitted two others. The verdict was patently ridiculous. The defendants had been charged with criminal conspiracy to murder, so jurors needed to find either that such a conspiracy existed or that it did not—in other words, the defendants could only be guilty of first-degree murder or innocent. But the court was determined to ensure that the majority of the defendants would see jail time and improvised a way to ensure that they were sent behind bars. Yet the verdict satisfied no one. The American Legion clamored for first-degree sentences, conceding the absurdity of second-degree findings. The defense also petitioned the state supreme court for an appeal on these grounds, but the court refused, fearing that a retrial might result in all the defendants going free. At least one of the jurors later declared that he had felt pressured to find the men guilty of something because they were Wobblies. He had sought a judgment that would spare the men the death penalty, which he feared they might receive from an even less sympathetic jury in the event of a retrial. The jurors' predicament was illustrated by their petition for leniency in sentencing. The petition was ignored, however, and each of the convicts received between twenty-five and forty years in jail. Several jurors were astonished by the sentence.[22]

Amnesty committees argued that the sentencing law had been erroneously applied, and ten years later, that argument began to find judicial and executive support. One of the Wobblies had already died in jail, but Roberts (who had been found insane but had been confined in general rather than special facilities) and five others were released on parole in the early 1930s. Ray Becker refused to accept parole, maintaining his innocence, and was not released until 1939.[23]

Though not communists, the Centralia Wobblies had been prosecuted as radicals and severely punished as a warning to all radicals on the left. Their families and supporters suffered along with them. Elmer Smith, who served as the Wobblies' assistant counsel, was disbarred for five years. One of the convicts, O. C. Bland, had a wife and dependents who were entitled to state support but never received it. The four legionnaires killed in Centralia were memorialized in the town square, while Everest was buried in a secret location beside a railroad. By the graveside of slain Lieutenant Warren O. Grimm, who had fought Reds in Siberia, the Legion's national commander, Franklin D'Olier, praised the Centralia legionnaires for having "died as heroically as though they had made the supreme sacrifice" in the European war. Yet Grimm's alleged final words were, "It served me right, I had no business being there."[24]

Tom Mooney and Warren Billings

On 22 July 1916, a huge explosion interrupted a Preparedness Parade along San Francisco's Market Street. Ten people were killed, and forty were injured. A terrified city bayed for the blood of those responsible. Authorities swiftly provided a handful of culprits. The principal suspects in the bombing were Thomas J. Mooney and Warren Knox Billings, both of whom were associated with the IWW and the Socialist Party and had previously been in trouble with the law.[25]

The trials of Mooney and Billings, like those of the Centralia Wobblies and Sacco and Vanzetti, were intrinsically marred by abuse of procedure. In fact, the San Francisco trials were arguably the most egregious. The prosecution failed to advance a convincing or material motive for the defendants' participation in the bombing. Like the Braintree killings, the event was explained, in the words of historian Richard Frost, simply as "the natural culmination of Mooney's and Billings' labor activities and anarchistic beliefs." They were also alleged to be German agents. All evidence pointing to the innocence of the suspects was ignored, including testimony of reputable witnesses suggesting that Mooney was on the roof of the building where he lived, some considerable distance from Market Street, five minutes before the explosion. The flimsy evidentiary basis for conviction was undermined by the testimony of prosecution witnesses, all of whom were exposed as perjurers or shown to be unreliable. One witness testified that although she had not seen Mooney and Billings at the scene of crime, their "astral bodies" had been revealed to her. Billings was sentenced to life imprisonment, while Mooney was sentenced to death by hanging. Both men remained imprisoned until 1939, so the case became as much a phenomenon of interwar as wartime political terror.[26]

Soon after the trials, the federal government appointed a commission of inquiry to investigate potential abuses of justice. It concluded that in Mooney and Billings's case, the district attorney was in such "constant association" with corporations against whom the defendants had agitated that he could not be "impartial or honest in the conduct of a case of this nature." The district attorney also was found to have been "cooperating with notorious jury and case fixers," to have "conspired to frame cases," and to have intimidated and blackmailed witnesses. Another prosecution witness admitted to having lied, and the prosecution's most important witness apparently tried to suborn another witness into perjuring himself during the trial. These findings helped to persuade Governor William D. Stephens to commute Mooney's sentence to life imprisonment but not to pardon either man.[27]

The circumstances of the case all but confirmed that Mooney and Billings were jailed for holding radical political opinions and associating with radical organizations. Their incarceration was arranged by the powerful corporations that employed the private detectives who assembled the prosecution's case (and that soon became strong sponsors of the Better America Federation). Yet the fact that the two men remained imprisoned for twenty-three years suggests that less tangible political and sociopsychological factors also influenced their treatment. Those who agitated for the conviction and continuing incarceration of the men in the face of overwhelming evidence of miscarriage of justice were guilty of willful denial and an attitude of expediency. Above all, they possessed an implicit desire to vent the most primitive urges of fury, vengeance, and tyranny against two representatives of a class of social undesirables. And as Mooney and Billings remained in prison into the 1930s, conflict surrounding their case became an important element in the struggle against communism in Southern California.

Supporters of the continuing confinement of Mooney and Billings advocated the perverse notion that a fuss had been made regarding their conviction only because they were Reds. One of the earliest proponents of this reasoning was former president Theodore Roosevelt, who stated in December 1917, "If Billings and Mooney were not anarchists, were not bomb throwers, were not murderers and were really entirely innocent, well behaved, law-abiding men, then the Bolsheviki people at home and abroad would be utterly indifferent to their fate."[28]

The Better America Federation also refused to accept the commission's findings. Because the investigator was the nephew of President Wilson's secretary of labor, William B. Wilson, a Progressive, the federation insisted that the commission had worked "hand in glove" with communists to save Mooney from the gallows.[29] In addition, others argued that the men should be imprisoned simply because they were Reds and that it was important to send their supporters a message about what politics the people of California would tolerate. These sentiments resonated with San Francisco's deputy district attorney, who responded to the exposure of witness perjury by fulminating, "If I knew that every single witness that testified against Mooney had perjured himself in his testimony, I wouldn't lift a finger to get him a new trial. If the thing were done that ought to be done, the whole dirty low-down bunch would be taken out and strung up without ceremony." Such rank prejudice convinced Mooney's trial judge, Franklin A. Griffin, that "the great obstacle in the way of Mooney's pardon" was "his alleged bad reputation," which was being used to justify his continuing incarceration regardless of his guilt. Such an idea, the judge reminded Governor Clement C. Young in 1927, was "more dangerous and pernicious than any Mooney [had] been accused of preaching."[30]

Griffin's counsel fell on deaf ears. Young's successor, James Rolph Jr., like Massachusetts's Fuller, sought to evade responsibility for freeing Mooney and Billings by establishing a special panel to review the case. It was headed by Matt Sullivan, a Progressive Democrat and lawyer from San Francisco who had briefly served as the state's chief justice. Sullivan's report used circular reasoning in finding that Mooney was guilty because he had been convicted. Dismissing the importance of perjured evidence and ignoring the posttrial recantations of other witnesses, Sullivan focused more on what Mooney had written in radical publications than on any material evidence. Mooney's attorney accused Sullivan of "permitting his prejudices to rule his judgment," keeping "an innocent man in prison from hatred of his labor views and activities." A number of eminent citizens agreed and signed an open letter to this effect. But Sullivan dismissed this

criticism, describing the signers as "parlor Bolsheviks, accommodating publicity seekers, intellectual irresponsibles and tricky special pleaders." Their "pro-
Mooney propaganda," he added, had been "liberally financed by Reds, radicals
and revolutionists throughout the world."[31]

But as the people of Massachusetts had earlier discovered, as Mooney and
Billings remained imprisoned, their role in California's political life and reputation grew. (Mooney was reputed to be one of the four best-known Americans
in Europe, joining Franklin Roosevelt, Charles Lindbergh, and Henry Ford.)
And just as broader interest in the fate of Sacco and Vanzetti had aroused defensive stubbornness in some denizens of Massachusetts, interest in Mooney
and Billings similarly affected some Californians. Leading supporters of their
convictions and imprisonment vilified anyone who actively defended the men
or campaigned for their release, in part because they reminded fellow citizens
that they were shutting their eyes to injustice and maladministration. The legal
practice of one attorney "was all but destroyed" by his involvement in the case.
Six young protesters brandishing "Free Tom Mooney" signs who ran around the
stadium track at the closing ceremony for the 1932 Olympic Games in Los Angeles were arrested for criminal syndicalism and then sentenced to nine months
jail for disturbing the peace. Their attorney, a prominent member of the ACLU,
was dismissed from his teaching post at a local law school. Observing "this local spleen," the *New Republic* described California as "the most stupidly reactionary state in the country." Upton Sinclair's 1934 bid for the governorship was
harmed by his commitment to pardoning Mooney and Billings, which allowed
his opponents to smear him as Red. When a woman in Los Angeles erected
"Free Mooney" billboards on her estate on Wilshire Boulevard, she was called
a communist. Mooney had become, *The Nation* wrote, California's "bogey man
extraordinary." The "hysteria with which he [was] hated and feared" was simply
beyond "reasoned argument."[32]

Mooney and Billings lost twenty-three years of their lives because a sufficient
number of their fellow citizens wanted someone to pay for the bombing. The
two men were sacrificed to the inadequacies of state legal authorities, corporate
interests, and the darker side of human nature. For years, citizens proffered irrelevant and unjustifiable excuses for the continuing incarceration of the men: their
pardon "would mean that the preparedness parade [was] unpatriotic and wrong
and should not have been held"; the death of a childhood friend in the "fright-
ful affair" would go unavenged. Such indifference to the importance of justice
was apparent also in responses to Governor Rolph's approval of the lynching of
two kidnap-murder suspects. Although Californians agreed that the murderers
of these alleged criminals should be pardoned, as Rolph promised, they were
disturbed that the governor had diminished his office by so nakedly approving
vigilantism. These citizens wanted the freedom to indulge their passion for tyr-

anny without having to face up to its responsibilities and consequences. Thus does political terror survive.[33]

Racism and Nativism

Any discussion about political terror in the United States in the interwar period should also acknowledge the prevalence and importance of racist and nativist campaigns of violence perpetrated by vigilante groups. The most well-known proponent and perpetrator of vigilante violence from the period, the Ku Klux Klan, enjoyed a major revival in the first half of the 1920s. However, contrary to popular perception, historian Thomas Pegram shows that participation in vigilante violence was actually "marginal to the experience of the vast majority of 1920s Klansmen." Few Ku Klux Klan members participated in or even witnessed Klan violence, which was "relatively rare" outside the South and Southwest. Even in the "violent heartland of hooded moral regulation," the Klan had basically eschewed violent vigilantism by the end of 1923.[34]

However, former Klansmen played a prominent role in forming and then leading the Black Legion, an "anti-labor terrorist organization" that, with the assistance of police and politician members, dominated the suppression of labor in Michigan, Ohio, Indiana, and Illinois in the mid-1930s. The group enrolled perhaps one hundred thousand members, becoming the nation's "largest and most formidable domestic fascist group in the 1930s." Formed around 1925 in Ohio, the Legion subsequently grew rapidly by recruiting white southern migrants who were competing with black southern and Eastern European migrants for increasingly scarce automotive manufacturing jobs. The Legion's size and its success in recruiting senior police and political figures and proprietors of leading industrial espionage firms helped to make it a formidable dispenser of (frequently lethal) industrial and social "justice," and it significantly inhibited labor organizing from 1933 to 1936. Police failed to investigate crimes committed by legionnaires, including murder and bombings, until a Catholic automotive worker who had never been a member of a labor union was murdered, ostensibly for beating his Protestant wife. This breach of the Legion's informal code and jurisdiction finally triggered official investigations, and when one Legion member testified for the prosecution, a horrific trail of murder, bombings, and beatings was finally revealed. In 1939, thirteen legionnaires were imprisoned for life for murder, while twenty-seven others received lengthy jail sentences. But the Legion and its leading members had already done much to help crush labor organization, arouse murderous anticommunist sentiment, and intimidate citizens. The Black Legion and similar groups helped ensure that the 1930s remained as fearful a time for many radicals and even liberals as the preceding decade had been.[35]

CHAPTER 11

The Mythology of Anticommunism

You probably would like to know how the Communists
operate. . . . They are the most skilled propagandists
in the world . . . and if they were so minded, they could
raid the White House and kidnap the President, and no
department of the Government would know anything about
it until they read it in the newspapers the next day.

—Hamilton Fish Jr.

The lifeblood of anticommunist propaganda was conspiracy theory. Anticommunism found its ultimate raison d'être in the notion that the United States was being subjected to unceasing subversion by an army of largely imported Bolsheviks, socialists, syndicalists, and anarchists. Anticommunist conspiracy theory maintained that this army was being aided by an even larger number of treacherous and gullible homegrown enemies: radicalized trade unionists, embittered African Americans, unfeminine feminists, softheaded peaceniks, Christian socialists, social progressives, and eccentric freethinkers. Like any conspiracy theory, anticommunism required a fantastically powerful and depraved antagonist. And the international communist movement, headed up by the Bolshevik regime in Russia, was made to order. So vicious was the Bolsheviks' reputation that anticommunists were able to project all fear of political, economic, and social revolution and even evolution onto doctrines and social elements that were easily characterized as "un-American," deranged, and evil.

For genuinely fearful anticommunists, the psychological posture of combating conspiracy could be addictive. The comfort of identifying an external source for the nation's many unresolved troubles and the personal conflict and trauma to which these troubles gave rise was often irresistible. However, conspiracy theory was also a political technique of choice for opportunistic and calculating anticommunists, who inflamed and manipulated emotions to advance their cause. Whatever their motives, anticommunists placed "Bolshevik" radical and union organizations and their Pink auxiliaries at the heart of a corpus of propaganda whose features were established by the early 1920s and remained fixed for several decades. According to this propaganda, American communists displayed the same military discipline and fanaticism as their Russian colleagues. What they lacked in numerical strength they more than made up for with furtive determination, sabotaging vital American institutions and organizations from within. The logic of conspiracy theory also required that the communist threat be associated with state-enforced free love, class warfare and murder, and forcible dispossession of property. As the Jazz Age unfolded, these associations were reinforced by exaggerated and often fantastic notions of Bolshevik depravity and power that became an intrinsic element of political "normalcy" in America. Focusing on the horrors of Bolshevism also prevented members of the Anticommunist Spider Web from having to acknowledge the humanity of their communist foes.

Anticommunist propaganda invested communists with a host of projected fears and desires. Anticommunists habitually claimed that their enemies did not want to be absorbed into the nation but instead wanted to seize control of it. Yet this was true only of the tiniest percentage of people tarred as "communists." Moreover, this idea both masked and legitimized the desire held by many anticommunists to expel from the United States those people they did not trust or wish to share a community with. The ultimate lesson of anticommunist conspiracy theory for its adherents, therefore, was to cease building a cooperative, pluralistic society. In its place, these anticommunists advocated the establishment of authoritarian government and the mass disenfranchisement, imprisonment, sterilization, deportation, and even execution of undesirable residents and citizens.

The Paranoid Position

The anticommunist conspiracy was a product of the human condition, American political culture and history, and contemporary events. It offered a classic example of both the "paranoid style" of politics and what Michael Paul Rogin describes as the "countersubversive" tradition of suppressing "alien threats to the American way of life" through "institutionalized . . . violent and exclusionary responses" justified by political "demonology."[1]

Conspiracy theory is one of the most powerful manifestations of the "paranoid style" of politics or the politics of the "paranoid position." The paranoid style of politics originates in psychic immaturity and turmoil. Rather than being a permanent or congenital condition, it is a position into which any person may fall. Those who espouse the paranoid position lose the hard-won and precarious ability to entrust the polity with a large measure of control over their fate. This lost ability is replaced by powerful feelings of insecurity that give rise to conspiracy theory and the desire to reconstitute society according to a schema with which those who are paranoid are more comfortable. The temptation to surrender to paranoid politics is strongly influenced by real, historical events. Throughout various periods in American history, state and society were continually redefined by episodes in which designated and demonized outsiders (Others) were destroyed or expelled from the national "imagined community." Beginning with crises of cohabitation with Native Americans and African slaves and continuing with threats represented by agents of the French Revolution, the Mormon Church, the Second Bank of the United States, Irish Catholics, abolitionists, southern slaveholders, and wet anti-Prohibitionists, challenges to a homogeneous American cultural and political identity induced paranoid-style reactions, including conspiracy theory. As Rogin has noted, the notion of "cultural adaptation" was repeatedly rejected as threatening a "dangerous and impossible" coexistence.[2]

Adherents (or prisoners) of the paranoid position understand that the restriction of community that they advocate must be morally justified. Conspiracy theory plays a crucial role in creating such a justification. As Eli Sagan has written, conspiracy theory permits paranoid people to believe that their "political passions are unselfish and patriotic," reconciling the "enormous psychological and moral ambivalence" their aggression creates. The psychological device of projection is equally "intrinsic" to paranoid-style behavior, through which occupants of the paranoid position attribute "to external figures . . . motivations, drives, or other tensions that are repudiated and intolerable in oneself." Thus, anticommunist mythology, created by men and women unwilling to tolerate the increasingly pluralistic evolution of American society, used a supposed grand communist conspiracy to destroy American democracy to justify the expulsion and disenfranchisement of unwanted political and racial types. At the same time, anticommunists enjoyed the benefits of a mythology of "national and personal disintegration," chiefly a sustaining "drama of survival and heroism," and the development of what Sagan has termed a "kinship" group, held together by "a tribal bond," to which the security of the nation could safely be entrusted.[3]

Inhabitants of the paranoid position take refuge in the kinship group when the "order of things" becomes unfamiliar and when the state appears to be incapable of guaranteeing the survival of that order. Having lost the sense that their cultural identity confers belonging in society's ruling group, those who are paranoid seek to re-create society by retaining only its pure elements. Enacting "rituals of empowerment," the paranoid renew their belief in their exclusive possession (or control) of their environment. (John Trevor's immigration reforms can be considered such a ritual.) Yet as anthropologist Ghassan Hage has observed, the belief "in the possibility of creating an ideal space" seldom brings the paranoid relief from his or her enormous psychological stress. Having convinced themselves that the community they are trying to save is the victim of a malign and mighty enemy, the paranoid experience heightened frustration as they fail to attain their "hopelessly demanding and unrealistic goals."[4]

Of course, not everyone who produced or subscribed to anticommunist propaganda was clinically paranoid, let alone suffering from paranoia; the calculating, materially motivated dimensions of anticommunism dispel such a notion. Further, belief in liberal democracy was an important motive for anticommunism. Nevertheless, anticommunist propaganda drew much of its power from and operated according to the logic of paranoid-style politics. Many members of the Anticommunist Spider Web inhabited the paranoid position for at least a significant period of their lives. And their propaganda, driven by conspiracy theory and manifesting all the characteristics of political demonology, was marshaled to defend material, political, and social privilege as well as to ward off the submersion of old, powerful, WASP America into what Ku Klux Klan imperial wizard William J. Simmons termed a multicultural "garbage can." The propaganda, therefore, featured a mélange of real and symbolic concerns. Interested and clearheaded observers noted that the Soviet communist regime perpetrated increasingly severe crimes against humanity throughout the interwar period, but these events went almost unobserved in the Anticommunist Spider Web's propaganda. Its concerns remained overwhelmingly domestic.[5]

Conspiracy Thinking

Paranoid conspiracy thinking is first expressed as a vague apprehension of danger from without before it is identified with defined forces; the paranoid first register their anxiety and only then search for its cause. The target of suspicion is mutable as well as cumulative and absorptive. In the United States, therefore, ethnic, religious, or political groups suspected of conspiracy were periodically supplanted by new objects of suspicion yet retained or only very slowly lost their status as symbols of disorder. Thus in the 1920s, the Klan continued to regard Roman Catholics as the nation's chief enemy. And as late as 1983, Secretary of the Interior James Watt spoke of Native Americans' tribal identity as a "socialistic" repudiation of individual "freedom" as the foundation of American life.[6]

Anticommunist conspiracy theory similarly was nourished by older conspiracy theories. Many decades of industrial turmoil birthed the "un-American" conspiracies of international and industrial unions. Later, when the United States waged war against Germany, America's large community of German immigrants became for a few years the paramount agent of conspiracy in the United States. With the end of the war, the rise of the Bolshevik regime, and the eruption of domestic industrial dispute, communism quickly supplanted the Hun as the principal demonic threat to America. Anticommunist propaganda was then hastily constructed, with crucial theoretical and political leadership provided by the Anticommunist Spider Web.

The Lusk Committee's delineation of the anticommunist conspiracy proceeded in accordance with the paranoid style. The committee asserted that the "very structure of American society" was being attacked by "various" loosely identified groups. The committee also popularized the paranoid conviction that the United States was the special target of these evil forces, arguing that the radical offensive against "prominent and useful public men" in America had no parallel "in any other country." This was a strange claim to make at the height of the Russian Civil War, but it was a necessary conclusion for people practicing paranoid politics as well as consistent with the idea of American exceptionalism.[7]

The Lusk Committee's conspiracy theory provided a structure for subsequent anticommunists to continually embellish. Powerful elements of the military and patriots seized on the identification of pacifism with Bolshevism to combat not just pacifism but also opposition to the militarization of educational institutions and social welfare reform. Schools, colleges, teachers, and professors were continually monitored by patriots, corporations, and state intelligence services for signs of communist treachery and student brainwashing. The US Army's Military Intelligence Division (MI), like the Better America Federation, spied on teachers, the American Association of University Women, and the National Students Forum. And major corporations and chambers of commerce paid Elizabeth Dilling and other nationally prominent patriots to examine the libraries of major colleges and professors.[8]

The role of Jews in communist conspiracy remained vital and, with the rise of the Nazis in Germany, became even more significant. Nazi sympathizers such as Harry Jung and Dilling were notorious purveyors of the notion that communism constituted a Jewish plot to take over America. This notion remained influential in business and national security sectors. During the Bonus March on Washington, for example, a MI colonel reported that one group of marchers from California was "100 per cent Jewish as to its controlling personnel" and had been sent by the studio heads at Metro Goldwyn Mayer to Bolshevize the veterans.[9]

Liberal clergy, identified by the Lusk Committee as a critical support for the pacifist phalanx of the Bolsheviks' "triangular" global army, were also prominent characters in anticommunist propaganda. The Federal Council of Churches of

Christ in America, slandered by the *Chicago Tribune* as a mouthpiece for the Comintern, was denounced as an "out and out" communist and "so-called Christian" organization by numerous ministers, several of whom were readers of Dilling's *Red Network*. It was also classified by the Office of Naval Intelligence (which had burgled its offices in the mid-1920s) as a "Communist Affiliated and Communist-Aiding Organization." Under such assault, many church leaders succumbed to conspiracy theory and established committees to monitor the distribution of "communistic literature" among parishioners. They also petitioned the Better America Federation and similar organizations for "data of the industrial condition."[10]

In the world of paranoid anticommunist conspiracy theory, differences of opinion were explicable only by treachery. A diverse range of liberal people and organizations thus found their way into the pantheon of communist traitors. Chief among these was the American Civil Liberties Union (ACLU). Congressman Hamilton Fish Jr. reckoned that about 90 percent of the organization's work involved "upholding the activities of the Communists in the U.S. seeking to destroy all civil liberties" in the country. Association with the group constituted confirmation of communist identity even for George Creel, the head of the Wilson administration's propaganda operation: Ralph Van Deman kept a file "a foot thick" on Creel and accused him "of every treason." The YMCA and YWCA, which committed the additional sin of supporting antilynching legislation, were denounced for their ACLU ties. Any organization advancing any cause that was not supported by the major political parties was also described as communist. Political prisoners' amnesty movements were a particularly unwelcome development because they directly challenged the notion that American justice was so vastly superior to the Soviet brand. MI linked the Committee of Forty-Eight, a progressive organization housing remnants of the Bull Moose Party, with single-taxers, the Socialist Party, the ACLU and the Nonpartisan League. Any citizen who supported the presidential candidacy of Senator Robert M. La Follette Sr. also found themselves labeled *Red*. Indeed, those described as subversives included farmers protesting their neighbors' evictions, bonus marchers, and members of an unemployed council during the depression. And simply being an intellectual with liberal leanings was a cause for infamy, as John Dewey (on whom the Bureau of Investigation kept a standing file), John Dos Passos, Felix Frankfurter, Sidney Hook, and Reinhold Niebuhr discovered.[11]

As anticommunist conspiracy theory stipulated that Bolsheviks had infiltrated every nook of American society, the Bolshevik enemy became a foe of fearsome magnitude and capacity. MI periodically attempted to put a precise figure on the numbers of Reds and Pinks in America. Circumventing a departmental ban on conducting domestic intelligence, the division routinely circulated questionnaires to reserve and recruiting officers to gauge the strength of the radical movement. Division headquarters would then interpret the returns with an opaque formula of uncertain provenance and publish a national membership figure for all "radical organizations"; radical "individuals belonging to semi-radical or semi-revolutionary organizations"; and individuals who "adhered" to these groups but were not registered as members, broken down into categories of aliens, African Americans, and criminals. A 1920 survey put the total number of American radicals and sympathizers at nearly 1,150,000, while domestic emergency manuals of the same period assumed that a "well organized movement for the overthrow of the Government" could immediately mobilize 600,000 militants and an additional 900,000 supporters "in thirty days." The strength of radical movements was also frequently measured by juxtaposing estimated membership numbers of radical and "loyal" organizations. This process was significantly compromised by professional and psychological imperatives, as the assistant chief of staff of the Chicago MI revealed when he informed his superiors that the figures for radical, organized wage earners in his area were "inclined more to a maximum than to a conservative estimate"; tripping over his material, he also stated that "30% of organized wage earners are radically inclined," and "25% of radically inclined wage earners are radical."[12]

MI at least attempted to produce an empirical study of radical numbers. This is more than can be said for J. Edgar Hoover, who as head of the General Intelligence Division seemed surprised to receive a request from MI's chief, Brigadier General C. E. Nolan, for precise data on the size of the radical movement. Discomfited, Hoover regretfully reported his inability to meet the request and instead advised, "We have found in the course of our work here that an estimate of the membership of the radical organizations is not a fair test of the amount of radical activity."[13]

Hoover trusted only his own unique perception, which was mired in the paranoid position, and as a result was usually ill informed, speculative, and just plain wrong. But the credit due to MI or any other agency seeking to quantify the strength of the communist threat should not be exaggerated, for the division's grasp of radical politics was so feeble as to make any data it collected worthless. As a 1920 document on "International Movements or 'Isms'" issued by the division shows, the institutional environment of MI made the communist threat so gargantuan that it became amorphous. For example, the division anticipated simultaneous assaults against America from the "important movements" of anarchism, labor, Bolshevism, "pan-Latinism," Islamism, "pan-Orientalism," "Jewry," and socialism. The division was also on guard against such "important international intrigues" as "International Jewry," "Japanese-Siberian," "Bolshevist-German-Islamic," and "Japanese-Russo-German."[14]

The communist movement's vast ideological and geographical reach led anticommunists to detect its effect in myriad incidents, some mundane, some extraordinary. The prosecuting attorney of Wayne County, Michigan, a colleague of Jacob Spolansky, informed the US Army's deputy chief of staff, General George Van Horn Moseley, that "expert plumbers" were "playing havoc" with the city's utilities, "fixing gas and electric meters so they do not register in the homes of Communists, particularly those unemployed." The designs of other communists were vastly more sophisticated and threatening. Few were more so than the schemes of Soviet überagent Carl Mostavenko. In the early 1930s, MI was panic-stricken by its failure to capture this Belorussian "with years of terrorist exploits to his record." Mostavenko was thought to be one of eleven members of a "Grand Committee of Decision of the Third International of Moscow," directing the "propaganda and terrorist activities" of the Soviet secret police throughout the world. Like the Klan, which was subconsciously impressed by the titles and regalia of the Catholic Church, MI endowed the Grand Committee of Decision with cabalistic and immensely powerful qualities. Mostavenko was described as a fearless fanatic possessing superhuman powers of persuasion. He was also degenerate and derived sexual pleasure administering torture. A fomenter of chaos and death, his reach was limitless. The army believed he had been a close associate of Béla Kun, the leader of the short-lived Hungarian Soviet Republic; had orchestrated armed clashes between Arabs and Jews in Jerusalem; and had even "prepared the revolutionary program in India . . . offsetting the passive, civil disobedience program of Mahatma Gandhi." A master of disguise and an "accomplished linguist," Mostavenko spoke "twenty languages fluently." Moreover, he had a phantom-like capacity to escape justice. When arrested in Palestine, he "successfully converted" his captors "to bolshevism" and "mysteriously" disappeared. Intelligence agents now worried that Mostavenko had recently left the USSR, posing as a "German tourist bound for the U.S." As the "practical leader in America of the Moscow secret police," he had been entrusted by the Politburo to disburse $1.5 million "for propaganda and sabotage." Since his arrival, he had organized an arson campaign that had devastated timberland and farming ranches in California, and MI had "no doubt" that he had perpetrated similar outrages elsewhere.[15]

Anticommunists had long detected the work of men such as Mostavenko in a series of calamities that overtook their political allies. Blair Coán, a former employee of the Department of Justice and publisher of a paranoid anticommunist tract, *The Red Web*, was certain that Red agents had destroyed attorneys general A. Mitchell Palmer and Harry Daugherty, neutered the Bureau of Investigation, and planned to seize the federal government through La Follette's presidential candidacy. Fred Marvin similarly alleged that the Teapot Dome scandal that ruined Daugherty had been planned by Politburo member and Comintern leader Grigorii Zinoviev. This allegation was reprinted by the *Army and Navy Journal* under the headline "Oil 'Scandals' Engineered by Radicals."[16]

The Bolsheviks' espionage capacity was not bought cheaply. Thus another enduring plank of anticommunist conspiracy theory was the myth that Soviet gold financed an enormous global espionage and terror network. The concept of Soviet gold became fundamental anticommunist dogma even before the Bolshevik victory in the Russian Civil War. The Senate committee inquiring into the activities of unofficial Soviet ambassador Ludwig Martens reported in April 1920 that he regularly received lump-sum payments of $150,000 from his superiors during his stay in the United States. By anticommunist standards, the committee's allegations were modest: MI accepted the claims of a Hearst journalist that the Bolsheviks had allocated $600 million in cash and an additional $150 million in gold reserves for propaganda in America. Jacob Spolansky informed intelligence authorities in Chicago that Martens had used this money to establish a local spy network. This assertion was "proven" by reports from Siberia alleging that radicals there had planted moles in government offices, hotels, railroads, and newspapers. Spolansky concluded that a similar plan to bribe government officials and security personnel was under way in the United States. Bolsheviks apparently could leap from Siberia to Chicago with terrifying ease. Several years later, Marvin adapted the myth, maintaining that the comptroller of domestic revolution, the ACLU, survived on "vast sums of money" it received from infamous parlor Reds. Chief among such wealthy Moscow stooges was Charles Garland, the son of a Wall Street stockbroker who founded the left-leaning American Fund for Public Service.[17]

After it exposed the social, cultural, political, and financial might of communism, anticommunist theory embedded communism deep in the history of conspiracy in America. This element of propaganda was underpinned by the paranoid belief that history itself is a conspiracy set in motion, as Richard Hofstadter has famously argued, by "demonic forces of almost transcendent power" whose objectives can be thwarted only by "an all-out crusade." The proof of this belief and its connection to communism came in the form of the mysterious Order of the Illuminati, of which the Bolsheviks were held to be the latest and deadliest incarnation. Fear of the Illuminati had been a factor in American politics since the late eighteenth century, when Scottish scientist John Robison's *Proofs of a Conspiracy against All the Religions and Governments of Europe, Carried on in the Secret Meetings of Free Masons, Illuminati, and Reading Societies* made its way across the Atlantic. The Order of the Illuminati was founded by Adam Weishaupt, a professor of law at the University of Ingolstadt in Bavaria, around the time of the American Declaration of Independence. Its teachings, although "spiced with an anticlerical animus," were consistent with Enlightenment rationalism, and according to Hofstadter, the order gained "fairly wide influence in Masonic lodges." Its views were thus consonant with those of several Founding Fathers. Yet the order ran afoul of European and American conservatives outraged by the French Revolution and the alleged revolutionary role of the Masonic movement. In the United States, fear of Masonic scheming melded with anxiety about the rise of Jeffersonian democracy, particularly among reactionary clerics in New England.[18]

Fear of the Illuminati played an inconsistent and inconstant role in American life over the next 120 years before it was revived by anticommunist conspiracy theory. And just as fear of the Illuminati was originally introduced from the British Isles, so, too, was the idea that the communist movement had its origins in the order. The original proponent of this notion was popular writer Nesta H. Webster. Webster came to two life-changing realizations during the first decade of the twentieth century: first, she was a reincarnated aristocrat who had lived through the French Revolution; second, this revolution had been "the dark design of 'illuminized Freemasonry' striving for world revolution and the destruction of Christian civilization." Wholly persuaded that conspiracy was the chief engine of history, Webster contended that the Illuminati and the Freemasons were now exercising power through the Bolshevik government in Russia. Consistent with paranoid fear, Webster identified her home, Great Britain, rather than the United States, as the "greatest stronghold of Christian Civilisation" and therefore the chief target of Bolshevik hostility. Nevertheless, her many American readers adapted her thesis to local conditions, substituting for democracy's great enemies American organizations that played the same role as the British Labour and Communist Parties and Sinn Féin. Webster further revised the Illuminati conspiracy by melding it with prevalent conceptions of Bolshevism as a distinctively Jewish cancer. Her identification of a "sinister confederacy" of international Jews as the cause of every subversive movement since the formation of the Illuminati found ready acceptance in her homeland, including by the minister for munitions and secretary of state for war, Winston Churchill, who based his 1920 speech "Zionism and Bolshevism" on her writings. Webster's ideas also held particular appeal for American anticommunists, who read with great interest her political pamphlets and above all her 1924 book, *Secret Societies and Subversive Movements* (which included the *Protocols of the Elders of Zion* in its appendixes).[19]

Although some historians have dated Webster's influence in the United States from the 1935 publication of a pamphlet by pro-Nazi evangelist and publisher Gerald B. Winrod, members of the Spider Web had embraced and popularized Webster's work much earlier. Richard Whitney's *Reds in America* (1924), whose frontispiece features a Russian cartoon depicting revolutionaries feasting on the executed Christ (figure 14), credited Webster with discovering the pivotal revolutionary role of "minorities, secretly organized, and working in secondary and tertiary minorities, also secretly organized, ultimately influencing vast numbers of people who knew not [their] objective and cared less." Having organized "disorder in France," Whitney explained, these secret orders moved into other countries and "counted upon reverberations as part of [their] political capital at home." When "the same organized movement appeared in [America] its advent caused George Washington and his coworkers considerable anxiety for they evidently could not understand its true significance." And "verily," Whitney concluded, "the scars of that agitation are still apparent in our political life."[20]

A few years later, Marvin placed the Illuminati at the center of Jewish-Bolshevik-Internationalist conspiracy. Claiming that Weishaupt had been dominated by "an oriental Jew known as Kolmer," Marvin stated that the "anti-civilization and Christianity" Illuminati had resolved to destroy government, patriotism, property and inheritance rights, religion, and family relations. The Illuminati-Bolsheviks had built themselves into an "advanced propaganda" organization through "deception, fraud, intrigue, secrecy and conspiracy." After going underground following its proscription in Bavaria, the order's leaders decreed that its name could never be used openly again to preserve the illusion of its destruction. This deception had proved so successful that the world now mistakenly believed Karl Marx to be the founder of socialism. Yet Marx had merely reactivated the doctrines of the Illuminati, which he had discovered in London libraries.[21]

The Webster-Marvin interpretation of the global revolutionary role of the Communist-Illuminati was thrust onto the national political stage by John E. Nelson, a five-term Republican congressman from Maine, who wrote an individual report on the deliberations of the Fish Committee. While accepting Marvin's arguments about the significance of the Illuminati, Nelson added a twist to the story in keeping with the paranoid tendency to interpret conspiracy "in apocalyptic terms" and to traffic "in the birth and death of whole worlds, whole political orders [and] whole systems of values." The date of the Illuminati's foundation, 1776, led Nelson to believe that divine will had created American republicanism at precisely the same time as Jewish international Bolshevism. The two "diametrically antagonistic and mutually exclusive" belief systems were fated to duel until one was exterminated. The global reach of communism demonstrated how dangerous the Illuminati remained, while the United States, the historical and spiritual bulwark of "noble and constructive principles of representative government and individual liberty," had to remain vigilant in self-defense. Nelson helpfully reduced Weishaupt's plan for "the destruction of Christianity and all existing governments" to "a simple formula" of six "abolitions": "monarchy and all ordered government; private property; inheritance; patriotism; the family

FIGURE 14. Frontispiece to Richard Whitney's *Reds in America* (1924), featuring a Russian cartoon depicting revolutionaries feasting on the executed Christ.

(i.e. of marriage and all orthodox morality, and the institution of the communal education of children); [and] all religion."[22]

Nelson's public airing of the Illuminati conspiracy profoundly affected anticommunist dogma. Few anticommunists were as influenced by Webster's theory as Amos Fries. Fries's *Communism Unmasked*, published in 1937, extensively referenced the work of Nelson and Webster and obsessively reiterated Weishaupt's founding role in international communism. Together with Elizabeth C. Barney

Buel, a pamphleteer for the Daughters of the American Revolution whom he also referenced, Fries seems to have believed that the international labor movement celebrated 1 May as Labor Day because this was the anniversary of the proclamation of the existence of the Order of the Illuminati. Fries and Buel distinguished their analysis of the conspiratorial role of the Illuminati from Webster's in two important ways. Buel rejected any association of late-eighteenth-century American reaction against the Illuminati with (paranoid) "panic," instead describing it as "a very real danger on which the clergy" of that era "had the courage to warn their congregations from pulpits all over the country." The patriotic foresight of these pastors contrasted strongly with contemporary clergy who preached "Communism and Socialism from their pulpits!" Perhaps aware of the revolutionary generation's interest in Freemasonry and the Illuminati, Fries felt compelled to state, "THE ILLUMINATI IS NOT MASONRY." And as he further explained, while the Masonic order "obtained a strong foothold . . . in several continental countries of Europe, it never got any hold on American Masonry and very little, if any, on English Masonry." The Illuminati, he concluded, was "never any more Masonry than a counterfeit silver dollar is money." These are archetypal examples of the process by which the paranoid justify conspiracy thinking, simply rejecting facts that contradict the neat separation of one's own community from its alien enemies.[23]

Justifying Conspiracy Theory

Anticommunist conspiracy theory sought always to make anticommunists' disavowal of what they termed communism credible and defensible. This disavowal was justified by contrasting communism and communists with "100% Americanism" and "loyal" citizens. Communists were routinely portrayed as foolish, perverted creatures who threatened the future of humanity. Such portrayals reflected the cardinal role of projection in the paranoid anticommunist conception of communism. Paranoid anticommunists were also obsessed with gathering facts to prove the veracity of their projected fantasies, even as they dismissed any facts or perspectives that contradicted their own beliefs.

The projected fantasies at the heart of anticommunist conspiracy theory concerned both what communists did and their intrinsic nature. Marvin thus developed the notion that communists spread propaganda into the idea that communists were directly responsible for the introduction of propaganda as a political method into the United States.[24]

The prism of racial inequality through which anticommunists surveyed the domestic landscape also led them to fear African Americans as especially vulnerable to communist infiltration. Yet their racism also offered some measure of comfort. MI officers, for example, concluded that the "vast majority of the Negroes [were] not sufficiently intelligent to grasp . . . Communistic doctrines." Nevertheless, they were unsure whether African Americans' "habitual easy-going docility" would prove to be "an asset or a liability" in the fight to protect America. And such uncertainty fueled projected hostility, which gave rise to the notion that enemy Others were fostering "hatred" of America and its traditions, particularly in minority ethnic communities. The Lusk Committee was disturbed by black Americans' "hatred" and "resentment" of the white majority. The Fish Committee similarly worried about the promotion in communist youth camps of "class hatred," which would "warp the minds of immature" foreign-born, African American, Japanese American, Chinese American, and Jewish American children, preventing them from appreciating the benefits of life in "a land of freedom and of equal opportunity." The ultimate expression of African American "hatred" was the "pan-Negro" miscegenation movement. And Spider Web members such as Van Deman and Jung were on perpetual guard against the formation of an "International League of the Darker Races," which they believed was being sponsored by Japan.[25]

Anticommunist conspiracy theory rationalized the fact that communists had made converts in the United States by imputing to such converts a susceptibility to moral corruption or infirmity. The Lusk Committee dismissed the attraction some Americans felt for left-wing political theory as sentimental and softheaded frailty. The committee also argued, like other anticommunists, that the beliefs of left-leaning clergy were attributable to venality. Such priests, aware that they were losing custom, began prostituting their congregations to cash in on fashionable notions. In fact, they "lost their belief in God."[26]

Another cherished means of accounting for political waywardness was the notion that communist dupes would readily renounce their heresy if only they were provided with the right information. The Lusk Committee thus chastised New York's "more conservative elements" who opposed the committee's education reforms for failing to understand their necessity. Jung similarly complained that "those unacquainted with the intricacies" of the communist movement were unable to recognize the omnipresent signs of its influence and "in their lack of accurate knowledge" scoffed at its existence.[27]

Other anticommunists did not bother even to try to account for deviant beliefs. Rather, they focused exclusively on destroying the communist message. Their fight against communism was reduced to its simplest level: the contest between right and wrong. As Dilling characteristically stated, it was all very well "to believe in the altruism and personal sincerity of the intellectual radical leader, [or] admire his learning or personal charm, just as we believe in the sincere religious devotion of the Hindu who, according to his religion, offers his baby girls for vile sex degradation and physical injury, jabs nails into himself, and offers bloody human sacrifices to his god 'Kali,' but we need not follow either."[28]

As these remarks suggest, a strong strand of anticommunist theory maintained that some communists were simply beyond salvation by virtue of their tainted racial stock or incorrigible perversity. A widely accepted truism in anticommunist milieu was that Bolshevism was uniquely corrupting as a result of its Jewish origins. It could disfigure even the soundest minds. Herbert Hoover had consequently counseled against using American troops to stem the tide of socialism in Europe: he doubted whether soldiers in that environment "could resist infection with Bolshevik ideas."[29]

The principal malady of communist infection was sexual depravity. Many anticommunists, including Fries, were obsessed with communist sexual decadence. Fries was specifically preoccupied with communists' nationalization of women, which he described as "the vilest proposal in the annals of times," conduct beneath even "the lowest types of savages or barbarians" that put "the mothers of men lower than the prostitute in the streets." Fries's fears were stoked by regular press reports of senior Soviet officials running prostitution and slavery rings and corrupting young girls with promises of government positions. The indignation caused by such reports melded with the projected horror of miscegenation and black revolution when newspaper headlines screamed "HIGH OFFICIALS OF RUSSIA BACK WHITE SLAVERS." And left-leaning nonconformists such as Charles Garland were derided as propagators of free love by such superpatriots as Dilling and Marvin, who alleged that Garland had established a "free love farm" to pursue "his individual ideas of liberalism . . . with sixteen women companions."[30]

Yet anticommunists protested communist sexual depravity a little too much. As Hofstadter has observed, if "anti-Catholicism [was] the pornography of the Puritan," anticommunism thrived on tales of Bolshevik debauchery and wickedness. Moreover, coinciding as it did with an unparalleled expansion of mass media technology, anticommunist conspiracy theory could furnish its adherents with descriptions of hate objects that were, in Hofstadter's words, "much more vivid . . . richer and more circumstantial in personal description and . . . invective" than those that had suffused anti-Masonry and anti-Catholicism. And advertising men played a significant role in the production and diffusion of anticommunist propaganda.[31]

In any event, devotees of the anticommunist conspiracy theory evinced no insight into such matters and paid special attention to portraying the sickness of communism in ways that consolidated the "interlocking directorates" theory of the Spider Web Chart and emphasized its organic (and therefore incurable and irremediable) quality. The Paul Reveres, for example, issued a cartoon, "The Body of Anarchy," that depicted the entire Political Left as a hideous half-man, half-simian beast. The creature's human half comprised a bespectacled "Parlor Pink" whose enormous sloping forehead and beaked nose topped an "arm of dupes," a "leg of socialism," and an ACLU foot "whose guiding spirit [was] an ex-convict." The bestial half was topped by the head of a "Gutter Red," an ape man with huge brows and lips, an "arm of adepts," a "leg of communism," and a supporting foot of "International Labor Defense." At the heart of this foul creature sat "The Garland Fund" and other radical stipends, while its gut housed the League of Industrial Democracy, "whose past president was [also] an ex-convict."[32]

While knowledge of communists' intrinsic character defects was important, anticommunists searched for other proof to substantiate their views. To combat devilishly capable communist propagandists and saboteurs, anticommunists found what they took to be hard facts invaluable in their crusade to rescue those elements of society that deserved salvation. They searched exhaustively for information about communist conspiracy and never lost an opportunity to publicize such evidence when it was found. Here, the intractable pursuit of indisputable truths as revealed by "proper" and "accurate knowledge" merged with the cornucopia of anticommunist "pornography." Aside from lurid stories, statistical information about communism was most prized because it bestowed scientific respectability on anticommunist claims. Yet because the drive to accumulate such information emanated from the paranoid position, the data collection and interpretive methods employed by anticommunists made such information worthless, as anticommunists themselves frequently and inadvertently admitted. In attempting to analyze the extent of communist involvement in strike activity, the Fish Committee merely aggregated the number of strikes in a given period to prove communist corruption of labor organizations. Perhaps as a result, after trawling for evidence for six months, the committee could conclude only that between fifty thousand and two million communists lived in the United States. The failure to produce precise data could always be blamed on the obsessive secrecy of the communist movement itself, which, as MI pointed out, guarded the activities of the "underground element . . . with the greatest caution," withholding sensitive information from even "the oldest Communists." With precise intelligence so difficult to obtain, some officers estimated the number of "actively and avowedly radical" persons "connected with" and "in sympathy with" communist organizations at three million (not including "Socialists or parlor Bolsheviks"); they were, however, prepared to vouch only that this figure was "based upon facts" that were "nearly correct."[33]

As such claims demonstrate, the collation of "proper" knowledge by anticommunists was not designed to facilitate "effective two-way communication with the world" and "least of all" with anyone who questioned the veracity of their views. The effort to amass "accurate" knowledge was primarily a defensive act, enabling anticommunists to shut off their "receptive apparatus" to avoid "having to attend to disturbing considerations that [did] not fortify [their] ideas."[34] Ironically, information gleaned from communists themselves was an especially important buttress for this "defensive act." Walter Steele, for example, quoted Moscow Communist Party boss Vyacheslav Molotov extensively to support the contention that the Soviets were deliberately destroying the global economy. The Fish Committee similarly accepted the Soviet State Planning Commission's claim that the production targets of the first five-year plan had been achieved by the end of the plan's fourth year. Again ironically, anticommunists involuntarily best accounted for the parasitic dependence of their conspiracy theory on communist rhetoric. As the Westchester Security League explained, "Since it is vital to know the nature of the enemy's attack, this phase of our effort has increased until it is almost the largest part of our current program, so important has it become . . . to know the 'pro' side of the story as well as the 'anti' side."[35]

Indeed, knowledge about the "pro" side of the communist conspiracy became in Hofstadter's view "almost the largest part" of the anticommunist program, because Red rhetoric was one of the few outside sources where anticommunists could glean information confirming the monstrous power of the global communist plot. For this reason, the testimony of renegade communists who came over to legitimate society was accorded "special authority." Having "been in the secret world of the enemy," such former radicals could verify the anticommunists' outlandish suspicions, "which might otherwise have been doubted by a skeptical world." More important, renegades offered anticommunists "living proof" that not all political conversions were "made by the wrong side" and brought "the promise of redemption and victory."[36]

Notwithstanding the importance of the facts and knowledge collected through their own and renegades' endeavors, anticommunists placed the greatest significance on the truths they held to be self-evident. In constructing anticommunist conspiracy theory, nothing could push them off course on their journey toward predetermined conclusions. The Lusk Committee, for example, discussed Bolshevik perfidy for many thousands of pages but restricted its criticism and analysis of systemic problems in American society to a mere two paragraphs. The committee declared itself "unable" to investigate the problem of inflation and expressed "regret" that no official inquiry into living standards had occurred. An association of expatriate Russian businessmen, the Russian Economic League, similarly struggled to divorce capitalism from its relationship to socialist revolution. While attempting to account for the success of Bolshevism in its homeland, the League conceded that "the causes of sympathies for Bolshevism" were rooted "in the great mistakes and even crimes of the bourgeois order of things." But it maintained that these great mistakes and crimes were not "connected with the nature" of that bourgeois order. One Bureau of Investigation agent observing "radical labor agitators" at an unemployment rally performed similar contortions to prove that the meeting had been called to foster revolution rather than employment. He suggested that the only way to discern the real purpose of the "exercise" was to "disregard" the entire question of "labor conditions." Doing so enabled one to see that the rally was really staged to enable "a large number of people to discuss . . . socialism." And to prove his theories about the connections among ethnic communities, intellectuals, and radical conspiracy, Trevor simply dispensed with the irritant of competing theories and evidence, remarking in an MI report on Indian radicalism and its connection with international communism, "It cannot be proved but it is a moral certainty money was given to the Hindus in Mexico by agents of . . . Albert DeSilver, director, National Civil Liberties Bureau, W. E. B. Du Bois, negro, director of the activities of the National Association for the Advancement of Colored People . . . Frederic C. Howe, too well known now to need comment [and] Frank P. Walsh, American spokesman for the Irish cause at the Peace conference in Paris."[37]

Anticommunists ultimately found all the evidence needed to justify their belief in communist conspiracy in either the circular processes of paranoid conspiracy theory or the postwar Social Darwinist zeitgeist. The impact of world war and the rise of communism destroyed belief, historian Gilman Ostrander has suggested, in a "changeless Newtonian universe" and heightened the popularity of notions of competition in nature and civilization. The perception that "man struggled in his universe like other animals" and was influenced "by forces over which he had little control" amplified the paranoid sense of battle between rival belief systems that formed the core of anticommunist conspiracy theory. Sensitive to the absence of what Ostrander has termed a "National Father" or "God" who could guarantee the socioeconomic order they prized, anticommunist kinship groups mobilized to perform this vital function. Anticommunist mythology thus taught its adherents that America's salvation paradoxically required an authoritarian, antidemocratic revolution; those who could no longer trust democracy would have to trust in government of, by, and for themselves.[38]

Constructing a Perfect America

In anticommunist conspiracy mythology, the United States was a unique nation deserving not mere loyalty but reverence. Indeed, anticommunists thought the protection of America the paramount task of all civilized people. Superpatriots such as Dilling habitually spoke of the United States as "the miracle of modern times." Its capitalist economy and system of government had made it "the greatest success in history" and "the envy of every nation on earth." Her fellow patriot James Horn averred that the "republican form of government in the United States" was the predestined result of the "slow process of civilization" and as "a plan of human association" was "far greater and much better than any heretofore devised and practiced." Anticommunists thus maintained that America provided its citizens with unprecedented and singular prosperity and equity. Americans wanted for nothing, and the strength of civic feeling and "Christian (not atheist) mercy" guaranteed that no American who asked for aid ever starved—even, it seems, at the height of the depression. Consistent with the anticommunist movement's strong corporatist roots and ethos, anticommunist mythology also emphasized America's unique capacity to encourage "maximum initiative and maximum output" and, Horn insisted, to reward the "industrious in proportion to skill and application."[39]

This idealization of life in America, contingent on the most obstinate refusal to admit or acknowledge internal fault or difficulty, made possible the portrayal of the United States as an intrinsically whole and pure object that by definition could once more be made whole and cleansed when its impure elements were purged. The presence of communism in the United States, therefore, was portrayed as thoroughly alien and separate. The pure water of America's Melting Pot now carried on its surface contaminating oil that had to be skimmed off; no longer could it subsume excess exotic flavor into its white Protestant (or at the very least Christian) stew. This reasoning influenced the Fish Committee when it declared that the disproportionate number of the foreign-born in the Communist Party proved that the party and communism itself were not really a part of America and had "but little contact or influence with the great masses of the workers in American industries."[40]

This delineation of the legitimate elements of American society was an essential justification for antidemocratic, authoritarian behavior. As the communist Other was symbolically purged from the nation, anticommunists compared the qualities of American and communist societies to rationalize this division. Anticommunist mythology thus always extolled the virtues of American conditions and policies while demonstrating the miserable and brutish realities of communism and doing so in absolute, crude terms. The grossly exaggerated virtues of American government and society were juxtaposed with only the worst realities of Soviet communism. Yet much of the misery and brutishness of which anticommunists complained concerned not the pitiless slaughter and mass deportation of the Russian peasantry (though it certainly concerned Fries) but rather the principles of social leveling underpinning socialism. Dilling regarded Soviet economic redistributive practices, particularly the use of income tax to help fund public housing and cooperative stores, as an inexcusable fetter on individual rights. But perhaps the most offensive result of such practices was the conversion of "suburban homes formerly owned by well-to-do families" into Workers' Clubs filled with "workers in undershirts," sitting around "hammering grand pianos."[41]

The Moscow correspondent for the *Saturday Evening Post*, Isaac F. Marcosson, was much animated by snobbery, and he illustrated the collapse of Russian life principally by describing the folly of class and biological inversion. Marcosson's readers were invited to reflect on the calamities suffered by the former aristocracy and bourgeoisie, who alone received his sympathy. Readers learned that rural properties were being redistributed to benefit the "usually shiftless" rural proletariat—the masses of peasants on whom the Bolsheviks apparently relied for support—at the expense of those farmers who worked at "a high state of efficiency." These policies were creating a "rural proletariat" that illegally hoarded its produce, enriching itself at the expense of the starving urban middle class. Disgracefully, "old paintings, works of art, beautiful furniture, and even jewels" were now hanging "in the houses of the peasants." Marcosson could not contain his hatred for Soviet social equality, which, he spluttered, covered "a multitude of sins and likewise an immense amount of dirt and smell." The rise of Bolshevism not only brought about the abolition of "royalty, aristocracy and a few other trifles like property rights" but also established "an astounding and equally devastating human level" that was "just another name for mediocrity." Such conceit was merely a screen for the paranoid fear of self-disintegration and union with "inferior" peoples. Moreover, this projected horror found expression in the Fish Committee's report, which not only denounced American communists' "open advocacy" of "complete social and racial equality between the Whites and Negroes even to the extent of intermarriage" but also refused to accept that anyone could genuinely believe in social equality. The committee concluded that communists were cynically using the doctrine of equality as a recruiting ploy.[42]

Anticommunist conspiracy theory's separation of communist and American life was made possible by an absence of empathy and blindness to double standards. It was not enough for Marcosson to condemn Bolshevik dictatorship. He was determined also to deprive the Russian masses of any measure of sympathy. The internal logic of his propaganda required him to castigate Russians for "choosing" the wrong path and repudiating partnership with the United States. In effect, Russia's vulnerable and weak, like their counterparts in the United States, bore the brunt of anticommunists' fear, frustration, and fury. While anticommunists were eager to document communists' belief in the necessity of violence to dispossess capitalists and destroy the institutions that maintained their property rights, they were loath to consider the decades-long deployment of violence by capital and the state in America against wage laborers. And as the anticommunist crusade matured, its proponents not only refused to acknowledge this inconsistency but also divorced not only communists but even the entire Russian people from the boundaries of humanity.

Sinners Justly Punished

An example of such division appeared in a 1930 *Saturday Evening Post* story, "The Red Flag (In the Workers' Paradise)."[43] Written by F. Britten Austin, it is both a compendium of anticommunists' projected fears and a culmination of the paranoid splitting process. Austin depicted the revolution as corrupt and immoral, deriving from the ambition of debased and misguided working-class activists. His protagonist, Muscovite factory worker Ivan Ivanovitch Kozlov, greets the revolt with mindless fervor. Rushing home to share the news with his young family, Kozlov rejoices that Russia now belongs to the working class. Quickly brainwashing his daughter and son, he teaches them to say, "Long live Lenin! Down with the *bourjoui!* All power to the proletariat!" The manner in which Ivan treats his children reveals much about the psychology of revolutionaries. Selfish, degenerate, and foolish, they destroy their inheritance. Sure enough, Ivan's Russia quickly falls apart. Transportation ceases to function, shops are looted and boarded up, and piles of dead men litter the streets. The Kozlovs live in "squalid" conditions, a situation that Ivan believes justifies thieving: he brings home jewelry from "a fine *bourjoui* house," horrifying his wife, Maria Petrovna Kozlova. Maria embodies the old Russia: pious, honest, simple, and family-oriented. She refuses the "gold trinkets," stating, "That isn't right Ivan Ivanovitch! God forbids us to steal!" Unimpressed, Ivan admonishes Maria, "Don't let me hear any more of those superstitions! We have deposed the *bourjoui* God. He doesn't exist anymore!"

Austin revisits the Kozlov family in 1923. The revolution has devoured its children. Every day, aching with fatigue, Ivan labors for piecework wages in an "insufficiently illumined . . . squalid factory." He earns less than 60 percent of his prewar wage, and payments are "months in arrears." By some "miracle," his family has survived recent famines. He and his fellow workers are denied a voice in the management of their lives; they are dominated by the party and subordinate trade unions. The experiment in worker management of industry has failed. Under worker control, industry has "been much damaged." And cooperative ownership has brought unwelcome intrusion into private life. Ivan and his "comrades" hurriedly flee their workplace at the end of the day, fearful of orders to remain and plan economic strategy. In their free time, men face interminable harangues at the Workers' Club, and officials regularly force laborers to demonstrate, marching "for hours about this, that or the other happening in some foreign country."

The destruction of industry is compounded by the ruin of social custom. No one is addressed by name and patronymic or as "Mr." or "Mrs." Every one is

"Comrade X." Informality has reached obscene proportions. Personal life is public business, and personal morality is sacrificed for revolutionary change. One day after work, Ivan is accosted by a party man, Strubin, who is concerned about Ivan's *bourjoui* marital behavior.

> "I got a divorce today," [Strubin] remarked.
>
> Ivan was but mildly interested. Strubin was always marrying and getting a divorce; one just went to the registrar and asked for it. It was the easiest thing possible.
>
> "Was that Lydia?" he asked.
>
> Strubin laughed. "No. Lydia was last month. This was Marousia. She doesn't know yet." He laughed again.
>
> "Why do you marry them?" asked Ivan. "You always divorce them a week later."
>
> "It makes it more regular, as I'm a Party man."

Finally, Strubin arrives at his purpose, asking Ivan, "You've never divorced, have you?" Ivan ponders the wisdom of a divorce. His wife has "become very plain featured, worn and haggard, and her temper . . . abominable." Worse, she is a poor citizen, "always quarreling with [their daughter] Nadezhda and [son] Nikolai, holding up her hands in horror when they came home from school full of their atheist doctrines. 'Your revolution is just wickedness!' she would scream. Several times she had got into trouble with the house committee about it. It had cost him more than one bribe to hush things up." It would be simple for Ivan to procure the necessary papers. Strubin advises him, "If Maria Petrovna makes a fuss, denounce her to the house committee for creating a counter-revolutionary disturbance. I did that when Nasha wouldn't go." The roots of this madness and dysfunction lie deep in Russian culture; it is all most Russians know. Ivan reminisces about his childhood in his home village, where peasants habitually drank themselves into a stupor after dancing and singing. The secret police then arrest Ivan in the dead of night and whisk him away to prison, where he languishes for six months, fearing insanity, accused of colluding with counterrevolutionaries. He eventually realizes that Strubin has set him up to advance his own career. Such are the perils of a system that makes war on its own citizens.

By 1927, Ivan is free again, and if his hopes of increased prosperity have been dashed, he at least takes pride in his daughter, a paragon of communist virtue. Nadezhda, an atheist, is conformist, arrogant, insolent, and impertinent. A member of Komsomol (the Communist Youth League) and a patron of the "anti-God center," she will soon be off to university and a student hostel. She will rise in the party. She worries that her younger brother might be expelled from Komsomol because he has missed "anti-God meetings," reflecting poorly on the family. Nadezhda's boyfriend, Dmitri Somenov, "an insolently self-assured young man," dresses "typically" for a communist, in a "black leather jacket, breeches and spurs." He strides into the Kozlov's home as if he owns it, "ignoring Ivan's polite salutation" and is manifestly unwilling "to bother with mere nonparty people." Somenov sees Maria Petrovna's Orthodox icons in a corner of the living room and rudely upbraids Ivan, displaying total contempt for the older man. Ivan, in contrast, is supine and debased. He "cringingly" clutches at Somenov and "humbly" explains that his daughter is right to excuse him for this counterrevolutionary behavior: his wife is "obstinately superstitious." As the young couple sweep out of the apartment, Ivan is awed by the formidable creature that is his daughter: "Very different was she from the sluttish working-class girls of his own youth. This was what the proletarian dictatorship had produced—hard, self-reliant, smart, her head filled with all sorts of exciting things far beyond his atavistic stupidity." If there is any redemption to be found in Ivan's world, it will come from his more "intelligent" son. Nikolai seeks to break through the ideological fog enveloping their lives. He wants to see the world for himself and draw his own conclusions from experience. He tells his father, "I'm getting sick of this anti-God propaganda. . . . [I]t's all so crude. It's just obscenity." He continues, "As one grows up father . . . there's a lot of things a fellow wants help about. One can't help asking oneself questions. [The party] doesn't believe in a fellow thinking things for himself. Comrade Vashka told me the other day that I was still fettered by *bourjoui* ideology. That's nonsense. . . . [I]t seems to me that a proletarian ought to be encouraged to think." Pure and gifted Nikolai is doomed. His inquisitiveness and love of knowledge and justice bring him death. It occurs on one of Ivan's few days off work, when Ivan wakes in the knowledge that he will soon have to march in a mass protest against the execution of "two comrades named Sacco and Vanzetti," about whom he knows nothing. In the communal kitchen below, he hears his wife arguing with other women, "each using her little primus stove; all of them flatly [declining] to use the communal cooking range." Nadezhda arrives home and reveals that she is pregnant. Just as Maria Petrovna prepares to celebrate, her daughter coldly advises her that she has visited "Comrade Sonia" at the state abortion clinic and will have the pregnancy terminated the following day. She scolds her weeping mother: "'There's no need to throw up your hands, mother. I'm merely stating a fact. We're emancipated nowadays from your old *bourjoui* superstitions. All the girl students have babies—or don't have them.' She smiled again queerly. 'It's their own affair. This is my affair. It doesn't call for sentimentalism. It's just a matter of physiology.'" Nadezhda refuses to jeopardize her professional career and warns her parents that Nikolai's apathy for party duties will bring him trouble. Ivan is confident that Nikolai knows what he is doing but knows nothing of his son's whereabouts or inner thoughts. Nadezhda is not surprised. Members of the younger generation will not seek counsel from their parents, since "none of the old ideas count any more." Just as she berates her parents for dealing with speculators in the early 1920s and for their complicity in the retreat from "communist principles" that necessitated the New Economic Policy, a neighbor arrives to tell the Kozlovs that Nikolai has been shot for associating with Menshevik counterrevolutionaries. Maria Petrovna immediately faints. Ivan is relieved that the rest of the family is not under suspicion, but Nadezhda, an inhuman monster, is triumphant:

> "Plotting counter-revolution you say? Serves him right!"
> "Nadezhda!" [Ivan] could not help that protest. "You forget he's your brother!"
> "Brother!" she said, in bitter scorn. "I have no brother who was a counter-revolutionary. We of the Party know no family. We know only comrades in the world revolution. And we exterminate traitors."
> [Ivan] shuddered. Never would he understand these young people.

Before leaving, Nadezhda reminds her father to participate in the Sacco-Vanzetti demonstration to avert suspicion. Ivan leaves Maria Petrovna in the care of a neighbor and prepares to go out. In a breathtakingly crude passage, Austin describes Ivan's response to his son's execution to illustrate the unbridgeable difference between communists and citizens of a capitalist republic:

> As he hurried down the stairs he thought of Nikolai. He would never see him any more. A despicable *bourjoui* emotion blurred his sight with tears, choked his throat. . . . An hour later he marched in the long procession under great double banners inscribed DOWN WITH THE AMERICAN CAPITALIST MURDERERS! . . . They marched, thousands upon thousands of them, in broad ranks, in endless serpents arriving and merging into one great mass, tramping in disciplined unison, left, right, left, right. In that mass his own individuality was swamped, blurred. He was one infinitesimal component in an immensity far transcending himself, part of the mass, the mass that was marching blindly, irresistibly, to a world victory. That sense of collective strength sustained him, weary though he was, made him think of Nikolai as something extraneous to it, something justly exterminated because he was hostile to that mass. It was odd that he should feel like that, for underneath it all he was heartbroken for Nikolai. That was because he was one of the old generation, who could never become fully revolutionary.

Austin's account of the degeneracy of Russian life encapsulates the entire scope of anticommunist mythology. It confirmed that communism utterly destroyed appreciation of religion, marriage, family, friendship, order, prosperity, privacy, achievement, knowledge, and justice, leaving no basis or justification for any form of relations between communists and the people of the United States. Consequently, communists' ideas and feelings could be entirely disregarded. Communism both abroad and at home was to be attacked, and the process of intellectual and emotional expulsion expressed in anticommunist propaganda gave birth to antidemocratic fantasies of purging the nation of its unwanted elements. Many anticommunists indeed set about achieving this task.

CHAPTER 12

Antidemocracy and Authoritarianism

It [is] impossible to have a democratic form of government in a nation of this size. . . . For the people of this
country to be called upon to vote directly upon every sort
of proposal [produces] nothing but dangerous confusion.

—Fred R. Marvin

Anticommunist conspiracy theory, anticommunist propaganda, and the actions of many anticommunists ultimately encouraged the destruction of democracy and its replacement by a system of government by kinship group or tribe. The propaganda issued by the Anticommunist Spider Web, stressing the inherent disloyalty and degeneracy of huge sections of the community, inevitably pointed toward the restriction of American citizenship to those who truly deserved it. Many Web members sought to restrict the franchise to people of the same ethnic background and religious and political beliefs. So even though anticommunist rhetoric emphasized the virtues of republican government and the universal basis of citizenship, it ultimately sought to legitimize an antidemocratic and even authoritarian society. This lesson was learned from the Spider Web Chart: because communists trawled the dregs of society to further their cause, anticommunists determined to do the opposite. And although some anticommunists recognized that the radical nature of their project was at odds with democratic political traditions, the Spider Web expended much energy developing elaborate theories to justify the radical restriction of the franchise and enlightened rule by members of the anticommunist fraternity.

Establishing Anticommunism

In spirit, anticommunism's antidemocratic thrust developed not only out of traditional antiunion and antiradical sympathy but also out of the recent impulse to eliminate antiwar sentiment. Further, the forces of Bolshevism, vastly more powerful and widespread than that of the kaiser, were thought to require even greater opposition. Thus the Lusk Committee described anticommunism as a crusade for the soul of humanity: the Bolshevik threat to the United States reached "down to the fundamentals of man's nature and the organization of society." Accordingly, the committee solicited the unreserved allegiance of "loyal Americans" and projected its argument for authoritarian control onto the nation. Maintaining that the United States needed "leadership" that could revive "religious and moral standards as the basis" of a new "political and economic program," the committee volunteered its services in this capacity. The committee ostensibly grounded its fight against socialism in democratic action: the community would be "appealed to . . . given the facts . . . made to see the causes and remedies . . . made to band itself together as a civic force." However, only a select few—purportedly a meritocratic body of public representatives but in reality a kinship group of "leading men"—could really be entrusted to lead America's crusade for righteousness. Because honest but weak-minded citizens would continue to be "turned to purposes of contamination [by] astute, hardworking, clearheaded revolutionists," it was essential that the anticommunist kinship group formulate and enforce state policy. Like philosopher kings, the kinship group would stamp out "disjointed, unprincipled, unpractical or sentimental altruism." It would make the errant "understand the realities and dangers" of their efforts" and lead them "to the camp of constructive action." Hence the committee professed the archetypal paranoid fantasy of total control of the external environment as its ultimate goal.[1]

Because anticommunist conspiracy theory preoccupied its adherents with allaying anxiety, they often acted without understanding their obligations and even their objectives. Anticommunists tended to plunge into repressive operations, careless of their legality. Only sometimes did they worry about justifying such operations after their commission. Those who did worry quickly persuaded themselves that their actions had been legitimate or denied their unconstitutional character with the aid of semantic and psychological devices. And ultimate measures were always sanctioned by moral rights and duties, themselves a curious mix of cynicism, opportunism, and antinomianism.

The Committee on Public Information was particularly adept at denial, perhaps because it was led by advertising men whose expertise in self-promotion and the manipulation of public perception made them important creators, distributors, and justifiers of anticommunist propaganda. George Creel spoke of the committee as an embodiment of and force for democratic action. However, its purpose and methods were wholly antidemocratic. Creel's method for mobilizing "democracy" sought not to incorporate multiple voices in consultation but rather to manage the minds of the masses under strict supervision. He wanted to make the American people the federal government's helpers and guardians, generating "no mere surface unity, but a passionate belief in the justice of America's cause that should weld the people of the United States into one white-hot mass instinct with fraternity, devotion, courage, and deathless determination." In spite of Creel's claims that America's fight was "for all that life has taught decent human beings to hold dear," his committee's chief objective was to make all citizens feel "a compulsion from within" to pursue the government's war aims— in other words, to enforce mass conformity. The committee behaved similarly abroad. Creel described its foreign section as "designed to clear away all points of misunderstanding and misconception that prevailed, or might prevail . . . in regard to America, its life, work, ideals, and opinions." Yet its operations in Europe and Russia were intended to ensure that as the "Poles, Czechs, Austrians, Hungarians, and Jugoslavs were crystallizing into new political shapes," they would "have the *facts*" about Bolshevism so that "their determinations might form along lines acceptable to the new world." Only self-delusion distinguished the committee's educational activities from propaganda. Creel reasoned that the committee's foreign success would come from the "friendship and support" of other nations, gained "by continuous presentation of facts." He did not accept that he was spreading propaganda and refused to acknowledge the common bond uniting the Bolshevik and US governments in their desire to control citizens' beliefs. Others, among them Senator John Sharp Williams, a Mississippi Democrat, distinguished American and Bolshevik propaganda on a moral basis: "American propaganda" did the work not of propagandists but of humanitarians, "just as Christ's cure of the sick and resurrection of the dead was, in the highest sense, propaganda work."[2]

Such denial and delusion were essential to the formulation and implementation of authoritarian anticommunism. Further, by isolating themselves from contrary opinions and influences, anticommunist kinship groups were encouraged to operate in a furtive and dictatorial manner, just like the communists they despised. The Lusk Committee summarily tried and convicted its enemies, seized and published citizens' private correspondence, and was responsible for the arrest, criminal conviction, and loss of employment of many citizens. The committee also evinced little trust in the public's political judgment and did not respect its sovereignty. Instead, it justified its actions with semantic exercises and appeals to fear, leveling baseless allegations while protecting its deliberations from scrutiny. The committee repeatedly claimed, for example, that it was obliged to withhold "much of the evidence" of communist perfidy that came into its possession for use in "criminal prosecutions." Yet such concerns never discouraged the committee from sweetening its report with hearsay that damned suspects by inference and association.[3]

Other anticommunist groups felt less restricted than government bodies in admitting to elitist and authoritarian designs. Business lobbies regularly proclaimed their God-given right to stand atop society, rationalizing the maintenance of rigid social and commercial hierarchies as the stamp of natural order. Business-funded anticommunists evinced such elitism in part because their propaganda was so compatible with the philosophy of individualism. The promise of egalitarian opportunity at the heart of American national identity had always been made on specific, onerous conditions. As Herbert Hoover put it, citizens were entitled to "equality of opportunity" only to the degree warranted by their "intelligence, character, ability, and ambition." The acceptance of inherent inequality was thus intrinsic to traditional political ideology and an article of faith for anticommunist kinship groups, who urged the populace to accept that political inequality was as necessary as economic and racial inequality. And for not a few anticommunists, belief in inequality was a pathway to abandoning the "mistaken idea," as Fred Marvin put it, "that 'The majority must rule.'"[4]

Marvin W. Littleton, a New York congressman and associate of Marvin, like many Web members, associated democracy with unacceptable risk to national security and prosperity. He took umbrage at the "not finally affirmed but supposed" idea that "the consent of the governed" best guaranteed "life, liberty and happiness" for all. A government's first duty was to secure the people's life, liberty, and happiness but not necessarily their consent. Democracy, Littleton averred, was too influenced by "sweet moralities." It was too easy for citizens to concern themselves primarily with "those things which are right and wrong" and about which "everybody" could have an opinion because forming that opinion did not require "much information." The difficult tasks of running a nation and an economy, by contrast, took a great deal of accurate information, accessible only to a select, hardheaded few. The US Army's Military Intelligence Division similarly distrusted the calamitous influence of democracy. Senior officers believed that "sweet moralists" and pacifists undermined "natural patriotic spirit and feeling" and imperiled specialists' proper control of America's foreign policy.[5]

Anticommunists sought to exercise this proper control of American domestic and foreign policy in numerous ways, none more important than the illegal and clandestine maintenance of enormous indexes of American radicals. The Anticommunist Spider Web's determination to document every facet of the domestic radical movement betrayed not just the self-interested desire to reestablish a

Red Scare–era intelligence network but also the belief that the members of the Web had a moral right and imperative to exceed the jurisdiction of democracy. These lists would enable the Spider Web to spring into action when needed to save American democracy from both the communists and itself.

Putting the Anticommunist House in Order

While gravely concerned with controlling society, Spider Web members were also anxious to bring their own organizations under firm control. Military commanders had long been concerned about communist infiltration and perversion of the armed forces. While they wanted to introduce exacting regulations to prevent the enlistment of "persons of communist affiliations," they had difficulty reforming the enlistment process, much to their chagrin. They had little objective cause to worry: in the interwar period, only two privates in Military Intelligence were court-martialed for communist activity. And when titillating legislative committees with tales of communist subversion, the military had to be careful to avoid calling into question the army's competence to control its own security.[6]

J. Edgar Hoover was similarly disgusted by the "absence of any federal statute prohibiting the so-called Communistic or radical activities" in federal agencies and the armed services. He regarded such legal impediments as a transitory nuisance as his response to the 1924 reform of the Bureau of Investigation illustrates. In 1936, he noted that "the activities of Communists and other ultra-radicals" had not "constituted a violation of Federal Statutes," meaning that his department "theoretically, [had] no right to investigate such activities." Regardless of the technical interpretations of its legal rights, Hoover believed that the bureau was obliged to act in whatever way he saw fit to defend the nation.[7]

Paranoid Authoritarianism

Opposition to democracy and a pluralist society was the inevitable and ultimate terminus of anticommunist conspiracy theory. This opposition was manifest in two major approaches to the development and implementation of anticommunist public policy: expelling and monitoring radical persons, and eradicating "false" beliefs from the community through "educative" means. In practice, these hard and soft approaches were not dissimilar. Both expressed not just political and economic advantage but also in some cases the reactionary psychology of the paranoid position, which could imprison anticommunists in debilitating psychic and rhetorical quagmires. In addition, the advocacy of authoritarianism— whether opportunistic or sincere—presented anticommunists with a difficult political challenge: deciding how public support should best be galvanized and incorporated into their crusade. To resolve this dilemma, anticommunists appealed especially to racial, religious, and ethnic prejudices to encourage public identification with a reconstituted and drastically shrunken national tribe. This appeal to prejudice was manifest in immigration restriction, the repression of foreign language and identity, and Americanization programs.

Support for authoritarian policies and actions in the Anticommunist Spider Web was unstinting and impervious to circumstances. Web members responded to the depression with sharpened fear of revolution and continuing advocacy of exclusionary and censorious measures. Some of these measures found support in the highest circles. President Hoover supported such national security measures as the forcible removal of "criminal aliens" through strengthened deportation laws and the stringent monitoring of migrants. Such monitoring would ideally occur through the issue of certificates to lawfully resident aliens, a scheme that was briefly realized in Michigan's Spolansky Act. It was axiomatic that such reform necessitated enlarging domestic surveillance powers, which constituted a significant motive for such reform. The Fish Committee, which saw the reinstatement of the Bureau of Investigation's Red Scare powers as one of its two prime objectives, expressed a hope that the agency would be able to devote its "entire time to investigating and preparing reports on the personnel of all [objectionable] entities, groups [and] individuals."[8]

The most common anticommunist responses to the depression included Lusk-style education measures. Yet Spider Web suspicions about colleges and instructors were generally misplaced. Far from being hotbeds of radicalism, institutions of higher education had an effective regime of self-censorship that kept them politically docile. Even after the repeal of the Lusk Acts, Ellen Schrecker has noted, a "normal" level of political repression suppressed "the academy's most outspoken and conspicuous radicals." Until the late 1930s, university faculties remained "apolitical, genteel, and essentially conservative," with "semi-feudal employment practices" that enabled them to purge any suspected radical instructors who lacked tenure. Nevertheless, fear of an upsurge in campus radicalism during the Great Depression increased the pressure placed on the academy from the Red-baiting mainstream press, the American Legion, the Catholic Church, and state legislators. Twenty-one states and the District of Columbia enacted new teacher loyalty oath laws by 1936. Such measures gained greater legitimacy with the Nazi-Soviet nonaggression pact of 1939 and revelations of Stalin's great purge of the Soviet Communist Party. As the idea of the party as a conspiracy became nearly universal, "previously reluctant liberals [endorsed] the anticommunist measures that right-wing politicians and journalists had been urging for years." By the close of the 1930s, the political environment for the Spider Web was as favorable as it had been since the Red Scare. As the nation moved rightward, according to Schrecker, the political "fringes which these traditional anti-communists inhabited" were brought closer to the political center, where "they had once been." Another Red scare was soon in full swing "in many segments of American society." Unions expelled communist leaders and communist-dominated locals. In 1940, Congress passed the Alien Registration Act (the Smith Act), which reiterated the criminality of advocating revolution and finally introduced the compulsory alien registration scheme for which anticommunists had long agitated. And anticommunists transformed the Rapp-Coudert Committee, a state legislative body originally established to inquire into the financial state of New York City schools, into "what was, until the height of the McCarthy era . . . by far the largest purge of politically undesirable professors" that had been conducted in America. The committee, chaired by Frederic "Fritz" Coudert III, son of a director of the American Defense Society, provided an important inspiration and resource for McCarthy era Red-baiters.[9]

To generate support for authoritarian policies, anticommunists relied heavily on propaganda. Yet anticommunist propaganda typically betrayed unacknowledged doubt about the political judgment of the American people. This propaganda also betrayed its propagators' lack of faith in the logic and persuasiveness of their own case. Anticommunists attempted to compensate by investing their beliefs with a sacred aura, asserting those beliefs with forceful language, and denying and dissociating themselves from the harmful effects of their policies and actions.

Anticommunist propaganda consistently exaggerated its proponents' identification with the American people, often at the climax of speeches or articles, to give an impression of sympathy with popular sentiment and appreciation for the broader public's sagacity. Yet these appeals constituted the propaganda's sole manifestation of populism or support for democracy. Anticommunists often expressed their passion for democracy rather suddenly at the conclusion of a rhetorical tirade. The first 231 pages of Blair Coán's 232-page *The Red Web*, for example, regard the "American people" with suspicion, deriding them as a disloyal, fickle mob unworthy of holding the franchise, let alone power. But in the final paragraph, Coán abruptly places the future of America in the hands of that mob and enjoins the American people to determine "the kind of government—red, pink or red-white-and-blue" that will administer the United States.[10]

The pressure anticommunists felt to establish ideological control was heightened by the fact that they had for the most part a limited understanding of historical processes and social structures. Anticommunist rhetoric strained to make complex theory and phenomena conform to its proponents' often infeasible and simplistic notions. Many anticommunists behaved as though they could separate revolution from class issues with forceful language alone. The task of differentiating Americanism from communism frequently stumped anticommunists. While confident in noting the symptoms of social collapse in Russia, they had greater difficulty ascribing its causation. One author cited in Elizabeth Dilling's *Red Network* attributed the revolution to "the loss of private ownership which always fosters personal interest and initiative," made apparent by "the dirty drab dilapidation in Russia, with its uncurtained, broken windows and unrepaired roofs."[11]

The level of knowledge and analysis in official intelligence circles was similarly rudimentary, as a 1923 lecture delivered by Military Intelligence Division lieutenant Ralph Duncan to his peers shows. Duncan's comprehension of contemporary global history and revolutionary processes was not only crude but also nonsensical. Rather like Fred Marvin and John E. Nelson, Duncan understood the "six principal aims of communism" to be the "abolition of private property . . . all rights of inheritance . . . the family . . . marriage . . . religion . . . and cities and towns." Just why communists should seek to abolish cities and towns, he did not explain. Nevertheless, he asserted that communists planned to seize control of the United States by dividing "the voting population . . . into three principal groups . . . the Women, the Farmers and Labor," each of which would be educated and mobilized for revolt. Unperturbed by the needless exclusion such a scheme would make of huge sections of the populace, Duncan turned to global politics, arguing that communism led "inevitably to a state of anarchy." To substantiate this claim, Duncan recalled "the fate of the Russian people" and the "conditions under the socialist dictatorship in Germany." It is not clear whether Duncan was referring to the short-lived socialist government of Munich or the Weimar Republic, but he likely had no real idea. His sole task was to motivate others to fight "the insidious, intellectual poison of communism," which was "mutually exclusive" of and "wholly incompatible" with "Christian civilisation." Verifying his assertions and organizing them into a coherent structure was of secondary importance.[12]

The failure of many anticommunists to think through their beliefs was especially apparent in their habit of cultivating horror and outrage with conditions thought to be unique to Soviet Russia. However, many of these conditions also existed in the United States. Anticommunist propaganda decried living conditions in Russia: the dearth of quality goods and services; rampant inflation; the general deprivation of infrastructure, agriculture, and industry; the censorship of opinion; the subjugation of trade unions; the deportation of millions of kulaks and ethnic minorities; the corrupt wealth of party members; and the ubiquity of the dreaded secret police. Yet millions of Americans were also impoverished by mass unemployment and enormous disparities of wealth and opportunity. Their labor organizations were suppressed and destroyed by state and corporate entities. And their public letters and opinions were censored. The Anticommunist Spider Web would not acknowledge these unpalatable facts, brushing them off with semantic contrivances. Thus government suppression of labor unions was typically described, as it was by the Fish Committee, as an act of benevolence, a lone "defense" of American workers "against communist attacks on industry." The Lusk Committee similarly described its education act as a pastoral gesture, disregarding the damage it caused to the morale of teachers, students, and ethnic and labor communities. Further, the committee failed to recognize the similarity of its antiradical measures to the "educational" activities of the much-hated Bolsheviks.[13]

For all the conviction with which they put forward their views, anticommunist propagandists were generally nervous about the intellectual deficiencies and crudity of their work. Indeed, they believed themselves to be at a particular disadvantage relative to their enemies on the left in comprehending and propagating social theory. This perception helped to foster resentment of intellectuals and antipathy toward humanistic education. The equanimity of some left-wing intellectuals also infuriated anticommunists, who were destabilized by these thinkers' apparent liberation from regressive and defensive political structures. Dilling expressed characteristic anti-intellectual distemper in her writings on "so-called" Christian pacifism, indicating her discomfort with any suggestion of reasoning with enemies. Also evincing hot contempt for those who threatened conservatives' exclusive identification with Christ, Dilling cited II Corinthians 7:14 and Matthew 12:29 to caution the "righteous" to avoid "communion with darkness" and to lambast the "sincere Christian pacifist" who "buried his head in the sand . . . blindly ignoring the fact that those most dominant in influencing, financing, boring from within, if not actually controlling the great majority of pacifist societies are Socialists and Communists who appear in the clothing of sheep crying 'Peace! Peace!' . . . like ravening wolves . . . agitating 'class struggle,' 'class war,' civil wars and bloody revolution."[14]

Illiberal anticommunists also projected their envy and fear of intellectuals into the notion that the Red and Pink intelligentsia improperly influenced government and disenfranchised mainstream America. The Westchester Security League articulated this concern to Congress in 1934. Although worried that governments were not taking seriously patriots' counsel, the League could not sustain this charge, and the vague, tortured quality of its rhetoric expressed its fundamental anxiety. Requesting an "investigation . . . broad and comprehensive enough to give the American people a complete picture of the radical movement," the League complained, "We feel that it, the radical movement, is greater and more dangerous than you seem to believe. During the past year the American people have had some intensive education as to the fundamental changes in principles of Government, as favored by many professors. The citizens have a right to know where those changed principles may lead them."[15]

Proponents of authoritarian anticommunism occasionally addressed its intellectual poverty. J. Howard Rhodes, an advertising executive engaged by the Westchester Security League to assist with publicity, acknowledged patriots' educational deficiency and counseled them to improve their intellectual training: "It is all right to stir up these young socialists, but some of the 'stirrers' should be prepared to snap back the answers to floor them, otherwise the members of the [League] will be put down as 'red-baiters' or fanatics. The 'liberal's' [sic] like nothing better than to try to make their opponents look ridiculous. See what they did to the Liberty League; to the DAR and others who have opposed them. . . . We 'conservative's' [sic] have everything in our favor but skill in the art of disputation. . . . It takes a Jew to beat a Jew."[16]

Yet while some anticommunists recognized the need to improve their education, their self-improvement efforts seem not to have matched their ambition. The anticommunist defense of capitalism continued to rest on the total denial of structural dysfunction in the economy, made possible only by comparing the United States favorably with the USSR and by never measuring America's equity and prosperity against its own ideals and laws. The Political Right recognized various criticisms as damaging and embarrassing; economic inequality was especially disturbing. Anticommunists' stock response to such criticism was to claim, as Dilling did, that "millions of Americans, a greater proportion of the population than in any other country," had invested in their nation, in "farms, homes, property, stock, savings or a business of some sort." The gross size of the economy was also emphasized, as was pride in the abstract achievement of national strength. In the teeth of America's greatest economic downturn, Republican congressman Hamilton Fish Jr., Swiss- and Harvard-educated, the son of a congressman and grandson of a secretary of state, simply shut his eyes to the radicalizing effects of decades of labor suppression in America, boasting, "For the last thirty years we in this country have been wiping out abuse after abuse to protect the wage earners and to give them better conditions." He continued by contending that the American economic system had made the country's wage earners "for many, many years the best paid, the best fed, the best clothed, the best housed, and the most contented in the world."[17]

While intellectual myopia helped anticommunists to rationalize their views and plans, it could not mask fundamental deficiencies in their political program or psychology. The kinship groups' failure to create viable alternative means of government clashed with national democratic traditions and elements of their own dogma, which forced them into a reluctant dialogue with communism and other ideologies. The burden of democracy and the legacy of republicanism compelled them to acknowledge the universality of political rights, even though they denied many citizens the capacity to responsibly exercise those rights. And the tension between the psychological drive to establish absolute control and traditional obligations of openness and power sharing helped to prevent the Anticommunist Spider Web from realizing many of its authoritarian schemes.

In addition to being impractical, anticommunist measures generally came too late to bring about desired change. Legislation expediting the deportation of undesirable alien internees, for example, passed Congress only after no such internees were left to deport. In this respect, the legislation proved as useful as the Immigration Act of 1903, which penalized membership in anarchist organizations years after they had essentially vanished from the political landscape. The Immigration Act of 1924 was another example of reactive, tardy activity. By the time the act came into effect, immigration restrictionists had in all but a symbolic sense lost their battle. Between 1880 and the 1924, twenty-five million immigrants entered the United States, permanently altering its ethnic profile and culture. The act thus stood with the Ku Klux Klan as an ultimately futile gesture aimed at preserving the racial and cultural purity and primacy of Protestant Anglo-Saxons.[18]

Aside from encouraging impractical public policy, cardinal tenets of anticommunism caused even its advocates discomfort. The patent injustices created or worsened by unmediated capitalism were particularly discomforting. And the tension caused by defending these injustices created problems for conservatives outside the Spider Web. It paralyzed such senior political figures as President Hoover. His inability to conceive public policy outside the framework of "American individualism" and "enlightened self-interest," according to his biographer, Joan Hoff, gravely compromised his attempt to "explain clearly the subtle difference between the uncontrolled, individual acquisitiveness and open-ended national expansion so characteristic of nineteenth-century America, and his dream of a humane, voluntarily controlled capitalistic system based on cooperatively sharing the abundance produced by technology."[19]

Rather than being accepted as a progressive capitalist, Hoover was pilloried for supporting crude and aged justifications of social stratification and for being indolent in the face of great misery. As the Great Depression worsened, these charges were routinely leveled against illiberal anticommunists and business advocates of the free market, whose public esteem fell so low that the Republican Party asked them to dissociate themselves from the 1936 presidential campaign. In any event, the members of the Anticommunist Spider Web surrendered to aggressive impulses and remained insensitive to the social harm they caused. The countless acts of legal and psychological abuse performed by its members occasioned at most an abstract and not-widely-shared sense of regret. But such regret was invariably overshadowed by the more dominant characteristics of ferocity, ignorance, viciousness, vengefulness, and incapacity for reflection. The intellectual, moral, and psychological paralysis of paranoid anticommunist conspiracy theory, engendered by the Spider Web and others between the Bolshevik Revolution and the Cold War, continued to influence American politics, even to the present day.[20]

Conclusion
Legacies of the Spider Web

The Russians [have been] a flop in other countries. Yet the
Russian bear dominates just about everything we do. I wonder how
much of my whole life and my generation has been influenced to
hate the Russians. Even when I didn't even know where it was.

—Eugene Larocque

The legacies of the Anticommunist Spider Web survive in myriad ways in the
extraordinary life span and significance of anticommunism in US politics,
economy, and culture. That significance can scarcely be overestimated. Allan
Lichtman, for example, has recently argued that anticommunism in the Cold War
became "the largest and most luminous planet orbiting the conservative sun"
and a "gospel" bonding "elite economic conservatives with religious conservatives and middle- and working-class populists." This doctrine "could never be
preached with too much fire and brimstone."[1]

Other historians attribute the phenomenon even greater importance. Frank
Donner has maintained that in the absence of positive "shared values," American
society has been defined primarily by its communist antithesis. Regardless of
whether one accepts these assessments, it is clear that throughout the twentieth
century, anticommunism placed the "stigma of unworthy," as Donner has put it,
on the same ideas and people whom the Spider Web identified as intrinsically
"un-American." The Web's descendants used the same arguments, rhetorical
tropes, and state and corporate instruments to pursue the political, economic,
and social agenda of their forebears. And the cooperation of liberals and labor
unions in the suppression of anything that smacked of "communism" restricted

public debate about how the Left might or should influence the future of America while creating an ideological void that the heirs of the Spider Web rushed to fill.[2]

The Triumph of the Surveillance State

Among the most important consequences of anticommunism was the creation of the surveillance state. The intelligence bureaucracy for nearly a hundred years was, as Donner has succinctly written, "the steward of American anti-communism." Adopting a counterrevolutionary mission similar to those of political police forces in authoritarian societies, the civil and military intelligence establishment strove to counter government intervention in the economy and society and to drive Marxism and other subversive (but almost exclusively left-wing) ideas from popular consciousness. To do so, the national security apparatus grew exponentially, evading the control of elected officials and encompassing civil law enforcement agencies. Reviving and expanding techniques of the Red Scare and the interwar period, the Federal Bureau of Investigation (FBI), police Red Squads, and federal and state legislative committees collaborated to expand the postwar fight against "communism" into almost every corner of US society. Following the rise of the Popular Front of labor, socialist, and communist organizations in the 1930s, FBI director J. Edgar Hoover persuaded President Franklin Roosevelt to allow the agency to resume its covert internal security operations. Hoover drove a truck through that clandestine legal fissure, creating a security empire over which he presided as "Minister for Internal Security and Propaganda." Holding responsibility both for domestic security and federal law enforcement, Hoover was vested with powers that the Soviet Politburo would not have dreamed of conferring on its secret police chiefs. Further, he was left essentially free to supervise his own operations.[3]

Starting in the mid-1930s, Hoover was empowered to annex state and local police into his virtual kingdom. While Roosevelt may have been concerned with avoiding a repeat of the anticommunist vigilantism of the Red Scare and the interwar period, the president's request that local and state police turn over to the FBI information relating "to espionage, counter-espionage, sabotage [and] subversive activities" encouraged numerous states to establish their own anti-subversive units and local police to engage in extensive electronic surveillance and wiretapping operations, which the bureau itself was prohibited from conducting. After the Second World War, the task of hunting Reds was institutionally separated from general policing and criminal detection. The duties of Red Squads, according to Donner, ranged from screening "questionable applicants for speaking permits on the basis of file data, traveling the luncheon circuits, and exchanging information with and answering inquiries from other cities, to selecting wiretap targets, running informers, and developing press outlets."[4]

Throughout his fifty-year reign as bureau director, Hoover and his police, military, and legislative allies relied on the specter of communism to justify the continuous surveillance of American citizens and organizations. Although the US Communist Party (CP) remained pitifully small, Hoover always brandished the example of the Bolsheviks before legislators, government officials, and the American public, reminding them that the American party could claim more members than Lenin's Bolsheviks had in 1917. The creation of federal law abridging First Amendment rights was Hoover's ultimate objective. However, it was also a defensive goal to distract attention from the patent absence of revolutionary threats in the United States. The ruse worked until Hoover's death in 1972. The FBI's surveillance of antiwar elements during the Vietnam War, for example, proceeded on the grounds that a supposed failure to monitor students during the Great Depression had allowed radical infiltration of the federal government. And although the bureau's counterintelligence program (which existed from roughly 1956 to 1971) weakened the Ku Klux Klan and other violent white hate groups, its efforts to disrupt "Black Nationalist-Hate" and "New Left" groups took in law-abiding civil rights organizations and activists. The bureau's civil-rights-era marriage of Red and black scares similarly perpetuated its war on long-vanished figures such as Marcus Garvey and more recent ones such as famed actor, singer, activist, and frequent visitor to the USSR Paul Robeson, against whom the bureau and the State Department waged a ten-year and almost lethal campaign.[5]

The labor movement remained a principal target of infiltration for security agencies and legislative committees. Although the CP was small, its influence on labor unions and the American Left was regarded, feared, and described as huge. Countersubversive organizations assumed that subversive elements in local unions and workforces were advancing the CP's program, an assumption that gave new life to old state criminal syndicalism laws. In Michigan, for example, the legislature revised state law to authorize the formation of a countersubversive unit "to discourage the employment of subversive individuals." According to Donner, these urban and state units "shared investigative information and files, conducted joint operations, and consulted in such matters as target selection" while strengthening their "role as an operational resource of federal agencies" including the FBI, the Immigration and Naturalization Service, and the House Un-American Activities Committee (HUAC).[6]

Although the US Army was supposed to defer to the FBI in such matters, intelligence units also monitored left-wing and antiwar movements until the early 1970s. The Counter Intelligence Corps spied on behalf of US senator Joseph McCarthy, including on the army itself, while the Joint Chiefs later authorized the services to indoctrinate civilians on the communist peril, leading to the re-generation of its Red Scare–era intelligence infrastructure.[7]

The men who ran the nation's security agencies brooked no limits on their power and regarded most efforts to supervise their activity as unwelcome and even treasonous meddling. No security official evinced this attitude with greater obduracy than J. Edgar Hoover. Hoover not only considered statutory limits on the FBI's jurisdiction "theoretical" but later deceived President Harry Truman and then President Dwight D. Eisenhower's attorney general by denying having illegally provided several governors with bureau files on alleged "communists employed in state agencies, including colleges and universities." The various legislators who staffed federal and state un-American activities committees similarly and serially violated rules governing their access to and right to dis-tribute information. The most (in)famous and important of these committees, HUAC, was not permitted to consult with the FBI except in expressly authorized instances. Covertly, however, the two enjoyed a symbiotic relationship. Hoover directed bureau staff to supply the committee with reports about investigative targets, and the committee would then subpoena these people without disclosing the bureau's role in impugning their reputations. The information the committee gathered was promptly divulged to the FBI, enabling Hoover to discredit people as "communist" threats to national security even though he lawfully could not investigate them.[8]

Having become accustomed to such latitude during the Cold War, security agencies continue to "leverage their coercive power," as Corey Robin has ob-served, targeting dissenters "posing no conceivable threat." In recent decades, the threat of terrorism has supplanted that of communism as security organizations' principal justification for assuming extraordinary powers, particularly after 11 September 2001. Since then, according to Robin, FBI and police officials have systematically interpreted "individual statements of opposition to U.S. foreign policy or the [incumbent] administration as a sign of possible terrorist inclina-tions" and have monitored the people uttering these statements. Members of the American Civil Liberties Union as well as Amnesty International, the Green Party, the "antiwar movement," and the Catholic Church have routinely been de-tained even though the FBI has acknowledged that it possesses no information suggesting that these organizations or individuals have ever planned "violent or terrorist activities." A former contractor with the National Security Agency, Edward Snowden, revealed the existence of a clandestine electronic surveillance program, monitoring the communications of almost everyone possessing a cell phone or Internet connection in the United States as well as in a host of foreign nations. The problem of inadequate oversight of the national security bureau-cracy remains: journalist Ryan Lizza has argued that most members of the Senate

Select Committee on Intelligence "treat senior intelligence officials like matinée idols." And security chiefs continue to regard congressional supervision of their activity as theoretical: the Obama administration's director of National Intelligence, James R. Clapper, deliberately misled the intelligence committee during 2013 hearings on National Security Agency activity and corrected the record only after Snowden's leaks forced his hand.[9]

Just as Cold War national security officials recognized no limits to their jurisdiction, they evinced a callous disregard and even outright cynicism regarding the consequences of their actions. Hoover in particular never forgot the cardinal lessons of the Red Scare: attend ceaselessly to the public image of his bureau and make maximum political capital out of even insignificant cases if doing so aided the overarching mission of destroying "communism." No longer willing to leave the FBI's reputation in the hands of the media, Hoover established a public relations arm, the "Crime Records Division," whose boss was responsible for shaping the bureau's public image and responding to criticism it received. According to historian Seth Rosenfeld, the division's head had "extensive contacts among news reporters, bureau supporters, and members" of the American Legion, which he also served as director of public relations. A significant part of the division's function was to ensure that the electorate retained confidence in the bureau, particularly in its efforts to root out Reds serving in the federal government. Soviet spies Julius and Ethel Rosenberg paid for this need with their lives after committing what Hoover described as the "Crime of the Century." Notorious though they were, the Rosenbergs were not regarded by US authorities as particularly important spies. Hoover himself acknowledged in confidential memoranda that the Soviets probably obtained secret details of the US atomic program from other, more effective agents. However, he raised no objection to their execution because the spies who had obtained the atomic secrets had eluded his bureau agents. Thus, the Rosenbergs were executed in part to conceal the bureau's fundamental ineffectiveness as a counterespionage agency, just as members of the Union of Russian Workers had been deported when the bureau failed to identify any Red Scare bombers.[10]

In any event, the raison d'être of Cold War anticommunism was never restricted to destroying communism. The growth of the national security apparatus and its anticommunist mission expressed not just a desire to eliminate all traces of "communism" from American life but also what Alfred McCoy has described as "the modern state's use of coercion . . . to extract information for heightened levels of social control." As Donner has observed, the gradual substitution of political "intelligence" operations for other "traditional interventionist practices" such as strikebreaking changed the focus of national, state, and local enforcement agencies from "passive monitoring" to outright "harassment and confrontation [of suspects] for allegedly deviant conduct or speech." Over time, the collection of political intelligence, always justified by the fight against communism, mutated from "an investigative means to a decision-making end" into a "punitive end itself." Further, because "neither external nor internal standards of target selection and operations were imposed" on police and national security agencies, they came to regard as their duty the suppression, as a Chicago Red Squad lieutenant put it, of "any organization that could create problems for the city or the country." But in focusing with increasing obsession on subversive ideology instead of criminal activity, the anticommunist intelligence state habitually attributed all social unrest to political conspiracy. Thus the state failed to predict the civil disturbances of the 1960s, which encompassed an unprecedented breadth and number of social groups: the "communist" revolution apparently had mushroomed to almost unfathomable size.[11]

The intelligence legacy of the Spider Web also encompasses the domestic and external sponsorship of anticommunist propaganda by the Central Intelligence Agency, the heir, in this respect, of the Committee on Public Information. Commencing in 1947, according to historian Hugh Wilford, the agency covertly sponsored the "Cold War propaganda battles" of an "astounding number of U.S. citizen groups," including the ever-pliable AFL, "university professors, journalists, aid workers, missionaries [and] civil rights activists." These activities were subsidized from 1950 to 1967 through the Congress for Cultural Freedom and its affiliates in the United States, Western Europe, the antipodes, Latin America, and the Third World.[12]

Partisan Politics

The consensus around postwar expenditure on containment and combating communism partially masked the partisan function of anticommunism, particularly HUAC's existence. Since its formation, Republicans had used the committee to damage their Democratic opponents. In the mid-1930s, Hoover put pressure on the Roosevelt administration by passing information to Republican committee member J. Parnell Thomas about the role the FBI's lack of surveillance powers had played in the alleged government employment of thousands of radicals. The committee also attempted to impeach Roosevelt's secretary of labor, Frances Perkins, for failing to deport Australian-born union leader Harry Bridges, the incident that prompted Roosevelt to remove the bureau's investigative leash. After the war, Republican power brokers aghast at losing the 1948 presidential election unleashed Senator McCarthy. Senator Robert Taft, a perennial presidential aspirant and coauthor of the Labor Management Relations Act, advised McCarthy to continue alleging communist infiltration of government until one of his charges stuck. Another Republican graduate of the anticommunist Class of '46, Richard Nixon, won an ugly Senate contest in 1950 by calling his Democratic opponent a communist "appeaser." Such charges, which had also been leveled against Truman, represented the Right's attempt to transfer to Democrats the stain of conservative support of fascism and Nazism. The McCarthyist charge that Democratic affinity for communism was proven by the detection on American soil of Soviet spies constituted a smokescreen: Republicans knew, as did President Truman, that the Soviets had already pulled their spies out of America, having essentially failed to penetrate the upper levels of the federal government.[13]

Communist infiltration of the government became a constant and difficult issue for Democratic administrations. In March 1947, Truman's sensitivity to charges of being soft on communism helped prompt him to establish what became known as the Federal Employee Loyalty Program. The program was essentially run by the FBI, which had sole authority to investigate the "loyalty" of prospective and current federal employees. In the event that the bureau rendered an unfavorable assessment of an employee or job applicant, that person would be called before a departmental board and asked to explain why he or she should not be dismissed or refused employment. While employees or applicants were made aware of the allegations against them, they were not privy to the FBI's reports that constituted the basis for the assessments. Thus, in the words of a contemporary lawyer, a determination by a board could "rest primarily upon the statements of unsworn witnesses whose names [were] known only to the FBI." Ellen Schrecker has estimated that in the first ten years of the program's operation, approximately twenty-seven hundred federal employees were dismissed for failing to satisfy employers that they opposed communism. Notwithstanding this high number, the program, which one historian has described as "mild, even meek [and] hardly aggressive," is generally regarded as having been "an ineffective way to address the problem" of employee treachery in government, as "the ostensible targets of the program [were] neither open [CP] members nor likely to be involved in [communist] front organizations."[14]

The program also proved ineffective in protecting the Truman administration from attacks on its competence to combat communism. These attacks gathered pace after the administration initially dismissed former communist Whittaker Chambers's August 1948 denunciation of State Department employee Alger Hiss. The president and his secretary of state, Dean Acheson, doubted the accusation, in part because they distrusted both Chambers and Hoover and suspected that the FBI was exaggerating the extent of Soviet espionage in the United States. Their suspicions of Hoover were warranted: senior officials and officers in the National Security Agency, the US Army, the FBI, and the Central Intelligence Agency had declined to inform the president that US agents had deciphered the code that the USSR used to communicate with its spies in the United States and had seized many cables. Instead, these agencies only selectively shared the information gleaned from the cables with Truman and Acheson, deceiving Truman into defending Hiss and damaging the president's anticommunist bona fides. Aside from damaging his administration, the deception of the president by the national security and military establishment helped create a political environment in which additional anticommunist measures could be sponsored, including the Internal Security Act (the McCarran Act), which passed over Truman's veto in 1950 and required communist organizations to register with the US attorney general, and the Communist Control Act of 1954, which outlawed the CP. The McCarran Act created the Subversive Activities Control Board, which was empowered to designate individuals or groups as "communist-action," "communist-front," or "communist-infiltrated," leading nearly two hundred left-wing groups to be designated as either communist or communist-front organizations. Eleven states subsequently passed statutes similar to the McCarran Act, and eight states outlawed the CP. At the end of 1950, thirty-two states had banned alleged subversives from working in government agencies; California even made all of its employees "civil defense workers." By the close of the 1960s, forty-five states had passed antisedition laws, thirty-two states subjected its employees to loyalty oaths, and five states required public school teachers and university professors to take Lusk-style oaths. By the end of the decade, between 65 and 75 percent of US state and local government employees were required to swear loyalty oaths.[15]

Although Jacob Spolansky had died by this time, he might well have been pleased to learn that government loyalty screening programs not only brought the private intelligence industry back from the dead but restored it to a state of health that exceeded its Red Scare prime. By the mid-1960s, the Rand Corporation calculated that the United States had more than four thousand "industrial security" agencies. As always, leading agencies were formed and staffed by former state security agents, fanatically anticommunist in their beliefs and strongly connected to national employer lobbies and HUAC.[16]

As these anticommunist measures took hold, the national security establishment continued to provide political assistance to senior Republican politicians, including Ronald Reagan, a former movie actor who was hoping to become governor of California. Having recruited him as an informant (classification "T-10") in 1946, the FBI and Hoover developed a close and mutually beneficial relationship with Reagan. Reagan helped derail the careers of several noted actors whose political views and associations he found objectionable and gave Hoover conspicuous awards for patriotism; in return, Hoover publicly endorsed Reagan's plan to establish a new police training academy with the help of the FBI, thus breaking with the bureau's practice of refraining from supporting any particular candidate for political office. More important, Hoover personally ensured that the bureau suppressed information that could have scuppered Reagan's 1966 campaign for governor: his son, Michael, had been associating with the son of one of America's most notorious mafia bosses, and a "reliable" source had informed the bureau that Reagan had secretly joined the fanatically anticommunist, extreme right-wing John Birch Society.[17]

The Resurrection of Big Business

The political-military-industrial complex was not the only powerful sector that exploited postwar anticommunism. Like the business lobbies of the interwar period, corporations (and the think tanks they established to promote their messages) used anticommunism throughout the Cold War to generate support for their objectives. What began with the renewed assault on labor organization in the late 1930s spread into a transfer of the tax burden to middle-class America and 1920s-style deregulation of labor markets, environmental protection standards, and other fetters on business. All of these initiatives were justified by the "folklore of capitalism," which pitted American "free enterprise" against the dastardly, impoverishing effects of socialism.[18]

That big business should succeed in reestablishing its pre–Great Depression power is the ultimate testament to the political utility of anticommunism. The depression, to which big business contributed so greatly, had damaged its social prestige and diminished its political clout. Although business still had the backing of the Republican Party, the GOP itself had little support. Notwithstanding massive corporate campaign spending, the Republicans were consistently annihilated in midterm and presidential elections in the 1930s. The party, Kim Phillips-Fein has written, "seemed nearly as obsolete as the Whigs they had displaced." Just as important, "a coherent body of conservative thought hardly existed," and even "forceful critics of the New Deal . . . took a skeptical approach to business, believing that excessive concentration of private economic power . . . limited freedom nearly as much as the state." With business's power somewhat muted, the labor movement set about creating a new middle class. In the first decades after the Second World War, stronger labor organization and economic growth helped to foster steady real rises in median incomes and a massive expansion in private pension plan and hospital insurance coverage. The political economy of these postwar years was truly anomalous in American history: never before had so much wealth been spread so broadly and deeply. Yet big business never accepted the legitimacy or merits of this political economy and began even before the war to reassert its priorities under the guise of fighting communism.[19]

In its postwar fight against the New Deal and the welfare state, big business relied heavily on the rhetorical tropes and tactics of the Anticommunist Spider Web. Even in the 1930s, lobbies such as the American Liberty League recycled pro-business boilerplate, explaining the distribution of income and profits with *Straight Shooter*–like homilies and fables and concealing operations behind fronts such as the Farmers' Independent Council. While the zeitgeist and the organization's own myopia strangled the League, industrialists enjoyed more success in the postwar environment, adopting the tactics of the Better America Federation and other Red Scare lobbies. In the name of "Boulwarism" (after staunchly antiunion General Electric manager Lemuel Ricketts Boulware), corporations bombarded staff with propaganda. Antiunion consultancies also produced antilabor literature, while business lobbies spent millions on advertising campaigns countering public perceptions of bosses as cigar-chomping plutocrats. The workday for the average corporate employee increasingly resembled that of the *Saturday Evening Post*'s Ivan Kozlov.[20]

Retaining its interwar conviction of cultural disadvantage in the face of a Left-dominated academy and world of letters, the Anticommunist Right attempted to address this deficiency through its own think tanks. Business lobbies were particularly eager, Phillips-Fein has noted, to bestow on its intellectual subsidiaries titles connoting "austere, noble, and pure" purposes: hence, for example, the American Enterprise Association redubbed itself the American Enterprise Institute.[21]

Following in the footsteps of the Anticommunist Spider Web, the forces of the Right described every political, economic, or social program that it opposed as "socialist." Right-wing journalist John T. Flynn popularized the term *creeping socialism* to describe the Truman administration's advocacy of national health insurance, antidiscrimination laws, housing programs, and federal education funding. These programs, like the Sheppard-Towner Act and the Child Labor Amendment, were equated with the covert introduction of communism through a British Fabian–style program of gradual reform. The American Medical Association continued to describe all government involvement in the delivery of health programs as "socialism." Merwin Hart's National Economic Council, where Archibald Stevenson concluded his Red-baiting career, similarly described the Fair Employment Practices Commission as of "communist origin." These voices were amplified by the arrival in the US Senate of a new champion, Barry Goldwater, whose denunciations of the welfare state and equation of laissez-faire with 100% Americanism helped secure him the 1964 Republican presidential nomination. In addition to adopting the Spider Web's rhetoric, the Right continued to use that motif to depict subversive networks operated by organizations such as the Federal Council of Churches. The reactionary Christian organizations that began to adopt the label *fundamentalist* in the 1920s had always been economic as well as theological Tories, and in the Cold War, new Christian groups funded by business lobbies spread the gospel of Christ the free marketeer. The Christian Right eventually birthed powerful politicized organizations, including Spiritual Mobilization and the Moral Majority. And the conservative female activism pioneered by the Woman Patriots was revived by Phyllis Schlafly's Eagle Forum and similar groups.[22]

The Postwar Anticommunist Spider Web

The ongoing utility of Spider Web rhetoric and explanatory designs mirrored the postwar careers of numerous Web members. Several of these members became leading lights in American fascist and Nazi movements. Boris Brasol and Elizabeth Dilling fed information to numerous US senators and representatives. Dilling befriended Gerald B. Winrod, a prominent anti-Semitic preacher and activist, and worked in the Mothers' Crusade with pro-Nazi seminarian and broadcaster Father Charles E. Coughlin. John B. Trevor and Walter Steele maintained close relations with John Snow's profascist League for Constitutional Government. Trevor also wrote speeches for Senator Robert Reynolds, a prominent opponent of immigration and Nazi appeaser who regularly inserted speeches by Winrod into the *Congressional Record*. After the war, Trevor's front committee, Ten Million Americans Mobilizing for Justice, attempted to prevent the censure of Senator McCarthy. Trevor's son, John B. Trevor III, carried on the pro-Nazi work of the American Coalition of Patriotic Societies, campaigning in 1962 for the release of prisoners jailed after the Nuremberg trials. Sitting on the board of the Pioneer Fund, he also funneled hundreds of thousands of dollars to Massive Resistance campaigns opposing school desegregation in the late 1950s. Hamilton Fish Jr.'s congressional career was curtailed by his association with Nazi agent George Sylvester Viereck. The National Economic Council was sponsored by corporate giants General Motors, Du Pont, and Otis Elevators and survived Merwin Hart's death by promulgating the paranoid, anticommunist fantasies of the John Birch Society, which was established in 1958. After Harry Jung's death in 1954, his antilabor files, described as the most extensive private archive of its kind in the 1930s, were bequeathed to the American Security Council, described by Lichtman as "the voice of the military-industrial complex."[23]

The military also remained a haven for fanatical anticommunists, particularly sympathizers and members of the John Birch Society. The society was mired in the paranoid style of politics. Its founder Robert Welch, a member of the board of the National Association of Manufacturers, believed that America's mortal fight against the Reds placed it "in circumstances where it [was] *realistic* to be *fan-*

tastic." For the Birchers, US Supreme Court chief justice Earl Warren, the Council of Foreign Relations, and the civil rights movement were all "Soviet-controlled." Army commanders fed their troops Bircher propaganda. So total was the conservative/reactionary outlook of the armed services in the Cold War that by the 1990s, fewer than 10 percent of officers identified as Democrats or liberals. And the legend of the Bolshevik Illuminati was subsequently embraced by presidential aspirant and Christian Coalition founder Pat Robertson and conservative cable-television and radio host Glenn Beck.[24]

Postwar Immigration Policy

The Spider Web wielded significant influence on immigration policy for the duration of the twentieth century. The deliberate omission of refugee provisions in the 1924 Immigration Act held for a generation. And the general fear of subversive immigrants was one of the spurs that prompted the convocation of HUAC, passage of the Alien Registration Act of 1940, and the transfer of administrative responsibility for immigration to the Department of Justice. Only in 1948 did the United States begin to admit refugees, and even then, only escapees from communist lands were allowed in. Both immigration restrictionists and liberalizers sought to legitimize their policies by stressing the damage that they would inflict on global communism. And the United States did not recognize the need to provide asylum to victims of right-wing governments until the 1970s. In the early- to mid-1950s, refugees were screened so rigorously for signs of communist belief that intake proceedings nearly ground to a halt. Only the 1956 Hungarian uprising uncorked the refugee bottle, moving the Eisenhower administration to expedite the rapid admission of tens of thousands of Hungarians using its long-dormant executive discretion to parole aliens into the country on an emergency basis. This mechanism became a major feature of immigration administration, with large numbers of Cubans and then Indochinese brought into the United States through this device. In 1965, racial quotas were finally removed from immigration law despite the objections and lobbying largesse of the Pioneer Fund, which operated in this instance through Trevor's other venerable vehicle, the American Coalition of Patriotic Societies. Yet the notion that refugee issues could be viewed outside the prism of the Cold War remained avant-garde. Even the fall of President Nixon heightened the influence of anticommunism on refugee policy as neoconservatives sought to discredit détente and provoke the USSR by campaigning for the admission of Soviet Jews and Indochinese. President Reagan continued to direct refugee admissions to asylum seekers from communist countries, particularly Latin America. Only with the end of the Cold War did refugee policy begin to focus on other victims of oppression.[25]

The Postwar Political Economy

While the heirs of the Spider Web made important contributions to the temper and shape of Cold War society, the Right's ultimate postwar focus, like that of the Web, was economic power. And despite the usefulness of anticommunist propaganda in making a case for the return of pre–New Deal "100% American" policy settings, big business could not have succeeded in recapturing control of the economy without the powerful legislative and regulatory backing it received. The Taft-Hartley Act, which crippled workers' capacity to organize and mount industrial action, was designed by Minnesota's employer lobbies, who formulated state legislation that the state's representatives brought to Washington and enshrined in Taft-Hartley. This "New Deal for America's Employers" proscribed secondary boycotts, the closed shop, and "jurisdictional strikes or boycotts." The act also excused companies from bargaining with unions not certified by federal regulators and restricted striking rights to a sixty-day negotiation period. Strikes regarded as injurious to the national welfare could be enjoined by presidential decree for eighty days. Shortly after the passage of Taft-Hartley, Congress overrode President Truman's veto to enact the Internal Security and Immigration Act and did so again to enact the Nationality Act. In addition to requiring communist groups to register with the government, these acts authorized the president to intern suspected subversives during a national emergency as well as the exclusion or deportation of immigrants and visitors found to profess ideologies that threatened national security. A few years later, the National Labor Relations Board empowered managers to conduct isolated face-to-face interviews with staff members and inquire whether they were union members.[26]

Even during their postwar heyday, unions were thoroughly subdued by these anticommunist measures, which unleashed a government- and business-fostered exodus from the labor movement. Union locals that supported communist-led unemployment councils, forged partnerships with progressive churches and community groups, and united black and white workers across industry lines were neutered, while employers and the FBI harassed the ablest union leaders into retirement and even early death. The AFL aided and abetted such repression, eager to reassert control over activist union locals and to destroy or at least curtail the influence of its rival, the Congress of Industrial Organizations (CIO). The AFL consequently sponsored Virginia representative Howard Smith's investigations into the National Labor Relations Board; the 1939 Act to Prevent Pernicious Political Activities (the Hatch Act), which targeted Reds and Pinks working in government; and the Alien Registration Act. Even union members who appreciated communists' efforts and the industrial education they offered were influenced by anticommunist rhetoric and ideology to reject "foreign," atheistic leadership and a panracial message. Political, business, and labor leaders attacked the "communist" reforms of the New Deal by appealing to the racial prejudice of the white working class and by describing endogenous, sometimes-Marxist industrial organization as Moscow-directed revolution. Thus, by the close of the 1940s, the CIO, like the American Civil Liberties Union before it, had adopted a policy of "voluntarist" anticommunism, purging its ranks of CP members and sympathizers and acquiescing in the passage of the Taft-Hartley Act. The CIO and the AFL eventually merged based largely on their now-inseparable stances toward communism.[27]

Even before but especially after the AFL-CIO nuptials, the State Department and the Central Intelligence Agency co-opted the peak American labor organizations into the international fight against communism. The AFL-CIO assisted noncommunist and anticommunist unions in Europe, Central and South America, Africa, and Asia. As late as the mid-1980s, AFL-CIO leaders were helping to organize anticommunist insurgencies in Central America. So important were the AFL-CIO's contributions to international anticommunist initiatives that historian Jennifer Luff has concluded, "American labor anti-communists made the greatest impact in these international campaigns, in countries where Communism was a much larger and more significant working-class movement than in the United States."[28] Yet by assisting in the construction and legitimization of anticommunism, America's most significant labor organizations significantly damaged the cause of labor and the broader Left. After America's manufacturing sector lost markets to cheaper foreign labor at the close of the 1960s, unions were unable to protect their members' benefits, conditions, and wages in the Taft-Hartley world they helped create. The financial sector then became the new command center of the US economy. Laborers found that they increasingly had no role and no legislative structure to protect them.[29]

The industrial relations regime created by Taft-Hartley remains essentially intact, and the act continues to inhibit labor organization in crucial ways. The act's "free speech" clause gave employers the right to share their opinions about unions with employees during shop election campaigns. Employers and management consultants, Robin has observed, quickly made an art form of threatening employees with the consequences of organizing without breaching the law. The National Labor Relations Act (the Wagner Act) imposes no financial penalties on employers who infringe it, and employees can wait years for the National Labor Relations Board to hear cases and perhaps impose minor sanctions on employers. The number and kinds of workers who do not enjoy the protection of the Wagner Act have also expanded. Whereas agricultural and domestic workers were originally excluded from its coverage, their ranks have been joined in many states by independent contractors and supervisors, managers, employees of religious institutions, private university professors, and public employees. Precise figures for employees who have been deprived of federal labor rights are unknown, but Robin has put the number in the millions. Fittingly, inveterate anticommunist and FBI informant Ronald Reagan led America into its current, full-scale revival of 1920s-style labor suppression when he dismissed thousands of air traffic controllers. The neoconservative assault on the union movement associated with Reagan relegitimized the practice of breaking strikes with non-union labor. In Minnesota and other states, employers have prevailed on courts to strike down laws prohibiting the employment of permanent replacement staff during strikes or lockouts. Since 1980, union membership has been reduced, in William Millikan's view, "to a tragic display of futility."[30]

The industrial relations legacies of anticommunism extend far beyond the restrictions on organizing rights, manifesting in the fear of dismissal that disorganized and vulnerable workers in myriad industries experience in modern America. What began in the interwar period as workplace political censorship enforced by spies and thugs grew during the Cold War into what Robin has described as a "feudal . . . internal social order," a "world less post-modern than pre-modern." In the contemporary United States, according to Robin, the "most salient political fear is . . . the fear among the less powerful of the more powerful, whether public officials or private employers": the American workplace has become "a vast terra incognita protected from public scrutiny by high towers of legal argument and political indifference," with a raft of threats and sanctions ensuring "workers don't talk back or act up." Modern firms no longer rely on men like Jacob Spolansky to police their workers, but they concern themselves with far more personal matters than their employees' political views. For manual laborers in particular, surveillance has created a workplace in which they may be instructed to urinate in their clothing rather than make "unauthorized expeditions to the toilet" and submit details of their menstrual cycles to human resource departments to avoid being labeled slackers.[31]

The disempowerment of labor unions and widespread exploitation of labor has been essential to big business's postwar economic project to restore Jazz Age norms of income and wealth distribution. Another essential pillar underpinning this program has been the steady transfer of corporate America's tax burden to the middle and working classes. Although this process was begun by the Kennedy administration, it reached its apotheosis in the Reagan era. While corporate and top-tier personal income taxes fell steadily between 1962 and the early 1980s, payroll taxes just as steadily increased. President Reagan's measures then delivered nearly two hundred billion dollars in tax relief to the affluent. In the first decade of the new millennium, income inequality reached levels not seen since the Great Depression. In 2005, the top 10 percent of earners collected 44.3

percent of national income, compared to 32.6 percent in 1975 but about equal to 1929's 43.8 percent. Similarly, in 2005, the top 1 percent of earners received 17.4 percent of the nation's income, compared to 8 percent in 1975 and 18.4 percent in 1929.[32]

Such a monumental transfer of wealth would not have been possible had business not recolonized the economy's principal regulatory agencies, as was the case during the 1920s. Yet while plutocrats shared control of such agencies in the Roaring Twenties, banking behemoth Goldman Sachs has taken for itself all regulatory power in the modern era: the US Treasury, the New York Federal Reserve, and the Commodities Futures Trading Commission have all been entrusted to former Goldman executives. Thus in 2008, while the United States plunged into its greatest recession in eighty years, Goldman Sachs paid fourteen million dollars in federal taxes, one-third the amount its chief executive officer was gifted. More broadly, two-thirds of American corporations paid no taxes at all between 1998 and 2005.[33]

The Military-Industrial Complex

Just as the device of war had been a cardinal instrument of domestic politics in the Progressive era, anticommunist foreign policy after the Second World War became a principal means of shaping the domestic political agenda, particularly among Democratic administrations eager to refute allegations of being soft on communism and among the political and economic interests promoting the extremely profitable rise of what President Eisenhower famously termed the military-industrial complex. As former diplomat and writer Lawrence Dennis prophesied in 1944, anticommunism eliminated the partisan contest over foreign policy, as military expenditure and "containment" of communism consumed federal government finances and diplomatic efforts. The twin features of this policy, articulated in an April 1950 National Security Council report, offered political salvation to President Truman, who had been buffeted by the Maoist revolution in China, the detonation of a Soviet atomic bomb, and the conviction of Alger Hiss as a communist spy. The Truman Doctrine called on the United States to "attain military superiority" over the USSR by making "significant domestic financial and economic adjustments"—shorthand for massive reductions in domestic social spending. The doctrine received strong bipartisan support, as evidenced by the fact that prominent conservative commentator William F. Buckley Jr. made the most strident case in its favor: the United States had to "accept Big Government for the duration, for neither an offensive nor defensive war [against communism] can be waged . . . except through the instrument of a totalitarian" US bureaucracy as well as "extensive and productive tax laws [to] support a vigorous anti-Communist foreign policy" that included "large armies and air forces, atomic energy, central intelligence, war production boards, and the attendant centralization of power in Washington." Buckley's call was heeded. The United States went to fight communists in Korea and Vietnam, and not until 1972 did a postwar federal budget spend more on domestic social programs than on military expenditures.[34]

The Right has dismantled labor and financial market regulations and reduced business's tax bill to virtually nothing but should not be regarded as being committed to small government. Rather, the Right remains a strong proponent of massive military expenditures at the expense of social programs, another position strongly influenced by anticommunism and its leading supporters. The American Security Council, with a corporate board stacked with commanding officers from all services, was a particularly effective lobbyist for military appropriations. Its "propaganda arm," according to Lichtman, sponsored several other anticommunist think tanks and it maintained "the closest ties with established power centers, especially Congress." It was instrumental in prolonging HUAC into the 1970s by reorienting it as a security committee focused on international terrorism. Outside of Congress, the council's most important supporters included Edward Teller, the father of the H-bomb. It claimed to hold files on two million communist organizations and individuals and drew support from almost two hundred corporate sponsors. In addition to becoming the home for Jung's labor files, the council absorbed John B. Trevor III's American Coalition of Patriotic Societies. Until the mid-1980s, Trevor, a professional military engineer, was a board member of the council, and in the mid-1980s, the coalition was headquartered with the American Security Council.[35]

Notwithstanding the paranoid delusions of the John Birch Society and its successors, most sensible observers understood by the mid-1970s that the United States had beaten the Soviet Union. So untroubled were right-wing think tanks by the Soviet threat that the Conservative Caucus, launched in 1974, did not bother even to mention communism, Russia, or China in its founding statement. This development troubled the military-industrial complex. To counter suggestions that defense expenditures should be reduced, the complex's political supporters revived the tactics used by the Wilson administration when it released the Sisson Papers to justify the invasion of Soviet Russia. In 1976, vexed by persistent Central Intelligence Agency reports that the Soviets "were by no means as formidable" as the Pentagon claimed, agency director George H. W. Bush appointed an "independent" group, dubbed Team B, to demonstrate, as team member and future deputy secretary of defense Paul Wolfowitz explained, "that it was possible to construct a sharply different view of Soviet motivation from the consensus view of the analysts." This view helped to rationalize a massive expansion of military spending on hardware manufactured by firms closely aligned with Team B members and senior Republican politicians. The political payoff of Team B's assessments was to expose Democratic president Jimmy Carter to the same accusations of failing to curb Soviet power that had damaged Harry Truman.[36]

Cynical as these maneuvers were, fear of or competition with communism still played a part during the 1980s in US support for the Contras in Nicaragua and for militant Islamic groups during the Soviet invasion of Afghanistan. Having fed the hand that would bite it so dramatically on 11 September 2001, Team B reconvened under President George W. Bush to prove the existence of a "mature symbiotic relationship" between Osama bin Laden's terrorist group, Al-Qaeda, and the state of Iraq. The invasion of the latter would prove a disastrous strategic blunder, hugely injurious to US military, diplomatic, and financial standing but extremely profitable for the handful of megacorporations licensed by an administration committed to "outsourcing" its quarter-baked occupation of a foreign land.[37]

Liberal Anticommunism in Practice and in History

One of the cardinal achievements of the Anticommunist Spider Web was to entrench its values and political responses in American society and political culture. Yet the degree to which the Web influenced anticommunism in general is a matter of debate among historians. Jennifer Luff has argued that rather than adopting the values and methods of the Spider Web, conservative trade union leaders developed a principled "commonsense" brand of anticommunism that stood broadly for the defense of liberalism and constitutional freedom but condoned the suppression of leftist radicalism. Richard Gid Powers, Jennifer Delton, Ellen Schrecker, and Corey Robin have also posited the importance of liberals to anticommunism in different ways and with starkly different levels of approval. In Robin's words, the political repression of the Truman and Eisenhower years constituted a "multidimensional movement" that "worked through the . . . contrivances of [both the] state and society" to discipline citizens and force them to abjure communist or radical alternatives to liberal capitalist democracy. In the view of all four of these authors, this repression resulted not so much from threats of "lethal violence" as from threats of "loss of a career or steady employment" that were issued by civic and professional bodies at least as much as by national security and legislative entities and individuals.[38] Anticommunism was therefore in significant part a product of liberal democracy.

Powers and Delton part with Schrecker and Robin—and indeed, me—in justifying much anticommunist repression as an intrinsically liberal response to the threat of communism that differed qualitatively from the illiberal anticommunist ideas and activity on which this book focuses. These authors explain "liberal" anticommunism in several ways: as a necessary assault on revolutionaries who had willingly forfeited the protection provided by the US Constitution; as a social and political purge limited to CP members; as an essential measure to preserve the Democratic Party and with it the legacy of the New Deal; and as an exercise in national spiritual revival.

The argument that CP members were agents of a hostile foreign power and consequently did not deserve the rights guaranteed to every "loyal" American citizen by the US Constitution has been influential since Sidney Hook articulated it in the 1930s. Hook argued that the repression of communists even by antidemocratic means could occur in a liberal democracy without threatening the institutional or social health of that polity because their suppression was "a matter of ethical hygiene, not of politics or persecution." As conspirators against American democracy, CP members and those who aided and abetted their conspiracy had placed themselves outside the realm of that democracy. They were, in effect, stateless—like Islamic terrorists today. Hook's philosophical journey to this conclusion epitomized the longer-term effects of anticommunism on many left-wing and liberal citizens' political outlooks and behavior. Yet while Hook's opposition to the USSR was understandable and principled (particularly after the revelations of the Stalinist purges, the mass deportation of kulaks, and the Gulag Archipelago), Hook's insistence that party membership alone automatically deprived American citizens of their constitutional rights and capacity to earn a living was no more liberal than J. Edgar Hoover and A. Mitchell Palmer's identical assertions during the Red Scare. It was a decidedly Bolshevik view. The reasons why Hook and others like him arrived at such a conclusion is less clear. Did ex-Marxists such as Hook want to punish their former associates for failing to divine the truth? Did party members' radicalism challenge Hook and others' conversion to liberalism? Did they hope that purging communists would prove their fidelity to America?

The related notion that liberal anticommunism affected only card-carrying communists and others who refused or failed to deny or disprove their party membership was expressed in numerous sectors of American society but seldom with greater effect or publicity than in Hollywood. While Ronald Reagan and some other actors denounced their left-wing colleagues to the FBI and HUAC, studio bosses commenced their own purge of the industry independent of the bureau and the committee. The president of the US Chamber of Commerce and longtime head of the Motion Picture Association of America, Eric Johnston, was the kind of "moderate corporate leader" who Delton argues made liberal anticommunism a force for good. Believing that the best way for the United States to "beat" communism was to make capitalism "work for all people," Johnston defended workers' right to organize and argued for "fiscal and tax policies that lifted all economic boats." He also criticized HUAC's "strong-arm tactics" and told the committee, "We are not willing to give up our freedoms to save our freedoms." Yet in December 1947, Johnston "initiated" the Hollywood blacklist and "ensured HUAC's presence in Hollywood to enforce it." This volte-face was explained by the argument that communists in Hollywood deserved to be persecuted because they had concealed their party membership. "As an anticommunist," Delton explains, "Johnston had no problem using [strong-arm] tactics against actual Communists." And when the group of screenwriters and directors known as the Hollywood Ten refused to answer a HUAC subpoena to discuss their party membership, Johnston decided that the industry should no longer tolerate communists.[39]

The role of liberal anticommunism in unifying the post-Roosevelt Democratic Party and safeguarding the legacies of the New Deal was perhaps its most popular justification. As foreign policy tensions between the United States and the USSR worsened and liberal antipathy toward the CP grew, the need to "appease" communists to preserve the Popular Front faded. Instead, Delton has argued, liberals were "forced to articulate the danger of communism and the great promise of the liberal agenda." An important voice calling for the marginalization of the CP was Arthur Schlesinger Jr., whose 1949 book, *The Vital Center*, provided a guiding philosophy and political arguments to use against communists in union and civic elections. For Schlesinger, "the real threat" communists posed to America was their capacity to divide the forces of the Left and imperil the New Deal. Their ostracism was a necessary act in liberalism's defense.[40]

The last defense of liberal anticommunism was that it promotes what Robin has called a "general spiritual awakening." Liberal philosophy, according to Robin, has always emphasized the importance of fear, especially political fear, as a stimulus to purpose and achievement. One of the most influential proponents of the positive power of fear was Schlesinger, whose call to liberals to cast communists out of the Progressive firmament ultimately sought to address the profound despondency and anxiety that he detected in his fellow citizens at the century's midpoint. Citizens of the West, he wrote, were "tense, uncertain [and] adrift," watching hopelessly as their "certitude . . . familiar ideas and institutions [vanished] like shadows in the failing dusk." Schlesinger's solution to this crisis was to transform the conflict between the world's last remaining superpowers "into a proving ground of self and society," enabling Americans to "thereby transform their existential anxiety into focused, galvanizing fear." For Schlesinger, a Stalin dwelled in the breast of even the most ardent 100% American. And the discipline that the CP offered to "lonely and frustrated people, craving social, intellectual and even sexual fulfilment" had to be provided by other, more agreeable sources.

Thus, anticommunism had to become a crusade to ensure that Americans would find the necessary strength to protect their liberal heritage.[41]

In the second decade of the twenty-first century, Soviet communism is long dead, but the American experience of anticommunism continues to generate fierce debate. Was the defense of democracy and capitalism truly democratic and principled? And was the harm that anticommunism caused—the many thousand shattered careers and lives, the suppression of free speech and thought, the neutering of the labor movement, the lives lost abroad in war, the entanglement in ugly foreign coups d'état and later scandals such as the Iran-Contra Affair—justified by the triumph of capitalism and liberal democracy?

The school of historians represented by Powers and Delton, answers these questions with an emphatic "*Yes*." For them, liberal anticommunism represents an entirely different strain of activism from what Delton has termed "hysterical and conservative" anticommunism. Further, in this view, "responsible" liberal anticommunism, not its "hysterical and conservative" relation, constituted the "most effective" bulwark against communist perversion of America's libertarian heritage. Finally, they maintain that the measures both liberals and even hysterical conservatives used to suppress communism were entirely justified to safeguard an "ascendant liberal political agenda" that came to dominate politics in the first decades of the postwar era. According to Delton, this "triumph of liberal assumptions and political power" was one of the principal outcomes of the Cold War: the "liberal consensus . . . was born out of liberals' anticommunist efforts."[42]

However, these arguments do not survive close inspection. In attempting to somehow surgically separate different effects of anticommunism and attribute responsibility for their origins to different segments of the American polity, scholars have attempted to unscramble the anticommunist omelet. Doing so is neither possible nor appropriate. To suggest that a distinctive "liberal" brand of anticommunism not only emerged but triumphed over a related "hysterical and conservative" brand during the Cold War ignores the fact that anticommunism had been continually developing and had already been woven into American society for about eighty years. The notion that two distinct forms of anticommunism both coalesced and then branched off from one another to enjoy quite different influences in Cold War America is anachronistic. It is also difficult to regard the late 1940s and 1950s as a time of triumph for a "liberal political agenda." Rather, the liberal reforms of the New Deal were subjected to a constant and intensifying assault that began before the Second World War. After all, the period is widely known (with all the problems this creates) as the "McCarthy era." In fact, little if any more "liberal consensus" existed in Cold War America than had existed previously. Workers' rights were still fiercely contested and steadily and substantially eroded. New Deal ambitions to bring domestic and agricultural workers into the ambit of federal labor laws were defeated and abandoned. The liberal dream of government-guaranteed health insurance remained out of reach. And blacklists continued to determine who could find work in any number of fields of employment, whether in colleges and schools, in Hollywood, in science laboratories, or on construction projects. As Robert Griffith remarks, in Cold War America, "the left was in virtual eclipse," and no real distinctions existed between liberal and conservative anticommunist principles and political techniques.[43]

To counter this conclusion, proponents of liberal anticommunism tie themselves in non sequiturs. In addition, they strive to cleave liberal and reactionary anticommunism in two by sheer force of rhetoric, rather like the Anticommunist Spider Web years before. Delton, for example, has accepted Hook's rationale that repression of communists could occur outside the realm of "politics or persecution." Conceding that such an attitude "seems to endorse a decidedly antiliberal vigilante mentality," she nevertheless puts this contradiction "aside" to conclude that "liberal principles were more effectively promoted by purging Communists than by defending their rights." Similarly, Delton has argued that Johnston's anticommunism was "entirely different from that of HUAC [because] it was modern, forward-looking, and above all dedicated to achieving a postwar liberal order." However, that order was open only to the vision of "a middle-class progressive or labor leader who just wanted to improve the conditions for the working class and other disenfranchised groups."[44]

The problem with communists, however, was that they were not Progressives who "just wanted to improve the conditions" of the downtrodden. Rather, they wanted to change the country's political and economic system. This goal was their right, however misguided or deluded it may have appeared then or now. Yet this right was ultimately as unacceptable to liberals as it was to conservatives and reactionaries. Stripped of rhetorical finery, Hook, Johnston, and myriad other liberal anticommunists showed that they were indeed willing to give up freedoms to save them;—or more accurately that they were willing to surrender the freedoms of people for whom they had little respect or sympathy. Thus, to argue that liberals were able to use the repressive machinery and ideology of anticommunism yet still transcend the brutal excesses of reactionary anticommunism is delusional or sophistry. Indeed, as Delton has unwittingly conceded, "To show that liberalism benefited from anti-communism is not the same as showing that liberals intentionally instigated it."[45]

Delton's claim that a distinct set of liberal anticommunist "achievements deserve to be recognized and even perhaps celebrated, not hidden, regretted, or equated with McCarthyism" is similarly insupportable. Liberal (and for that matter, labor union leaders') anticommunism did not appreciably moderate the antilabor and capitalist precepts of Cold War anticommunism. Rather, liberals and conservative labor leaders shared or adopted many values of the Anticommunist Spider Web. And under vigorous political, economic, and social pressure, they abandoned many Progressive dimensions of their own platforms and professed beliefs, delivering what Michael Harrington has described as "an abject capitulation by liberalism to illiberalism." And while Delton may have argued that "it is a mistake to assume that J. Edgar Hoover or HUAC could have had much power without the cooperation of liberals who wanted Communists identified and driven out of their organizations," it is more insensible to discount the galvanizing force that reactionary anticommunists exercised on their liberal cocitizens. As Robin has remarked, one of the cardinal lessons of America's long experience with anticommunism is just how coercive state power can be and just "how small a constituency is required to use it repressively." This lesson holds true even in a federated, bifurcated, democratic system of government. In numerous instances, separate branches of government in the United States competed or collaborated with one another to enforce anticommunism. If anything, Robin has understated the problem by claiming the existence of a "duplication of coercive repression during the Cold War." In fact, a triplication of repression occurred, encompassing local as well as federal and state authorities and the judiciary as well as the executive and legislatures. Moreover, this tripartite repression antedated the Cold War by several decades.[46]

As for the role of civil society in anticommunist repression, Tocqueville's "tyranny of public opinion" often endorsed and even anticipated illiberal action by the state. Just as Hollywood moguls volunteered to do much of HUAC's work, other purveyors of culture, such as the American Writers Association, volunteered to "combat communism" and "noisy, vicious, un-American elements." It is hard not to conclude that liberal anticommunists too often failed to live by and show real faith in their principles. Johnston once proclaimed, "Communists can hang all the iron curtains they like, but they'll never be able to shut out the story of a land where free men walk without fear and live in abundance."[47] If he truly believed these words, it is difficult to see what liberal purpose a blacklist could serve.

Afterword

Nearly a century after the Bolshevik Revolution, how is American anticommunism best characterized? Writing about this question in 2015, as opposed even to 2007, is an interesting exercise, for events in the interim (most notably the global financial crisis) encourage the application of a different analytical framework. This framework also needs to encompass the great sweep of American history over the past 150 or so years to allow the full contextual meaning of American anticommunism to emerge.

Anticommunism was fundamentally a device, albeit one of unprecedented power, for perpetuating and then reviving prejudices, fears, and doctrines that America's powerful have used since the country's foundation to protect their social, political, and economic control at the expense of the great majority of its citizens. Anticommunism divided many social groups from each other, moderating or entirely preventing their collaboration. The poor and the working classes; native-born citizens and immigrants; whites and blacks; social progressives and radicals; the professional middle classes and manual workers—all failed as often as not to collaborate in the development of broadly acceptable solutions to America's diverse political, economic, and social problems. As a diversion from systemic flaws in domestic policies and conditions, anticommunism was a spectacular success. It made impossible the creation of a welfare state that would provide its people with the protections that citizens of comparable Western democracies have for decades enjoyed. It led to the sacrifice of hundreds of thousands of American soldiers' lives in external wars of choice. It justified the violent overthrow of democratically elected governments in Latin America and Iran. And when it had served its purpose, it simply faded away, to be replaced by new "wars" on drugs and terror.[1]

In the final analysis, little good can be said about anticommunism. Even the promotion and defense of Western democracy was typically compromised rather than aided by anticommunism. As Frances Stonor Saunders has pondered, what sort of freedom could be advanced by the deception of the Congress for Cultural Freedom and the repression of the Federal Bureau of Investigation's counterintelligence program? How fragile a concept was democracy that it should need such protection? How fragile was the commitment of America's political elites to democracy if they could not believe that it would outlast Soviet communism by developing, as Saunders has written, according to the "fundamental processes of organic intellectual growth . . . free debate and the uninhibited flow of ideas"? Even supporters of anticommunism tacitly agree. The very title of a book such as Richard Gid Powers's *Not without Honor* confesses the betrayal of liberal values at the heart of anticommunism: a double negative hardly constitutes a positive endorsement.[2]

Another cardinal lesson to draw from America's anticommunist experience is how "constituent elements in the . . . polity can be both instruments of freedom and weapons of fear." As Corey Robin has argued, "Too often in the United States, we assume that political fear arises outside our political system, beyond the Constitution and institutions of civil society." While James Madison and the Constitution's Framers had theorized that a healthy civil society comprising "so many separate descriptions of citizens" would "render an unjust combination of a majority of the whole very improbable," they did not foresee the extent to which "civil society, even in the most liberal polities, is often either a supplement to state repression or a repressive agent in its own right [because] where state power is limited, elites have every incentive to use civil society to promote fear."[3]

This book has explored hundreds of instances of civilian promotion of fear and with it sectional political, economic, and social objectives associated with anticommunism. The importance of this form of repression prior to the Cold War was as established as the state repression that gave rise to McCarthyism. This was as true a form of voluntarist anticommunism as existed, for there was no constitutional provision that required corporate employees unconditionally to support laissez-faire or that forbade attorneys from defending CP members or sympathizers. Rather, anticommunism was a fundamental instance of a pluralist society's capacity to withdraw support for the liberties that it might at other times and in other circumstances grant.[4]

Ironically, the great service that communism performed for the West is infrequently discussed: forcing American policymakers and business elites to offer a real and better alternative to life in the Soviet bloc. Yet as the West gradually won the war on communism, the doctrine of anticommunism helped to deliver control of the US economy back into the hands of the business elites that controlled it from the mid-nineteenth century until the Great Depression. The economic stewardship of these elites has perhaps been even more disastrous than that of their predecessors. While warring nineteenth-century railway barons merely debased the workforce of a few industries, the interconnectivity of the globalized economy has meant that twenty-first-century financiers have taken entire national economies to the brink of ruin. In the 1870s, railroad workers, coal miners, and their families paid for the greed of their bosses. In the 2010s, all workers and taxpayers are socializing the debts of the finance industry. As the US Treasury has paid off the self-incurred debts of the (surviving) megabanks, these banks have exacerbated the collapse of the real economy by driving up the price of commodities through speculation, devastating regional economies, and denuding state and local governments of vital revenue. In the face of this crisis in public finance, right-wing administrations such as that of Wisconsin governor Scott Walker have sought permanently to deflate the state's costs by driving down public-sector wages. Once the manufacturing powerhouse of the global economy, the United States is now hollowed out, in debt and failing to provide prosperity and hope to tens of millions of the unemployed and working poor. It has become an "Intern Nation," requiring legions of undergraduate students to labor without pay or purpose for lengthy periods just to qualify for the privilege of work.[5]

One need not be a devotee of Karl Marx to see that history is being repeated in the United States as both tragedy and farce. Not surprisingly, the failure of the major political parties to meet the needs of many citizens has spawned third-party insurrections, just as it did in the Gilded Age. In America today, the presidential election has again become, in Matt Taibbi's pithy description, "a drama that . . . Americans have learned to wholly consume as entertainment, divorced completely from any expectations about concrete changes in [their] own lives." As "crass show-business manipulations" take the place of "real political movements and real change," Taibbi argues, corporate America on the one hand dresses up moderates "who don't question the corporate consensus," including President Barack Obama, in the clothing of "revolutionary leaders" and on the other spawns "wonderfully captive opposition diversions like the Tea Party," which Taibbi describes as "a fake movement for real peasants." The Tea Party, like previous woolly headed rebellions, blames the wrong people for the nation's crises and proposes precisely the solutions that created the ills of which its adherents complain. According to Taibbi, this ostensibly libertarian movement exhibits an "oxymoronic love of authority figures coupled with a narcissistic celebration of its own 'revolutionary' defiance" and can profitably be thought of as "fifteen million pissed-off white people sent chasing after Mexicans on Medicaid by the small handful of banks and investment companies who advertise on Fox and CNBC." The corporate-backed orchestrators of the Tea Party have sought to persuade their followers that the mom-and-pop investors who could not afford their subprime mortgages caused the financial meltdown. Tea Party leaders have also led the fight against the Obama administration's Affordable Care Act, rousing public fear by warning of government-appointed "death panels" authorized to euthanize the elderly and sick and justifying the shutdown of the federal government in late 2013 as a necessary defense against a "socialist" health care scheme. Thus, the Affordable Health Care Act is not only described in Red Scare terms but also being obstructed in the same way the Sheppard-Towner Act was—by Republican-held states that refuse to accept federal funds to expand their programs.[6]

Some historians and other commentators blame liberal as much as paranoid anticommunists for bringing the United States to this juncture. Critics such as Chris Hedges have argued that by embracing anticommunism and "national security" as the highest priorities, liberals colluded for decades in "political passivity and imperial adventurism." Losing their commitment to classical liberalism, they forfeited any meaningful role in the political culture. "Cornered and weak," they "engaged in the politically safe game of attacking the barbarism of communism—and, later, Islamic militancy—rather than attempting to fight the mounting injustices and structural abuses of the corporate state." Hence, in Hedges's view, "an ideological vacuum" was created on the left, and "the language of rebellion" was ceded to the Far Right. Whereas "capitalism was once viewed by workers as a system to be fought," liberals and the working classes now obediently sing its praises.[7]

Yet even this analysis misses another great and sad legacy of anticommunism—the perpetuation of the aged and oppressive notion that Americans should remain atomized and free to make their way in life (or not) solely by dint of their own effort, suppressing "politics at the prepolitical level" and channeling political discontent into problems of their personal lives.[8]

Notes

Introduction

1. Klehr and Haynes, "Revising Revisionism"; Haynes and Klehr, *In Denial*.

2. Schrecker, *Many Are the Crimes*; Phillips-Fein, *Invisible Hands*; Katznelson, *Fear Itself*.

3. On public-private or state-society collaboration, see McCoy, *Policing America's Empire*; Schrecker, *Many Are the Crimes* (for the role of the American Legion, see 61–64); Talbert, *Negative Intelligence*. Other recent studies exploring the New Deal origins of modern conservatism and antilabor politics include Lichtenstein and Shermer, *Right and Labor in America*.

4. Hofstadter, *Paranoid Style*. Murray, *Red Scare* is the standard study but is marred by its persistent attribution of events to the will of the "American people," "many Americans," and so on.

5. McCoy, *Policing America's Empire*, 11–24.

6. By the end of the twentieth century, as many as 70 percent of Americans identified themselves as anticommunists; only 49 percent placed themselves in the next-largest social category, religious persons (Kovel, *Red Hunting*, 4).

7. McCoy, *Policing America's Empire*; Goldstein, *Political Repression*; Schrecker, *Many Are the Crimes*, 52–55.

8. Rogin, *Ronald Reagan*; Hofstadter, *Paranoid Style*.

9. This book places significantly more emphasis on the importance of anticommunism to immigration policy than does Ngai, *Impossible Subjects*.

10. Schrecker, *Many Are the Crimes*, shares this view (64).

11. On anticommunist networks and the political rise of Ronald Reagan, see Rosenfeld, *Subversives*.

12. Kovel, *Red Hunting*, 8–10.

13. Jennifer Luff coined the term *armchair anticommunism* to distinguish those anticommunists who "worked like armchair detectives, collecting stacks of documents and bits

of intelligence" from the commonsense craft union members who "had direct experience with Communist [activity] on a regular basis" (*Commonsense Anticommunism*, 133, 136).

14. On liberal and trade union contributions to anticommunism, see Luff, *Commonsense Anticommunism*; Delton, "Rethinking Post–World War II Anticommunism"; Powers, *Not without Honor*.

Chapter 1. The Origins of American Anticommunism, ca. 1860–1917

1. On the origins and purpose of the Civil War, see Goodwin, *Team of Rivals*, 141–43, 180–81, 191; David Williams, *People's History*, 3, 32. On the Jacksonian reform tradition, see Beatty, *Age of Betrayal*, 12.

2. Goodwin, *Team of Rivals*, 166–69; Beatty, *Age of Betrayal*, 153–55, 187; Rogin, *Ronald Reagan*, 63–65.

3. Beatty, *Age of Betrayal*, 89–90, 103–8.

4. Brands, *American Colossus*, 7; David Williams, *People's History*, 484.

5. Beatty, *Age of Betrayal*, 193–95, 203, 250–54; Lens, *Labor Wars*, 36; Brands, *American Colossus*, 42–49.

6. Beatty, *Age of Betrayal*, 192–99, 224, 246, 254.

7. David Williams, *People's History*, 109; Beatty, *Age of Betrayal*, 91–103, 385–86.

8. Brands, *American Colossus*, 30–31, 96; Beatty, *Age of Betrayal*, 83.

9. David Williams, *People's History*, 121–23; Brands, *American Colossus*, 53–56.

10. Beatty, *Age of Betrayal*, 76–80.

11. Norwood, *Strikebreaking and Intimidation*, 8–9.

12. Donner, *Protectors of Privilege*, 7–8.

13. Rogin, *Ronald Reagan*, 64.

14. Ibid., 45–51.

15. Ibid., 56–58; Donner, *Protectors of Privilege*, 8; David Brion Davis, *Slave Power Conspiracy*.

16. Rogin, *Ronald Reagan*, 58–63.

17. Ibid., 57, 63.

18. Ibid., 272–87; Hofstadter, *Paranoid Style*; Sagan, *Honey and the Hemlock*.

19. Heale, *American Anticommunism*, 15–20; Gutman, "Tompkins Square 'Riot'"; *New York Times*, 14 January 1874; Rogin, *Ronald Reagan*, 64.

20. Gutman, "Tompkins Square 'Riot,'" 45–55; *New York Times*, 14 January 1874.

21. Gutman, "Tompkins Square 'Riot,'" 53; *New York Times*, 14 January 1874.

22. Gutman, "Tompkins Square 'Riot,'" 54, 60; *New York Times*, 13 January, 4, 26 February 1874; Pacyga, *Chicago*, 78–80.

23. Gutman, "Tompkins Square 'Riot,'" 48–69; Rogin, *Ronald Reagan*, 64; Beatty, *Age of Betrayal*, 154.

24. Kenny, *Molly Maguires*, 8–9, 229; Lens, *Labor Wars*, 29.

25. Kenny, *Molly Maguires*, 9–12; Lens, *Labor Wars*, 13, 19–22.

26. Lens, *Labor Wars*, 11, 22–24; Kenny, *Molly Maguires*, 11–12, 219–20, 238; Bimba, *Molly Maguires*, 71.

27. Beatty, *Age of Betrayal*, 299.

28. Anarcho-syndicalists believed that no state could be the workers' friend and that workers' and producers' cooperative organizations had to form the basis of a new society, governing through federation. Anarcho-syndicalists thus combined the notion of anarchy (abolition of the state) with the foundational supremacy of the *syndicat* (the French term for a trade union).

29. Messer-Kruse, *Haymarket Conspiracy*, 4. This book thoroughly documents newspaper reactions to the events.

30. Lens, *Labor Wars*, 92–97; Brands, *American Colossus*, 470.

31. Brands, *American Colossus*, 469–473; Lens, *Labor Wars*, 99–106; Archer, *Why Is There No Labor Party?*, 122–23.

32. Gutman, "Tompkins Square 'Riot,'" 58.

33. Kenny, *Molly Maguires*, 235–41.

34. Archer, *Why Is There No Labor Party?*, 122; Donner, *Protectors of Privilege*, 12, 15.

35. Bimba, *Molly Maguires*; Kenny, *Molly Maguires*, 229–35; Morn, *"The Eye That Never Sleeps."*

36. Norwood, *Strikebreaking and Intimidation*, 3–5, 52–53, 173; McCormick, *Seeing Reds*, 15; Archer, *Why Is There No Labor Party?*, 123.

37. Theoharis, *FBI and American Democracy*, 16.

38. Beatty, *Age of Betrayal*, 154, 294; Lens, *Labor Wars*, 55–65; Pacyga, *Chicago*, 88, 94–99; Goldstein, *Political Repression*, 40–43.

39. Beatty, *Age of Betrayal*, 281–82, 286–87; Donald, "National Problems," 536–37; Pacyga, *Chicago*, 88; Archer, *Why Is There No Labor Party?*, 123.

40. Donner, *Protectors of Privilege*, 12; Archer, *Why Is There No Labor Party?*, 120–23.

41. Beatty, *Age of Betrayal*, 286–92.

42. Brands, *American Colossus*, 469–73; Lens, *Labor Wars*, 96–109; Archer, *Why Is There No Labor Party?*, 122–23; Beatty, *Age of Betrayal*, 165–81, 203.

43. Kenny, *Molly Maguires*, 235.

44. Bimba, *Molly Maguires*, 64, 129–30; Kenny, *Molly Maguires*, 239–40, 286–87; Donner, *Protectors of Privilege*, 11, 25.

45. Pacyga, *Chicago*, 86–93; Donner, *Protectors of Privilege*, 13; Lens, *Labor Wars*, 55–63.

46. Lens, *Labor Wars*, 56–57.

47. Ibid., 55–65; Pacyga, *Chicago*, 88, 94–99; Goldstein, *Political Repression*, 40–43.

48. Lens, *Labor Wars*, 65; Pacyga, *Chicago*, 98–99; Donner, *Protectors of Privilege*, 14–15. For a recent discussion of the tactics of the defendants' lawyers and the defendants' attitudes toward their predicament, see Messer-Kruse, *Haymarket Conspiracy*.

49. Donner, *Protectors of Privilege*, 4–5.

50. Ibid., 5–22, 32; McCoy, *Policing America's Empire*, 25; Schrecker, *Many Are the Crimes*, 52. The Chicago Police Department received one hundred thousand dollars from the business community each year for five years after the Haymarket bombing to continue to hunt down Reds. Similar deals existed in Los Angeles, New York City, and Detroit (Donner, *Protectors of Privilege*, 5–22).

51. Archer, *Why Is There No Labor Party?*, is the most comprehensive and insightful study

of its kind. On the different character of American and Australian anticommunism, see Fischer, "American Protective League"; Fischer, "Australian Right."

52. Archer, *Why Is There No Labor Party?*, 96, 121.

53. Ibid., 95, 104–5.

54. Ibid., 31–36, 98–99, 106.

Chapter 2. The First World War and the Origins of the Red Scare

1. Sources both partial and hostile to Wilson essentially agree on this point. See Robert W. Tucker, *Woodrow Wilson*; Karp, *Politics of War*, 176–219.

2. Karp, *Politics of War*, 76–77; Beatty, *Age of Betrayal*, 389.

3. Karp, *Politics of War*, 196, 223, 227.

4. Rogin, *Ronald Reagan*, 55–57.

5. Goldstein, *Political Repression*, 66–69, 79; Scott Miller, *President and the Assassin*.

6. McCoy, *Policing America's Empire*, 99–100, 112–15.

7. Sellars, *Oil, Wheat, and Wobblies*; Sims, "Idaho's Criminal Syndicalism Act"; Whitten, "Criminal Syndicalism"; Cain, *Origins of Political Surveillance*; Burgmann, *Revolutionary Industrial Unionism*.

8. McCoy, *Policing America's Empire*, 299–300.

9. Karp, *Politics of War*, 216, 241, 325.

10. Ibid., 229; O'Toole, *When Trumpets Call*, 275, 364–66.

11. Peterson and Fite, *Opponents of War*, 14–15, 20; *New York Call*, 18 April, 17 May 1917; Peterson, *Propaganda for War*, 230.

12. O'Toole, *When Trumpets Call*, 308.

13. McCormick, *Seeing Reds*, 3–4.

14. Ibid., 28, 33, 46.

15. Ibid., 12; McCoy, *Policing America's Empire*, 296, 300.

16. Theoharis, *FBI and American Democracy*, 18–19; McCormick, *Seeing Reds*, 10.

17. McCormick, *Seeing Reds*, 4; McCoy, *Policing America's Empire*, 40, 50, 82–90, 176–77, 295.

18. Peterson and Fite, *Opponents of War*, 90–91; Preston, *Aliens and Dissenters*, 88–91; Goldstein, *Political Repression*, 65.

19. Thompson and Bekken, *Industrial Workers of the World*, 1–9; Lens, *Labor Wars*, 151–52; Sellars, *Oil, Wheat, and Wobblies*, 10; McCormick, *Seeing Reds*, 62.

20. Preston, *Aliens and Dissenters*, 59; Whitten, "Criminal Syndicalism," 6–7, 16; Sellars, *Oil, Wheat, and Wobblies*, 68–73; Lens, *Labor Wars*, 169–86.

21. McCormick, *Seeing Reds*, 12–13, 32.

22. Whitten, "Criminal Syndicalism"; Sellars, *Oil, Wheat, and Wobblies*; Sims, "Idaho's Criminal Syndicalism Act"; *New York Call*, 30 September 1917.

23. Sellars, *Oil, Wheat, and Wobblies*, 99; Preston, *Aliens and Dissenters*, 103; Peterson and Fite, *Opponents of War*, 53–58; Whitten, "Criminal Syndicalism," 18; McCoy, *Policing America's Empire*, 309.

24. Taft, "Bisbee Deportation"; Sellars, *Oil, Wheat, and Wobblies*, 99; Sims, "Idaho's Criminal Syndicalism Act," 514–17; Preston, *Aliens and Dissenters*, 99–102.

25. Preston, *Aliens and Dissenters*, 99–111; Peterson and Fite, *Opponents of War*, 54–55; McCoy, *Policing America's Empire*, 310–11; Taft, "Bisbee Deportation," 14–22.

26. Whitten, "Criminal Syndicalism," 18; Sellars, *Oil, Wheat, and Wobblies*, 102–3; Peterson and Fite, *Opponents of War*, 171–75; Taft, "Bisbee Deportation," 30–37; Millikan, *Union against Unions*, 109–11; *New York Call*, 30 September 1917.

27. Peterson and Fite, *Opponents of War*, 39, 41; *New Day*, 4 March 1922; William Cunningham, *Green Corn Rebellion*, vi–xv.

28. Peterson and Fite, *Opponents of War*, 64–66, 156; Rome Brown, "Americanism versus Socialism" (address delivered before the Middlesex County Bar Association of Boston, December 1919), Senate Doc. 260, *Congressional Record*, 66th Cong., 2nd sess.; Nielsen, *Un-American Womanhood*, 37.

29. Peterson and Fite, *Opponents of War*, 189; Creel, *How We Advertised America*, 179–80.

30. McCormick, *Seeing Reds*, 73–74.

31. Jensen, *Price of Vigilance*, 10–41.

32. Ibid., 25–26.

33. Ibid., 22–26; McCoy, *Policing America's Empire*, 301–3.

34. Jensen, *Price of Vigilance*, 48, 131–41; APL membership records, Records of the American Protective League, Records of the Federal Bureau of Investigation, US National Archives and Records Administration.

35. Jensen, *Price of Vigilance*, 138–41.

36. Ibid.; McCormick, *Seeing Reds*, 12.

37. Jensen, *Price of Vigilance*, 48, 155–56; Preston, *Aliens and Dissenters*, 99–109, 131–49, 163–68; Harris, *Bloodless Victories*, 221–25; Sellars, *Oil, Wheat, and Wobblies*, 114; McCormick, *Seeing Reds*, 19–26.

38. Stone, *Perilous Times*, 187–88; David M. Kennedy, *Over Here*, 80; *Spy Glass* 1, nos. 1, 7–10. Many BI files pertaining to "German Aliens" in fact related to American educators and libertarians such as John Dewey and Roger Baldwin (Records Relating to German Case Files, Records of the Federal Bureau of Investigation, US National Archives and Records Administration, OG 105400).

39. Jensen, *Price of Vigilance*, 45–49, 135, 145–50; McCoy, *Policing America's Empire*, 303.

40. Peterson and Fite, *Opponents of War*, 17–20; Trask, *AEF and Coalition Warmaking*, 14; Jensen, *Price of Vigilance*, 10–23, 37–41; McCoy, *Policing America's Empire*, 295; Keith, *Rich Man's War*.

41. *Spy Glass* 1, nos. 7–9, 12; Chief Examiner, St. Louis Immigration and Naturalization Service, to APL, 26 July 1918, Records of the American Protective League, US National Archives and Records Administration.

42. Jensen, *Price of Vigilance*, 237–88; Coben, *A. Mitchell Palmer*, 118–65; McCoy, *Policing America's Empire*, 295. Australian observers were completely taken in by the APL's claims that it stringently policed itself, meticulously evaluated the suitability of members before they were enrolled, and expelled members who behaved improperly. The league's boast to the Australians that it was "responsible for the quietness of the German and Irish sympathizers of the Central powers," however, had at least some basis in fact. Australian officials did not, however, create an APL counterpart. See Fischer, "American Protective League."

43. Peterson and Fite, *Opponents of War*, 24.

44. Ibid.

45. McCormick, *Seeing Reds*, 46–63, 79; Luff, *Commonsense Anticommunism*, 32–43; Rehnquist, *All the Laws but One*, 173–75.

46. Rehnquist, *All the Laws but One*, 175–78; "A Talk with Mr. Burleson," *The Public*, 12 October 1917; Peterson and Fite, *Opponents of War*, 95–97.

47. Peterson and Fite, *Opponents of War*, 94–101.

48. Karp, *Politics of War*, 227; *La Follette's Magazine*, May 1916; Peterson and Fite, *Opponents of War*, 100–101; *New York Call*, 18 April, 17 May 1917; Peterson, *Propaganda for War*, 230.

49. Creel, *How We Advertised America*, 85–87, 184; US Committee on Public Information, *Complete Report*, 2–3, 29.

50. Hedges, *Death of the Liberal Class*, 76; US Committee on Public Information, *Complete Report*, 2–4, 46.

51. Creel, *How We Advertised America*, 5, 20.

52. C. L. Keep to A. Bruce Bielaski, 11 May 1918, Records of the American Protective League, US National Archives and Records Administration; Karp, *Politics of War*, 334.

53. Schrecker, *Many Are the Crimes*, 54. The Wilson administration ultimately brought 2,168 citizens to trial for violations of the Espionage and Sedition Acts.

Chapter 3. Here Come the Bolsheviks! The Russian Revolution and the Red Scare

1. According to the Julian calendar in use in Russia at the time, the date was 25 October.

2. Discussion of domestic repression is informed by Peterson and Fite, *Opponents of War*, 37, 149, 151, 259–63; *Evening Call*, 7, 10, 13 December 1917; Anna Louise Strong to Department of Justice, 14 December 1917, Investigative Case Files of the Bureau of Investigation, Records of the Federal Bureau of Investigation, US National Archives and Records Administration; "Where Miss Strong Stands: Statement by Anna Louise Strong, Member of Seattle School Board," *Shingle Weaver*, 2 March 1918; *Seattle Union Record*, 2 March 1918; Norman Thomas, *War's Heretics*.

3. Rogin, *Ronald Reagan*, 92–94; Burton, *Learned Presidency*, 179.

4. Van Der Pijl, "Arab Revolts," 41–44.

5. Ibid., 42–44.

6. Ibid.; William Appleman Williams, "American Intervention," 64–66.

7. Moynihan, *Comrades*, vii, 9, 106; Morgan, *Reds*, 13, 25–26; Kennan, *Soviet-American Relations*, 15–17, 38–40, 44–45; Dispatches to the Secretary of State, Report no. 304, Communiqué to the State Department, 15 May 1917, Overview of the United States, Consulate (Petrograd, Russia), Dispatches, Hoover Institution.

8. Communiqués from Russia to the War College, Washington, D.C., 24 November, 12, 17, 28 December 1917, 27 January 1918, "U.S. Colonel's Russian Note Stirs Up Row—Unofficial O.K. on General Peace Denounced," [*Chicago Daily Tribune*?], 4 December 1917, all in Judson Papers, Newberry Library; William Appleman Williams, "American Intervention," 61, 64; Moynihan, *Comrades*, 201–2. Wilson told Congress on 2 April 1917 that "Russia

was known by those who knew it best to have been always in fact democratic at heart, in all the vital habits of her thought, in all the intimate relationship of her people that spoke their natural instinct, their habitual attitude towards life" (Whiticker, *Speeches*, 34). Wilson offered similar bromides on Russia in a speech delivered in Billings, Montana, on 11 September 1919 (Egbert Papers, Hoover Institution).

9. Ambassador Francis's incompetence again proved crucial: he mislaid his cipher books and could not relay to Washington an offer from the Bolshevik government to continue fighting Germany in exchange for American military and financial aid (Morgan, *Reds*, 34–35).

10. US Committee on Public Information, *German-Bolshevik Conspiracy*, 3; US Committee on Public Information, *Complete Report*, 108; Kennan, *Soviet-American Relations*, 50–52, 416–19, 447–50.

11. *New York Globe*, January 1919 (clipping), *New York Post*, 19, 22 January 1919, all in Egbert Papers, Hoover Institution. On the prior release of papers describing German plans to reward Mexico, see Karp, *Politics of War*, 296.

12. Mitchell, *1919*, 74–75; Coben, *A. Mitchell Palmer*, 219; press clippings, Egbert Papers, Hoover Institution. At least one Bureau of Free Love was indeed established in revolutionary Russia. It was the handiwork of (undoubtedly male) provincial staff of the Commissariat for Social Welfare, perverting Commissar Alexandra Kollontai's objective of liberating women from oppressive marriages and sexual slavery. The liberalization of divorce law in Russia was used by some to justify licentious and callous behavior; the divorce rate rocketed to twenty-six times the rates recorded in some regions of "bourgeois Europe." The US government had no knowledge of these developments. See Figes, *People's Tragedy*, 741–42.

13. Creel, *How We Advertised America*, 243, 376–78, 393–95; US Committee on Public Information, *Complete Report*, 216–18, 251–52.

14. William Appleman Williams, "American Intervention," 59; Memorandum to President Wilson, 28 March 1919, "Preliminary Drafts on Bolshevik Manifestations," 25 April 1919, both in Hoover Papers, Hoover Institution. An example of sanguine American views regarding the possibility of domestic revolution appeared in the November 1918 issue of the *Literary Digest*, which concluded that "America was immune to the Bolshevik virus, because nearly all Americans belonged to the decent, literate, property-loving classes" (Slotkin, *Lost Battalions*, 383). On the position of Russian and European peasantry, see Pipes, *Russia*, 492–93.

15. Edward Egbert and Ben Williams to John Sharp Williams, 7 August 1917, Creel to Egbert, 14 February 1918, H. R. Burton to Creel, 12 March 1918, Elliot H. Goodwin to Egbert, 29 March 1918, Charles Stewart Davison to Egbert, 27 December 1918, Egbert to Creel, 14 February 1918, all in Egbert Papers, Hoover Institution. For details of the fund's executive membership, see *The Catherine Breshkovsky Russian Relief Fund—Prospectus of Its Scope and Activities*, letterhead for the American Central Committee for Russian Relief, both in Egbert Papers, Hoover Institution; Breshkovsky, *Message*; Figes, *People's Tragedy*, 456.

16. Smith, "American Foreign Relations," 69; Morgan, *Reds*, 48. The last American troops left Russia in April 1920. Anti-Bolshevik operations cost nearly six hundred

Americans their lives. In 1959, Soviet premier Nikita Khrushchev still remembered US intervention as the lowest point in US-Soviet relations (Morgan, *Reds*, 52).

17. O'Toole, *When Trumpets Call*, 308; John L. Thomas, "Progressivism and the Great War," 676; Coben, *A. Mitchell Palmer*, 173; Schrecker, *Many Are the Crimes*, 55–56.

18. Hanson, *Americanism versus Bolshevism*, vii, 7–8, 18; Preston, *Aliens and Dissenters*, 163–68.

19. Hanson, *Americanism versus Bolshevism*, viii.

20. Ibid., 57–71, 87–91, 247, 298–99; Donner, *Protectors of Privilege*, 37; Murray, *Red Scare*, 65–66; Nielsen, *Un-American Womanhood*, 16.

21. Slotkin, *Lost Battalions*, 382.

22. Archibald Stevenson, testimony, 19–21 January 1919, in US Senate, Committee on the Judiciary, *Brewing and Liquor Interests*, 2690–2729; George E. Chamberlain, "Present Dangers Confronting Our Country," Senate Doc. 78, *Congressional Record*, 65th Cong., 3rd sess.; LeBaron Colt, "Shall Civilization Survive?: An Address on the Vital Issues Involved in This War," Senate Doc. 265, *Congressional Record*, 65th Cong., 3rd sess.; Rome Brown, "Americanism versus Socialism (address delivered before the Middlesex County Bar Association of Boston, December 1919), Senate Doc. 260, *Congressional Record*, 66th Cong., 2nd sess.

23. Pacyga, *Chicago*, 208–13; John L. Thomas, "Progressivism and the Great War," 693; McCoy, *Policing America's Empire*, 313.

24. Gompers regarded socialism as a slow-fuse bomb lit by Germany's Iron Chancellor, Otto von Bismarck (in office 1871–90) (Luff, *Commonsense Anticommunism*, 56).

25. Ibid., 2, 6, 53.

26. Ibid., 32–33, 40–50, 56.

27. Ibid., 53, 63–73.

28. Ibid., 58, 67–75; Dowell, *History*, 63; Peterson and Fite, *Opponents of War*, 174–76; Preston, *Aliens and Dissenters*, 129, 142. On the American Legion, see Schrecker, *Many Are the Crimes*, 70; Nehls, "American Legion," 35.

29. McCormick, *Seeing Reds*, 136.

30. Donner, *Protectors of Privilege*, 38; McCormick, *Seeing Reds*, 137.

31. Whitten, "Criminal Syndicalism," 19; Morgan, *Reds*, 57–60; Theoharis, *FBI and American Democracy*, 24; Coben, *A. Mitchell Palmer*, 176–79, 205–6.

32. Powers, *Secrecy and Power*, 42, 45, 64.

33. Murray, *Red Scare*, 192; Whitten, "Criminal Syndicalism," 34–35, 38; Sellars, *Oil, Wheat, and Wobblies*, 140–41; Dowell, *History*, 48–49.

34. Murray, *Red Scare*, 182–89; Copeland, *Centralia Tragedy*, 57.

35. Better America Federation, *Weekly Letter*, 10 December 1919, Kerr Papers, Hoover Institution; Theoharis, *FBI and American Democracy*, 25; McCormick, *Seeing Reds*, 146.

36. Preston, *Aliens and Dissenters*, 194–236; "CLARA ROFSKY, Chicago, Illinois, 10110-1584-1," in *U.S. Military Intelligence Reports*, ed. Boehm, reel 15; McCormick, *Seeing Reds*, 158.

37. McCormick, *Seeing Reds*, 118–19, 160–61, 169, 204.

38. Buckingham, *America Sees Red*, 26–27; Coben, *A. Mitchell Palmer*, 232–44; Preston,

Aliens and Dissenters, 200, 214; Peterson and Fite, *Opponents of War*, 294; Gage, *Day Wall Street Exploded*, 325–26; "Explosive Stores All Accounted For," *New York Times*, 17 September 1920; Theoharis, *FBI and American Democracy*, 26–28; Donner, *Protectors of Privilege*, 39.

39. Dallek, "Modernizing the Republic," 704; Murray, *Red Scare*, 262.

40. For works that rely on these inappropriate explanations for the events of the Red Scare, see Murray, *Red Scare*; Buckingham, *America Sees Red*; Peterson and Fite, *Opponents of War*; Coben, *A. Mitchell Palmer*; Preston, *Aliens and Dissenters*; Higham, *Strangers in the Land*.

41. On Palmer, see Murray, *Red Scare*, 256–57; Post, *Deportations Delirium*, 302–3; Schmidt, *Red Scare*, 313–17. Senator George H. Moses of the Committee on Foreign Affairs was one important ally Hoover cultivated. Moses helped facilitate Hoover's appointment and supported his claim to be made permanent director, particularly on the basis of his experience in hunting Reds (Moses to Hoover, 7 March 1929, Hoover Papers, Hoover Institution).

Chapter 4. The Spider Web Chart

1. Brophy, "Origins," 217–19, 223–26; McCoy, *Policing America's Empire*, 298.

2. van Courtland Moon, "United States Chemical Warfare Policy," 496; Jensen, "All Pink Sisters," 208–11.

3. Jensen, "All Pink Sisters," 211–12; Reports, 2, 10, 17 February 1923, in *U.S. Military Intelligence Reports*, ed. Boehm, reel 22.

4. Jensen, "All Pink Sisters," 212; Hapgood, Howard, and Hearley, *Professional Patriots*, 11, 103.

5. Lemons, *Woman Citizen*, 215; Suskin, *Show Tunes*, 46–47.

6. J. Edgar Hoover to Lucia R. Maxwell, 19 May 1923, R. M. Whitney to Maxwell, 14 June 1923, both in *U.S. Military Intelligence Reports*, ed. Boehm, reel 19; Hapgood, Howard, and Hearley, *Professional Patriots*, 103, 106; Jensen, "All Pink Sisters," 212–13; Talbert, *Negative Intelligence*, 218–20; Whitney, *Reds in America*.

7. Reports, 2, 10, 17 February 1923, in *U.S. Military Intelligence Reports*, ed. Boehm, reel 22; Lemons, *Woman Citizen*, 215–17; Nielsen, *Un-American Womanhood*, 77, 173.

8. Numerous organizations had already called on Weeks to discipline Fries. Weeks assured them Fries would desist from slandering such organizations, but "shortly after this the spider-web chart appeared." See Jensen, "All Pink Sisters," 213; Hapgood, Howard, and Hearley, *Professional Patriots*, 219; Nielsen, *Un-American Womanhood*, 76, 78.

9. Talbert, *Negative Intelligence*, 220; Lemons, *Woman Citizen*, 217–18; Nielsen, *Un-American Womanhood*, 80, 83; Wilson, *Women's Joint Congressional Committee*, 154; Hapgood, Howard, and Hearley, *Professional Patriots*, 103. The president of the National Association of Manufacturers was just one of many anticommunists with poor information about Russian affairs. Kollontai, a founding member of the Workers' Opposition faction of the Bolshevik Party, had been removed from political power in 1923 and exiled to the Soviet diplomatic service (Figes, *People's Tragedy*, 765).

10. Ida L. Jones to Colonel James H. Reeves, 26 April 1927, Colonel Stanley H. Ford to Jones, 20 May 1927, in *U.S. Military Intelligence Reports*, ed. Boehm, reel 19.

11. "R. M. Whitney Dies Suddenly in Hotel," *New York Times*, 17 August 1924; Maxwell, *Red Juggernaut*; Nielsen, *Un-American Womanhood*, 76; Fries, *Communism Unmasked*; for Key Men, see Felt Collection, Loyola University of Chicago; Hapgood, Howard, and Hearley, *Professional Patriots*, 167.

Chapter 5. Mapping a Political Network: The Anticommunist Spider Web

1. This remained the case even during the Popular Front, when the pressures of economic depression and fascist, Nazi, and Falangist bellicosity condensed the Left's common cause.

2. Robin, *Fear*, 216.

3. Hapgood, Howard, and Hearley, *Professional Patriots*, 3, 7, 54.

4. Ibid., 102, 159; Luff, *Commonsense Anticommunism*, 2, 40–45, 54, 63–66, 70, 87, 100–101, 163–66, 171–73, 232, also discusses the close relationship between the AFL, the NCF, the national security apparatus and the House Un-American Activities Committee.

5. Hapgood, Howard, and Hearley, *Professional Patriots*, 102, 120, 122; Talbert, *Negative Intelligence*, 221–23; Millikan, *Union against Unions*, 225; Theoharis, *FBI and American Democracy*, 29–33; Donner, *Protectors of Privilege*, 41, 47–54.

6. Hapgood, Howard, and Hearley, *Professional Patriots*, 8, 9, 12.

7. Ibid., 43, 76; on Easley, see Cyphers, *National Civic Federation*, 20; on Hough, see Wylder, *Emerson Hough*, 60–62, 121–22.

8. Hapgood, Howard, and Hearley, *Professional Patriots*, 159–60; Nielsen, *Un-American Womanhood*, 57.

9. Hapgood, Howard, and Hearley, *Professional Patriots*, 21, 159.

10. Coudert's son, Fritz Coudert III, made his reputation as a Red-baiter when he co-chaired a 1940 New York state witch hunt for teachers holding communist beliefs (see chap. 12).

11. Hapgood, Howard, and Hearley, *Professional Patriots*, 21–24, 133–37.

12. On Walker, see Carlson, *Under Cover*, 218; Nielsen, *Un-American Womanhood*, 57.

13. See Martin Wade to Charles Frey, 27 March, 23 April 1918, Frey to Wade, 2 April 1918, all in Records of the American Protective League, Records of the Federal Bureau of Investigation, US National Archives and Records Administration.

14. US House of Representatives, Committee on Un-American Activities, *Testimony*, 2–4; *New York Times*, 22 February 1956; Carlson, *Under Cover*, 130, 196, 218–19, 228, 456–59, 509; Talbert, *Negative Intelligence*, 225.

15. Hapgood, Howard, and Hearley, *Professional Patriots*, 96, 162–65; American Civil Liberties Union, *Story of Civil Liberty*, 30; Carlson, *Under Cover*, 246, 390–93, 456–57, 460, 468. Robert McCormick was a member of the harvesting machine dynasty. His father's first cousin, Cyrus McCormick Jr., launched attacks on union labor that helped spark the Haymarket tragedy. Robert's brother, Joseph Medill McCormick, was a state and federal legislator who married Ruth Hanna, the daughter of Republican power broker and industrialist Mark Hanna (see Pacyga, *Chicago*, 94, 96).

16. Advisory Council, *Key Men of America*, National Clay Products Industry Association

circular by Harry Jung, 13 September 1927, both in Felt Collection, Loyola University of Chicago; *New York Times*, 22 February 1956; Millikan, *Union against Unions*, 171; Nielsen, *Un-American Womanhood*, 80, 85; Hapgood, Howard, and Hearley, *Professional Patriots*, 87, 90–91, 161.

17. Hapgood, Howard, and Hearley, *Professional Patriots*, 156, 167–68, 181; Jeansonne, *Women of the Far Right*, 16; Talbert, *Negative Intelligence*, 234–35, 249; McCoy, *Policing America's Empire*, 319–23.

18. Hapgood, Howard, and Hearley, *Professional Patriots*, 23, 45, 53, 95, 132–33, 159–60, 204; Nielsen, *Un-American Womanhood*, 55; Jeansonne, *Women of the Far Right*, 22.

19. Dilling, *Red Network*; Jeansonne, *Women of the Far Right*, 11–18, 21–23, 27–28; Talbert, *Negative Intelligence*, 252.

Chapter 6. John Bond Trevor, Radicals, Eugenics, and Immigration

1. "Obituary, John B. Trevor," *New York Times*, 24 December 1890; "J. B. Trevor Marries Miss Wilmerding," *New York Times*, 26 June 1908; "$4,000,000 Fund Tangle," *New York Times*, 13 March 1924; "John Trevor Dies: Urged Alien Law," *New York Times*, 21 February 1956.

2. Polenberg, *Fighting Faiths*, 167–69.

3. Slotkin, *Lost Battalions*, 383.

4. "John Trevor Dies: Urged Alien Law," *New York Times*, 21 February 1956; Polenberg, *Fighting Faiths*, 167–69.

5. Bendersky, *"Jewish Threat,"* xi–xii, 124–25; Polenberg, *Fighting Faiths*, 167–69. The description of ethnic maps comes from the acknowledgments section of New York Legislature, Joint Committee, *Revolutionary Radicalism*, vol. 1, pt. 1, iv.

6. Bendersky, *"Jewish Threat,"* 66–67, 129; Slotkin, *Lost Battalions*, 385.

7. The Black Hundreds attracted international opprobrium in 1913 for attempting to frame a Jewish man, Mendel Beiliss, for the murder of an ethnic Ukrainian child. Brasol at this time worked for justice minister I. G. Schleglovitov. Both the minister and Tsar Nikolai II were aware of Beiliss's innocence, but according to Figes justified Beiliss's prosecution "in the belief that his conviction would . . . 'prove' that the Jewish cult of ritual murder [of Christian boys] was a fact." Brasol was perhaps MI's "most dedicated anti-Semite." Known as "Agent B-1," Brasol commenced work with MI in the summer of 1918 and enjoyed the confidence of its most senior staff. See Higham, *Strangers in the Land*, 280, 314; Bendersky, *"Jewish Threat,"* 64–66, 125, 127; Talbert, *Negative Intelligence*, 87–88; Hapgood, Howard, and Hearley, *Professional Patriots*, 47–48; Carlson, *Under Cover*, 203–4; Figes, *People's Tragedy*, 241–44. For Trevor's intelligence reports and their widespread use, see Boehm, *U.S. Military Intelligence Reports*, reels 14–19, 22–24.

8. Polenberg, *Fighting Faiths*, 167–69; "Fingerprint Each Person in America, Stevenson Demands," *Evening Call*, 3 December 1917; US Senate, Committee on the Judiciary, *Brewing and Liquor Interests*, 2690; Pfannestiel, *Rethinking the Red Scare*, 13.

9. Polenberg, *Fighting Faiths*, 169; "Union League to Study Bolshevist Movement," *New York Times*, 10 January 1919; Pfannestiel, *Rethinking the Red Scare*, 19.

10. US Senate, Committee on the Judiciary, *Brewing and Liquor Interests*, 2691–2729.

11. Ibid.; Pfannestiel, *Rethinking the Red Scare*, 13.

12. Slotkin, *Lost Battalions*, 385–89. The idea that Trotsky had a strong association with New York was misplaced. Trotsky's personal acquaintance with the United States consisted of a three-month stay in New York in early 1917. He thoroughly antagonized American Jewish socialists, whom he chided for excessive loyalty to their adopted homeland (Service, *Trotsky*, 154–59).

13. US Senate, Committee on the Judiciary, *Brewing and Liquor Interests*, 2702–17; "Deplores Pacifist List," *New York Times*, 28 January 1919; Polenberg, *Fighting Faiths*, 170; Talbert, *Negative Intelligence*, 148–49.

14. "New York State Probe of Bolshevism Asked," *National Civic Federation Review*, 25 March 1919, 12–13; Pfannestiel, *Rethinking the Red Scare*, 20–21; "Stevenson's 'Personally Conducted' Raid," *New York Call*, 15 June 1919; Luff, *Commonsense Anticommunism*, 65–66.

15. Pfannestiel, *Rethinking the Red Scare*, 12–24.

16. Ibid., 25, 110, 125; Hapgood, Howard, and Hearley, *Professional Patriots*, 107. Lusk's gubernatorial ambitions were dashed because he was found to have accepted an expensive silver service from lobbyists working for the New York City police department, whose members were seeking a pay raise.

17. Pfannestiel, *Rethinking the Red Scare*, 25–27; "Lusk Committee Spent $80,000," *New York Times*, 30 January 1920; "Travis Assails 'Reds,'" *New York Times*, 12 February 1920; New York Legislature, Joint Committee, *Revolutionary Radicalism*, vol. 1, pt. 1, iv; Talbert, *Negative Intelligence*, 176–78; Tunney, *Throttled!*

18. Pfannestiel, *Rethinking the Red Scare*, 26; "Stevenson's 'Personally Conducted' Raid," *New York Call*, 15 June 1919; "Cure of Radicalism Seen in Education," *New York Times*, 18 January 1920; New York Legislature, Joint Committee, *Revolutionary Radicalism*, vol. 1, pt. 1, iv.

19. "Search Warrants and Prosecutions," in New York Legislature, Joint Committee, *Revolutionary Radicalism*; Lusk, "Radicalism under Inquiry."

20. Pfannestiel, *Rethinking the Red Scare*, 31–34, 75–80; Bendersky, *"Jewish Threat,"* 127; New York Legislature, Joint Committee, *Revolutionary Radicalism*, vol. 1, pt. 1, 20.

21. A Senate committee estimated on specious grounds in 1920 that no less than $150,000 had been funneled to the bureau. See "Russian Propaganda," Senate Rpt. 526, 14 April 1920, *Congressional Record*, 66th Cong., 2nd sess. See also Pfannestiel, *Rethinking the Red Scare*, 34, 44, 52–56, 71; Bendersky, *"Jewish Threat,"* 129.

22. Pfannestiel, *Rethinking the Red Scare*, 52, 59–60, 62–63, 68–69; "Stevenson's 'Personally Conducted' Raid," *New York Call*, 15 June 1919; "Search Warrants and Prosecutions," in New York Legislature, Joint Committee, *Revolutionary Radicalism*.

23. Pfannestiel, *Rethinking the Red Scare*, 75–79; Talbert, *Negative Intelligence*, 180.

24. Pfannestiel, *Rethinking the Red Scare*, 19, 80–86, 123.

25. Ibid., 84, 89–95, 126; "Search Warrants and Prosecutions," in New York Legislature, Joint Committee, *Revolutionary Radicalism*.

26. Lusk, "Radicalism under Inquiry."

27. New York Legislature, Joint Committee, *Revolutionary Radicalism*, vol. 1, pt. 1, 7; Lusk, "Radicalism under Inquiry."

28. Lusk, "Radicalism under Inquiry"; J. B. Trevor, *Introduction and Historical Review of Conditions and Agencies Tending to Create the Present Tendency toward Radicalism*, in *U.S. Military Intelligence Reports*, ed. Boehm, reel 15; New York Legislature, Joint Committee, *Revolutionary Radicalism*, vol. 1, sec. 2, 502.

29. New York Legislature, Joint Committee, *Revolutionary Radicalism*, vol. 1, sec. 2, 502; Lusk, "Radicalism under Inquiry."

30. Lusk, "Radicalism under Inquiry"; New York Legislature, Joint Committee, *Revolutionary Radicalism*, vol. 1, pt. 1, 10, 12.

31. Bendersky, *"Jewish Threat,"* 131; Trevor, *Introduction*; Tunney, *Throttled!*, 3, 5.

32. New York Legislature, Joint Committee, *Revolutionary Radicalism*, vol. 1, pt. 1, 11, 16–18, sec. 2, 1112–20; Lusk, "Radicalism under Inquiry."

33. Pfannestiel, *Rethinking the Red Scare*, 19, 85; Lusk, "Radicalism under Inquiry"; New York Legislature, Joint Committee, *Revolutionary Radicalism*, vol. 2, pt. 1, 1476–1512, 1517–19.

34. Trevor, *Introduction*.

35. Lusk, "Radicalism under Inquiry"; Trevor, *Introduction*.

36. "Search Warrants and Prosecutions," in New York Legislature, Joint Committee, *Revolutionary Radicalism*; "To Fight Red Periodicals," *New York Times*, 21 September 1919; "Russian Archbishop Urges War on Reds—Utters Warning to Jews," *New York Times*, 15 July 1919; "Lusk Answers Socialist Charges," *New York Times*, 10 January 1920; "Republicans Split on Assembly's Act Barring Socialists," *New York Times*, 10 January 1920; "Sweet Defends Assembly's Action against Socialists," *New York Times*, 11 January 1920; "Sweet Defends Ban on Socialists," *New York Times*, 16 January 1920; "Union League Report Indorses Assembly," *New York Times*, 15 February 1920; "Union League Club Approves Barring of the Socialists," *New York Times*, 20 February 1920; Pfannestiel, *Rethinking the Red Scare*, 98–99.

37. New York Legislature, Joint Committee, *Revolutionary Radicalism*, vol. 1, pt. 1, 17–19; Pfannestiel, *Rethinking the Red Scare*, 99–117; "To Test Teachers' Loyalty," *New York Times*, 25 April 1922; US President, "Americanization Work in the Public Schools of the District of Columbia," Senate Doc. 320, *Congressional Record*, 67th Cong., 4th sess.; American Civil Liberties Union, *Record of the Fight*, 20; Pegram, *One Hundred Percent American*, 19, 115; American Civil Liberties Union, *Free Speech, 1926*, 22.

38. New York Legislature, Joint Committee, *Revolutionary Radicalism*, vol. 1, pt. 1, v–xxx; Boehm, *U.S. Military Intelligence Reports*, reels 16–19, 22–24; *Daily Data Sheet of the Key Men of America (Dealing with Radical and Subversive Movements)*, Felt Collection, Loyola University of Chicago; Dilling, *Red Network*, dedication.

39. *Report of Special Committee*, 4–11; Adamic, "Aliens and Alien-Baiters," 571; Luff, *Commonsense Anticommunism*, 150–51.

40. New York Legislature, Joint Committee, *Revolutionary Radicalism*, vol. 1, pt. 1, 14.

41. Higham, *Strangers in the Land*, 314; Bendersky, *"Jewish Threat,"* 147.

42. Hannaford, *Race*, 31, 187–88, 330. The notion that humanity was "divided into material classes, genera, and species" emerged after the Reformation in the late seventeenth century.

43. McCoy, *Policing America's Empire*, 100–101.

44. Higham, *Strangers in the Land*, 301; Pula, "American Immigration Policy."

45. Ngai, *Impossible Subjects*, 19; Higham, *Strangers in the Land*, 40–41, 101. On literacy tests in the South, see Kelley, *Thelonious Monk*, 7–8.

46. Higham, *Strangers in the Land*, 102–5; Hannaford, *Race*, 338–39; Pula, "American Immigration Policy," 14.

47. Higham, *Strangers in the Land*, 151–53; Pula, "American Immigration Policy," 14–20; Beatty, *Age of Betrayal*, 163. Boas himself maintained that "the inference that various populations are composed of individuals belonging to various races is . . . objectively unproved" (Hannaford, *Race*, 371). Eugenicists nevertheless applied his research into hereditary deficiencies to wider racial categories. The Court of Appeals's broad defense of constitutional liberty in *In re Ah Fong* was issued after lobbying by prostitution rings profiting from the unrestricted employment of aliens brought to the United States from Asia.

48. "Albert Johnson," *Biographical Directory of the U.S. Congress*; Hillier, "Albert Johnson," 193–99.

49. Hillier, "Albert Johnson," 199–204; US Committee on Public Information, *Complete Report*, 38; Higham, *Strangers in the Land*, 202–4; Daniels, *Asian America*, 149.

50. Higham, *Strangers in the Land*, 155–56, 271, 313–14.

51. Hannaford, *Race*, 260, 328–30, 356–58; Higham, *Strangers in the Land*, 156–57, 306. The notion that an anti-Bolshevik Russian counterrevolution would result in a deathly campaign against Jews was widely accepted in national security circles. White Russian informants working with MI secured President Wilson's "support for their . . . aspirations" by minimizing "the role of their people in anti-Jewish violence" and excusing cases of such violence "on the ground that the Jews were responsible for Bolshevism." Army intelligence officers, conditioned "to accept the idea that racial conflicts inevitably provoke extraordinary and exterminating violence," were easily persuaded that opposition to Bolshevism would culminate in a retaliatory pogrom: Russian Jewish Bolsheviks had to be tamed, just as Jim Crow had to lynch African Americans. See Slotkin, *Lost Battalions*, 384.

52. Hannaford, *Race*, 346, 357, 359; Higham, *Strangers in the Land*, 272–73, 307; "Lusk Would Eradicate Anarchy in Schools," *New York Times*, 2 May 1921.

53. Higham, *Strangers in the Land*, 305–13; Ngai, *Impossible Subjects*, 19.

54. Higham, *Strangers in the Land*, 314.

55. Ibid., 310–11.

56. Ibid., 301–11; Hillier, "Albert Johnson," 204–5; Ngai, *Impossible Subjects*, 20.

57. Higham, *Strangers in the Land*, 315; Hillier, "Albert Johnson," 205–6.

58. Higham, *Strangers in the Land*, 315–18, 320; Hillier, "Albert Johnson," 206–10; Trevor, *Analysis*, 5, 7; Ngai, *Impossible Subjects*, 19.

59. Trevor, *Analysis*, 54–56, 61; Higham, *Strangers in the Land*, 321.

60. Higham, *Strangers in the Land*, 322–23.

61. Pula, "American Immigration Policy," 12; Higham, *Strangers in the Land*, 323–24; Hillier, "Albert Johnson," 207–8; Trevor, *Analysis*, 15–16; Bendersky, *"Jewish Threat,"* 166; Ngai, *Impossible Subjects*, 23.

62. Trevor, *Analysis*, 14, 18–19, 21, 60.

63. Ibid., 5, 7, 19; Hillier, "Albert Johnson," 208.

64. Ngai, *Impossible Subjects*, 7–9.

65. Ibid., 10, 19. On Shipley, see McCormick, *Seeing Reds*, 11; "Ruth B. Shipley, Ex-Passport Head," *New York Times*, 5 November 1966.

66. Bon Tempo, *Americans at the Gate*, 21–26, 95–97.

67. Grant et al., "Third Report"; Adamic, "Aliens and Alien-Baiters," 567–69; "John Trevor Dies: Urged Alien Law," *New York Times*, 21 February 1956; "Deaths," *New York Times*, 21 February 1956; Bendersky, *"Jewish Threat,"* 131.

68. Carlson, *Under Cover*, 219; Adamic, "Aliens and Alien-Baiters," 561–63; American Civil Liberties Union, *Liberty under the New Deal*.

69. Adamic, "Aliens and Alien-Baiters," 566–69; Ngai, *Impossible Subjects*, 35, 53; "Urges Federal Ban on Red Propaganda," *New York Times*, 3 October 1930; Hillier, "Albert Johnson," 210; Morse, *While Six Million Died*, 165–67, 260–61, 267; "Says We Are Next on Hitler's List," *New York Times*, 2 December 1940; Bendersky, *"Jewish Threat,"* 280; Daniels, *Asian America*, 193–96. Hoover's opposition to the scheme stemmed from concern that the quota would too severely restrict family immigration among midwesterners of German and Scandinavian heritage, who were important Republican voters. Johnson had also been eager to place a quota on Mexican immigration and frequently used statistics provided by Edythe Tate Thompson, the chief of the California Tuberculosis Bureau, to argue his case on public health grounds.

70. In a series of opinion polls conducted between 1939 and 1946, respondents "consistently chose 'the Jews' over the Japanese or the Germans" as the greatest threat to the United States (Nirenberg, *Anti-Judaism*, 457–58).

71. Carlson, *Under Cover*, 120, 127, 130, 194–96, 456–57; Jeansonne, *Women of the Far Right*, 152–64; W. H. Tucker, *Funding of Scientific Racism*, 61.

72. Adamic, "Aliens and Alien-Baiters," 571; Powers, *Not without Honor*, 162; Bellant, *Old Nazis*, 33; American Civil Liberties Union, *Story of Civil Liberty*, 30–31.

73. W. H. Tucker, *Funding of Scientific Racism*, 6–7, 11–42, 58–62; Bellant, *Old Nazis*, 32; Ngai, *Impossible Subjects*, 25; quotations taken from the Pioneer Fund website, http://www.pioneerfund.org/ (website no longer available); "Fund Backs Controversial Study of 'Racial Betterment,'" *New York Times*, 11 December 1977. Stoddard argued in 1927 that immigration restriction and eugenics should be discussed not in terms of "theorizing about superiors and inferiors" but rather in terms of "the bedrock of *difference*" (Hannaford, *Race*, 346). In addition to the younger Trevor, Pioneer Fund directors included the fund's principal financial benefactor, Draper; Laughlin (who died in 1943); Frederick Henry Osborn, Henry Fairfield Osborn's nephew and a railroad and investment banking multimillionaire; jurist Charles Codman Cabot; and future US Supreme Court associate justice John Marshall Harlan (for whom Weyher clerked) .

74. The ACPS also opposed fluoridation of water, the National Council of Churches, and the World Federation of Mental Health (W. H. Tucker, *Funding of Scientific Racism*, 63). See also "Fund Backs Controversial Study of 'Racial Betterment,'" *New York Times*, 11 December 1977; Bon Tempo, *Americans at the Gate*, 102. Regarding the denial of linkages

between Nazism and eugenics, see the Pioneer Fund webpage, which states, "The idea that a few crypto-Nazi, Anglo-Americans dominated the eugenics movement is ludicrous and wrong." The fund also complains that "innuendo, falsehood, and name-calling" has damaged its reputation (http://www.pioneerfund.org/ [website no longer available]). For John B. Trevor Jr.'s obituary, see *New York Times*, 30 August 2006.

Chapter 7. Jacob Spolansky: The Rise of the Career Anticommunist Spook

1. McCoy, *Policing America's Empire*, 12.

2. Weiss, "Private Detective Agencies," 87–97; Theoharis, *FBI and American Democracy*, 15.

3. Spolansky, *Communist Trail*, 1–3; Figes, *People's Tragedy*, 80; www.familysearch.org; www.ellisisland.org; www.jewishgen.org.

4. Spolansky's first commanding officer in this Negative Branch was Major Thomas B. Crockett, a relative of the famous Davy and one of two MI officers on the board of the American Protective League. Crockett ran "by far the most active army intelligence center" in the United States, collaborating with the league, the Illinois attorney general's office, and the Chicago Police Anarchist Squad and running similar operations in Cincinnati, Indianapolis, Cleveland, and Gary. See Talbert, *Negative Intelligence*, 184.

5. Spolansky, *Communist Trail*, 5–9, 16; Klug, "Labor Market Politics," 15; Theoharis, *FBI and American Democracy*, 24; Donner, *Protectors of Privilege*, 32; Jensen, *Price of Vigilance*, 25; Talbert, *Negative Intelligence*, 95; Jacob Spolansky, interview by Theodore Draper, 24 November, 20 December 1954, Theodore Draper Research Files, Emory University.

6. Weiss, "Private Detective Agencies," 97–98; Theoharis, *FBI and American Democracy*, 24–26.

7. Theoharis, *FBI and American Democracy*, 27–29; Weiss, "Private Detective Agencies," 98–100; Post, *Deportations Delirium*, 55–56; Donner, *Protectors of Privilege*, 42.

8. The prosecution's resources for the Bridgman trials were bolstered by the services of Archibald Stevenson, whom Ralph Easley loaned to the Michigan commissioner of public safety. The National Civic Federation paid for Ruthenberg's trial after Michigan authorities declined to shoulder the expense. A grateful Burns then leaked trial material to the federation. See Spolansky, *Communist Trail*, 23, 26; Jacob Spolansky, "Dauntless Daredevils: Behind the Red Lines, the Story of K-97," unpublished manuscript, ca. 1950, Draper Research Files, Emory University; Weiss, "Private Detective Agencies," 101; Southern, Department HQ, to MI Director, 12 July 1920, in *U.S. Military Intelligence Reports*, ed. Boehm, reel 19; Hapgood, Howard, and Hearley, *Professional Patriots*, 99; "Charges Inciting of Red Outrages," *New York Times*, 13 February 1923; "Death Threat Here Laid to Burns Man in Spy's Testimony," *New York Times*, 14 February 1923; "Says Reds Plotted Armed Revolt Here for a Dictatorship," *New York Times*, 16 March 1923; "Link W. Z. Foster with Red Meeting," *New York Times*, 17 March 1923; " 'K-97' Quit Job in Shipyard to Unmask Reds' Leaders," *New York Times*, 8 April 1923; Luff, *Commonsense Anticommunism*, 98; Donner, *Protectors of Privilege*, 43.

9. Spolansky, *Communist Trail*, 12, 142; Theoharis, *FBI and American Democracy*, 32–33; Luff, *Commonsense Anticommunism*, 97–99.

10. *Chicago Daily News*, 17 October 1924.

11. Klug, "Labor Market Politics," 16; Spolansky, *Red Trail*; *Textile Strike Bulletin* (Trade Union Educational League), 8, 15 July 1926; Weisbord, *Passaic*, 52; McCormick, *Seeing Reds*, 92–94.

12. Spolansky, *Communist Trail*, 10, 44; Weisbord, *Passaic*, 39.

13. Weisbord, *Passaic*, 12–39; Foner, *History*, 144, 153, 155; Jacob Spolansky, interview by Theodore Draper, 24 November, 20 December 1954, Theodore Draper Research Files, Emory University; Draper, *Roots*, 227–36.

14. Spolansky, *Communist Trail*, 45–47.

15. Klug, "Labor Market Politics," 3–4, 13; Millikan, *Union against Unions*, 5–43; Feurer, *Radical Unionism*; Harris, *Bloodless Victories*.

16. Klug, "Labor Market Politics," 3–19; Jacob Spolansky, interview by Theodore Draper, 24 November, 20 December 1954, Theodore Draper Research Files, Emory University.

17. *Detroit Saturday Night*, 30 July 1927.

18. Klug, "Labor Market Politics," 19–22; Donner, *Protectors of Privilege*, 53.

19. Klug, "Labor Market Politics," 19–22.

20. Ibid., 22–25.

21. Ibid., 25–32; Spolansky, *Communist Trail*, 47–48.

22. Klug, "Labor Market Politics," 32; Spolansky, *Communist Trail*, 11, 52, 61; Donner, *Protectors of Privilege*, 54; McCormick, *Seeing Reds*, 186.

23. Spolansky, *Communist Trail*, 52, 61. General Motors also built a company store of tear gas. Only Ford maintained its own in-house labor espionage service, the "Service Department," arguably the world's largest private army, which established the "most extensive and efficient espionage system in American industry." The department employed between thirty-five hundred and six thousand members—roughly one for every twenty-five plant workers. See Norwood, *Strikebreaking and Intimidation*, 172–83, 203–4.

24. Norwood, *Strikebreaking and Intimidation*, 172–78, 181–82; Phillips-Fein, *Invisible Hands*, 15; "G.M.C. Has Dropped Spies, Says Chief," *New York Times*, 16 February 1937; Auerbach, "La Follette Committee." The La Follette Committee estimated that in the mid-1930s, US industry was supporting at least forty thousand labor spies at an annual cost of eighty million dollars.

25. Spolansky, *Communist Trail*, 55–57; "Says Stalin Aimed to Destroy A.F.L.," *New York Times*, 19 October 1938; Donner, *Protectors of Privilege*, 57.

26. Spolansky is presumably describing communist efforts to frustrate the March 1941 Lend-Lease Act, which provided Great Britain with access to US-manufactured munitions and credit. Later that year, the United States entered the Second World War as an ally of the USSR, and communist subversion abruptly ceased.

27. Spolansky, *Communist Trail*, 77, 80, 196–202; Morgan, *Reds*,188.

28. "Books Published Today," *New York Times*, 10 April 1951; Orville Prescott, "Books of the Times," *New York Times*, 11 April 1951; Frank S. Adams, "Commie Hunting Is His Business," *New York Times*, 15 April 1951; "Nero in New Musical," *New York Times*, 4 July 1951. On Russian secret police brutality, see Conquest, *Great Terror*.

29. "Center for Taft Will Open in City," *New York Times*, 26 November 1951; "G.O.P. Action Group Formed by Taft Men," *New York Times*, 11 August 1952. On Taft, see Morgan,

Reds, 346, 393; Dallek, "Global Setting," 781. On the FBI, see Theoharis, *FBI and American Democracy*, 65, 174; Jacob Spolansky, interview by Theodore Draper, 24 November, 20 December 1954, Theodore Draper Research Files, Emory University. For Draper's ancestry, see "Theodore Draper, Freelance Historian, Is Dead at 93," *New York Times*, 22 February 2006; "Scholar, Historian Theodore Draper," *Washington Post*, 23 February 2006. Private detective agencies were not the only strikebreaking forces to rely on criminals. In 1935, Michigan's governor appointed the head of Ford's Service Department, Harry Bennett, to serve on the state parole board. This position enabled Bennett to recruit paroled murderers, rapists, armed burglars, and drug pushers whose freedom hinged on satisfying Bennett's will. See Norwood, *Strikebreaking and Intimidation*, 181–82.

30. For Spolansky's death certificate, see www.familysearch.org; Klug, "Labor Market Politics," 13.

Chapter 8. The Better America Federation and Big Business's War on Labor

1. Schrecker, *Many Are the Crimes*, 49.

2. Harris, *Bloodless Victories*; Millikan, *Union against Unions*; Feurer, *Radical Unionism*; Archer, *Why Is There No Labor Party?*

3. Silverberg, "Citizens' Committees," 17, 31; Millikan, *Union against Unions*, 7–12, 16–19, 30, 158–59.

4. Harris, *Bloodless Victories*, 59–61, 64, 71; Millikan, *Union against Unions*, 14–15, 34; Feurer, *Radical Unionism*, 8; McCormick, *Seeing Reds*, 30; Norwood, *Strikebreaking and Intimidation*, 176.

5. Feurer, *Radical Unionism*, xiv, 1, 7, 9, 97; Harris, *Bloodless Victories*, 78, 83–84, 179, 236–37, 392; Millikan, *Union against Unions*, 28, 35, 37.

6. Donner, *Protectors of Privilege*, 30; Harris, *Bloodless Victories*, 158, Feurer, *Radical Unionism*, 9, Millikan, *Union against Unions*, 44–45; Beatty, *Age of Betrayal*, 379; Silverberg, "Citizens' Committees," 18, 20, 34–35.

7. Carter, "Labor Unions," 25–33.

8. Harris, *Bloodless Victories*, 247; Millikan, *Union against Unions*, 50–58.

9. Silverberg, "Citizens' Committees," 28–29; Millikan, *Union against Unions*, 13–15, 30, 86, 162, 170; McCormick, *Seeing Reds*, 122; Phillips-Fein, *Invisible Hands*, 39.

10. Millikan, *Union against Unions*, 150; Silverberg, "Citizens' Committees," 28; Putnam, "Persistence of Progressivism," 398–99.

11. Harris, *Bloodless Victories*, 105; Silverberg, "Citizens' Committees," 28; Millikan, *Union against Unions*, 57, 168.

12. Harris, *Bloodless Victories*, 82, 247.

13. Ibid., 246–47; Millikan, *Union against Unions*, 174. The American Plan's name may have been inspired by the monthly bulletin of the CA in Ramsay and Dakota Counties, Minnesota.

14. Harris, *Bloodless Victories*, 247; Feurer, *Radical Unionism*, 14; Millikan, *Union against Unions*, 130, 140–41.

15. Millikan, *Union against Unions*, 102–9; Feurer, *Radical Unionism*, 11.

16. Harris, *Bloodless Victories*, 246–73; Feurer, *Radical Unionism*, 12; *Report of the Industrial Conference*, 6 March 1920, Hoover Papers, Hoover Institution.

17. Goldstein, *Political Repression*, 170; Millikan, *Union against Unions*, 176; American Civil Liberties Union, *Year's Fight*, 6.

18. Scott Miller, *President and the Assassin*, 194–95; Murray, *Red Scare*, 261; Goldstein, *Political Repression*, 170.

19. Powers, *Not without Honor*, 69–70; American Civil Liberties Union, *Year's Fight*, 4; Goldstein, *Political Repression*, 183–84.

20. Circular to US district attorneys, 23 August 1922, and H. Daugherty to J. M. Dickinson, 28 October 1922, both in US Department of Justice, *Appendix*; Goldstein, *Political Repression*, 183–84; Luff, *Commonsense Anticommunism*, 31, 82–83.

21. Scott Miller, *President and the Assassin*, 196–211; American Civil Liberties Union, *Fight for Free Speech*, 4; American Civil Liberties Union, *Record of the Fight*; American Civil Liberties Union, *Free Speech in 1924*; American Civil Liberties Union, *Free Speech 1925–1926*; American Civil Liberties Union, *Fight for Civil Liberty, 1927–28*; American Civil Liberties Union, *Fight for Civil Liberty: The Story of the Activities of the ACLU, 1928–29*.

22. Radosh, "Corporate Ideology," 75–83; Preston, *Aliens and Dissenters*, 259; Feurer, *Radical Unionism*, 15.

23. Layton, "Better America Federation," 137.

24. "Causes Leading up to the Organization of the Commercial Federation and Accomplishments to Date," [1918 or 1919], BAF Organizational Profile, 27 December 1950, *Weekly Letter*, 22 June 1920, all in Kerr Papers, Hoover Institution; Layton, "Better America Federation," 137; Haldeman, interview, California State Archives; Tygiel, *Great Los Angeles Swindle*, 77–80, 183–84, 301; Mike Davis, *City of Quartz*, 114.

25. Layton, "Better America Federation," 137–40; Hapgood, Howard, and Hearley, *Professional Patriots*, 64, 134; "Association for Betterment of Public Service: Principles and Purposes," Kerr Papers, Hoover Institution; Mike Davis, *City of Quartz*, 114.

26. *Weekly Letter*, 7 January, 22 June 1920; Hapgood, Howard, and Hearley, *Professional Patriots*, 65, 133; Layton, "Better America Federation," 138–40; regarding American Liberty League, see Phillips-Fein, *Invisible Hands*.

27. *Weekly Letter*, 19, 31 October, 3 December 1919, 7 January 1920; E. G. Pratt to J. G. Riethmeier, W. W. Andrew, and James T. Kent, 28 April 1920, circular letter to "Members and Friends," drafts and final, 20, 22, 23 August 1918, all in Kerr Papers, Hoover Institution.

28. "Causes Leading up to the Organization of the Commercial Federation and Accomplishments to Date," [1918 or 1919], Kerr Papers, Hoover Institution.

29. Ibid.; *Weekly Letter*, 26 November 1919, 17 February 1920; Layton, "Better America Federation," 140–45.

30. *Weekly Letter*, 6 August, 26 November, 10 December 1919, 17 February 1920.

31. Ibid., 31 October, 10 December 1919, 17 February 1920; BAF mission statement and "Association for Betterment of Public Service: Principles and Purposes," both in Kerr Papers, Hoover Institution.

32. *Weekly Letter*, 22 June 1920; on the activities of the Taxpayers' Association, see Putnam, "Persistence of Progressivism," 400.

33. *Weekly Letter*, 31 October, 10 December 1919; Harris, *Bloodless Victories*, 347. In December 1919, with full knowledge that 120,000 American soldiers had been killed in the Great War, the federation called on the US government to intervene in the Mexican civil war on behalf of manufacturers in San Francisco and Los Angeles. As the map on the BAF letterhead shows, the federation considered Baja California to be part of the United States (see figure 10).

34. As in other major cities, the files of the disbanded American Protective League went to the Los Angeles Red Squad rather than to US attorneys, as should have been the case.

35. Donner, *Protectors of Privilege*, 33, 39.

36. Ibid., 36, 43; Layton, "Better America Federation," 147; American Civil Liberties Union, *Record of the Fight*; American Civil Liberties Union, *Story of Civil Liberty*; American Civil Liberties Union, *Fight for Civil Liberty 1930–1931*; American Civil Liberties Union, *"Sweet Land of Liberty"*; American Civil Liberties Union, *Liberty under the New Deal*.

37. Dowell, *History*, 100–109, 122, 127, 147; Whitten, "Criminal Syndicalism," 54, 63; Donner, *Protectors of Privilege*, 35; Hapgood, Howard, and Hearley, *Professional Patriots*, 65, 133.

38. Whitten, "Criminal Syndicalism," 60–61; Hapgood, Howard, and Hearley, *Professional Patriots*, 17; Sims, "Idaho's Criminal Syndicalism Act," 525.

39. Donner, *Protectors of Privilege*, 42; Whitten, "Criminal Syndicalism," 52–58; Dowell, *History*, 132; Sellars, *Oil, Wheat, and Wobblies*, 161–65.

40. Whitten, "Criminal Syndicalism," 58–61.

41. Ibid.; Sellars, *Oil, Wheat, and Wobblies*, 167–73; Sims, "Idaho's Criminal Syndicalism Act," 525.

42. Sims, "Idaho's Criminal Syndicalism Act," 525–26; Whitten, "Criminal Syndicalism," 51–52, 62–63; Dowell, *History*, 123–27; BAF, "1923 Resume of Activities," Kerr Papers, Hoover Institution.

43. "Causes Leading up to the Organization of the Commercial Federation and Accomplishments to Date," [1918 or 1919], material addressed to teacher organizations in California, 1919, *Weekly Letter*, 24 December 1919, all in Kerr Papers, Hoover Institution. On the failure of the teacher bill, see Layton, "Better America Federation," 146.

44. BAF material addressed to teacher organizations and 1923 résumé, both in Kerr Papers, Hoover Institution; Hapgood, Howard, and Hearley, *Professional Patriots*, 149.

45. Millikan, *Union against Unions*, 206–7; American Civil Liberties Union, *Fight for Civil Liberty, 1930–1931*; Hapgood, Howard, and Hearley, *Professional Patriots*, 9.

46. "Causes Leading up to the Organization of the Commercial Federation and Accomplishments to Date," [1918 or 1919], Kerr Papers, Hoover Institution; Hapgood, Howard, and Hearley, *Professional Patriots*, 26–27, Silverberg, "Citizens' Committees," 25; Millikan, *Union against Unions*, 231.

47. Hapgood, Howard, and Hearley, *Professional Patriots*, 33.

48. McCormick, *Seeing Reds*, 136.

49. *Straight Shooter* annual report, Kerr Papers, Hoover Institution.

50. Harris, *Bloodless Victories*, 289.

51. *Straight Shooter* annual report, sheet 5, Kerr Papers, Hoover Institution.

52. *Straight Shooter*, sheets 11, 42, in ibid.

53. BAF, 1923 résumé, *Weekly Letter*, 3 February 1920, Elmer W. Benedict to BAF (soliciting "data of the industrial condition"), 16 March 1920, W. S. Grassie to BAF, 27 March 1920, *Straight Shooter* annual report, all in Kerr Papers, Hoover Institution; Hapgood, Howard, and Hearley, *Professional Patriots*, 175. On Atwood, see "Queries and Answers," *New York Times*, 11 April 1920; "Harry Fuller Atwood, Lawyer, Dies at 61," *New York Times*, 14 December 1930. On Baroness De Ropp, see *Los Angeles Daily News*, 14 August 1923; *Berkeley Daily Gazette*, 30 October 1926.

54. Layton, "Better America Federation," 142, 145; Roberts, *"Laughing Horse"* (quoting from Upton Sinclair's *The Goose-Step: A Study of American Education* [1923], which in turn sourced Haldeman's comments from the *San Francisco Call*, 20 January 1922); Hapgood, Howard, and Hearley, *Professional Patriots*, 146.

55. Hapgood, Howard, and Hearley, *Professional Patriots*, 80, 146–49; Layton, "Better America Federation," 145. On constitutional originalism, see Lepore, "Commandments."

56. Feurer, *Radical Unionism*, 9; Millikan, *Union against Unions*, 329–33; Hapgood, Howard, and Hearley, *Professional Patriots*, 147, 151.

57. Silverberg, "Citizens' Committees," 29; *Weekly Letter*, 25 September, 17 October 1919, 9 March 1920; Pula, "American Immigration Policy," 24.

58. *Weekly Letter*, 31 October, 19 November 1919; Layton, "Better America Federation," 143.

59. *Weekly Letter*, 6 August, 19 October 1919.

60. Ibid., 10 December 1919; Layton, "Better America Federation," 142, 147.

61. Tygiel, *Great Los Angeles Swindle*, 232.

62. Ibid., 8; Goldstein, *Political Repression*, 171.

63. Phillips-Fein, *Invisible Hands*, 13; Harris, *Bloodless Victories*, 358–63; Lichtman, *White Protestant Nation*, 53, 82; Murphy, "Sources and Nature"; Layton, "Better America Federation," 143, 146.

64. "Study on Subversives," 6 June 1927, in *U.S. Military Intelligence Reports*, ed. Boehm, reel 23; Talbert, *Negative Intelligence*, 225–44; McCoy, *Policing America's Empire*, 322.

65. Charles H. Titus to W. H. Wilson, 7 February 1933, in *U.S. Military Intelligence Reports*, ed. Boehm, reel 23; Murphy, "Sources and Nature," 67.

66. Miscellaneous papers, ca. 1934–36, Kerr Papers, Hoover Institution; Millikan, *Union against Unions*, 329–30. On farm lobby fronts, see Feurer, *Radical Unionism*, 92; Phillips-Fein, *Invisible Hands*, 21–22. For business's use of farmers' antilabor rhetoric, see *Weekly Letter*, 2 March 1920.

67. James E. Davis to California Oil and Gas Association, 18 January 1936, Kerr Papers, Hoover Institution. Davis was later stripped from command for his role in the Wineville Chicken Coop murder case, dramatized in the 2008 motion picture *The Changeling*.

68. Charles Kramer to BAF, 15 May 1935, Kerr Papers, Hoover Institution. In the 1930s, the BAF sometimes coordinated its anticommunist testimony to Congress with the National Civic Federation, where Archibald Stevenson was now assisting Ralph Easley (Luff, *Commonsense Anticommunism*, 149).

69. Federation material, 1942 and 1948, letterhead, 27 December 1950, subscriber

sheet, 1 November 1951, letterhead, ca. 1955, anticommunist literature, 1963, M. A. Kerr to J. Edgar Hoover, 17 July 1964, Hoover to Kerr, 22 July 1964, all in Kerr Papers, Hoover Institution; McCoy, *Policing America's Empire*, 328, 332.

70. Haldeman, interview, California State Archives; Tygiel, *Great Los Angeles Swindle*, 301. H. R. Haldeman continued to attempt to burnish his grandfather's reputation, informing an interviewer in 1991 that he "was a little bit into real estate investing and bought all the wrong things and held them for the wrong lengths of time" (Haldeman, interview, California State Archives).

Chapter 9. Political Repression and Culture War

1. See Case Files on Mexican, Japanese, and Radical Matters, Records of the Federal Bureau of Investigation, US National Archives and Records Administration; American Civil Liberties Union, *Free Speech in 1924*, 21–22.

2. American Civil Liberties Union, *Fight for Civil Liberty: The Story of the Activities of the ACLU, 1928–29*, 3, 12; American Civil Liberties Union, *Story of Civil Liberty*, 10–13.

3. American Civil Liberties Union, *Fight for Civil Liberty 1930–1931*, 4–5.

4. Auerbach, "La Follette Committee," 445; Schrecker, *Many Are the Crimes*, 55; Luff, *Commonsense Anticommunism*, 97, 140.

5. Luff, *Commonsense Anticommunism*, 3, 171, 188; Delton, "Rethinking Post–World War II Anti-Communism," 29.

6. Schrecker, *Many Are the Crimes*, 23–25.

7. American Civil Liberties Union, *Free Speech in 1924*, 38; American Civil Liberties Union, *Fight for Civil Liberty, 1927–28*, 24; American Civil Liberties Union, *Fight for Civil Liberty 1930–1931*, 21.

8. American Civil Liberties Union, *Year's Fight*, 35; American Civil Liberties Union, *Record of the Fight*, 24; American Civil Liberties Union, *Story of Civil Liberty*, 28; American Civil Liberties Union, *Fight for Civil Liberty 1930–1931*, 14; American Civil Liberties Union, *"Sweet Land of Liberty"*; American Civil Liberties Union, *Liberty under the New Deal*, 14.

9. Edward Brennan to BI Chief, 3 August 1920, Case Files on Mexican, Japanese, and Radical Matters, Records of the Federal Bureau of Investigation, US National Archives and Records Administration.

10. Pegram, *One Hundred Percent American*, esp. 69–71.

11. American Civil Liberties Union, *Record of the Fight*, 19; Pegram, *One Hundred Percent American*, 19, 114–15.

12. Nehls, "American Legion," 34; *Centralia Case*, 76.

13. *Centralia Case*, 77–78.

14. Ibid.

15. American Civil Liberties Union, *Free Speech in 1924*, 27–28; American Civil Liberties Union, *Free Speech 1925–1926*, 22; American Civil Liberties Union, *Free Speech, 1926*, 20; American Civil Liberties Union, *Fight for Civil Liberty, 1927–28*, 26–28; American Civil Liberties Union, *Fight for Civil Liberty 1930–1931*, 13.

16. American Civil Liberties Union, *Fight for Civil Liberty, 1927–28*, 27–28.

17. *Summary of Proceedings, Fifteenth Annual Convention of the American Legion*, Chicago, 2–5 October 1933, National Republic Records, Hoover Institution.

18. Mrs. G. Frederick Hawkins, document describing the history of the Westchester Security League, *Westchester Security League, Inc. Annual Reports*, 1934–35, 1935–36, Westchester Security League internal report, ca. 1935, *Early Contacts of Westchester Security League*, all in Westchester Security League Records, Hoover Institution.

19. Mrs. G. Frederick Hawkins, document describing the history of the Westchester Security League, *Westchester Security League, Inc. Annual Reports*, 1934–35, 1935–36, Westchester Security League internal report, ca. 1935, *Early Contacts of Westchester Security League*, all in Westchester Security League Records, Hoover Institution.

20. Higham, *Strangers in the Land*, 232, 254; Creel, *How We Advertised America*, 198–99.

21. Hapgood, Howard, and Hearley, *Professional Patriots*, 186–87; US Patriotic Society, *Makers of History—Preserve the Ideals for Which Our Ancestors Sacrificed Their Lives*, 1929, National Republic Records, Hoover Institution.

22. US Patriotic Society, *Makers of History—Preserve the Ideals for Which Our Ancestors Sacrificed Their Lives*, 1929, National Republic Records, Hoover Institution.

23. Norwood, *Strikebreaking and Intimidation*, 18–20; Anthony Lewis, "A Hero of American Justice," *New York Review of Books*, 11–24 February 2010, 30. Lowell restricted the number of Jewish students attending Harvard and circulated a petition opposing Louis Brandeis's nomination to the US Supreme Court.

24. Norwood, *Strikebreaking and Intimidation*, 20.

25. Ibid., 20–27.

26. McCoy, *Policing America's Empire*, 40, 295; Rogin, *Ronald Reagan*, 59–60.

27. Lemons, *Woman Citizen*, 240–41; Nielsen, *Un-American Womanhood*, 45, 89–90.

28. Nielsen, *Un-American Womanhood*, 3–4, 7, 42–45; Scott Miller, *President and the Assassin*, 193. The term *Founding Fathers* had only recently been coined by then-US senator Warren Harding.

29. Nielsen, *Un-American Womanhood*, 5, 12, 16.

30. Ibid., 6, 33–34, 65–66, 92, 101, 114.

31. Ibid., 29; Lemons, *Woman Citizen*, 210.

32. O'Neill, *Everyone Was Brave*, 25–29.

33. Nielsen, *Un-American Womanhood*, 18, 37, 40–41; Millikan, *Union against Unions*, 155.

34. Nielsen, *Un-American Womanhood*, 51–57, 61, 115; Hapgood, Howard, and Hearley, *Professional Patriots*, 9.

35. Lemons, *Woman Citizen*, 153–72.

36. Nielsen, *Un-American Womanhood*, 105, 107.

37. Pegram, *One Hundred Percent American*, 94; Abbott, "Child Labor Amendment," 229–35; Emery, *Examination*, 9, 14.

38. Aldous, "Political Process," 75, 77–78, 85; Emery, *Examination*, 21; Nielsen, *Un-American Womanhood*, 93.

39. Aldous, "Political Process," 82–83; Emery, *Examination*, 8; Nielsen, *Un-American Womanhood*, 56, 68, 80, 95; Millikan, *Union against Unions*, 246.

40. Aldous, "Political Process," 74–77, 86; Nielsen, *Un-American Womanhood*, 93–103,

134; Lemons, *Woman Citizen*, 220; Abbott, "Child Labor Amendment," 229; Emery, *Examination* 3–4, 7–8, 16, 22, Grinnell, "So-Called 'Child Labor' Amendment"; Figes, *People's Tragedy*, 743; Millikan, *Union against Unions*, 249.

41. "The 116 Organizations Opposed to the 20th Amendment," *Woman Patriot*, 15 January 1925; "Bureaucrats and Bolsheviks," *Woman Patriot*, 15 July 1925.

42. Nielsen, *Un-American Womanhood*, 5, 112, 117–27, 136–38; Lemons, *Woman Citizen*, 225.

43. Lemons, *Woman Citizen*, 240–41; Wilson, *Women's Joint Congressional Committee*, 102–3; Pegram, *Battling Demon Rum*. It is ironic that passage of this amendment would have made impossible the Twenty-Second Amendment, which a still-smarting conservative movement so heartily endorsed to avoid having another four-term Democratic president.

44. Lepore, "Commandments," 74.

45. Auerbach, "La Follette Committee," 440; Katznelson, *Fear Itself*, 16.

46. Katznelson, *Fear Itself*, 241–42.

47. Auerbach, "La Follette Committee," 442, 453. For more on the American Liberty League, see Phillips-Fein, *Invisible Hands*.

48. Auerbach, "La Follette Committee," 443, 446–47.

49. Ibid., 449–55.

50. Katznelson, *Fear Itself*, 267, 271.

51. Ibid., 9, 273–74.

52. Quinn, *Furious Improvisation*, 76–78.

53. Schechner, "Invasions Friendly and Unfriendly," 102; Ladurie, *Carnival in Romans*, 322; Quinn, *Furious Improvisation*, 281.

54. Quinn, *Furious Improvisation*, 79–80.

55. Ibid., 243–48; "WPA Witness Says Soviet Trained Him in Street Fighting," *New York Times*, 7 June 1939.

56. Quinn, *Furious Improvisation*, 241–42, 278–82.

Chapter 10. Anticommunism and Political Terror

1. Peterson and Fite, *Opponents of War*, 267–69; Karp, *Politics of War*, 348.

2. Talbert, *Negative Intelligence*, 80–81; Preston, *Aliens and Dissenters*, 257–59.

3. Kohn, *American Political Prisoners*, 83–157. Two wartime prisoners happened to be named Edgar Hoover and Joseph McCarthy (Preston, *Aliens and Dissenters*, 259).

4. Preston, *Aliens and Dissenters*, 261–72; American Civil Liberties Union, *Year's Fight*, 10, 14; American Civil Liberties Union, *Record of the Fight*, 14; Peterson and Fite, *Opponents of War*, 276.

5. Indicating the laxity of judicial supervision of the immigration bureaucracy, the director of immigration in Portland, Oregon, lamented in 1932 that the courts were "beginning to take exception to the practice, long in use, of using alternative charges in deportation hearings." Worse, his officers were suddenly being required to make a "definite charge, or several charges . . . fit the particular case" (Raphael P. Bonham to Harry E. Hull, 4 October 1932, in *U.S. Military Intelligence Reports*, ed. Boehm, reel 23).

6. American Civil Liberties Union, *Free Speech in 1924*, 11; American Civil Liberties Union, *Free Speech, 1926*, 7; American Civil Liberties Union, *Fight for Civil Liberty, 1927–28*; American Civil Liberties Union, *"Sweet Land of Liberty"*; American Civil Liberties Union, *Liberty under the New Deal*.

7. Peterson and Fite, *Opponents of War*, 272; Kohn, *American Political Prisoners*, 183–92.

8. Theoharis, *FBI and American Democracy*, 28; Frost, *Mooney Case*, 413; American Civil Liberties Union, *Free Speech 1925–1926*; American Civil Liberties Union, *Fight for Civil Liberty 1930–1931*.

9. American Civil Liberties Union, *Free Speech in 1924*, 5, 14, 25–27.

10. Frankfurter, "Case of Sacco and Vanzetti."

11. Ibid.

12. Ibid.; John Davis, *Sacco and Vanzetti*, 3.

13. Frankfurter, "Case of Sacco and Vanzetti," "American Tragedy," both reproduced in John Davis, *Sacco and Vanzetti*, 3, 93.

14. Bruce Bliven, "Boston's Civil War," in *Sacco and Vanzetti*, ed. John Davis, 65–70;

15. John Dos Passos, Letter to the Editor, *Nation*, 9 August 1927, in *Sacco and Vanzetti*, ed. John Davis, 97–99. Lowell was personally attacked for his National Council for the Prevention of War membership by the commander of Fort Bragg, Major General Albert J. Bowley. Lowell's "patriotic" organization of student strikebreakers during the Boston police strike seemingly did not inoculate him against suspicion. See Hapgood, Howard, and Hearley, *Professional Patriots*, 117.

16. John Davis, *Sacco and Vanzetti*, 7–9; "American Tragedy," in *Sacco and Vanzetti*, ed. John Davis, 96; for cartoons, see *Chicago Daily News*, 10 August 1927, *Detroit Saturday Night*, 30 July 1927, both in Felt Collection, Loyola University of Chicago.

17. Howard Zinn, "Upton Sinclair and Sacco and Vanzetti" (introduction to Upton Sinclair's *Boston: A Documentary Novel*), in *Sacco and Vanzetti*, ed. John Davis, 113.

18. *Centralia Case*, 60, 76–77; McCoy, *Policing America's Empire*, 315.

19. *Centralia Case*, 9–10, 13, 18–19, 38–39, 42–44, 55–56, 65, 90.

20. Ibid., 19–20, 29–30, 74, 83–84.

21. Ibid., 20–27, 85–86, 90.

22. Ibid., 30–34, 132–34, 141–42.

23. Ibid., 35, 49; Copeland, *Centralia Tragedy*, 185.

24. *Centralia Case*, 68, 74, 78–79, 121.

25. Frost, *Mooney Case*, 11–25, 30–36.

26. *Story of Mooney and Billings*, 16, 19–21; Frost, *Mooney Case*, 100, 108, 115.

27. *Story of Mooney and Billings*, 12, 22; Frost, *Mooney Case*, 483–86.

28. Frost, *Mooney Case*, 264.

29. *Weekly Letter*, 26 November 1919.

30. Frost, *Mooney Case*, 383; *Story of Mooney and Billings*, 12, 14.

31. *Story of Mooney and Billings*, 8–9; Frost, *Mooney Case*, 408–11.

32. *Story of Mooney and Billings*, 7; Frost, *Mooney Case*, 115–16, 375–76, 417, 422–25, 470.

33. Frost, *Mooney Case*, 383, 469.

34. Pegram, *One Hundred Percent American*, 157–61.

35. Norwood, *Strikebreaking and Intimidation*, 196–201; Schrecker, *Many Are the Crimes*, 52. Norwood estimates that about one hundred members of the Black Legion were also members of the Detroit Police Department, including the commissioner, Heinrich Pickert, a virulent fascist and anti-Semite.

Chapter 11. The Mythology of Anticommunism

1. Hofstadter, *Paranoid Style*; Rogin, *Ronald Reagan*, 44–45.

2. Hofstadter, *Paranoid Style*, 3–6; Rogin, *Ronald Reagan*, 50, 57; David Brion Davis, *Slave Power Conspiracy*, 3, 6. On the paranoid position, see Sagan, *Honey and the Hemlock*. On the nation as an imagined community, see Benedict R. Anderson, *Imagined Communities*.

3. Hofstadter, *Paranoid Style*, 4; Sagan, *Honey and the Hemlock*, 17–19, 147, 301; Hage, *White Nation*, 225.

4. Hage, *White Nation*, 211–17, 241; Hofstadter, *Paranoid Style*, 31.

5. David Brion Davis, *Slave Power Conspiracy*, 6; Rogin, *Ronald Reagan*, 272–80; Pegram, *One Hundred Percent American*, 12.

6. Rogin, *Ronald Reagan*, 47.

7. New York Legislature, Joint Committee, *Revolutionary Radicalism*, vol. 1, pt. 1, 7.

8. Talbert, *Negative Intelligence*, 228; Jeansonne, *Women of the Far Right*, 20. The Los Angeles Chamber of Commerce, a partner of the Better America Federation, asked Dilling to investigate the presence of communism on the campus of the University of California at Los Angeles. The Ford Motor Company also paid Dilling five thousand dollars to determine the strength of communism at the University of Michigan (Jeansonne, *Women of the Far Right*).

9. Talbert, *Negative Intelligence*, 226, 239; Carlson, *Under Cover*, 216; Jeansonne, *Women of the Far Right*, 26.

10. "Moscow's Hand Directs 12 U.S. Organizations—Bare More Links in Chain Forged by Reds," *Chicago Tribune*, 28 March 1924; First Baptist Church, Paso Robles, California, to Walter Steele, ca. June 1936, National Republic Records, Hoover Institution; Talbert, *Negative Intelligence*, 223, 249; Elmer W. Benedict to Better America Federation, 16 March 1920, Kerr Papers, Hoover Institution.

11. Fish, "Menace of Communism," 58; Talbert, *Negative Intelligence*, 69, 72, 215, 218, 242–43, 247; Jeansonne, *Women of the Far Right*, 15; US Federal Bureau of Investigation Miscellaneous Records, Hoover Institution.

12. Walter Steele, "An Analysis of Communism," March 1931, National Republic Records, Hoover Institution; Fish, "Menace of Communism," 54; H. A. Jung, circular, 13 September 1927, Felt Collection, Loyola University of Chicago; Talbert, *Negative Intelligence*, 201–4; Assistant Chief of Staff, Chicago, to MI Director, Washington, D.C., 30 April 1920, in *U.S. Military Intelligence Reports*, ed. Boehm, reel 19.

13. J. Edgar Hoover to C. E. Nolan, 3 November 1920, in *U.S. Military Intelligence Reports*, ed. Boehm, reel 19.

14. Talbert, *Negative Intelligence*, 224–25; MI Director to Office of the Assistant Chief of Staff for Intelligence, 14 October 1920, in *U.S. Military Intelligence Reports*, ed. Boehm, reel 19. A 1927 staff study on radicalism in America inflated the number of radicals to five

million by including the presidential vote for Robert M. La Follette Sr. on the grounds that his program had been "more or less socialistic" (MI Director to Office of the Assistant Chief of Staff for Intelligence, 14 October 1927, in *U.S. Military Intelligence Reports*, ed. Boehm, reel 19).

15. Prosecuting Attorney, County of Wayne, Michigan, to George Van Horn Moseley, 10 August 1932, in *U.S. Military Intelligence Reports*, ed. Boehm, reel 23; Report on Mostavenko, HQ 8th Corps Area Office of Corps Area Commander, filed 15 September 1930, File 10110-2617 9, Colonel F. H. Payne to W. W. Husband, [25?] October 1930, Husband to Payne, 6 November 1930, all in *U.S. Military Intelligence Reports*, ed. Boehm, reel 23. On the Ku Klux Klan's inspiration in the Catholic Church, see Hofstadter, *Paranoid Style*. MI's fantasies about Mostavenko reveal its fundamental incompetence. Even moderately informed observers of Soviet affairs knew that the Comintern exercised no authority over the Soviet secret police. On the contrary, the former had good reason to fear the latter.

16. Coán, *Red Web*, 223; Hapgood, Howard, and Hearley, *Professional Patriots*, 88, 92–93; Hedges, *Death of the Liberal Class*, 75.

17. "Russian Propaganda," Senate Rpt. 526, 14 April 1920, *Congressional Record*, 66th Cong., 2nd sess.; Boston MI report on Martens and Alleged Bolshevik Activities, 13 June 1919, W. L. Moffat to J. Trevor, 22 March 1919, and reports from Chicago, 29 May, 23 June 1919 (both furnished by Jacob Spolansky), all in *U.S. Military Intelligence Reports*, ed. Boehm, reel 14; "Liberalism and Its Work," *Daily Data Sheet*, 22 July 1927; Dilling, *Red Network*, 163. The myth of Soviet gold persists. Harvey Klehr and John Earl Haynes insist that "secret Soviet funding" Communist Party of the United States "was much more extensive than . . . suspected, beginning with very generous subsidies in the party's first decade" ("Revising Revisionism," 458). Yet even the final three-million-dollar donation given by Moscow in 1988 was fairly trivial. It is difficult to imagine how large sums could have been made available for such purposes in the 1920s, when the Bolshevik government was preoccupied with civil war, famine, and collapsing industrial and agricultural productivity.

18. Hofstadter, *Paranoid Style*, 4, 10–11.

19. Ibid.; Lee, "Nesta Webster," 88–92; Lichtman, *White Protestant Nation*, 45. Like Henry Cabot Lodge and Theodore Roosevelt, Webster was profoundly influenced by Gustav Le Bon's theory of race psychology, which led her to postulate that the French "masses" could not conceivably have led the revolution of 1789 without (in this case, perverse) leadership from another race.

20. Lee, "Nesta Webster," 95, cites Bennett, *Party of Fear*, on the widespread adoption of Webster's work in the United States. See also Whitney, *Reds in America*, 5–6.

21. *Daily Data Sheet*, 10, 12 November 1927.

22. *Report of Special Committee*.

23. Fries, *Communism Unmasked*, 61, 63–64, 76–77, 143.

24. "Questions and Answers," *Daily Data Sheet*, 28 October 1927.

25. Talbert, *Negative Intelligence*, 129, 237, 243; *Report of Special Committee*, 8.

26. New York Legislature, Joint Committee, *Revolutionary Radicalism*, vol. 1, pt. 1, 1117.

27. Ibid., 17–18; H. A. Jung, circular, 13 September 1927, Felt Collection, Loyola University of Chicago.

28. Dilling, *Red Network*, 257.

29. Herbert Hoover to Woodrow Wilson, 28 March 1919, Hoover Papers, Hoover Institution.

30. Peterson and Fite, *Opponents of War*, 65; "Liberalism and Its Work," *Daily Data Sheet*, 22 July 1927; Dilling, *Red Network*, 163; Jeansonne, *Women of the Far Right*, 16; Fries, *Communism Unmasked*, 5, 39; *Chicago Tribune*, 23 February, 23 October 1924; *Chicago Daily News*, 8 January 1925.

31. Hofstadter, *Paranoid Style*, 20–21, 24. Anticommunists' sexual anxieties might have been assuaged if they had known that V. I. Lenin "in sexual matters . . . was as conservative as any other nineteenth-century bourgeois," considering free love "completely un-Marxist" (Figes, *People's Tragedy*, 741–42).

32. "The Body of Anarchy," National Republic Records, Hoover Institution.

33. *Report of Special Committee*, 5, 8; MI report from Minneapolis, 9 March 1926, in *U.S. Military Intelligence Reports*, ed. Boehm, reel 23.

34. Hofstadter, *Paranoid Style*, 38.

35. "An Analysis of Communism," March 1931, National Republic Records, Hoover Institution; *Report of Special Committee*, 11; untitled circular, ca. 1930, Westchester Security League Records, Hoover Institution.

36. Hofstadter, *Paranoid Style*, 35.

37. New York Legislature, Joint Committee, *Revolutionary Radicalism*, vol. 1, pt. 1, 9–10; Russian Economic League pamphlet, Egbert Papers, Hoover Institution; W. W. Grimes, report regarding Samuel Beardsley and Robert Fechner, 17 February 1919, Records Relating to German Aliens, Records of the Federal Bureau of Investigation, US National Archives and Records Administration; J. B. Trevor, *Introduction and Historical Review of Conditions and Agencies Tending to Create the Present Tendency toward Radicalism*, in *U.S. Military Intelligence Reports*, ed. Boehm, reel 15.

38. Ostrander, "Revolution in Morals," 130; Hage, *White Nation*, 217.

39. Dilling, *Red Network*, 14, 94; Horn, *From Anarchy to Reason*, 14.

40. *Report of Special Committee*, 4. The committee's claim was strange, since the body also insisted that the United States might have two million active communists and since it had received its commission because fear of revolution had risen with the radicalizing effects of the depression.

41. Fries, *Communism Unmasked*, 93–94; Dilling, *Red Network*, 12–13.

42. "After Lenine—What? The War on Capital," *Saturday Evening Post*, 15 November 1924, 8, 12, 140; *Report of Special Committee*, 9. Fish, who first traveled to the USSR in the early 1920s with a congressional delegation, also professed to be disturbed by the impoverishment of the better classes of Russians, although his discomfort did not prevent him from purchasing "a fine collection of art and jewelry at distress prices" (Powers, *Not without Honor*, 88).

43. All quotations in this section from "The Red Flag (In the Workers' Paradise)," *Saturday Evening Post*, 4 October 1930, 33–64.

Chapter 12. Antidemocracy and Authoritarianism

1. New York Legislature, Joint Committee, *Revolutionary Radicalism*, vol. 1, pt. 1, 14.

2. Creel, *How We Advertised America*, xiii–xiv, 4–5, 17, 85–97, 184, 417–21; Higham, *Strangers in the Land*, 256; John Sharp Williams to Woodrow Wilson, 6 September 1917, Egbert Papers, Hoover Institution.

3. New York Legislature, Joint Committee, *Revolutionary Radicalism*, vol. 2, pt. 1, 657, 969, 1088.

4. Excerpt from *American Individualism*, 9–10, in "Compilation of Public Statements on Various Selected Subjects, 1920–1932," Hoover Papers, Hoover Institution; "Radicalism in Churches," *Daily Data Sheet*, 23 September 1927; "Questions and Answers," *Daily Data Sheet*, 12 November 1927.

5. Littleton and Marvin, *Radicalism in Washington*, 7; Richard A. Charles, Study on Subversives Submitted to Chief of Staff, 6 June 1927, in *U.S. Military Intelligence Reports*, ed. Boehm, reel 23; Hapgood, Howard, and Hearley, *Professional Patriots*, 51–54.

6. Talbert, *Negative Intelligence*, 224, 248; Andrew Moses to Office of Assistant Chief of Staff, ca. 1935, in *U.S. Military Intelligence Reports*, ed. Boehm, reel 22.

7. J. Edgar Hoover to Harry E. Knight, 3 February 1936, in *U.S. Military Intelligence Reports*, ed. Boehm, reel 22.

8. "Compilation of Public Statements on Various Selected Subjects, 1920–1932," Hoover Papers, Hoover Institution. Hoover issued two statements to Congress on the subject of deportation, on 2 December 1930 and 8 December 1931; *Report of Special Committee*, 14. In sanctioning funding increases for the Bureau of Investigation for immigration purposes, the Fish Committee revealed its ignorance of federal departmental jurisdiction. Administration of immigration was (and remained for several more years) the responsibility of the Department of Labor.

9. Schrecker, *No Ivory Tower*, 63–64, 67–69, 71–77, 83; Veenswijk, *Coudert Brothers*.

10. Coán, *Red Web*, 232.

11. Dilling, *Red Network*, 9, 257.

12. Ralph E. Duncan, "Communism—A World-Wide Program of Conquest and Revolution," 31 October 1923, in *U.S. Military Intelligence Reports*, ed. Boehm, reel 23.

13. *Report of Special Committee*, 8; New York Legislature, Joint Committee, *Revolutionary Radicalism*, vol. 1, pt. 1, 341–44.

14. Dilling, *Red Network*, 61–63.

15. Westchester Security League to Henry T. Rainey, 31 March 1934, Westchester Security League Records, Hoover Institution.

16. J. Howard Rhodes to Mrs. Phelps, ca. 1937, in ibid.

17. Dilling, *Red Network*, 92 (from an article, "Capitalism—Hewer and Chiseler"); Fish, "Menace of Communism," 56.

18. Preston, *Aliens and Dissenters*, 21, 251; Hage, *White Nation*, 240–41.

19. "Americanism and the World," 29 October 1919, Hoover Papers, Hoover Institution; Hoff, *Herbert Hoover*, 27.

20. Phillips-Fein, *Invisible Hands*, 20.

Conclusion: Legacies of the Spider Web

1. Lichtman, *White Protestant Nation*, 15–16.

2. Donner, *Age of Surveillance*, 10–11.

3. Ibid., 4, 55, 65–78, 83, 91–92; Rosenfeld, *Subversives*, 22. For decades, Hoover based much of his authority on a vague presidential order that may have been confined to the surveillance of communist and Nazi agents. Throughout Franklin Roosevelt's presidency, according to Rosenfeld, Congress "exercised virtually no oversight of the FBI, even as it [grew] more than tenfold from fewer than 400 agents in 1932 to 4,370 in 1945."

4. Donner, *Protectors of Privilege*, 46.

5. Donner, *Age of Surveillance*, 13–14, 49; Lichtman, *White Protestant Nation*, 273–74; David Cunningham, *There's Something Happening Here*, 6, 77; Duberman, *Paul Robeson*.

6. Donner, *Protectors of Privilege*, 57–59.

7. Donner, *Age of Surveillance*, 290–94; Talbert, *Negative Intelligence*, 253, 271–74, 292. The analysis of the army's postwar intelligence files has been frustrated by their seemingly deliberate misplacement within the Military History Center. Talbert reports that the army claims that the files were sent to and lost by the National Archives.

8. Rosenfeld, *Subversives*, 30–35, 88–89. Beginning in 1951, Hoover ran a clandestine "Responsibilities Program" that spread derogatory information on almost one thousand citizens employed in state agencies, perhaps half of whom were fired, quit, or otherwise left their employment (Rosenfeld, *Subversives*, 31–35).

9. Robin, *Fear*, 189; Lizza, "State of Deception." Intelligence remains a lucrative field for operatives seeking to enrich themselves. According to Lizza, the officials running a Department of Defense program, Total Information Awareness, that began in 2002 contemplated creating "a futures market in which anonymous users could place bets on events such as assassinations and terrorist attacks, and get paid on the basis of whether the events occurred." The supervisor of the program, Admiral John Poindexter, resigned soon after the futures-market idea was exposed. Poindexter had previously been convicted on several counts of lying to Congress and obstructing its investigation of the Iran-Contra Affair, although the convictions were appealed and reversed on technical grounds.

10. Rosenfeld, *Subversives*, 27, 64.

11. McCoy, *Policing America's Empire*, 20; Donner, *Protectors of Privilege*, 3–4. J. Edgar Hoover's obsession with "communist" ideology perverted the work of the FBI down to its remuneration structure. Hoover handed out "cash bonuses" to agents who successfully conducted illegal surveillance of CP premises. Although by 1964 the FBI had opened more than 440,000 "subversion" files and civil rights investigations into the lawful activity of American citizens (according to the 1976 report of the US Senate Select Committee to Study Governmental Operations with Respect to Intelligence Activities), the agency was still generally responding to rather than anticipating much of the decade's political activity. See Rosenfeld, *Subversives*, 14, 177.

12. Saunders, *Cultural Cold War*; Wilford, *Mighty Wurlitzer*, 3–4, 10.

13. Donner, *Protectors of Privilege*, 62; Talbert, *Negative Intelligence*, 252–53; Lichtman, *White Protestant Nation*, 175, 178, 201.

14. Richardson and Truman, "Federal Employee Loyalty Program," 549; Schrecker, *Many Are the Crimes*, 43–47; Delton, "Rethinking Post–World War II Anticommunism," 25.

15. Delton, "Rethinking Post–World War II Anticommunism," 24–25; Robin, *Fear*, 204–5, 211–12.

16. Donner, *Protectors of Privilege*, 425.

17. Rosenfeld, *Subversives*, 122–40, 297–98, 303–4, 333–34. According to Rosenfeld, in 1951, Gale Sondergaard, who had won the inaugural Academy Award for Best Supporting Actress, was forced out of Hollywood after she refused to testify before HUAC and was blacklisted. She did not know that Reagan, her union leader, had informed the FBI that he suspected her dubious associations and beliefs, leading directly to her subpoena by the committee.

18. Phillips-Fein, *Invisible Hands*, 23.

19. Lichtman, *White Protestant Nation*, 89, 92; Phillips-Fein, *Invisible Hands*, 23, 88, 269.

20. Phillips-Fein, *Invisible Hands*, ix–x, 10–22, 59, 100, 193, 206; Rosenfeld, *Subversives*, 293.

21. Phillips-Fein, *Invisible Hands*, 66, 166.

22. Lichtman, *White Protestant Nation*, 28, 59, 123–24, 150,158, 167, 321, 402; Phillips-Fein, *Invisible Hands*, 120, 130; Donner, *Protectors of Privilege*, 419.

23. Talbert, *Negative Intelligence*, 225; Carlson, *Under Cover*, 120–22, 166, 195–96, 206–7, 211–13, 228–31, 414–15; Lichtman, *White Protestant Nation*, 72, 225, 275; Donner, *Protectors of Privilege*, 423. Steele was an important contact for the FBI. A legally admissible brief of evidence the bureau prepared from 1945 to 1947 to outlaw the CP was informed by material furnished by Steele and a handful of other trusted civilians (Schrecker, *Many Are the Crimes*, 42). In December 1954, Spolansky informed historian Theodore Draper that Jung's archives were probably the largest of their kind and estimated their value at $250,000 (Spolansky, interview by Draper, 20 December 1954, Draper Research Files, Emory University). Spolansky also informed Draper that Jung had died a few weeks earlier.

24. Phillips-Fein, *Invisible Hands*, 59; Lichtman, *White Protestant Nation*, 236, 238; Bennett, *Party of Fear*, 245, 317, 423; Wilentz, "Confounding Fathers."

25. Bon Tempo, *Americans at the Gate*, esp. 13–20, 44, 55, 67–70, 85–87, 104–7, 133, 148, 188–89, 201–2; Lichtman, *White Protestant Nation*, 267.

26. Millikan, *Union against Unions*, 349–62; Lichtman, *White Protestant Nation*, 176; Phillips-Fein, *Invisible Hands*, 105.

27. Feurer, *Radical Unionism*, 15, 31–33, 74–86, 121–22, 226–29; Luff, *Commonsense Anticommunism*, 30, 188–90, 192–94, 217–18; Donner, *Protectors of Privilege*, 58–59.

28. Luff, *Commonsense Anticommunism*, 220–21.

29. On the evolution of America's postwar political economy and its effects on the labor movement, see Perry Anderson, "Homeland."

30. Robin, *Fear*, 243–46; Millikan, *Union against Unions*, 362–64.

31. Robin, *Fear*, 20–21.

32. Lichtman, *White Protestant Nation*, 235, 292, 353, 446.

33. Taibbi, *Griftopia*, 224.

34. Lichtman, *White Protestant Nation*, 133, 203, 294.

35. Donner, *Age of Surveillance*, 423; Lichtman, *White Protestant Nation*, 222; Bellant, *Old Nazis*, 33.

36. Lichtman, *White Protestant Nation*, 331; Cockburn, *Rumsfeld*, 40–41.

37. Cockburn, *Rumsfeld*, 101, 105; Lichtman, *White Protestant Nation*, 441. For an excoriating account of how corporations received sizable fortunes to run the second Bush administration's occupation of Iraq and defrauded the US Treasury while doing it, see Marx, "I Was a Propaganda Intern."

38. Robin, *Fear*, 14, 19; Luff, *Commonsense Anticommunism*; Delton, "Rethinking Post–World War II Anticommunism"; Powers, *Not without Honor*; Schrecker, *Many Are the Crimes*.

39. Delton, "Rethinking Post–World War II Anticommunism," 35–36.

40. Ibid., 15–18.

41. Robin, *Fear*, 4, 13, 87, 97.

42. Delton, "Rethinking Post–World War II Anticommunism," 2, 4. Both Powers, *Not without Honor*, and Luff, *Commonsense Anticommunism*, refer to "common-sense" liberal anticommunism, and Powers also favors the term *respectable*.

43. Robert Griffith, "American Politics and the Origins of McCarthyism," quoted in Delton, "Rethinking Post–World War II Anticommunism," 8.

44. Delton, "Rethinking Post–World War II Anticommunism," 12, 30, 33, 36.

45. Ibid., 21.

46. Ibid., 2, 41; Robin, *Fear*, 201–4, 212.

47. "Fight Radicals in WPA: American Writers Association Forms to Curb Communism," *New York Times*, 21 March 1936; Delton, "Rethinking Post–World War II Anticommunism," 37.

Afterword

1. President Richard Nixon formally declared a "war on drugs" and revived the long-standing policy of criminalizing the use and distribution of specified illicit substances in a special message to Congress on 17 June 1971, as America's inability to win the Vietnam War became increasingly clear. See Dufton, "War on Drugs."

2. Saunders, *Cultural Cold War*, 5.

3. Robin, *Fear*, 200, 216.

4. Ibid., 216–17.

5. Taibbi, *Griftopia*, 132–47; Yates, *Wisconsin Uprising*; Perlin, *Intern Nation*.

6. Taibbi, *Griftopia*, 10–12, 17–18; Hertzberg, "Lies"; Gawande, "States of Health."

7. Hedges, *Death of the Liberal Class*, 7–8, 15.

8. Rogin, *Ronald Reagan*, 59.

Bibliography

Archival and Manuscript Collections

CALIFORNIA STATE ARCHIVES, SACRAMENTO

H. R. Haldeman Interview, conducted by Dale E. Trevelen, 18, 25 June 1991

EMORY UNIVERSITY, ATLANTA

Theodore Draper Research Files

HOOVER INSTITUTION, STANFORD UNIVERSITY, STANFORD, CALIF.

Edward H. Egbert Papers
Sidney Hook Papers
Herbert Hoover Papers
Margaret Anne Kerr Papers
Myers G. Lowman Papers
National Republic Records
Overview of the United States, Consulate (Petrograd, Russia), Dispatches
US Federal Bureau of Investigation Miscellaneous Records
Westchester Security League Records

LOYOLA UNIVERSITY OF CHICAGO, CHICAGO

Dorr E. Felt Collection

NEWBERRY LIBRARY, CHICAGO

William Vorhees Judson Papers
Graham Taylor Papers

US NATIONAL ARCHIVES AND RECORDS ADMINISTRATION, WASHINGTON, D.C.

Records of the Federal Bureau of Investigation (RG 65)
Case Files on Mexican, Japanese, and Radical Matters, 1919–20 (RG 65.2.2)
Investigative Case Files of the Bureau of Investigation, 1908–22 (M-1085)
Records of the American Protective League, 1917–19 (RG 65.5)
Records Relating to German Aliens (Old German Files), 1915–20 (RG 65.2.2)

Published Works

Abbott, Grace. "The Child Labor Amendment." *North American Review*, December 1924, 223–37.
Adamic, Louis. "Aliens and Alien-Baiters." *Harper's*, November 1936, 561–74.
Aldous, Joan. "The Political Process and the Failure of the Child Labor Amendment." *Journal of Family Issues* 18, no. 1 (January 1997): 71–91.
American Civil Liberties Union. *The Fight for Civil Liberty, 1927–28: The Story of the Year 1927*. New York: American Civil Liberties Union, 1928.
———. *The Fight for Civil Liberty, 1930–1931*. New York: American Civil Liberties Union, 1931.
———. *The Fight for Civil Liberty: The Story of the Activities of the ACLU, 1928–29*. New York: American Civil Liberties Union, 1929.
———. *The Fight for Free Speech—A Brief Statement of Present Conditions in the U.S., and of the ACLU against the Forces of Suppression*. New York: American Civil Liberties Union, 1921.
———. *Free Speech in 1924: The Work of the American Civil Liberties Union, January to December 1924*. New York: American Civil Liberties Union, 1925.
———. *Free Speech 1925–1926*. New York: American Civil Liberties Union, 1926.
———. *Free Speech, 1926: The Work of the American Civil Liberties Union*. New York: American Civil Liberties Union, 1927.
———. *Liberty under the New Deal—The Record for 1933–34*. New York: American Civil Liberties Union, 1934.
———. *The Record of the Fight for Free Speech in 1923: The Work of the American Civil Liberties Union, January to December 1923*. New York: American Civil Liberties Union, 1924.
———. *The Story of Civil Liberty—1929–1930*. New York: American Civil Liberties Union, 1930.
———. *"Sweet Land of Liberty" 1931–1932*. New York: American Civil Liberties Union, 1932.
———. *A Year's Fight for Free Speech: The Work of the American Civil Liberties Union from Sept. 1921, to Jan. 1923*. New York: American Civil Liberties Union, 1923.
"An American Tragedy." *The Nation*, 13 August 1927.
Anderson, Benedict R. *Imagined Communities: Reflections on the Origin and Spread of Nationalism*. London: Verso, 1983.
Anderson, Mary, and Mary N. Winslow. *Woman at Work: The Autobiography of Mary Anderson, as Told to Mary N. Winslow*. Westport, Conn.: Greenwood, 1973.
Anderson, Perry. "Homeland." *New Left Review*, May–June 2013, 5–32.
Archer, Robin. *Why Is There No Labor Party in the United States?* Princeton: Princeton University Press, 2007.

Auerbach, Jerold S. *American Labor: The Twentieth Century*. Indianapolis: Bobbs-Merrill, 1969.

———. *Labor and Liberty: The La Follette Committee and the New Deal*. Indianapolis: Bobbs-Merrill, 1966.

———. "The La Follette Committee: Labor and Civil Liberties in the New Deal." *The Journal of American History* 51, no. 3 (December 1964): 435–59.

Bailyn, Bernard, ed. *The Great Republic: A History of the American People*. Lexington, Mass.: Heath, 1985.

Beatty, Jack. *Age of Betrayal: The Triumph of Money in America, 1865–1900*. New York: Knopf, 2007.

Bell, Daniel. *The Radical Right: The New American Right*. Garden City, N.Y.: Doubleday, 1963.

Bellant, Russ. *Old Nazis, the New Right, and the Republican Party*. Boston: South End, 1991.

Bendersky, Joseph W. *The "Jewish Threat": Anti-Semitic Politics of the U.S. Army*. New York: Basic Books, 2000.

Bennett, David H. *The Party of Fear: From Nativist Movements to the New Right in American History*. New York: Vintage, 2005.

Benowitz, June Melby. *Days of Discontent: American Women and Right-Wing Politics, 1933–1945*. DeKalb: Northern Illinois University Press, 2002.

Berger, Raoul. *Memoir*. Interview by Jerold S. Auerbach. New York Times Oral History Program. Sanford, N.C.: Microfilming Corp. of America, 1982.

Bimba, Anthony. *The Molly Maguires*. New York: International, 1932.

Biographical Directory of the U.S. Congress, 1774–1961. Washington, D.C.: US Government Printing Office, 1961.

Boehm, Randolph, ed. *U.S. Military Intelligence Reports, Surveillance of Radicals in the United States, 1917–1941*. Frederick, Md.: University Publications of America, 1984.

Bon Tempo, Carl J. *Americans at the Gate: The United States and Refugees during the Cold War*. Princeton: Princeton University Press, 2008.

Bradley, James. *The Imperial Cruise: A Secret History of Empire and War*. New York: Little, Brown, 2009.

Brands, H. W. *American Colossus: The Triumph of Capitalism, 1865–1900*. New York: Doubleday, 2010.

Breshkovsky, Catherine. *A Message to the American People*. Intro. George Kennan. New York: Russian Information Bureau in the United States, 1919.

Brophy, Leo P. "Origins of the Chemical Corps." *Military Affairs* 20, no. 4 (Winter 1956): 217–26.

Buckingham, Peter H. *America Sees Red: Anticommunism in America, 1870s to 1980s: A Guide to Issues and References*. Claremont, Calif.: Regina, 1988.

Burgmann, Verity. *Revolutionary Industrial Unionism: The Industrial Workers of the World in Australia*. Cambridge: Cambridge University Press, 1995.

Burton, David Henry. *The Learned Presidency: Theodore Roosevelt, William Howard Taft, Woodrow Wilson*. Rutherford, N.J.: Fairleigh Dickinson University Press, 1988.

Cain, Frank. *The Origins of Political Surveillance in Australia*. London: Angus and Robertson, 1983.

Cannistraro, Philip V., Gerald Meyer, and Paul Avrich. *The Lost World of Italian American Radicalism: Politics, Labor, and Culture*. Westport, Conn.: Praeger, 2003.

Carlson, John Roy. *Under Cover: My Four Years in the Nazi Underworld of America—The Amazing Revelation of How Axis Agents and Our Enemies within Are Now Plotting to Destroy the United States*. New York: Dutton, 1943.

Carter, Saalim A. "Labor Unions and Antitrust Legislation: Judicial Activism vs. Judicial Restraint from 1890–1941." *Penn State McNair Journal* 13 (Summer 2006): 1–92.

Catton, Bruce. *Mr. Lincoln's Army*. Garden City, N.Y.: Doubleday, 1951.

The Centralia Case: Three Views of the Armistice Day Tragedy at Centralia, Washington, November 11, 1919: The Centralia Conspiracy. New York: Da Capo, 1971.

Coán, Blair. *The Red Web: An Underground Political History of the United States from 1918 to the Present Time, Showing How Close the Government Is to Collapse, and Told in an Understandable Way*. Chicago: Northwest, 1925.

Coben, Stanley. *A. Mitchell Palmer: Politician*. New York: Columbia University Press, 1963.

Cockburn, Andrew. *Rumsfeld: His Rise, Fall, and Catastrophic Legacy*. New York: Scribner, 2007.

Coleman, James William. "Law and Power: The Sherman Antitrust Act and Its Enforcement in the Petroleum Industry." *Social Problems* 32, no. 3 (February 1985): 264–74.

Conquest, Robert. *The Great Terror: A Reassessment*. London: Pimlico, 1990.

Copeland, Tom. *The Centralia Tragedy of 1919: Elmer Smith and the Wobblies*. Seattle: University of Washington Press, 1993.

Creel, George. *How We Advertised America: The First Telling of the Amazing Story of the Committee on Public Information That Carried the Gospel of Americanism to Every Corner of the Globe*. New York: Harper, 1920.

Cunningham, David. *There's Something Happening Here: The New Left, the Klan, and FBI Counterintelligence*. Berkeley: University of California Press, 2004.

Cunningham, William. *The Green Corn Rebellion: A Novel*. Norman: University of Oklahoma Press, 2010.

Cushman, Barry. *Rethinking the New Deal Court: The Structure of a Constitutional Revolution*. New York: Oxford University Press, 1998.

Cyphers, Christopher J. *The National Civic Federation and the Making of a New Liberalism, 1900–1915*. Westport, Conn.: Praeger, 2002.

Dallek, Robert. "A Global Setting for the Modern Republic, 1941–1952." In *Great Republic*, ed. Bailyn.

———. "Modernizing the Republic, 1920 to the Present." In *Great Republic*, ed. Bailyn.

Daniels, Roger. *Asian America: Chinese and Japanese in the United States since 1850*. Seattle: University of Washington Press, 1988.

David, Henry. *The History of the Haymarket Affair: A Study in the American Social-Revolutionary and Labor Movements*. New York: Russell and Russell, 1958.

Davis, David Brion. *The Slave Power Conspiracy and the Paranoid Style*. Baton Rouge: Louisiana State University Press, 1970.

Davis, John, ed. *Sacco and Vanzetti: Italian Immigrants and Anarchists, Framed by the State and Executed for Murder in Boston during the Red Scare of the 1920s*. Melbourne: Ocean, 2004.

Davis, Mike. *City of Quartz: Excavating the Future in Los Angeles*. New York: Vintage, 1992.

Delton, Jennifer A. "Rethinking Post–World War II Anticommunism." *Journal of the Historical Society* 10, no. 1 (March 2010): 1–41.

Dilling, Elizabeth Kirkpatrick. *The Red Network: A "Who's Who" and Handbook of Radicalism for Patriots*. Chicago: the author, 1934.

Donald, David Herbert. "National Problems, 1865–1877." In *Great Republic*, ed. Bailyn.

Donner, Frank J. *The Age of Surveillance: The Aims and Methods of America's Political Intelligence System*. New York: Knopf, 1980.

——. *Protectors of Privilege: Red Squads and Police Repression in Urban America*. Berkeley: University of California Press, 1990.

Dowell, Eldridge Foster. *A History of Criminal Syndicalism Legislation in the United States*. New York: Da Capo, 1969.

Draper, Theodore. *The Roots of American Communism*. New York: Viking, 1957.

Duberman, Martin B. *Paul Robeson*. New York: Knopf, 1988.

Dufton, Emily. "The War on Drugs: How President Nixon Tied Addiction to Crime." *Atlantic*, 26 March 2012. http://www.theatlantic.com/health/archive/2012/03/the-war-on-drugs-how-president-nixon-tied-addiction-to-crime/254319/.

Ellis, Joseph J. *Founding Brothers: The Revolutionary Generation*. New York: Knopf, 2000.

Emery, James A. *An Examination of the Proposed Twentieth Amendment to the Constitution of the United States*. New York: National Association of Manufacturers of the United States of America, 1924.

Feurer, Rosemary. *Radical Unionism in the Midwest, 1900–1950*. Urbana: University of Illinois Press, 2006.

Figes, Orlando. *A People's Tragedy: The Russian Revolution, 1891–1924*. New York: Penguin, 1998.

Fischer, Nick. "The American Protective League and the Australian Protective League: Two Responses to the Threat of Communism, c. 1917–1920." *American Communist History* 10, no. 2 (August 2011): 133–49.

——. "The Australian Right, the American Right, and the Threat of the Left, 1917–1935." *Labour History* 89 (November 2005): 17–36.

——. "The Founders of American Anti-Communism." *American Communist History* 5, no. 1 (June 2006): 67–101.

Fish, Hamilton, Jr. "The Menace of Communism." *Annals of the American Academy of Political and Social Science* 156 (July 1931): 54–61.

Foner, Philip S. *History of the Labor Movement in the United States*. Vol. 10, *The T.U.E.L., 1925–1929*. New York: International, 1994.

Fones-Wolf, Elizabeth A. *Selling Free Enterprise: The Business Assault on Labor and Liberalism, 1945–60*. Urbana: University of Illinois Press, 1994.

Frankfurter, Felix. "The Case of Sacco and Vanzetti." *Atlantic Magazine*, March 1927. http://www.theatlantic.com/magazine/archive/1927/03/the-case-of-sacco-and-vanzetti/306625/.

Freund, Paul Abraham. *Memoir*. Interview by Jerold S. Auerbach. New York Times Oral History Program. Sanford, N.C.: Microfilming Corp. of America, 1982.

Fries, Amos Alfred. *Communism Unmasked*. Washington, D.C.: Georgetown, 1937.

Frost, Richard H. *The Mooney Case*. Stanford, Calif.: Stanford University Press, 1968.

Gage, Beverly. *The Day Wall Street Exploded: A Story of America in Its First Age of Terror*. New York: Oxford University Press, 2009.

Gawande, Atul. "States of Health." *New Yorker*, 7 October 2013. http://www.newyorker .com/magazine/2013/10/07/states-of-health.

Goldstein, Robert Justin. *Political Repression in Modern America from 1870 to the Present*. New York: Schenkman, 1978.

Goldstone, Lawrence. *Dark Bargain: Slavery, Profits, and the Struggle for the Constitution*. New York: Walker, 2005.

Goodwin, Doris Kearns. *Team of Rivals: The Political Genius of Abraham Lincoln*. New York: Simon and Schuster, 2005.

Gorky, Maksim. *Untimely Thoughts; Essays on Revolution, Culture, and the Bolsheviks, 1917–1918*. New York: Eriksson, 1968.

Gould, Lewis L. *Grand Old Party: A History of the Republicans*. New York: Random House, 2003.

Grant, Madison, Charles W. Gould, Lucien Howe, Roswell H. Johnson, Francis H. Kinnicut, John B. Trevor, and Robert DeC. Ward. "Third Report of the Sub-Committee on Selective Immigration of the Eugenics Committee of the United States of America: The Examination of Immigrants Overseas, as an Additional Safeguard in the Processes of Enforcing American Immigration Policy." *Journal of Heredity* 16, no. 8 (August 1925): 293–98.

Green, Marguerite. *The National Civic Federation and the American Labor Movement, 1900–1925*. Washington, D.C.: Catholic University of America Press, 1956.

Grinnell, Frank W. "The So-Called 'Child Labor' Amendment." *Virginia Law Review* 11, no. 2 (December 1924): 121–22.

Gutman, Herbert G. "The Tompkins Square 'Riot' in New York City on January 13, 1874: A Re-Examination of Its Causes and Its Aftermath." *Labor History* 6, no. 1 (1965): 44–70.

Hage, Ghassan. *White Nation: Fantasies of White Supremacy in a Multicultural Society*. Annandale, N.S.W.: Pluto, 1998.

Hannaford, Ivan. *Race: The History of an Idea in the West*. Baltimore: Johns Hopkins University Press, 1996.

Hanson, Ole. *Americanism versus Bolshevism*. Garden City, N.Y.: Doubleday, Page, 1920.

Hapgood, Norman, Sidney Coe Howard, and John Hearley. *Professional Patriots*. New York: Boni, 1927.

Harris, Howell John. *Bloodless Victories: The Rise and Fall of the Open Shop in the Philadelphia Metal Trades, 1890–1940*. New York: Cambridge University Press, 2000.

Haynes, John Earl, and Harvey Klehr. *In Denial: Historians, Communism, and Espionage*. San Francisco: Encounter, 2003.

Heale, M. J. *American Anticommunism: Combating the Enemy Within, 1830–1970*. Baltimore: Johns Hopkins University Press, 1990.

Hedges, Chris. *Death of the Liberal Class*. New York: Nation, 2010.

Hertzberg, Hendrik. "Lies." *New Yorker*, 21 September 2009. http://www.newyorker.com/magazine/2009/09/21/lies-2.

Higham, John. *Strangers in the Land: Patterns of American Nativism, 1860–1925*. New York: Atheneum, 1963.

Hillier, Alfred J. "Albert Johnson, Congressman." *Pacific Northwest Quarterly* 36, no. 3 (July 1945): 193–211.

Hoff, Joan. *Herbert Hoover, Forgotten Progressive*. Boston: Little, Brown, 1975.

———, ed. *The Twenties—The Critical Issues*. Boston: Little, Brown, 1972.

Hofstadter, Richard. *The Paranoid Style in American Politics, and Other Essays*. New York: Knopf, 1965.

Horn, James B. *From Anarchy to Reason, Not in Defense of Capital but Sound Reason*. Philadelphia: Horn, 1923.

Horowitz, David, ed. *Containment and Revolution: Western Policy towards Social Revolution, 1917 to Vietnam*. London: Blond, 1967.

Jeansonne, Glen. *Women of the Far Right: The Mothers' Movement and World War II*. Chicago: University of Chicago Press, 1996.

Jensen, Joan M. "All Pink Sisters: The War Department and the Feminist Movement in the 1920s." In *Decades of Discontent*, ed. Scharf and Jensen.

———. *The Price of Vigilance*. Chicago: Rand McNally, 1969.

Karp, Walter. *The Politics of War: The Story of Two Wars Which Altered Forever the Political Life of the American Republic. 1890–1920*. New York: Franklin Square, 2003.

Katznelson, Ira. *Fear Itself: The New Deal and the Origins of Our Time*. New York: Liveright, 2013.

Keith, Jeanette. *Rich Man's War, Poor Man's Fight: Race, Class, and Power in the Rural South during the First World War*. Chapel Hill: University of North Carolina Press, 2004.

Kelley, Robin D. G. *Thelonious Monk: The Life and Times of an American Original*. New York: Free Press, 2009.

Kennan, George F. *Soviet-American Relations, 1917–1920*. Princeton: Princeton University Press, 1956.

Kennedy, David M. *Over Here: The First World War and American Society*. New York: Oxford University Press, 1980.

Kennedy, Ross A. "Woodrow Wilson, World War I, and an American Conception of National Security." *Diplomatic History* 25, no. 1 (January 2001): 1–31.

Kenny, Kevin. *Making Sense of the Molly Maguires*. New York: Oxford University Press, 1988.

Klehr, Harvey, and John Earl Haynes. "Revising Revisionism: A New Look at American Communism." *Academic Questions* 22, no. 4 (December 2009): 452–62.

Klug, Thomas A. "Labor Market Politics in Detroit: The Curious Case of the 'Spolansky Act' of 1931." *Michigan Historical Review* 14, no. 1 (Spring 1988): 1–32.

Kohn, Stephen M. *American Political Prisoners: Prosecutions under the Espionage and Sedition Acts*. Westport, Conn.: Praeger, 1994.

Kovel, Joel. *Red Hunting in the Promised Land: Anticommunism and the Making of America*. New York: Basic Books, 1994.

Ladurie, Emmanuel Le Roy. *Carnival in Romans*. New York: Braziller, 1979.

Layton, Edwin. "The Better America Federation: A Case Study of Superpatriotism." *Pacific Historical Review* 30, no. 2 (May 1961): 137–47.

Lee, Martha F. "Nesta Webster: The Voice of Conspiracy." *Journal of Women's History* 17, no. 3 (Fall 2005): 81–104.

Lemons, J. Stanley. *The Woman Citizen: Social Feminism in the 1920's*. Urbana: University of Illinois Press, 1973.

Lens, Sidney. *The Labor Wars: From the Molly Maguires to the Sitdowns*. Garden City, N.Y.: Doubleday, 1973.

Lepore, Jill. "The Commandments: The Constitution and Its Worshippers." *New Yorker*, 17 January 2011, 70–76.

Lichtenstein, Nelson, and Elizabeth Tandy Shermer. *The Right and Labor in America: Politics, Ideology, and Imagination*. Philadelphia: University of Pennsylvania Press, 2012.

Lichtman, Allan J. *White Protestant Nation: The Rise of the American Conservative Movement*. New York: Atlantic Monthly Press, 2008.

Littleton, Martin Wilie, and Fred Richard Marvin. *Radicalism in Washington: A Notable Address of National Importance Delivered at the First Annual Conference Dinner of Patriotic Societies, under the Auspices of the Key Men of America at the Hotel Roosevelt, New York, April 18, 1927*. New York: Key Men of America, 1927.

Lizza, Ryan. "State of Deception." *New Yorker*, 16 December 2013. http://www.newyorker .com/magazine/2013/12/16/state-of-deception.

Luff, Jennifer. *Commonsense Anticommunism: Labor and Civil Liberties between the World Wars*. Chapel Hill: University of North Carolina Press, 2012.

Lusk, Clayton R. "Radicalism under Inquiry: Conclusions Reached after a Year's Study of Alien Anarchy in America." *Review of Reviews*, February 1920, 167–71.

Marx, Willem. "I Was a Propaganda Intern in Iraq." *Harper's Magazine*, September 2006, 51–59.

Maxwell, Lucia. *The Red Juggernaut*. Washington, D.C.: Library Press, 1932.

McCormick, Charles. *Seeing Reds: Federal Surveillance of Radicals in the Pittsburgh Mill District, 1917–1921*. Pittsburgh: University of Pittsburgh Press, 1997.

McCoy, Alfred W. *Policing America's Empire: The United States, the Philippines, and the Rise of the Surveillance State*. Madison: University of Wisconsin Press, 2009.

Mertes, Tom. "American Duopoly." *New Left Review* 49 (January–February 2008): 123–35.

Messer-Kruse, Timothy. *The Haymarket Conspiracy*. Urbana: University of Illinois Press, 2012.

Miller, Nathan. *Star-Spangled Men: America's Ten Worst Presidents*. New York: Scribner, 1998.

Miller, Scott. *The President and the Assassin: McKinley, Terror, and Empire at the Dawn of the American Century*. New York: Random House, 2011.

Millikan, William. *A Union against Unions: The Minneapolis Citizens Alliance and Its Fight against Organized Labor, 1903–1947*. St. Paul: Minnesota Historical Society Press, 2001.

Mitchell, David J. *1919: Red Mirage*. London: Cape, 1970.

Mitrani, Sam. *The Rise of the Chicago Police Department: Class and Conflict, 1850–1894*. Urbana: University of Illinois Press, 2013.

Morgan, Ted. *Reds: McCarthyism in Twentieth-Century America*. New York: Random House, 2003.

Morn, Frank. *"The Eye That Never Sleeps": A History of the Pinkerton National Detective Agency*. Bloomington: Indiana University Press, 1982.

Morse, Arthur D. *While Six Million Died: A Chronicle of American Apathy*. Woodstock, N.Y.: Overlook, 1983.

Mowry, George Edwin. *Theodore Roosevelt and the Progressive Movement*. Madison: University of Wisconsin Press, 1946.

Moynihan, Brian. *Comrades: 1917—Russia in Revolution*. London: Hutchison, 1992.

Murphy, Paul L. "Sources and Nature of Intolerance in the 1920s." *Journal of American History* 51, no. 1 (June 1964): 60–76.

Murray, Robert K. *Red Scare: A Study in National Hysteria, 1919–1920*. Minneapolis: University of Minnesota Press, 1955.

Nehls, Christopher. "The American Legion and Striking Workers during the Interwar Period." In *Right and Labor*, ed. Lichtenstein and Shermer.

New York Legislature. Joint Committee Investigating Seditious Activities. *Revolutionary Radicalism: Its History, Purpose, and Tactics, with an Exposition and Discussion of the Steps Being Taken and Required to Curb It*. Vol. 1, pts. 1–2. 1920; New York: Da Capo, 1971.

Ngai, Mae M. *Impossible Subjects: Illegal Aliens and the Making of Modern America*. Princeton: Princeton University Press, 2004.

Nielsen, Kim E. *Un-American Womanhood: Antiradicalism, Antifeminism, and the First Red Scare*. Columbus: Ohio State University Press, 2001.

Nirenberg, David. *Anti-Judaism: The Western Tradition*. New York: Norton, 2013.

Norwood, Stephen H. *Strikebreaking and Intimidation: Mercenaries and Masculinity in Twentieth-Century America*. Chapel Hill: University of North Carolina Press, 2002.

O'Neill, William L. *Everyone Was Brave: A History of Feminism in America*. Chicago: Quadrangle, 1971.

O'Toole, Patricia. *When Trumpets Call: Theodore Roosevelt after the White House*. New York: Simon and Schuster, 2005.

Ostrander, Gilman M. "The Revolution in Morals." In *Twenties*, ed. Hoff.

Pacyga, Dominic A. *Chicago: A Biography*. Chicago: University of Chicago Press, 2009.

Pegram, Thomas R. *Battling Demon Rum: The Struggle for a Dry America, 1800–1933*. Chicago: Dee, 1998.

———. *One Hundred Percent American: The Rebirth and Decline of the Ku Klux Klan in the 1920s*. Chicago: Dee, 2011.

Perlin, Ross. *Intern Nation: How to Earn Nothing and Learn Little in the Brave New Economy*. Brooklyn: Verso, 2011.

Peterson, H. C. *Propaganda for War: The Campaign against American Neutrality, 1914–1917*. Port Washington, N.Y.: Kennikat, 1968.

Peterson, H. C., and Gilbert Courtland Fite. *Opponents of War, 1917–1918*. Madison: University of Wisconsin Press, 1957.

Pfannestiel, Todd J. *Rethinking the Red Scare: The Lusk Committee and New York's Crusade against Radicalism, 1919–1923*. New York: Routledge, 2003.

Phillips-Fein, Kim. *Invisible Hands: The Making of the Conservative Movement from the New Deal to Reagan.* New York: Norton, 2009.

Pipes, Richard. *Russia under the Bolshevik Regime.* New York: Knopf, 1993.

Polenberg, Richard. *Fighting Faiths: The Abrams Case, the Supreme Court, and Free Speech.* New York: Viking, 1987.

Post, Louis F. *The Deportations Delirium of Nineteen-Twenty: A Personal Narrative of an Historic Official Experience.* New York,: Da Capo, 1970.

Powers, Richard Gid. *Not without Honor: The History of American Anticommunism.* New York: Free Press, 1995.

———. *Secrecy and Power: The Life of J. Edgar Hoover.* New York: Free Press, 1987.

Preston, William, Jr. *Aliens and Dissenters: Federal Suppression of Radicals, 1903–1933.* New York: Harper and Row, 1966.

Pula, James S. "American Immigration Policy and the Dillingham Commission." *Polish American Studies* 37, no. 1 (Spring 1980): 5–31.

Putnam, Jackson K. "The Persistence of Progressivism in the 1920s: The Case of California." *Pacific Historical Review* 35, no. 4 (November 1966): 395–411.

Quinn, Susan. *Furious Improvisation: How the WPA and a Cast of Thousands Made High Art out of Desperate Times.* New York: Walker, 2008.

Radosh, Ronald. "The Corporate Ideology of American Labor Leaders." In *Twenties*, ed. Hoff.

Rehnquist, William H. *All the Laws but One: Civil Liberties in Wartime.* New York: Knopf, 1998.

Report of Special Committee to Investigate Communist Activities and Propaganda in the United States in Accordance with House Resolution No. 220, House of Representatives, 71st Cong., 2nd sess. Supplement to the *United States Daily* (newspaper). Washington, D.C.: United States Daily, 19 January 1931.

Richardson, Seth W., and Harry S. Truman. "The Federal Employee Loyalty Program." *Columbia Law Review* 51, no. 5 (May 1951): 546–63.

Roberts, William M. "*The Laughing Horse*: A Horse Laugh at the University." *Chronicle of the University of California*, Spring 2002, 13–18.

Robin, Corey. *Fear: The History of a Political Idea.* New York: Oxford University Press, 2004.

Rogin, Michael Paul. *Ronald Reagan, the Movie, and Other Episodes in Political Demonology.* Berkeley: University of California Press, 1987.

Rosenfeld, Seth. *Subversives: The FBI's War on Student Radicals, and Reagan's Rise to Power.* New York: Farrar, Straus, and Giroux, 2012.

Sagan, Eli. *The Honey and the Hemlock: Democracy and Paranoia in Ancient Athens and Modern America.* New York: Basic Books, 1991.

Saunders, Frances Stonor. *The Cultural Cold War: The CIA and the World of Arts and Letters.* New York: New Press, 2000.

Scharf, Lois, and Joan M. Jensen, eds. *Decades of Discontent: The Women's Movement, 1920–1940.* Westport, Conn.: Greenwood, 1983.

Schechner, Richard. "Invasions Friendly and Unfriendly: The Dramaturgy of Direct Theatre." In *Critical Theory and Performance*, ed. Janelle G. Reinelt and Joseph R. Roach. Ann Arbor: University of Michigan Press, 1992.

Schlesinger, Arthur M. *The Age of Jackson.* Boston: Little, Brown, 1945.

Schmidt, Regin. *Red Scare: FBI and the Origins of Anticommunism in the United States, 1919–1943*. Copenhagen: Museum Tusculanum, 2000.

Schrecker, Ellen. *Many Are the Crimes: Mccarthyism in America*. Boston: Little, Brown, 1998.

——. *No Ivory Tower: McCarthyism and the Universities*. New York: Oxford University Press, 1986.

Sellars, Nigel Anthony. *Oil, Wheat, and Wobblies: The Industrial Workers of the World in Oklahoma, 1905–1930*. Norman: University of Oklahoma Press, 1998.

Service, Robert. *Trotsky: A Biography*. Cambridge: Belknap Press of Harvard University Press, 2009.

Silverberg, Louis G. "Citizens' Committees: Their Role in Industrial Conflict." *Public Opinion Quarterly* 5, no. 1 (March 1941): 17–37.

Sims, Robert C. "Idaho's Criminal Syndicalism Act: One State's Response to Radical Labor." *Labor History* 15, no. 4 (1974): 511–27.

Slotkin, Richard. *Lost Battalions: The Great War and the Crisis of American Nationality*. New York: Holt, 2005.

Smith, Robert Freeman. "American Foreign Relations, 1920–1942." In *Twenties*, ed. Hoff.

Spolansky, Jacob. *The Communist Trail in America*. New York,: Macmillan, 1951.

——. *The Red Trail in America*. Chicago: Open Shop Review, ca. 1925.

Stone, Geoffrey R. *Perilous Times: Free Speech in Wartime from the Sedition Act of 1798 to the War on Terrorism*. New York: Norton, 2004.

The Story of Mooney and Billings. New York: National Mooney-Billings Committee (American Civil Liberties Union), 1928.

Suskin, Steven. *Show Tunes: The Songs, Shows, and Careers of Broadway's Major Composers*. New York: Oxford University Press; 2010.

Taft, Philip. "The Bisbee Deportation." *Labor History* 13, no. 1 (1972): 3–40.

Taibbi, Matt. *Griftopia*. Melbourne: Scribe, 2010.

Talbert, Roy. *Negative Intelligence: The Army and the American Left, 1917–1941*. Jackson: University Press of Mississippi, 1991.

Theoharis, Athan G. *The FBI and American Democracy: A Brief Critical History*. Lawrence: University Press of Kansas, 2004.

Thomas, John L. "Progressivism and the Great War." In *Great Republic*, ed. Bailyn.

Thomas, Norman M. *War's Heretics: A Plea for the Conscientious Objector*. New York: Civil Liberties Bureau of the American Union against Militarism, 1917.

Thompson, Fred W., and Jon Bekken. *The Industrial Workers of the World: Its First 100 Years*. Cincinnati: Industrial Workers of the World, 2006.

Trask, David F. *The AEF and Coalition Warmaking, 1917–1918*. Lawrence: University Press of Kansas, 1993.

Trevor, John Bond. *An Analysis of the American Immigration Act of 1924*. New York: Carnegie Endowment for International Peace, 1924.

Tucker, Robert W. *Woodrow Wilson and the Great War: Reconsidering America's Neutrality, 1914–1917*. Charlottesville: University of Virginia Press, 2007.

Tucker, Robert W., Linda Wrigley, Theodore Draper, and Lehrman Institute. *The Atlantic Alliance and Its Critics*. New York: Praeger, 1983.

Tucker, W. H. *The Funding of Scientific Racism: Wickliffe Draper and the Pioneer Fund*. Urbana: University of Illinois Press, 2002.

Tunney, Thomas J. *Throttled!: The Detection of the German and Anarchist Bomb Plotters*. Boston: Small, Maynard, 1919.

Tygiel, Jules. *The Great Los Angeles Swindle: Oil, Stocks, and Scandal during the Roaring Twenties*. New York: Oxford University Press, 1994.

US Committee on Public Information. *Complete Report of the Chairman of the Committee on Public Information, 1917: 1918: 1919*. Washington, D.C.: US Government Printing Office, 1920.

———. *The German-Bolshevik Conspiracy*. Washington, D.C.: US Government Printing Office, 1918.

US Department of Justice. *Appendix to the Annual Report of the Attorney General of the United States for the Fiscal Year 1922*. Washington, DC: US Government Printing Office, 1924.

US House of Representatives. Committee on Un-American Activities. *Testimony of Walter S. Steele Regarding Communist Activities in the United States: Hearings before the Committee on Un-American Activities, 80th Congress, 1st Session, on H.R. 1884 and H.R. 2122: Bills to Curb or Outlaw the Communist Party in the United States*. Washington, D.C.: US Government Printing Office, 1947.

US Senate. Committee on the Judiciary. *Brewing and Liquor Interests and German Propaganda: Hearings before a Subcommittee of the Committee on the Judiciary, United States Senate, Sixty-Fifth Congress, Second and Third Sessions*. Washington, D.C.: US Government Printing Office, 1919.

van Courtland Moon, John Ellis. "United States Chemical Warfare Policy in World War II: A Captive of Coalition Policy?" *Journal of Military History* 60, no. 3 (July 1996): 495–511.

Van Der Pijl, Kees. "Arab Revolts and Nation-State Crisis." *New Left Review* 70 (July–August 2011): 27–49.

Veenswijk, Virginia Kays. *Coudert Brothers: A Legacy in Law: The History of America's First International Law Firm, 1853–1993*. New York: Talley/Dutton, 1994.

Weisbord, Albert. *Passaic: The Story of a Struggle against Starvation Wages and for the Right to Organize*. Chicago: Daily World, 1926.

Weiss, Robert P. "Private Detective Agencies and Labour Discipline in the United States, 1855–1946." *Historical Journal* 29, no. 1 (March 1986): 87–107.

Whiticker, Alan J. *Speeches That Shaped the Modern World*. Frenchs Forest, N.S.W.: New Holland, 2005.

Whitney, Richard Merrill. *Reds in America: The Present Status of the Revolutionary Movement in the U.S. Based on Documents Seized by the Authorities in the Raid upon the Convention of the Communist Party at Bridgman, Mich., Aug. 22, 1922, Together with Descriptions of Numerous Connections and Associations of the Communists among the Radicals, Progressives, and Pinks*. New York: Beckwith, 1924.

Whitten, Woodrow C. "Criminal Syndicalism and the Law in California: 1919–1927." *Transactions of the American Philosophical Society* 59, no. 2 (1969): 3–73.

Wilentz, Sean. "Confounding Fathers: The Tea Party's Cold War Roots." *New Yorker*, 18 October 2010. http://www.newyorker.com/magazine/2010/10/18/confounding-fathers.

Wilford, Hugh. *The Mighty Wurlitzer: How the CIA Played America*. Cambridge: Harvard University Press, 2008.

Williams, David. *A People's History of the Civil War: Struggles for the Meaning of Freedom*. New York: New Press, 2005.

Williams, William Appleman. "American Intervention in Russia: 1917–1920." In *Containment and Revolution*, ed. Horowitz.

Wilson, Jan Doolittle. *The Women's Joint Congressional Committee and the Politics of Maternalism, 1920–1930*. Urbana: University of Illinois Press, 2007.

Wylder, Delbert E. *Emerson Hough*. Boston: Twayne, 1981.

Yates, Michael. *Wisconsin Uprising: Labor Fights Back*. New York: Monthly Review Press, 2012.

Zimmermann, Warren. *First Great Triumph: How Five Americans Made Their Country a World Power*. New York: Farrar, Straus, and Giroux, 2002.

Zinn, Howard, and Anthony Arnove. *Voices of a People's History of the United States*. New York: Seven Stories, 2009.

Index

Union of Russian Peasant Workers, 103
Union of Russian Workers, 27, 65, 66, 68, 260
Union Oil Company of California, 165, 174
unions, labor. *See* labor, organized
Union Theological Seminary, 6
United Kingdom, 228, 229
United Mine Workers, 66
Universal Portland Cement Company, 92
University of California, 167
University of Minnesota, 184
University of Southern California, 174
University of Virginia, 184
Unlawful Associations Act (Australia), 30
US Army, 17, 26–27, 33, 79; BAF and, 172;
    Chemical Warfare Service, 72, 73, 79, *91*,
    116; and Navy Officers' Club, 94; parti-
    san politics and, 262; surveillance state
    and, 258–59. *See also* Military Intelligence
    (MI), US Army
US Catholic Conference, 185
US Census Bureau, 120
US Chamber of Commerce, 57, 147, 274
US Department of Education, 88
US Navy Office of Naval Intelligence, 32–33,
    35, 42, *91*, 93, 99, 131; conspiracy think-
    ing and, 225
US Shipping Board, 99
USSR. *See* Russia/USSR
US Steel, 85

Van Deman, Ralph, 33, 41, 63, 65, 86, 90, 129;
    BAF and, *89*, 172, 174; conspiracy think-
    ing and, 225, 233; John Trevor and, *87*, 93,
    96, 124
Vanderveer, George, 214
Vanzetti, Bartolomeo, 178, 180, 209–12, *213*,
    214, 218
Viereck, George Sylvester, 266
Vietnam War, 258, 272
Vital Center, The (Schlesinger), 275

Wade, Martin, 90, 168
Walker, Flora A., 86
Walker, Scott, 281
Walsh, Frank P., 237
Walsh, Thomas J., 38
War Industries Board, 153
Warren, Earl, 267
Washington, George, 96

Washington Post, 124
Watson, James E., 155
Watt, James, 223
Webster, Nesta H., 229–30, 231, 309n19
Weeks, John W., 73, 77
Weishaupt, Adam, 228, 230, 231
Weiss, Robert, 131
Welch, Robert, 266
Welsh, Francis Ralston, 94
Westchester Security League, 90, *91*, 184–85,
    252–53
Western Gulf Oil, 174
Weyher, Harry Frederick, Jr., 126
What America Means to Me (Cash), 186
White Slave Traffic (Mann) Act of 1910, 33
Whitney, Richard Merrill, 76, 77, 78–79, 82,
    229–30, *231*
Wilcox, James, 201
Wilcox, Thomas, 141
Wiley, Alexander, 200
Wilford, Hugh, 261
Willett, Thomas, 96
Williams, John Sharp, 246
Wilmerding, Caroline Murray, 96
Wilson, William B., 37, 65, 67, 68, 149, 156,
    217
Wilson, Woodrow, 26, 98, 102, 131, 133, 170;
    APL and, 40–44; Bolshevik Revolution
    and, 51, 52; constitutional amendments
    and, 197; cultural repression under, 37;
    disloyalty policing and, 30–31; efforts at
    silencing dissent, 29, 31–32; First World
    War and, 27–28; immigration laws un-
    der, 118; industrial unions and, 34–38;
    intervention in Russia, 1917–1920, 53–58;
    open shop movement and, 149–50; politi-
    cal prisoners under, 206, 207; post–First
    World War economy and, 59; and Russian
    people, views on, 288n8; stroke suffered
    by, 65
Winrod, Gerald B., 229–30, 266
Wobblies. *See* Industrial Workers of the
    World (IWW)
Wolfowitz, Paul, 272
Woman Patriot, The, 78, 176, *193*, 196
Woman Patriots, *91*, 189, 195, 266; constitu-
    tional conservatism and, 197
Woman's Christian Temperance Union, 74,
    188

NICK FISCHER is Adjunct Research Fellow of the School of Philosophical, Historical and International Studies at Monash University, Melbourne.

The University of Illinois Press
is a founding member of the
Association of American University Presses.

University of Illinois Press
1325 South Oak Street
Champaign, IL 61820-6903
www.press.uillinois.edu